INVESTING IN WHAT WORKS

FOR AMERICA'S COMMUNITIES

ESSAYS ON PEOPLE, PLACE & PURPOSE

FEDERAL RESERVE BANK OF SAN FRANCISCO & LOW INCOME INVESTMENT FUND

FEDERAL RESERVE BANK OF SAN FRANCISCO
101 Market Street
San Francisco, CA 94105

LOW INCOME INVESTMENT FUND
100 Pine Street, Suite 1800
San Francisco, CA 94111

Senior Editors:
Nancy O. Andrews
David J. Erickson

Contributing Editors:
Ian J. Galloway
Ellen S. Seidman

ISBN 978-0-615-68152-8

Library of Congress Control Number: 2012947084

Printed in the United States of America

In Memory of
Cushing Niles Dolbeare

Cushing N. Dolbeare was often called the grandmother of the modern day housing movement. Her unflinching honesty and unassuming demeanor allowed her to find common ground along the entire political spectrum. Cushing inspired the pioneers of the community development movement, many of whom are acknowledged in the pages of this book. Her example is one that we will emulate for decades to come.

TABLE OF CONTENTS

▌▌ OPEN FORUM: VOICES AND OPINIONS FROM LEADERS IN POLICY, THE FIELD, AND ACADEMIA

FROM LEADERS IN POLICY

FROM LEADERS IN THE FIELD

III MAPPING THE FUTURE: SYNTHESIZING THEMES AND IDEAS FOR NEXT STEPS

ACKNOWLEDGEMENTS

This book is a joint project of the Low Income Investment Fund (LIIF) and the Federal Reserve Bank of San Francisco. The book would not have been possible without the support of the Citi Foundation, which provided LIIF with a grant to help free up staff for this effort and gave encouragement and valuable feedback throughout the process.

Our nationally drawn advisory panel also deserves special acknowledgement. They provided inspiration, guidance, and suggestions. We could not have created this book without their wisdom and advice. We are also of course indebted to our authors, whose diverse points of view broadened our horizons.

Erika Poethig, the Acting Assistant Secretary for Policy Development and Research at the U.S. Department of Housing and Urban Development deserves special note. Thanks to her efforts, along those of Luke Tate, now with the White House

Domestic Policy Council, we were able to secure the combined reflections of Secretaries Donovan, Sebelius, and Duncan on the future of community development in fighting poverty in the United States.

We received first-rate copy editing and formatting from Barbara Ray and her team at Hiredpen, Inc. The cover art and layout was handled by C&G Partners LLC, who deserve the credit for giving the book its distinctive look. And Burness Communications was invaluable in helping us position the book within the larger and important narrative of poverty reduction.

Many others contributed intelligence, work, and patience as we completed this effort: Feather Moy-Welsh, Stephanie Huang, Samantha Hojo, Christopher Kramer, and Elisabeth Roth of the Low Income Investment Fund; Naomi Cytron, Scott Turner, and Laura Choi of the Federal Reserve Bank of San Francisco. Douglas Jutte, Elaine Arkin, and our friends at the Robert Wood Johnson Foundation helped provide some of the original inspiration that led to this project.

And last but not least, the Board of the Low Income Investment Fund and John Williams and Joy Hoffmann at the Federal Reserve Bank of San Francisco deserve our gratitude for providing an atmosphere of support, enthusiasm, and encouragement as we spent two years bringing such an ambitious endeavor to reality.

Thanks to all of you from the bottoms of our hearts – it takes a village, a network, and a thousand friends with kind words and helping hands to make a project like this possible.

Nancy O. Andrews and David Erickson, Senior Editors
Ian Galloway and Ellen Seidman, Contributing Editors

Advisory Committee

Alan Berube
Senior Fellow, Metropolitan Policy Program
Brookings Institution

Raphael Bostic
Bedrosian Chair in Governance
USC, Price School of Public Policy

Antony Bugg-Levine
Chief Executive Officer
Nonprofit Finance Fund

Pam Flaherty
President and CEO
Citi Foundation

Ingrid Gould Ellen
Professor of Urban Planning and Public Policy
New York University

Douglas Jutte
Assistant Adjunct Professor
UC Berkeley, School of Public Health

Jeff Lubell
Executive Director
Center for Housing Policy

Sr. Lillian Murphy
Chief Executive Officer
Mercy Housing

Mark Pinsky
President and CEO
Opportunity Finance Network

Erika Poethig
Acting Assistant Secretary of Policy Development and Research
U.S. Department of Housing and Urban Development

BUILDING SUSTAINABLE COMMUNITIES[1]

Elizabeth A. Duke, Governor
Board of Governors of the Federal Reserve System

PEOPLE AND PLACES

At one time, policy discussions revolved around whether community development was about people or places. I would argue that the debate is over and both sides won. Successful community development is based on attention to both the physical infrastructure, whether housing or commercial spaces, and the health and welfare of the residents therein. Safe and affordable housing will always be an important concern for lower-income Americans, but the recent recession and resulting damage to communities across the country make it clear that communities are more than physical structures. Sustainable communities—those that can weather economic downturns—not only provide decent housing, but also have the resources to support individuals and families and to create a dynamic business environment. For this reason,

---

1 Based on a speech delivered by Governor Duke at the National Interagency Community Reinvestment Conference on March 27, 2012 in Seattle, WA. Text of the speech is available at http://www.federalreserve.gov/newsevents/speech/duke20120327a.htm.

community development today is a multidisciplinary exercise that challenges us to think holistically about how housing relates to jobs, educational opportunities, transportation, health care, and other services and amenities.

UNEMPLOYMENT

The foreclosure crisis that resulted from unsustainable subprime lending has persisted largely because of high unemployment rates. Thus, in order to be successful, any effort to stabilize and revitalize lower-income neighborhoods will need to consider housing through the lens of access to jobs and educational opportunities. The Federal Reserve System currently has an initiative underway to better understand the relationship between community development activities and successful workforce development strategies. We anticipate that this research will provide valuable information for bankers and their community partners as they address the needs of their communities.

Of course, having a job is one thing. Getting to it is another. With good reason, transportation considerations have become more common in community development plans in recent years. More communities are taking public transportation into account when planning residential projects. Given the high cost of owning and operating a car, transportation options are a significant factor in a neighborhood's overall affordability. Demographic shifts over the last decade have resulted in the suburbanization of poverty, and now dictate that communities work together to create transportation options, including buses, light rail, and even car-sharing arrangements.

Even so, as the Federal Reserve Bank of Richmond has discovered in its work on car ownership for low-income workers, public transportation is not always sufficient to solve the transportation problems of the poor. Some jobs, such as construction work, require that workers report to different locations. Shift workers, whether security guards, airport baggage handlers, or hospital workers, may not have easy access to public transportation at night.

One of the more innovative solutions to this issue that I have seen was developed by an organization in Dallas that aims to move the jobs to the workers, rather than vice versa. Lone Star Investment Advisors LLC is a private equity fund that invests in Texas companies located in, or willing to move to, low-income census tracts. The fund's managers have focused on manufacturing and distribution companies that can create jobs in the state's lower-income communities. One of the businesses in the fund's portfolio, PrimeSource Food Service Equipment, moved from an affluent northern Dallas suburb to South Dallas, where the poverty rate was higher than 40 percent, relocating more than 100 employees and hiring new employees from South Dallas. I raise this example because it demonstrates what a little imagination can do to solve the problem of connecting people with jobs. Moreover, this double bottom-line approach to investments—making a profit while benefitting the community—makes this kind of activity attractive to bankers with Community Reinvestment Act (CRA) obligations and other socially-minded investors.

COMMUNITY DEVELOPMENT: AN ENTREPRENEURIAL ENTERPRISE

Successful community development is an entrepreneurial enterprise. Thinking about community development this way reminds me of a presentation made at a recent Federal Reserve research conference on small business and entrepreneurship.[2] Amy Wilkinson, Senior Fellow at Harvard's Kennedy School Center for Business and Government, has conducted research to identify the skill sets of high-impact entrepreneurs and small business leaders. The skills she identified are, not surprisingly, applicable to community development. They include being able to spot opportunities that others don't see, managing complexity, reiterating ideas and revamping plans repeatedly, experimenting and failing wisely, networking to create solutions, and, as Amy

---

2 Speech by Amy Wilkinson delivered at the Small Business and Entrepreneurship during an Economic Recovery Conference, Federal Reserve Board of Governors, November 10, 2011 available at http://www.federalreserve.gov/mediacenter/files/wilkinson-transcript-20111110.pdf.

put it, "unleashing generosity" in ways that create reciprocity within the network.

No doubt these sound familiar. Community development is an ongoing process of identifying and understanding the complicated interaction of people and places. Solutions are found through the cycle of experimentation and adjustment. Successes look easy but they mask hard work and, often, failed attempts. Transformational changes in communities rarely happen without the involvement and support of a network that includes residents, business owners, community organizations, financial institutions, and local government. Sustained interaction among these stakeholders is what makes the opportunity known and the solution successful.

The city of Rochester, New York, put these principles to work and managed to weather the bankruptcy of the city's largest employer. Eastman Kodak once employed some 61,000 Rochester residents and invested significantly in the city's educational and cultural institutions; three decades later, it employs fewer than 7,000 people and recently filed for bankruptcy protection.[3] This is not an uncommon story, except for the fact that Rochester managed to gain a net of 90,000 jobs during the three decades of employment decline at Kodak.

How did Rochester manage this transition so successfully? The city recognized early on the need to diversify its economic base and, some 20 years ago, created a network of private and nonprofit partnerships to leverage the city's assets, the same universities and cultural institutions Kodak had supported. Together with local government, this network trained entrepreneurs and supported new business ventures, many of which are in optics and photonics. Through foresight and the collaboration of government, private and nonprofit partners, and committed citizens, Rochester was able to build on the Kodak legacy, effectively turning lost jobs at Kodak into new local opportunities.

---

3 Peter Applebome, "Despite Long Slide by Kodak, Company Town Avoids Decay," New York Times, January 16, 2012 available at www.nytimes.com/2012/01/17/nyregion/despite-long-slide-by-kodak-rochester-avoids-decay.html.

HEALTHY COMMUNITIES

In addition to housing and employment, residents need communities that support their health and well-being in a variety of ways. Community developers play a critical role in supporting healthy lifestyles by planning for sidewalks, parks, and other open spaces connecting housing and commercial areas in ways that also provide places for people to meet and children to play. Renovation and new construction plans increasingly adhere to standards that incorporate "green" materials and technologies not only because they lower utility costs, which is important, but also because they improve health results, such as asthma rates, among residents.

One of the most obvious ways to support healthy lifestyles in lower-income neighborhoods is by making healthy food accessible. In the face of increasing rates of obesity, low-income neighborhoods are notably underserved by grocery stores. This is beginning to change because of programs like The Pennsylvania Fresh Food Financing Initiative, which is supported by a partnership between The Reinvestment Fund, a nonprofit developer, and two community organizations, The Food Trust and the Greater Philadelphia Urban Affairs Coalition. This partnership stepped in to fill a financing need where infrastructure costs were not met by conventional financial institutions. Their original objective was to make fresh food available in low-income neighborhoods. But they have achieved much more. The grocery stores the partnership helped to establish create an anchor for other retail needs in the area. Moreover, the stores hire local workers and train them in both the required job skills and in the workplace etiquette necessary to succeed in any job. One of the original groceries financed under the program has also added in-store financial services and a health clinic. As this grocery operator discovered, access to health care is another critical need in many low-income communities.

In Chicago, residents have taken it upon themselves to fill the need for primary and specialty health care by establishing the Lawndale Christian Health Center. Ownership in the Center is retained by residents to ensure that it continues to meet the needs of its neighborhood. In another example of a community facility meeting more than one need, the Center has expanded over time to provide leadership development and organizational capacity building services to its members in addition to health services.

CONCLUSION

I could go on to recite more examples of programs that respond to community needs, but I think you get my point: Taking an entrepreneurial approach to community development results in innovative and effective programs, making communities more desirable places to live and more resilient in hard times. The CRA regulations encourage banks and thrifts to invest in activities that provide affordable housing or financial services for individuals, promote economic development, or revitalize or stabilize low- or moderate-income areas.

At a time when the needs of these communities are so great and the resources available to meet those needs are so scarce, it behooves financial institutions to think broadly about their CRA obligations. By partnering with other community stakeholders, these institutions can help address existing community needs and lay the groundwork for stronger credit demand in the future.

I don't want to underestimate the difficulty of the task. The recession damaged communities of all types, but particularly lower-income neighborhoods, and economic recovery has been stubbornly slow. Nonetheless, the commitment and innovation demonstrated in communities all across the country is encouraging. Taking an entrepreneurial approach to community development and thinking about the needs of both people and places will, I believe, make for stronger, more resilient communities in the future.

ELIZABETH A. DUKE *took office as a member of the Board of Governors of the Federal Reserve System on August 5, 2008, to fill an unexpired term ending January 31, 2012. Prior to her appointment to the Board, Ms. Duke was Senior Executive Vice President and Chief Operating Officer of TowneBank, a Virginia-based community bank. Prior to this, she was an Executive Vice President at*

Wachovia Bank, and an Executive Vice President at SouthTrust Bank. Earlier in her career, Ms. Duke was President and Chief Executive Officer of Bank of Tidewater, based in Virginia Beach, Virginia. Ms. Duke was the Chairman of the American Bankers Association from 2004 to 2005 and the President of the Virginia Bankers Association from 1999 to 2000. She served on the board of directors of the Federal Reserve Bank of Richmond from 1998 to 2000. Aside from her work in the banking industry, Ms. Duke has held many civic positions, including service on the boards of directors of the Virginia Council on Economic Education, the Hampton Roads Partnership, the Old Dominion University Foundation, and the Economics Club of Hampton Roads. She also served on the Virginia Legislative Subcommittee to Study Capital Access and Business Financing and served on the Board of Commissioners of the Norfolk Airport Authority. Ms. Duke received her bachelor's degree from the University of North Carolina at Chapel Hill and her MBA from Old Dominion University. She received an honorary doctor of humane letters degree from Old Dominion University.

I

COMMUNITY DEVELOPMENT

Past and Present

THE PAST, PRESENT, AND FUTURE OF COMMUNITY DEVELOPMENT IN THE UNITED STATES

Alexander von Hoffman[1]
Harvard University

F or more than a century, American reformers have struggled to remedy the problems of poverty in the places where low-income people live. At first, these social improvers could muster only a few isolated solutions, but by the end of the twentieth century, they had expanded their efforts to a large, dynamic, and sophisticated field of action. Today thousands of nonprofit community development organizations operate in the poorest urban and rural areas of the country. More impressively, they have helped stabilize community life and help individuals and families in some of the most forsaken neighborhoods in the country. The South Bronx, once

---

1   "The Past, Present, and Future of Community Development in the United States." Copyright © 2012 Alexander von Hoffman. This article cannot be reproduced in any form without written permission from Alexander von Hoffman. Permission requests should be sent to alexander_von_hoffman@harvard.edu.

the most infamous slum district in the United States, has became livable and vibrant.

To build a decentralized system of neighborhood improvement and individual betterment was not easy. The community development field had to emerge from the shadow of the top-down approach embodied in the urban renewal and public housing bureaucracies. The antipoverty crusaders realized that they had to combine a passion for social justice with viable management and business practices. They learned to keep practitioners accountable for their work and to measure their accomplishments.

And the movement's leaders had to grow and change, which they did by adopting new strategies aimed at building up the finances and assets of individuals, as opposed to simply looking at the problems of places.

To keep a decentralized system viable, of course, costs money. The current community development world could flourish only when new financial institutions along with philanthropic organizations, and especially government, offered sufficient financial support.

From the beginning, community development advocates have pursued the vision of a truly comprehensive strategy, one that would integrate approaches and overcome the barriers between types of services and the government and nongovernment entities that provide them. Now, in the twenty-first century, the vision of broadly collaborative approaches seems more feasible than at any time in the long and rich history of community development.

And yet to fulfill this vision the community development field must overcome the worst economic and financial circumstances its supporters have faced in the last 25 years.

COMMUNITY DEVELOPMENT: THE EARLY DAYS
To Fight the Slums
The concept of community development originated in the late nineteenth century when reformers discovered America's

"backward" areas. Socially committed women and men in Settlement Houses and charitable organizations confronted the ills of industrial capitalism: poorly paid immigrant and racial minority wage workers crowded into tenement apartments, cottages, and shacks in seedy neighborhoods near docks, trains, and factories. During the Progressive Era of the early twentieth century, urban reformers connected poverty, overcrowding, crime, youth delinquency, and sundry other social ills to the unsanitary and unsightly slums where the working poor and indigents lived.

The sweeping Progressive agenda of political, social, and physical reform anticipated later comprehensive antipoverty strategies. The women who led many of the reform movements liked to call the totality of their efforts "municipal housekeeping." Others talked of dealing with "the social question," and historians later labeled it progressivism. But under any name, their wide-ranging attack on the evils of modern urban society embraced a welter of labor, education, and welfare measures, including attempts to improve the lives of the lower classes through better housing. But if Progressive reformers left the useful legacy of trying to counter the many aspects of poverty, they also handed down the less useful principle that outside experts would save society by imposing reforms on the people they were trying to help.

New Deal Community Building: Comprehensive but Top-Down

For the most part the Progressive reformers agitated in local and state government until the 1930s when the Great Depression and the election of Franklin D. Roosevelt gave outlets for their social programs in the federal government. True to its Progressive roots, Roosevelt's New Deal encompassed a remarkably wide array of reforms, both visionary and practical. At times it seemed that he created a new agency to solve each individual social problem.

The idea of comprehensive physical and social planning ran through the diverse array of New Deal community development programs. At the large scale, the Roosevelt administration strove to develop rural regions, most notably through the Tennessee Valley Authority, which built electric power dams, taught new agricultural methods, and planned new towns in the impoverished Tennessee River basin. At the local level in America's cities and rural counties, New Dealers rebuilt slums with public housing projects, which they designed as small planned communities.

Although New Deal programs were idealistic and well-intentioned, their top-down administrative structure was undemocratic. Like their Progressive forebears, the New Dealers believed that enlightened experts such as themselves should dictate the terms of the bright shining new world they would create. Although they would work with leaders of labor, religious, and racial organizations, the reformers in the 1930s for the most part failed to include ordinary people in their decision-making process.

The defect of this approach appeared early in the history of the public housing program in the form of the "neighborhood composition" rule. Responding to requests from field officers for a rule for selecting tenants for housing projects in racially mixed neighborhoods, Secretary of the Interior Harold Ickes set down the guideline that members of whichever race had predominated prior to demolition of the slums would be the *only* group to be admitted. This segregation policy would hamper the program for decades to come.

The Slum Returns as the Ghetto

World War II brought great changes to America's cities. The construction of rapid transit systems and the Depression had in different ways helped decongest the densely packed immigrant city neighborhoods, but now the inner city filled up again. The boom in wartime industrial jobs started a migration of African Americans and people from other racial minorities in search of economic opportunity that lasted into the Cold War. But racism in white neighborhoods, real estate practices, and federal government policies combined with the newcomers' relatively low incomes to keep increasing numbers of blacks locked into racial ghettos. Soon crowded homes and decrepit buildings like those that had horrified reformers at the turn of the century were back.

Despite obvious racial issues—whites in Chicago, Detroit, and other large cities rioted and violently assaulted blacks who moved into their neighborhoods—and growing welfare needs, mid-twentieth century political leaders and reformers saw only physical problems. With little regard for the social dimension, they fixated on slum clearance as a remedy for the cities' social and economic problems.[2]

Doubling Down on Top-Down

The Housing Act of 1949 inaugurated a new federal program, urban redevelopment, later known as urban renewal, in which a government agency staffed by experts took "blighted and slum areas" by eminent domain, demolished the buildings therein, and turned the properties over to private developers to rebuild. Realtors and urban planners had devised urban redevelopment as a way to staunch the departure of the upper middle class to the suburbs and stop physical and economic deterioration. Needless to say, this top-down program had no mechanism for consulting those whose businesses and homes were to be taken. Within a few years, civil rights advocates, angered at the demolition of massive numbers of African American homes, would deride the program as "Negro removal." Yet the urban renewal projects that destroyed the predominantly white working-class West End in Boston to build luxury high-rise apartment buildings and razed the Mexican-American Chavez Ravine neighborhood in Los Angeles for a professional baseball stadium shamefully demonstrated that the program laid waste to low-income communities of other ethnic backgrounds as well.

The 1949 Housing Act also revived the public housing program, on hiatus during the war, with a fresh round of authorizations. The downtown powers of American cities—the mayors, businessmen, and civic leaders—thought public housing would

---

2 Robert C. Weaver, The Negro Ghetto (New York: Harcourt, Brace, 1948); Charles Abrams, Forbidden Neighbors: A Story of Prejudice in Housing (New York: Harper and Brothers, 1955); Arnold Hirsch, Making the Second Ghetto: Race and Housing in Chicago, 1940–1960 (Cambridge: Cambridge University Press, 1983); Thomas Sugrue, The Origins of the Urban Crisis: Race and Inequality in Postwar Detroit (Princeton: Princeton University Press, 1996).

kill two birds with one stone: clear the awful-looking slums and provide upwardly mobile African Americans with a new lot in life. They overlooked that public housing only provided for a fraction of the houses that were demolished, and they hardly ever thought about helping the displaced find new homes. Worse, during the 1950s, big-city officials built modernist public housing towers in racial ghettos to keep African Americans from moving to white neighborhoods, perpetuating the program's tradition of racial segregation. The U.S. Interstate highway program, enacted in 1956, probably demolished more low-income neighborhoods, if it were possible, than either urban renewal or public housing.[3] If the purpose of these postwar programs was to contain the poor and stop the spread of blight, they failed completely, largely because the destruction simply forced those low-income families who lost their homes to move to new areas.

THE REDISCOVERY OF POVERTY
The Other America

Starting about the mid-1950s, observers of American cities began to sound increasingly anxious. At first, many believed that urban problems stemmed primarily from the breakdown of physical planning and government services. In 1957, *Fortune* magazine produced a special issue, later a book, of essays that detailed the effects of the car, city government, the slums, sprawl, and, in Jane Jacobs' provocative debut of her urban theories, the failure to revive downtown. As more neighborhoods turned into low-income minority communities, social problems, particularly the old issue of "juvenile delinquency," entered the discussion about cities. From films like *The Blackboard Jungle* to *West Side Story*, America's popular culture gave iconic form to the urban street gangs and by extension the neighborhoods in which they lived.

---

3 Alexander von Hoffman, "A Study in Contradictions: The Origins and Legacy of the Housing Act of 1949," Housing Policy Debate, 10 (3) (Summer 2000): 299–326; Hirsch, Making the Second Ghetto; Raymond A. Mohl, "Race and Space in the Modern City: Interstate-95 and the Black Community in Miami." In Urban Policy in Twentieth-Century America, edited by Arnold R. Hirsch and Raymond A. Mohl (New Brunswick, NJ: Rutgers University Press, 1993), pp. 100–158; "The Interstates and the Cities: Highways, Housing and the Freeway Revolt." Research Report (Washington, DC: Poverty and Race Research Action Council, 2002), pp. 30–38.

Nonetheless, the increasing affluence of Americans made it shocking to discover that grinding poverty persisted. In 1962, Michael Harrington published a searing portrait of deprived and invisible poor people in *The Other America*, a book that caught the attention of many of the nation's leaders, including President John F. Kennedy. The dawning realization of poverty in the midst of plenty gave rise to a new generation of wide-ranging efforts to fight urban and rural social problems.

As in the past and many times since, reformers realized that solving the problems of the poor depended on coordinating a variety of efforts for economic development and human development. In 1958, two members of the faculty of the Columbia School of Social Work, Richard Cloward and Lloyd Ohlin, started Mobilization for Youth to combat juvenile delinquency on Manhattan's Lower East Side. Cloward and Ohlin blamed slum conditions and racial discrimination for juvenile delinquency and in response set up Mobilization for Youth as a broad attack—including job training, mental health counseling, and educational programs—on neighborhood social conditions. Although Mobilization for Youth succeeded in galvanizing low-income residents to act on their own behalf, school officials, welfare workers, and other professionals became defensive. Many of the efforts broke down in mutual hostility.

In 1961, Paul Ylvisaker, an officer of the Ford Foundation concerned with urban and racial issues, started the Gray Areas programs in Boston, Oakland, New Haven, Philadelphia, and Washington, DC. With grants from the Ford Foundation to local school departments, governments, and nonprofit agencies, he hoped to reform the delivery of social services to respond in innovative ways to the needs of the residents of low-income racial minority neighborhoods. The engine of this experiment in comprehensive community development was to be a nonprofit agency. Although these trials gave form to approaches that would soon resurface in federal policy, the failure of Ylvisaker and his foundation colleagues to think through ways to coordinate disparate agencies or to allow low-income African Americans to participate meaningfully in planning the improvement of their neighborhoods undermined the Gray Areas projects.[4]

LBJ Declares a Comprehensive War on Poverty

The Kennedy administration responded to the growing sense of urgency about American poverty. Attorney General Robert Kennedy nurtured youth programs through the President's Committee on Juvenile Delinquency, most famously Harlem Youth Opportunities Unlimited (HARYOU) in New York City, formed in 1962. Just days before he was assassinated, President Kennedy approved plans to launch a trial program as an attack on poverty in America. Soon after succeeding to the presidency, Lyndon B. Johnson raised the stakes by declaring not an attack but a full-fledged War on Poverty. In August 1964, Congress passed the Economic Opportunity Act, and Johnson named Sargent Shriver to head the ambitious new agency that would carry it out.

As implemented by Shriver, the War on Poverty reflected the anti-poverty experiments but with an even wider scope. In the Office of Economic Opportunity (OEO) and subsequent programs such as Model Cities, the Johnson administration strove for systematic approaches to help Americans lift themselves out of poverty. Through "comprehensive community action programs," Johnson declared in signing the Economic Opportunity Act, "We will strike at poverty's roots." He reeled off numerous approaches, including remedial education, job training, health and employment counseling, and neighborhood improvement. In the following years, the administration would add more education and human development elements: preschool learning through Head Start, itself a comprehensive approach that was to provide "health, educational, nutritional, social, and other services" to

---

4   Robert Halpern, Rebuilding the Inner City: A History of Neighborhood Initiatives to Address Poverty in the United States (New York: Columbia University Press, 1995), pp. 89–101; G. William Domhoff, "The Ford Foundation in the Inner City: Forging an Alliance with Neighborhood Activists" (Santa Cruz, CA: University of Southern California, WhoRulesAmerica.net, 2005), available at http://www2.ucsc.edu/whorulesamerica/local/ford_foundation.html.

low-income children and their families; food stamps; Upward Bound for college preparation; and the child nutrition program.

The idea of comprehensiveness permeated the antipoverty measures of the 1960s. To coordinate the federal government's multipronged attack on poverty, the Economic Opportunity Act set up an Economic Opportunity Council made up of the president's cabinet secretaries and named the OEO director as its chairman. The fundamental concept of the 1966 Model Cities program was that focusing diverse programs and approaches in a concentrated area would transform a slum neighborhood and its low-income inhabitants. The OEO, and even more explicitly Model Cities, relied on an integrated approach to uplift that would break down the barriers between different types of social services. In practice, however, effectively coordinating separate and often jealous government agencies often proved infeasible.

The Rise of People Power

While elite policymakers mulled over what was the best way to solve poverty, on the streets of America's cities the people had begun to act for themselves. The civil rights movement took center stage in the nation's domestic affairs, blowing from south to north and country to city and raising expectations of African Americans for a better day. After dramatic confrontations such as the marches in Selma, AL, and the triumphant achievements of the Voting Rights Act and the 1965 Civil Rights Act, civil rights leaders such as Martin Luther King Jr. pivoted to northern cities. In cities from Boston to Seattle, civil rights activists crusaded against racial discrimination in education, employment, and housing. The increasing appeal of black nationalism, which ranged from black pride to "black power," and the emergence of militant nationalists, such as H. Rap Brown, challenged leaders like King who preached nonviolence and racial integration.

Meanwhile, in Chicago, a close-to-the-ground approach to urban problems known as community organizing had taken root. In the late 1930s, Saul Alinsky, a former criminologist, applied union organizers' methods to help residents of the city's Back of the Yards, an impoverished polyglot immigrant neighborhood, gain political power to force local government and institutions to respond to their needs. Alinsky then set up the Industrial Areas Foundation to organize the powerless of all stripes—Mexican-Americans, Puerto Ricans, and African Americans—in their home communities. During the 1960s, Alinsky's brand of community organizing gained national attention, as Charles Silberman publicized Alinsky's work in the best-selling book, *Crisis in Black and White*, and members of the New Left turned to the organizer to learn political tactics. Many years later Alinsky's ideas would influence a young organizer in Chicago named Barack Obama.

Taking It to the Streets

The spirit of resistance that flourished in the 1960s also inspired citizens to take to the streets to stop large-scale urban renewal and highway projects. Across the nation, they rallied to stop the government from tearing down their homes for a small number of public or luxury housing and from slicing 10-lane expressways through their neighborhoods to benefit suburbanites. Although not always successful, especially at first, the protests gained champions who articulated the intellectual case for their cause. In her landmark book *The Death and Life of Great American Cities* (1961), Jane Jacobs, an editor at *Architectural Forum,* laid out a devastating critique of city planning that destroyed old buildings and neighborhoods and built instead monolithic public housing projects and soulless civic centers. In *The Urban Villagers* (1962), liberal sociologist Herbert Gans portrayed the residents of Boston's West End not as alienated slum dwellers but as members of a vital community. Martin Anderson, a scholar of finance and management, blasted urban renewal from a conservative perspective in *The Federal Bulldozer* (1964).

If the antipoverty experiments encouraged a comprehensive approach, the grassroots campaigns fed the idea that any plan to combat urban ills should involve, or better yet be written by, the people who were the objects of the initiative. Thus, a signature piece of the War on Poverty was the community action program, whose local agencies would carry out the panoply of antipoverty programs and legal services for the poor. The rule for the community action program was "maximum feasible participation" of the poor in the design and implementation of the programs that would affect them. Some community action agencies took this goal literally, threatening the local political status quo. In response, vexed southern and big-city politicians let Johnson and Shriver feel their ire in no uncertain terms. The Johnson administration in turn gave mayors more say-so in OEO and Model Cities, but never entirely rejected the principle of participation. Hence, in contrast to public housing, urban renewal, and highway construction, the antipoverty and community development projects of the 1960s enshrined, at least to some degree, a bottom-up approach.

Perhaps because they were situated close to the people they were trying to help, community action agencies, Model Cities organizations, and community development corporations survived the political opposition and in the following decades slowly began to multiply across the United States.

TOWARD BUSINESS REMEDIES
Urban Crisis

Despite the civil rights movement victories, Johnson's massive government antipoverty project, and the other community efforts, from 1964 to 1968 violence rocked big-city ghettos. Each summer an incident, usually involving the police, sparked riots in which angry blacks fought police, started fires, and looted stores. In 1964, sporadic violence broke out in several cities, most notably in New York. The following summer the Watts section of Los Angeles erupted for an entire week, with rioters crying out, "Burn, baby, burn!" When it was over, 34 were dead, hundreds injured, and almost 4,000 people arrested. In 1966, violence struck the West Side of Chicago and the Hough section of Cleveland, and the next year numerous cities exploded. The worst was Detroit, in which four days of upheavals left 43 dead and more than 7,200 arrested. After the assassination of Martin Luther King Jr. in April 1968, rioting hit numerous cities, to deadly effect in Chicago, Baltimore, and Washington, DC.

As the upheavals sent shockwaves through the country, the nation's increasingly anxious leaders cast about for explanations and solutions. While the fires were still smoldering in Detroit, President Johnson named the National Advisory Commission on Civil Disorders—known as the Kerner Commission after its chairman, Illinois governor Otto Kerner—to determine what was causing the violence and how it could be stopped. Some observers called for a crackdown on lawlessness, but many believed that deep-rooted problems were to blame for the violence. Reformers had long condemned the slums as a source of disorder, so it was unsurprising that numerous leaders, including the members of the Kerner Commission, concluded that conditions in the ghettos had helped spur a violent revolt.[5]

Bringing Big Business to Save the Ghetto

Hence, in the late 1960s, Americans redoubled their efforts to cure the slums and ghettos of their cities. Somewhat surprisingly given the leftward political tilt of the 1960s, lawmakers and government leaders seized on the idea that the private sector should play a central role in solving what many called the "urban crisis." New York Senator Robert F. Kennedy became a leading proponent of the idea of tapping the power and wealth of corporate America for social betterment. Deeply unhappy with Johnson's efforts to rescue America's ghettos—there was no love lost between LBJ and the martyred president's younger brother—Bobby Kennedy sought an alternative to the big government programs of the Great Society.

Kennedy turned to big business. In 1966, he and his aides conceived the idea of a "community development corporation," a prototype of which they worked to set up in Brooklyn's Bedford-Stuyvesant neighborhood. As Daniel Patrick Moynihan put it, the Bedford-Stuyvesant project would "get the market to do what the

---

5 The Kerner Commission singled out three major underlying causes of the riots: discrimination and segregation (in employment, education, but also housing); black migration and white departure from central cities (causing "concentration of impoverished Negroes"); and black ghettos. Report of the National Advisory Commission on Civil Disorders (New York: Bantam, 1968), pp. 203–204.

bureaucracy cannot."[6] With the support of New York Republican leaders Senator Jacob Javits and Mayor John Lindsay, Kennedy persuaded Congress and the administration in November 1966 to amend the Economic Opportunity Act by adding the "Special Impact Program" to fund community development ventures in urban poverty areas, beginning with Kennedy's Bedford-Stuyvesant Restoration Corporation.[7] In December Kennedy announced that two new nonprofit organizations—one made up of local leaders and another of top business executives—would lead the effort to revive Bedford-Stuyvesant. Kennedy had convinced several corporate heavyweights—including Thomas Watson, chairman of IBM, and George S. Moore, chairman of First National City Bank (later renamed Citibank)—to serve on the businessmen's advisory committee.

Not long after, the project directors dropped the awkward idea of a white corporate over-board. A locally based organization under Franklin Thomas, a rising African American star in New York City political circles, took over the direction of the effort, and the Manhattan executives were relegated to fundraising. The group would face other hurdles in the years to come, but something called a community development corporation (CDC) had been established in the federal law and on the mean streets of an American city.[8]

---

6   William P. Ryan, "Bedford-Stuyvesant and the Prototype Community Development Corporation." In Inventing Community Renewal: The Trials and Errors that Shaped the Modern Community Development Corporation, edited by Mitchell Sviridoff (New York: Community Development Research Center, New School University, 2004), pp. 67–96; Jeff Shesol, Mutual Contempt: Lyndon Johnson, Robert Kennedy, and the Feud that Defined a Decade (New York: W.W. Norton, 1997), p. 249 (Moynihan quotation).

7   Alice O'Connor, "Swimming Against the Tide: A Brief History of Federal Policy in Poor Communities." In Urban Problems and Community Development, edited by Ronald Ferguson and William Dickens (Washington, DC: Brookings Institution Press, 1999), pp. 105–108.

8   Kimberley Johnson, "Community Development Corporations, Participation, and Accountability: The Harlem Urban Development Corporation and the Bedford-Stuyvesant Restoration Corporation," Annals of the American Academy of Political and Social Science 594 (1) (July 2004): 117–120.

Private Sector Enlists

In the 1960s the social mission of business took many forms. Corporations such as General Electric and IBM operated urban centers for the federal government's Job Corps program, a key part of the War on Poverty. Employees of private firms helped to run hundreds of government, nonprofit organizations, and corporate charitable programs. Some aimed to employ the "disadvantaged," whereas others provided housing, education, safety measures, and social services. In September 1967, 348 life insurance companies pledged to commit a billion dollars to mortgage financing of low-income housing and other investments to help the impoverished sections of America's cities.

To take advantage of the blossoming sense of social responsibility among business people, the Johnson administration set up the Job Opportunities in Business Sector (JOBS) program, in which the federal government would train the "hard-core unemployed" and a volunteer organization, National Alliance of Businessmen, would find the trainees gainful employment. In 1968, after consulting with a presidential commission led by industrialist Edgar Kaiser, Congress passed a sweeping new housing bill that created two powerful new low-income programs, one for rental apartments and the other for single-family home purchases. Both were to be carried out not by public housing authorities but rather by private sector builders and real estate agents.

Black Business and the Rise of Local Economic Development

The private business approach also took hold locally in African American communities. The Reverend Leon H. Sullivan pioneered black economic development in Philadelphia. In 1964 he founded the Opportunities Industrialization Center, an employment training program. He then persuaded the members of his congregation to tithe themselves in what he called the 10-36 plan (they were to contribute $10 for 36 months) to establish the Zion Non-Profit Charitable Trust (ZNPCT). With this endowment the ZNPCT started a number of programs, including a for-profit subsidiary, Progress Investment Associates, which built moderate-income housing.

As businesses and government departments applied business techniques to solve America's pressing social problems, philanthropic institutions took up the idea of making interest-bearing investments in socially motivated enterprises. In 1967 John Simon of the Taconic Foundation organized the Cooperative Assistance Fund, a nonstock corporation made up of nine philanthropic foundations capitalized with $3.8 million, to invest in minority business enterprises. Simon had worked out the legal grounds for philanthropic investments based on social goals rather than maximum profit. He was joined by Louis Winnick, who was interested in making loans on projects, such as buildings, that would create an asset for low-income people. As a program officer at the Ford Foundation, Winnick helped persuade his board to become one of the members of the Cooperative Assistance Fund and then in 1968 to launch a "program-related investments" program that would channel Ford's capital funds as loans into projects with social purposes.[9]

As both the community development and civil rights movement progressed, policy intellectuals began an argument that continues today. Some believed that the poor and racial minorities should move to upper-middle-class neighborhoods where they could benefit from nearby jobs and better schools. Others questioned the practicality and political wisdom of moving the populations to integrate entire metropolitan areas and suggested the energy would be better spent improving the places where the poor currently lived. In fact, racial integration of housing and community development are not mutually exclusive goals, and reformers have pursued both successfully.[10]

---

9 Ford Foundation, "Program-Related Investments: A Different Approach to Philanthropy" (New York: Ford Foundation, 1974), pp. 5–6, 16; "Investing for Social Gain: Reflections on Two Decades of Program-Related Investments" (New York: Ford Foundation, 1991), pp. 5–7.

10 Frances Fox Piven and Richard A. Cloward, "The Case Against Urban Desegregation," Social Work 12 (1) (January 1967): 12–21; "Desegregated Housing—Who Pays for the Reformers' Ideal?" New Republic, December 17, 1966; John F. Kain and Joseph J. Persky, "Alternatives to the Gilded Ghetto," The Public Interest 14 (Winter 1969): 74–83; John F. Kain, "The Spatial Mismatch Hypothesis: Three Decades Later," Housing Policy Debate 3 (2) (1992): 371–460.

THE EMERGENCE OF A NATIONAL COMMUNITY DEVELOPMENT SYSTEM

The Inner City Spirals Downward

The ghetto riots of the 1960s, it turned out, were only a harbinger of bad times to come in the inner city. Apparently many inner-city residents agreed with the outside society that their neighborhoods were wanting and began to depart. From the late 1960s, the number of crimes rose, while street gangs and drug traffickers took over large areas of turf. A national building boom, chiefly in the suburbs, sank inner-city real estate values into the negative numbers, with the result that landlords abandoned and sometimes burned their properties. Local stores shut down and local government services dried up. As the stream of people departing inner-city neighborhoods turned into a flood, the local populations shriveled, such that by 1990 some were as little as one-third their size of only 10 or 20 years earlier. The exodus, sociologist William Julius Wilson has pointed out, deprived the neighborhoods of stable African American middle- and working-class families who could serve as models of how to get ahead in society. Left behind were the poor and elderly.[11] Yet even as the inner city spiraled downwards, the embryonic community development movement began to grow into a national force.

From Small Acorns Grow Large Oaks

Out of many small local efforts—and the increasing support for them of government and philanthropies—grew a complex national community development system. A key to the system was the creation of national institutions, called financial inter- mediaries, that provided loans and grants to local organizations. Although the people who worked at the local nonprofit groups and the well-endowed national intermediaries had different perspectives and roles, they shared a commitment to the idea that the combination of social mission and business practices would

---

11 William Julius Wilson, The Truly Disadvantaged: The Inner City, the Underclass, and Public Policy (Chicago: University of Chicago Press, 1987).

produce practical and effective ways to boost downtrodden communities and the people who lived in them.

In 1968, Dorothy Mae Richardson and her friends in a block club in Pittsburgh's Central Northside neighborhood were fighting slum rats and landlords. The club's efforts to get housing loans for their low-income neighbors attracted the attention of local bankers and foundation officers. After thinking it through together, the block club, a local bank, and the foundation set up a novel program to give home improvement loans and advice to residents whose incomes made them look too risky for fearful conventional bankers. They called the new lending agency Neighborhood Housing Services (NHS).

In 1970, Federal Home Loan Bank (FHLB) board members, who were visiting Pittsburgh to conduct special training for savings and loan officers, discovered and were impressed by the NHS experiment. Three years later, FHLB joined the Department of Housing and Urban Development (HUD) under Richard Nixon to create a task force that would expand the NHS concept across the country. The taskforce helped organize the Neighborhood Housing Services of America to operate a secondary market for the NHS high-risk loan funds and to provide technical assistance to the individual Neighborhood Housing Services. In 1978, with 60 Neighborhood Housing Services now operating around the country, Congress turned the task force into an independent entity, Neighborhood Reinvestment Corporation, now called NeighborWorks America, to support and strengthen the NHS system. After an initial period of struggle, NeighborWorks America began to grow by strengthening its affiliates—beginning with a rural NHS group in West Rutland, VT—and attracting investments from national financial partners. The program also launched successful home ownership campaigns. The little experiment in Pittsburgh would produce a national housing network.

During the late 1960s and 1970s, various nonprofit organizations began to appear in many inner-city and rural areas where poor people lived. In Los Angeles, with the help of the community action program, Mexican-American activists organized the East Los Angeles Community Union (TELACU), and African Americans, led by local United Auto Workers official Ted Watkins, set up Watts Labor Community Action Committee for that distressed district. In many riot-torn areas, residents set up community action agencies or development corporations such as the Hough Area Development Corporation in Cleveland. In 1968 in the Hunts Point section of the Bronx in New York City, a Roman Catholic priest, Father Louis Gigante, founded the South East Bronx Community Organization Development Corporation (SEBCO) as a Model Cities agency to serve impoverished Puerto Ricans. In the countryside, activists set out to improve the depressed conditions with organizations such as the Kentucky Highlands Investment Corporation.

Watering the Grass Roots

At the Ford Foundation, Mitchell Sviridoff had replaced Ylvisaker as head of urban operations and shifted the philanthropy's emphasis from strictly social services to economic development and housing. Sviridoff, the former director of the Gray Areas organization in New Haven, thought the nonprofit development organizations held great potential for social uplift. On the train returning from a trip to Baltimore to visit local CDCs in 1979, a Ford Foundation trustee challenged Sviridoff by asking him what he would do if he had $25 million to help the fledgling groups. It would take Sviridoff a year to answer that question. But with the help and support of Franklin Thomas, the former head of the Bedford-Stuyvesant Restoration Corporation who had recently become president of the Ford Foundation, Sviridoff worked out the idea for a large independent organization to assist CDCs. Using a grant of $9.3 million from the Ford Foundation and six major corporations, Sviridoff in 1980 established the Local Initiatives Support Corporation (LISC) to give loans, grants, and technical assistance to CDCs. Four years later LISC had obtained more than $70 million from 250 corporations and foundations and three federal agencies and set up 31 branch offices, which raised funds from local sources.[12]

Idealistic real estate developer James Rouse set up the third national financial intermediary. As in the other cases, his idea germinated from a small beginning. Terry Flood and Barbara Moore, two women who were part of a social mission group of the ecumenical Church of the Saviour in Washington, DC, wanted to save two decrepit apartment buildings in the Adams Morgan neighborhood. They turned to their fellow church member Rouse for help. Although he counseled against the idea, he supported the church members when they formed a nonprofit community development organization, Jubilee Housing, to renovate rundown properties for poor people in Adams Morgan. Impressed, Rouse and his wife Patricia decided to create a national institution, and in 1982 founded the Enterprise Foundation to assist entities of all types interested in developing low-income housing. Like LISC, the Enterprise Foundation (now called Enterprise Community Partners) grew quickly. In 1982 it supported six groups in six locations; six years later, Enterprise had made $5.8 million in loans and grants and had expanded its network to 54 organizations in 27 locations. In the years that followed, both LISC and Enterprise would continue to expand their operations and finances by leaps and bounds.[13]

The Emergence of Social Loan Funds

As the financial intermediaries and philanthropies demonstrated new ways to support nonprofits, activists in different parts of the country began creating social banks that would make loans to nonprofits for projects that regular banks shunned. One of the first of these social lenders was ShoreBank, which began in 1973 when four idealistic friends purchased a bank in the South Shore

---

12 Avis C. Vidal, Arnold M. Howitt, and Kathleen P. Foster, "Stimulating Community Development: An Assessment of the Local Initiatives Support Corporation." Research Report R86-2 (Cambridge, MA: John F. Kennedy School of Government, Harvard University, June 1986), pp. 3–6.

13 Y. Thomas Liou and Robert C. Stroh, "Community Development Intermediary Systems in the United States: Origins, Evolution, and Functions," Housing Policy Debate 9 (3): 585–586; Enterprise Foundation, Many Roads Home. Annual Report (Washington: Enterprise Foundation, 1993), pp. 3, 41.

neighborhood of Chicago to counteract the departure of other banks from an area undergoing a racial and economic transition. After a few years of losing money on its loans to struggling local stores, the bank's owners found customers who both brought in profits and fulfilled a social purpose. By making loans to mom-and-pop landlords who wanted to rehabilitate their apartment buildings, ShoreBank helped stabilize working-class neighborhoods. Soon others founded new banks devoted to working in lower-income neighborhoods. From the broader credit union movement, for example, came community development credit unions, such as that started by the Center for Community Self-Help to help low-income African Americans, women, and rural residents in North Carolina.[14]

Meanwhile, religious groups had begun to build a movement to provide capital to social mission projects. Inspired by the Second Vatican Ecumenical Council (declared by Pope John XXIII in 1962), the civil rights, antiwar, and women's liberation movements, Catholic women's religious orders led the way to faith-based community investing as it is known today. In 1978, the Adrian Dominican Sisters, who had joined other denominations in the Interfaith Center on Corporate Responsibility, established its own Community Investment Program, as a way to provide for the growing number of their order's retired nuns and at the same time work toward social justice. At first, the Adrian Sisters had difficulty finding financially viable nonprofits, but eventually they discovered nonprofit food banks, housing organizations, and community land trusts to invest in.[15]

In the early 1980s, social investment in the United States gathered momentum. Along with their grants and technical assistance, the large financial intermediaries, LISC and the Enterprise

---

14 Ronald Grzywinski, "The New Old-Fashioned Banking," Harvard Business Review 69 (3) (May-June 1991): 87–98; Richard P. Taub, Community Capitalism (Boston: Harvard Business School Press, 1992); ShoreBank, 1996 Annual Report (Chicago: Shorebank, 1996), available at http://self-help.org/about-us.

15 Portfolio Advisory Board, "History of the Adrian Dominican Sisters' Socially Responsible Investments" (Adrian, MI: Adrian Dominican Sister, n.d.), available at http://pab.adriando-minicans.org/AboutUs/History.aspx.

Foundation, began making social purpose loans. In 1982 the Enterprise Foundation, for example, formalized its lending by starting the Enterprise Community Loan Fund. In 1983, local activists organized the New Hampshire Loan Fund with the support of the Adrian Sisters and other religious investors. On the West Coast, San Francisco reformers grew frustrated with the biases of mortgage lenders and in 1984 founded the Low Income Housing Investment Fund to set a good example. Over the next 15 years it grew exponentially and, renamed the Low Income Investment Fund (LIIF), made loans for building child care and education facilities as well. On the opposite coast, socially conscious financiers in 1985 pooled resources to found Boston Community Capital, which invested in housing, child care, youth programs, and commercial real estate in poor neighborhoods.[16]

In 1994 Congress responded to the increase in community development lending by establishing the Community Development Financial Institutions Fund in the Treasury Department. Since that time, the Fund has made equity-like investments in hundreds of community development financial institutions (CDFIs). This has allowed the CDFIs, which include banks, credit unions, and a wide variety of loan funds directed at social progress, to vastly increase their lending to organizations working to help low-income communities.[17]

Government Tools for Community Development

Although philanthropic and nonprofit support helped the movement to grow, government funding, especially federal funding, was essential if community development was to thrive on any significant scale. Under both Republican and Democratic presidents, the federal government gradually became an indispensable source of funds for the community development system.

---

16 Thomas Miller, Bridges to Dreams: The Story of the Low Income Investment Fund, Celebrating 25 Years of Impact: 1984-2009 (San Francisco: Low Income Investment Fund, 2009), available at http://liifund.org/wp-content/uploads/2011/03/Bridges-to-Dreams-The-Story-of-LIIF-2009_LRes.pdf.

17 Mark Pinsky, "Taking Stock: CDFIs Look Ahead after 25 Years of Community Development Finance." (Washington, DC: Brookings Institution and Joint Center for Housing Studies, 2001).

Congress took a major step when, after years of haggling with the Nixon administration over its proposed bill, it passed the landmark Housing and Community Development Act of 1974. The law replaced the unpopular urban renewal program and the idealistic but poorly conceived Model Cities and other categorical programs with community development block grants (CDBGs) to local governments. Although the act allowed governments to use block grants for a range of activities, it required that at least some of the funds help low-income families. Three years later, the Carter administration reinforced this goal through the Urban Development Action Grant program to target additional funds to inner-city areas in extreme economic distress. With these prods, many local government agencies began to contract redevelopment work to neighborhood nonprofit organizations, including community action agencies and CDCs.

Besides the numerous antipoverty aids such as child care, meals for the elderly, and loans to small and minority businesses, government programs specifically targeted low-income housing. The 1974 act created the federal Section 8 housing program, which subsidized rents for tenants in newly constructed, rehabilitated, and existing apartment buildings. In combination with federal tax benefits for real estate investors, the Section 8 subsidies provided a set of financial incentives that produced a surge of privately owned, low-income housing developments.

Although in 1986 Congress eliminated key tax incentives for real estate development, it replaced them with the Low Income Housing Tax Credit, which proved to be one of the most powerful housing programs ever devised. Unlike the earlier system, which relied on small-scale investors, the Low Income Housing Tax Credit opened the door to large banks and corporations to pour hundreds of millions of dollars into housing projects. To date, the program has helped finance more than 2.5 million homes. And in 1990 the government specifically recognized the work of nonprofits by setting aside funds for them in the HOME program.[18]

State governments too supported the community development system. By 1980, 42 states had established housing finance agencies, which issued state bonds to finance the construction of low-income housing. In the face of Ronald Reagan's cuts in housing spending, the remaining eight states soon followed. Some states went further. Massachusetts led the way by creating one corporation to finance community and economic development projects; another entity to give technical assistance and consulting services to nonprofit organizations carrying out housing, job training, local economic development, and improvements to child care facilities; and another program to provide crucial operating support to CDCs.[19]

Local activists gained another tool when federal regulators began to implement the Community Reinvestment Act (CRA), which was aimed at overcoming banks' refusal to lend in inner-city neighborhoods. The act had been passed in 1977, but only became effective in the mid-1990s. There were two main reasons. The first was that regulators, under pressure from political agitation and legislation that changed their reporting requirements, began to reveal publicly banks' lending behavior. The second reason was that after a steep increase in the number of banks seeking to merge with other banks, the regulators indicated that they would not grant approval for the mergers unless the requesting bank fulfilled its local lending obligations under CRA. To comply with the regulations, many banks seeking approval for mergers began providing capital to CDFIs and making loans to developers of the Low Income Housing Tax Credit deals.

---

18 David J. Erickson, The Housing Policy Revolution: Networks and Neighborhoods (Washington, DC: Urban Institute Press, 2009); David Erickson and Nancy Andrews, "Partnerships among Community Development, Public Health, and Health Care Could Improve the Well-Being of Low-Income People," Health Affairs 30 (11) (2011): 2058.

19 Margaret M. Brassil, The Creation of a Federal Partnership: The Role of the States in Affordable Housing (Albany: State University of New York Press, 2010), pp. 48, 51–54; Alexander von Hoffman, House by House, Block by Block: The Rebirth of America's Urban Neighborhoods (New York: Oxford University Press, 2003), p. 86.

In this way, CRA encouraged investment in inner-city and rural neighborhoods. From 1977 to 1991, according to the National Community Reinvestment Coalition, financial lenders and community organizations negotiated $8.8 billion in CRA credit agreements. Spurred undoubtedly by a strong economy and a variety of new banking and securitization practices, from 1992 through 2007 lenders committed an astonishing $4.5 trillion in CRA loans.[20]

Community Development, the Leading Edge of Revival

By the 1980s, forces that would encourage the revitalization of the inner city began to gather momentum. During the 1980s, immigrants, attracted by economic opportunity greater than that in their homelands, began to arrive in increasing numbers. Often low-wage workers, they sought and found inexpensive shelter in low-income neighborhoods of large "gateway" cities, such as New York, Washington, Chicago, Los Angeles, and Miami. At the same time, a small but noticeable number of artists and white-collar professionals began to take up residence in central cities. For them the city held attractions: historic homes, which some of the arrivals took great care to renovate, lively cultural life, and proximity to downtown jobs.

But during the 1980s and 1990s, the community development movement provided the most visible signs of new life in the inner city. Across the United States, but especially along the East and West Coasts and in the Midwest, the number of local CDCs in storefronts and church basements began to multiply.

---

20 The Financial Institutions Reform, Recovery and Enforcement Act of 1989 required federal bank regulators to release CRA evaluations and changed the rating system from a numeric to verbal grades. The Riegle-Neal Interstate Banking and Branching Efficiency Act of 1994 allowed mergers of banks in different states. William Apgar et al., "The 25th Anniversary of the Community Reinvestment Act: Access to Capital in an Evolving Financial Services System," prepared for the Ford Foundation (Cambridge, MA: Joint Center for Housing Studies, Harvard University, March 2002); Eric S. Belsky, Michael Schill, and Anthony Yezer, "The Effect of the Community Reinvestment Act on Bank and Thrift Home Purchase Mortgage Lending." (Cambridge, MA: Joint Center for Housing Studies, 2001); Eric S. Belsky, Matthew Lambert, and Alexander von Hoffman, "Insights Into the Practice of Community Reinvestment Act Lending: A Synthesis of CRA Discussion Groups." (Cambridge, MA: Joint Center for Housing Studies, 2000); National Community Reinvestment Coalition, CRA Commitments (Washington, DC: NCRC, September 2007), p. 5, available at http://community-wealth.org/_pdfs/articles-publications/cdfis/report-silver-brown.pdf.

In the shambles of a neighborhood that was West Garfield Park in Chicago, the Lutheran Church in 1979 started a community development organization called Bethel New Life. The name expressed the hope that these organizations brought to the depressed and abandoned inner-city neighborhoods.

Learning by Trial and Error

Yet the road to community development was rough. The original notion, dating from Kennedy's experiment in Brooklyn, was that ghettos were backward places of low employment. Hence, in the 1970s and 1980s, community development advocates endeavored to lure large corporations to set up factories in the inner city, with only mixed success. The Bedford-Stuyvesant Restoration Corporation was able to persuade IBM to open a small manufacturing plant in the neighborhood. Yet old buildings were not necessarily efficient for modern production, locations were not always near highways, and sometimes labor costs were too high. No other large corporations followed IBM, which closed its plant but stayed in Brooklyn until the early 1990s. Similarly, the Stride Rite shoe corporation and the Digital Equipment Corporation agreed in the late 1970s to operate factories in Boston's Roxbury neighborhood. But in December 1992, both companies announced that they would shut the doors of the facilities.[21]

Because of their economic development goals, leaders of CDCs also tried to stimulate small-scale enterprises, a treacherous undertaking under any circumstances. Community development groups that invested directly in local supermarkets and restaurants often lived to rue the day, if they survived the ordeal. In 1981, for example, the Codman Square Community Development Corporation in Boston's Dorchester district tried to replace the neighborhood's recently closed supermarket with its own, but the store quickly went bankrupt and took the CDC down with it. Bedford-Stuyvesant Restoration was more successful than some, but was forced to liquidate its ice

---

21 Ryan, "Bedford-Stuyvesant and the Prototype Community Development Corporation"; Barry Bluestone and Mary Huff Stevenson, The Boston Renaissance: Race, Space, and Economic Change in an American Metropolis (New York: Russell Sage Foundation, 2000), pp. 68–70.

cream shop and fashion design firms. And Restoration's efforts at starting new businesses, according to its historian, "proved almost impossibly difficult." Even with lavish backing from the federal government and corporations, Restoration undercapitalized its business startups and lacked the management skills to help the fledgling companies.[22]

These kinds of early business failures were valuable, if painful, learning experiences for the new grassroots practitioners of community development. Gradually they gained professional skills in real estate development, finance, and management. Just as importantly, local community development directors and project managers began to appreciate that business methods and discipline were necessary tools for the pursuit of their social and economic goals.

Through trial and error, the community developers learned that housing, for which there was both subsidies and demand, provided a viable business model. With a commitment for federal government's Section 8 rental assistance or the allocation of a Low Income Housing Tax Credit, a nonprofit could make a reasonably accurate financial plan of revenue for a low-income housing project. That plan, in turn, could convince lenders to back the deal. Nonprofit community development groups usually had to find multiple lenders to back their deals, but despite this serious burden, they developed hundreds of thousands of homes, either by constructing new attractive buildings or by renovating old apartment buildings inside and out.

In the Inner City, a New Day Dawns

Across the country the new wave of housing developments stabilized the lives of low-income people and served notice that their neglected neighborhoods were worthy places in which to live and invest. The most spectacular example of the transformative effect of housing development on dying communities came in New York's South Bronx, the international symbol of urban

---

22 von Hoffman, House by House, Block by Block, p. 85; Ryan, "Bedford-Stuyvesant and the Prototype Community Development Corporation," p. 88.

degradation. In 1986, Mayor Edward Koch declared a 10-year plan to rebuild homes on the rubble of abandoned and arson-destroyed apartment buildings that pocked the city's landscape. Unlike the old central command model of the public housing and urban renewal programs, the Koch administration opened the city's coffers to anyone who had a plausible project. The city eventually put up $5 billion to develop or renovate more than 180,000 dwellings, and the largest share (65,300 units) went to the troubled borough of the Bronx. Yet diverse developers—large and small, nonprofit and for-profit—using an array of approaches and programs rebuilt New York. In the process, CDCs—including the colorfully named Mid-Bronx Desperadoes and Banana Kelly in the Bronx and St. Nicholas Neighborhood Preservation Corporation in Brooklyn—demonstrated their abilities to lenders and boosted the number and size of their projects.[23]

By the late 1990s, buoyed by an expanding economy and an influx of immigrants, areas of the Bronx and Brooklyn had undergone a startling makeover. In the vicinity of community development efforts, property values were rising and crime rates falling. Gone were the abandoned buildings, raging fires, and open drug markets, and in their stead were well-maintained apartment buildings, newly built row houses, and bustling boulevards of shoppers. Young people played sports in well-maintained parks. So normal looking was the South Bronx that when a delegation from inner-city Baltimore arrived there in 1995 to learn about community development, they initially thought their trip had been a waste of time. Looking around, the first-time visitors had decided that such a normal-looking place could not possibly offer lessons in how to save blighted neighborhoods.

Although no other city would match the scale of New York's massive effort, CDCs during the 1980s and 1990s sparked similar revivals in inner-city neighborhoods from coast to coast. In the Roxbury and Dorchester neighborhoods of Boston, on

23 Michael Schill, Ingrid Ellen, Amy Ellen Schwartz, and Ioan Voicu, "Revitalizing Inner City Neighborhoods: New York City's Ten Year Plan for Housing," Housing Policy Debate 13 (3) (2002): 529–566.

the West Side of Chicago, and in South Central Los Angeles, savvy CDC directors helped fill in the unsightly and dangerous vacant lots and buildings on their streets. In Washington, DC, the pioneering efforts of Jubilee Housing in Adams Morgan and the Development Corporation of Columbia Heights helped ignite a process that by the 2000s would turn these formerly crime ridden and dwindling communities into booming fashionable districts. If community development was stronger in coastal cities and the Midwest than in the South and Southwest, it nonetheless had a visible impact on inner-city neighborhoods that had been left to die not long before.

Although new housing development could make a dramatic impact on fortunes of a low-income neighborhood, the leaders of the effective groups believed that housing was only one component of community development. In addition to housing development, groups such as the Vermont-Slauson Economic Development Corporation in Los Angeles and Greater Southwest Development Corporation in Chicago helped to start or expand businesses and revive inner-city commercial thoroughfares. Organizations such as Newark's New Community Corporation offered a broad array of social services including child care, job training, and drug rehabilitation. Some groups introduced medical clinics to their neighborhoods. A few such as South Bronx Churches operated schools. In Atlanta, the Reynoldstown Revitalization Corporation developed housing and ran parenting classes, classes for school dropouts, and an antidrug program. But its centerpiece program has been the Wheelbarrow Summer Theater, an annual community arts festival.[24]

New Visions of Comprehensiveness

The broad range of activities pursued in the name of community development reflected the recurring theme of holistic urban revitalization that appeared in the nineteenth-century Settlement

---

24 For the range and accomplishments of community development groups in the 1990s, see von Hoffman, House by House, Block by Block; Carol F. Steinbach, "Coming of Age: Trends and Achievements of Community-Based Development Organizations." (Washington, DC: National Congress for Community Economic Development, 1999); Avis C. Vidal, "Rebuilding Communities: A National Study of Urban Community Development Corporations." (New York: Community Development Research Center, 1992).

Houses, reemerged in the New Deal projects, and had inspired Great Society antipoverty efforts. During the heyday of community development, it reappeared specifically in the form of comprehensive community initiatives (CCIs). These initiatives, often spurred by program officers in philanthropies and financial intermediaries, aimed to coordinate a set of locally determined and collaboratively diverse programs that would uplift impoverished neighborhood and residents together.

The forerunner and a prototype of comprehensive neighborhood renewal efforts is the Dudley Street Neighborhood Initiative (DSNI) in Boston, which like many CCIs emerged under unique circumstances that may not be easily replicable. When an alliance of local social service agencies, CDCs, and churches founded the DSNI in 1984 to upgrade an area of approximately 1.5 square miles in the Roxbury section of Boston, for instance, it garnered an extraordinary amount of interest among the local residents. The reason was fear: the Boston Redevelopment Authority had recently proposed an urban renewal plan that, with its call for construction of office towers and luxury hotels, raised the specter of demolition and gentrification of the Dudley Street neighborhood. A group of concerned residents took over the DSNI and transformed what was supposed to be a large-scale social service operation into a new kind of locally based redevelopment-planning entity.[25]

With the backing of a local foundation, the DSNI's new leaders were committed to strong neighborhood representation and community organizing. Their first executive director was an experienced community organizer, Peter Medoff, who won credibility for the group by leading a successful campaign to force the city government to get rid of abandoned cars and illegal trash transfer stations that plagued the neighborhood. To counter the Boston Redevelopment Authority's urban renewal plan, the DSNI put together a series of well-attended community workshops in which

---

25 Peter Medoff and Holly Sklar, Streets of Hope: The Fall and Rise of an Urban Neighborhood (Boston: South End Press, 1994); Dudley Street Neighborhood Initiative, "From the Bottom Up: The Dudley Street Neighborhood Initiative Strategy for Sustainable Economic Development." (December 1997), available at http://dsni.org.

residents devised a master plan for developing an "urban village" of houses, parks, and shops for the Dudley Street neighborhood. In an unprecedented accomplishment for a community-based nonprofit, the DSNI in 1988 acquired the power of eminent domain from the city's redevelopment agency to supervise the development of the neighborhood's 177 acres of vacant lots. Within the next 10 years, the DSNI oversaw the development of 300 vacant lots into 225 new homes, playgrounds, gardens, and community buildings.

The DSNI took a broad approach to the problems of the Dudley Street neighborhood. Besides physical development, the DSNI addressed issues of public safety, youth development, and environmental justice. From the beginning the organization was committed to organizing and resident participation, and so residents themselves determined the areas in which the DSNI would be active. Whenever possible, the DSNI did not manage projects directly but instead encouraged and coordinated local agencies and nonprofits to carry out the DSNI agenda.

The DSNI relied on local CDCs and minority developers to develop or rehabilitate housing and started the Agency Collaborative to coordinate human service programs within the neighborhood. The wide range of programs it adopted helped inspire the comprehensive community initiatives of the 1990s.[26]

In 1991, an officer of the Surdna Foundation started the Comprehensive Community Revitalization Program (CCRP) in the Bronx, creating another prototype for comprehensive community development. With funds from several foundations, Anita Miller, a veteran Ford Foundation and LISC program officer, instituted a $10 million program to improve six Bronx neighborhoods. Having helped a number of Bronx CDCs get off the ground, Miller was able to identify experienced and successful organizations to help to diversify their programs.[27]

---

26 Medoff and Sklar, Streets of Hope; von Hoffman, House by House, Block by Block, pp. 92–94, 107–108.

27 Xavier De Souza Briggs, Anita Miller, and John Shapiro, "Planning for Community Building: CCRP (Comprehensive Community Revitalization Program) in the South Bronx," Planners' Casebook 17 (Winter 1996): 1-6.

Like the DSNI, the organizers and funders of the CCRP placed great store in local participation and community planning. To carry out "quality-of-life physical planning" in each neighborhood, the local CDC put together a task force of its own leaders, residents active in community affairs, service providers such as police and teachers, and local merchants. The task forces in turn organized neighborhood forums in which local residents and government representatives and officials, with the help of planning consultants, drew up plans for their neighborhoods. The leaders of the CCRP also believed that collaboration was a powerful tool for community development. They felt that bringing together representatives of various elements of neighborhood life was in itself an achievement because it would lead to later collaborations to solve the problems raised in the community forums.[28]

Under the CCRP, the participating CDCs moved into or expanded their efforts in new areas of community development. One of the most impressive results was the creation of five new family practice health clinics in areas of the Bronx in which the local residents were forced to obtain most of their health care in hospital emergency rooms. True to the goal of collaboration, the CDCs provided the facilities for the primary health-care clinics, and the city's large hospitals ran them. In addition, four of the CDCs participated in a state program of immunization and lead screening. Other projects that grew out of the CCRP included employment training centers to teach basic job skills, professionally run child care centers, the development of new public parks, neighborhood safety efforts, and several economic development enterprises.[29]

Comprehensive Community Development Catches On

Following these stirring examples of wide-ranging community development, foundations during the 1990s created numerous

28 CCRP, "Summaries of Quality-of-Life Physical Plans." (New York: CCRP, 1995), pp. 1–2.

29 Gerri Spilka and Tom Burns, "Final Assessment Report: The Comprehensive Community Revitalization Program in the South Bronx." (New York: CCRP, OMG Center, 1998), pp. 15–30. See also Anne C. Kubisch et al., Voices from the Field III (Washington, DC: Aspen Institute, 2010).

comprehensive community initiatives. Begun in 1990 by the Ford Foundation, the Neighborhood and Family Initiative targeted poor neighborhoods in Detroit, Milwaukee, Memphis, and Hartford. The Ford Foundation worked through a philanthropic foundation in each city to guide the formation of a collaborative committee. In the collaborative committees, neighborhood residents, business owners, and professionals developed a local agenda, for which representatives of the city's government agencies, corporations, and nonprofit organizations served as resources. The same year, the Enterprise Foundation and the City of Baltimore began the Neighborhood Transformation Initiative, a multipronged effort—including education, social services, job training, and community organizing—to address in systematic fashion the social, economic, and physical conditions of Sandtown-Winchester, an impoverished district of Baltimore. In 1993 the Annie E. Casey Foundation's Rebuilding Communities Initiative began to fund existing community organizations in Denver, Detroit, Philadelphia, and Boston to lead campaigns for comprehensive renewal in their home neighborhoods. Other foundations such as The Pew Charitable Trusts followed with their own comprehensive initiatives.[30]

In general, the collaborative groups created by these comprehensive initiatives took on a diverse range of neighborhood issues— such as safety, education, housing, social services, employment, and collective action—and accomplished a great deal of good. Yet the projects tended to be isolated "one-off" deals, which the new collaborative organizations either maintained as specialized activities or let expire once the funding ran out. More to the point, the holistic improvement of a neighborhood by many parties working together synergistically never happened. Despite a new school, new houses, and useful programs, the

---

30 Robert J. Chaskin, Selma Chipenda-Dansokho, and Amanda K. Toler, "Moving Beyond the Neighborhood and Family Initiative: The Final Phase and Lessons Learned." (Chicago: Chapin Hall Center for Children at the University of Chicago, 2000); Winton Pitcoff, "Redefining Community Development, Part I: Comprehensive Community Initiatives," Shelterforce 96 (November/December 1997) (Special Section): 2–14; Winton Pitcoff, "Redefining Community Development, Part II: Collaborating for Change," Shelterforce 97 (January/February 1998) (Special Section): 2–16.

Sandtown-Winchester neighborhood remains impoverished and untransformed.

As in the past, the leaders of these efforts at comprehensive community development aimed higher than their reach. Looked at more closely, neither the DSNI nor the CCRP was truly comprehensive. By far the DSNI's greatest accomplishment lay in land planning, in which it had been fortunate to have enjoyed the crucial support of the mayor and the head of the city's neighborhood development agency. In the Bronx, the purpose of the CCRP was less to transform communities completely than to expand the accomplishments of local CDCs beyond housing.

Other comprehensive community initiatives bogged down for a variety of reasons: vague goals; strained relationships between the visionary officers of sponsoring foundations and leaders of local organizations; lengthy deliberations of community groups over the agenda; and strategies that were not always lined up with other community efforts. As a result, reformers and philanthropic program officers began to question whether a systematic, all-embracing approach to community improvement was practical. With some notable exceptions such as the MacArthur/LISC New Communities Program in Chicago, many philanthropic organizations by the 2000s had backed away from comprehensiveness as a goal.[31]

Nonetheless, the federal government committed heavily to the goal of comprehensive community development through HOPE VI, a program intended to replace crime-ridden and physically deteriorated public housing projects with wholesome living environments. Beginning in 1993, HUD and local housing authorities demolished public housing projects, replaced them with houses that resembled and sometimes included private-market homes, and rented them to families with a range of low incomes. Although an expensive and controversial program, HOPE VI has produced several showcases—such as the Townhomes on

---

31 Anne C. Kubisch, "Lessons to Improve the Design and Implementation of Community Change Efforts." In Kubisch et al., Voices from the Field III.

Capitol Hill in Washington, DC or the Villages of East Lake in Atlanta. One of the program's key goals has been to create vital communities for low-income people, and in pursuit of that goal many housing authorities—often in partnerships with nonprofit agencies—have taken a holistic approach by incorporating child care, job training, recreation, and health care into the new developments.[32]

THE CHANGING WORLD OF COMMUNITY DEVELOPMENT
Redrawing the Map of Poverty

By the start of the new millennium it was clear that the map of poverty had changed once again. In the large cities where the community development movement was strongest, the changes that had begun in inner-city communities now reached or passed a tipping point. Where once only a CDC or a few urban pioneers had seen the potential value of a neighborhood, an influx of upper-middle-class and wealthy professionals had driven up rents and home prices far above what unsubsidized low-income families could pay. In such gentrified places, subsidized affordable housing projects built in an earlier era of economic need now helped maintain a mixed-income character. Immigration also transformed the ethnicity of neighborhoods. The arrivals from Latin America, the Caribbean, and Asia had begun to write their own chapters of the history of their neighborhoods. Longtime residents of Los Angeles were startled to realize that the majority of people in the city's historically African American neighbor-hoods—Watts, for example—were now Mexicans. Poverty had by no means disappeared, and after a long decline began rising again. By 2010, with the nation feeling the effects of the Great Recession, the proportion of Americans whose incomes fell below the poverty line hit 15.1 percent, the highest level since 1993.[33]

---

32 Arthur J. Naparstek et al., "HOPE VI: Community Building Makes a Difference." (Washington: U.S. Department of Housing and Urban Development, 2000); Susan J. Popkin et al., "A Decade of HOPE VI" (Washington, DC: Urban Institute, 2004).

33 Sabrina Tavernise, "Soaring Poverty Casts Spotlight on 'Lost Decade,'" New York Times, September 13, 2011.

Complicating the problem were population movements that expanded the geography of poverty. Some poor people continued to reside in the old inner-city neighborhoods, some of which had extremely high rates of poverty. But increasingly low-income Americans, like their better-off fellow citizens, moved outwards in search of better homes, schools, and recreation. Both low-income African Americans and immigrants, long associated with inner-city neighborhoods, moved to the suburbs. Between 2000 and 2010, the number of poor people living in suburbs soared by 53 percent, twice the rate it grew in cities. Two-thirds of this increase took place during the recession after 2007. The great problem was that the governments of the towns where low-income people now made their homes often lacked the budgets, staff resources, and access to state and federal programs that large city administrations had.[34]

Community Development Gets Personal

Meanwhile, many in the community development field began to seek new approaches that were not necessarily "place-based" as were so many earlier efforts. During the 1990s, some in the field grew frustrated that too many community development efforts were restricted to one or another form of real estate development. In Los Angeles, for example, the comprehensive effort known as Rebuild Los Angeles evolved into an effort more tightly focused on small business development. Denise Fairchild left her position as LISC program officer to work on organizing trade associations for small ethnic businesses and increasing technological skills of inner-city workers. Whether because of an aversion to the real estate approach, the inability to devise a truly comprehensive strategy, or general intellectual restlessness, many national and community foundations chose not to support place-based project work directly.[35]

---

34 Sabrina Tavernise, "Outside Cleveland, Snapshots of Poverty's Surge in the Suburbs," New York Times, October 24, 2011.

35 von Hoffman, House by House, Block by Block; Kubisch, "Lessons to Improve the Design and Implementation of Community Change Efforts," p. 135.

Perhaps the greatest change in thinking in the antipoverty field was the widespread adoption of the concept of asset building. The community development movement that emerged in the 1970s and 1980s was built on the idea of improving the economic and community life of the places where low-income residents lived. If this generally included a host of programs that helped individuals directly, the emphasis was on the community. Indeed, CDCs often found that when successful, their efforts to increase the opportunity and skills of local people undermined their goal of a healthy community because individuals who prospered often chose to move elsewhere. The idea of asset building changed the overall priorities by focusing on increasing the wealth of individuals, not improving neighborhoods.

The theories of Michael Sherraden, a social work professor at Washington University, particularly influenced the officers of private funding agencies concerned with helping people escape poverty. Sherraden defined assets as wealth, including property and financial holdings, and his writings sometimes seemed to suggest that there was nothing that increasing poor people's assets could not do. In one article Sherraden asserted that asset building would increase household stability, make people plan their future, "provide a foundation for risk-taking," enhance a sense of well-being, elevate social status, and increase community involvement and civic participation and the well-being and life chances of the family's children.[36]

Finance for Individuals

One of the most popular policies that Sherraden championed to help poor people increase their wealth was individual development accounts (IDAs). Typically in these schemes, funding agencies and local nonprofit organizations match the amount of money that an individual saved. Sometimes IDAs were targeted

---

36 Michael Sherraden, Assets and the Poor: A New American Welfare Policy (Armonk, NY: M.E. Sharpe, 1991); Michael Sherraden and Deborah Page-Adams, "Asset-based Alternatives in Social Policy." In Increasing Understanding of Public Problems and Issues: Proceedings of the 1995 National Public Policy Education Conference (Oak Brook, IL: Farm Foundation, 1995), pp. 65–83; Deborah Page-Adams and Michael Sherraden, "Asset Building as a Community Revitalization Strategy," Social Work 42 (5) (September 1997): 423–434.

for specific goals such as school tuition or the purchase of a home. In that IDAs are a direct cash transfer, albeit for a special purpose, they are extremely beneficial to people whose chief problem is a lack of money.

Sherraden also advocated another individual asset program, microenterprise, which involved lending small sums of money to individuals. Activists working with very poor people in South Asia, South America, and Africa had devised the program to encourage the informal businesses that proliferate in the global slums. Conditions in the United States, however, differ from those in developing regions. Here the poor frequently lack tightly knit clan-type social groups, even the smallest businesses are regulated, and for better or worse credit is available to almost anyone. Nonetheless, the American version of support for microenterprise has grown dramatically. By 2002, more than 500 organizations offered either credit—including small seed grants and equity investments—and financial services or financial training and technical assistance. ACCION, the largest agency by far, had lent approximately $148 million to more than 15,000 entrepreneurs, with an average loan of $5,300.[37]

There's No Place Like Home
Home purchases, which IDAs could help achieve, became the other popular form of asset building. People in the community development field had long praised the effect of homeownership on neighborhoods: low-income homeowners, like other home-owners, worked hard to maintain their houses and yards and were engaged in community affairs. In addition to these beneficial aspects of owning a home, reformers now extolled the idea that houses were an asset that, like a bank account, could be drawn against in the future. At the same time, presidents Bill Clinton and George W. Bush both declared that expanding the percentage

---

37 Elaine Edgcomb and Joyce Klein, Opening Opportunities, Building Ownership: Fulfilling the Promise of Microenterprise in the United States (Washington, DC, Aspen, Colorado: Aspen Institute, 2005), p. 24; William Burrus, "Innovations in Microenterprise Development in the United States." Paper for Microcredit Summit Campaign, 2006, pp. 9, 16, available at http://microcreditsummit.org/papers/Workshops/12_Burrus.pdf; Mark Schreiner and Gary Woller, "Microenterprise Development Programs in the United States and in the Developing World," World Development 31 (9) (2003): 1569–1570.

of homeownership in the United States was a high priority for the nation. Thanks to a number of changes in mortgage lending, credit that had been so hard to come by in the past was now available to low-income households.

Nonprofit organizations such as the Neighborhood Housing Services groups across the country offered first-time home buyer classes as well as loans. These careful programs required that the novice mortgage borrowers take classes to prepare them for the challenges of homeownership and also offered them well structured fixed-rate loans. As a result, the first-time homebuyer programs had few defaults.

As is well known, however, subprime mortgage companies that were more interested in quick profits were not so careful and in some cases operated fraudulently. In numerous cases, unscrupulous lenders lured unsuspecting borrowers—who were disproportionately African American and Hispanic—into disastrous refinancing schemes, eventually causing millions of defaults and foreclosures. The concentration of foreclosures in low-income neighborhoods, especially those in the Midwest, undid decades of hard-won progress.

In the end, those low-income homebuyers who were able to complete their purchases had acquired their own homes, which is perhaps the most important benefit of the purchase. They often, however, did not possess an appreciating asset. Their houses were likely to be located in neighborhoods with stagnant or declining property values. Therefore, even if they were able to retain their homes, low-income homeowners often could not trade up or borrow against their houses for future investments as upper-middle-class owners in appreciating land markets might do.

The Return of Economic Community Development

Place-based community development was hardly dead. Rather it returned to its roots in economic development. To stimulate "economic opportunity in America's distressed communities," in 1994 the Clinton administration instituted the Empowerment Zone/Enterprise Community program, which channeled billions of dollars in tax incentives, performance grants, and loans to more than 100 designated urban and rural places. Twenty-seven years earlier, Robert Kennedy had proposed a similar concept, but it was Jack Kemp, HUD Secretary under President George H. W. Bush, who first established "enterprise zones" to provide financial incentives to help expand businesses and employment in economically depressed areas.

Following business professor Michael Porter's research on the hidden economic potential of the inner city, a coalition of 65 business and community leaders and government officials in 1997 concluded that private-sector investment in areas considered economically broken would actually pay off. Three years later, the federal government passed the New Markets Tax Credit program to stimulate "community capitalism." Similar in concept to Low Income Housing Tax Credits, the program allocated tax credits to organizations (including affiliates of many CDFIs) to attract investment in businesses in low-income communities. And similar to the response to the Low Income Housing Tax Credit, both local community developers and corporate investors quickly embraced the New Markets Tax Credit program.

The Maturing of Community Development

By the early years of the twenty-first century, community development activities and institutions had spread across the United States. The once experimental organization known as the community development corporation had become established in the American landscape. By 2005 the number of CDCs had multiplied to 4,600, and they could be found in large cities and rural areas in each of the country's major regions.[38]

A large financial and technical infrastructure buttressed community development efforts. At present, the community capital field boasts more than 1,000 CDFIs in cities, rural areas, and Native

---

38 The community development movement, nonetheless, is stronger in some regions—the Northeast, Midwest, and West Coast, especially—than others. National Congress for Community Economic Development, "Reaching New Heights: Trends and Achievements of Community-Based Development Organizations." (Washington DC: NCCED, 2005); Edward Goetz, "Local Government Support for Nonprofit Housing: a Survey of U.S. Cities," Urban Affairs Quarterly 27 (3) (March 1992): 424.

American reservations. In 2008, the authors of an industry study found that a sample of 495 CDFIs had $20.4 billion in financing outstanding and originated $5.53 billion in new community development financing.[39] The Low Income Investment Fund, to name just one example, to date has served more than one million people and through loans and grants has invested its billionth dollar, which leveraged an additional $6 billion to help pay for tens of thousands of homes, school facilities, and child care spaces in low-income communities.

Since 1980 LISC has invested $11.1 billion ($1.1 billion in 2010 alone) in community development, which contributed to $33.9 billion in total development of 277,000 affordable homes, millions of square feet of retail and community space, not to mention schools, child care facilities, and children's playing fields. Similarly, since 1982 Enterprise Community Partners has collected more than $11 billion in equity, grants, and loans to help build or preserve nearly 300,000 affordable rental and for-sale homes and provide more than 410,000 jobs nationwide. By 2000, NeighborWorks America and its affiliates had reached an annual direct investment in economically distressed communities of $1 billion. The network included 235 local nonprofit organizations, which served more than 4,500 neighborhoods. Since the economic downturn, its prodigious home buying and counseling machinery has turned to foreclosure mitigation counseling and

---

39 The figure for financing originated in 2008 was based on a smaller sample of 423 respondents and thus understates the totals for all 495 CDFIs. CDFI Fund, "List of Certified Community Development Financial Institution (CDFIs) with Contact Information as of December 31, 2011." (Washington, DC: U.S. Department of Treasury, 2011), in Excel file, "Certified CDFIs and Native CDFIs – Sortable," available at http://cdfifund.gov/ what_we_do/programs_id.asp?programID=9#certified; CDFI Data Project, "Development Financial Institutions: Providing Capital, Building Communities, Creating Impact, 2008." (Washington DC: Opportunity Finance Network, 2008), pp. 2, 9, 10, 11, available at http:// opportunityfinance.net/store/downloads/cdp_fy2008.pdf; Low Income Investment Fund, 2011 Annual Report (San Francisco: Low Income Investment Fund, 2011), available at http://liifund.org/annual-report.

administering mortgage payment relief to homeowners with falling income stemming from unemployment.[40]

Even as the government, banking, and philanthropic systems of financial support grew strong in the new millennium, community development organizations were forced to confront new and not always pleasant realities. The leaders of the founding generation had aged, and many now retired from the business. Sometimes the new leaders had trouble coping with changed circumstances. In some cities, boosted by the real estate boom, the areas that the CDCs served had indeed revived, raising the question of the necessity of such organizations.

In any case, a lack of vacant lots or decrepit buildings and the high costs of land limited the scope of what local community development organizations were able to do. As opportunities for community development lessened, so too did the need for many nonprofits operating in the same city. Meanwhile, not all the leaders of community development organizations could avoid missteps: in some cases, the search for new projects distracted them from managing the company's real estate assets, which could be financially disastrous. For such reasons, the ranks of community development organizations thinned significantly, dropping from about 8,400 CDCs in 2002 to perhaps half that number in 2010.[41]

The nonprofit field adjusted to the new conditions. CDCs increasingly turned to partnerships with other organizations and institutions as a way of stretching their resources and the scope of their activities. Some CDCs expanded into new service areas, either to

---

40 LISC, "Our Mission." (New York: LISC, n.d.), available at http://lisc.org/section/aboutus/mission; Enterprise Community Partners, "Mission and Strategic Plan." (New York: Enterprise Community Partners, n.d.), available at http://enterprisecommunity.com/about/mission-and-strategic-plan; NeighborWorks America, "History of NeighborWorks America and the NeighborWorks Network," available at http://nw.org/network/aboutUs/history/default.asp.

41 von Hoffman, House by House, Block by Block, pp. 16, 272n14. For conservative estimates of the number of CDCs, see National Congress for Community Economic Development, "Reaching New Heights," p. 4. The general sentiment of those who work in the community development field is that for several years the ranks of CDCs have been thinning.

take up the slack of groups that had gone out of business or to inaugurate community development in new territories.

Increasingly local groups and governments turned to large specialized nonprofit housing companies for housing development. Regional and national groups such as Mercy Housing, National Church Residences, BRIDGE Housing Corporation, and The Community Builders operated with the kind of business acumen—including asset management officers—and the size of real estate portfolios that compared well with for-profit real estate companies. With such skilled and yet socially committed organizations, it did not seem necessary for as many small groups to develop housing on their own.

Innovation Lives

For all the unsettling changes, community development was in many ways stronger than ever. The growing popularity of investing to achieve a social goal, against which specific results could be measured, channeled new funds and new energy into community development. A number of efforts demonstrated the persistent appeal of integrated, if not absolutely comprehensive, approaches to effect social change. As before, the many betterment programs took place in housing developments. At the Edgewood Terrace housing complex in Washington, DC, the Community Preservation and Development Corporation instituted a computer technology programs for the residents, which garnered widespread acclaim.

The most innovative of the new generation of community development projects sprang from areas other than housing. Perhaps the most celebrated has education at its core. Led by Geoffrey Canada, the Harlem Children's Zone in New York City focused a wide range of efforts on a defined area—originally a single block expanded in 1997 to a 24-block area, and in 2007, to a section of central Harlem that extends from 116th to 143rd streets. The group created a 10-year business plan and led the way for nonprofits by carefully evaluating and tracking the results of its programs so its staff could adjust the implementation of programs that were not achieving their objectives. As its name suggests, the Harlem Children's Zone first concerned itself with helping local schools and in 2004 helped start the Promise Academy, a high-quality public charter school. Its goal is "to create a 'tipping point' in the neighborhood so that children are surrounded by an enriching environment of college-oriented peers and supportive adults, a counterweight to 'the street.'" To do so, Canada and his colleagues expanded their efforts to include parenting workshops, a preschool program, a health program to counter asthma, and an antiobesity program for children. [42]

The Harlem Children's Zone has inspired the Obama administration to institute the Promise Neighborhoods program. Significantly, this community development program resides not at HUD but in the Department of Education. Its purpose is to nurture young people starting from the cradle and ending with a career. To create excellent schools and strong systems of family and community support, the Promise Neighborhoods program takes an approach that would sound familiar to those who invented the Model Cities program 50 years ago: by coordinating and integrating programs across agency boundaries.[43]

Health care is another entering wedge for community development. The best known example is the Codman Square Health Center located in a neighborhood in the Dorchester section of Boston. Although the organization dates from 1979, in 1995 it had grown to the point that it expanded into a multi-million dollar medical facility created out of a former nursing home. Its broadly defined mission is "to serve as a resource for improving the physical, mental and social well-being of the community." From the start, its leader William Walczak believed that health

---

42 Harlem Children's Zone, "The HCZ Project: 100 Blocks, One Bright Future," available at http://hcz.org/about-us/the-hcz-project; Will Dobbie and Roland G. Fryer, Jr., "Are High-Quality Schools Enough to Increase Achievement Among the Poor? Evidence from the Harlem Children's Zone," Federal Reserve Community Affairs Research Conference, Arlington, Virginia, April 29, 2011, available at http://frbsf.org/community/conferences/201 1ResearchConference/docs/5-dobbie-fryer-paper.pdf.

43 U.S. Department of Education, "Promise Neighborhoods." (Washington, DOE, Office of Innovation and Improvement, 2012), available at http://www2.ed.gov/programs/promise-neighborhoods/index.html.

care could serve as a tool for community development and often partnered with the local CDC located across the street from the health center. Hence, besides an array of medical and health services, the community clinic offers access to adult education, "financial health" classes (such as personal finance workshops), and youth services, and in conjunction with Dorchester House Multi-Service Center (a surviving local Settlement House!), civic engagement activities.[44]

CONCLUSION: TOWARD A NEW VISION FOR COMMUNITY DEVELOPMENT

The field of community development has grown immeasurably since the dark days of top-down policies such as urban renewal. In urban and rural areas, local and regional nonprofit organizations are developing real estate and delivering a range of services to once forgotten communities. Thanks to government programs, an array of philanthropic institutions and financial intermediaries such as CDFIs, the field has developed pipelines of funding. As experience in management and business progressed, so too did the sophistication of measures to gauge the results of community development efforts. If comprehensiveness has continued to prove elusive, the multifaceted approach has succeeded in numerous ways to uplift and enrich economically stressed neighborhoods. Innovative approaches as embodied in the Harlem Children's Zone and Codman Square Health Center hold bright promise for the future.

At the same time, current conditions pose great obstacles to the community development. First and foremost are the effects of the Great Recession. The economic downturn has brought a wave of foreclosures in low-income neighborhoods and modest suburban subdivisions. It also has created, or revealed, a new dimension of poverty in the millions of long-term unemployed. Once again homes are abandoned and communities are in peril. Some cities

---

44 Codman Square Health Center, "Mission Statement," available at http://www.codman.org/about-us/; "Community Services," available at http://codman.org/community-services. See also Sandra Braunstein and Risa Lavizzo-Mourey, "How The Health And Community Development Sectors Are Combining Forces to Improve Health and Well-Being," Health Affairs, 30 (11) (November 2011): 2042–2051.

never caught the wave of community development and urban revival. Cities such as Detroit, Baltimore, and New Orleans pose extreme cases of shrinking populations and empty streets. At the same time, the community development field has yet to establish a significant number of organizations in the suburbs, where the poor increasingly live.

As the plight of poor and working-class Americans grows increasingly dire, however, government social policy is in retreat. In response to plummeting tax revenues and gaping budget deficits, federal, state, and local, have cut back funds for a wide variety of social and economic programs. The new austerity directly imperils community development.

Hence, today the community development field stands on the threshold of new synergies, but it also faces challenges as never before. The people in this dynamic industry must apply the knowledge gained through past experiences to new and difficult circumstances. If history is a guide, they will rise to the occasion.

ALEXANDER VON HOFFMAN *is a senior fellow at the Joint Center for Housing Studies of Harvard University and a lecturer in the urban planning and design department at Harvard's Graduate School of Design. He is the author of* House by House, Block by Block: The Rebirth of America's Urban Neighborhoods; *Fuel* Lines for the Urban Revival Engine: Neighborhoods, Community Development Corporations, and Financial Intermediaries; *and* Local Attachments: The Making of an American Urban Neighborhood, 1850 to 1920. *Von Hoffman has written numerous scholarly articles on urban history as well as general interest essays on housing and urban development for periodicals such as* The Atlantic Monthly, The New York Times, *and the* Washington Post.

THE CONTINUING EVOLUTION OF AMERICAN POVERTY AND ITS IMPLICATIONS FOR COMMUNITY DEVELOPMENT

Alan Berube
Brookings Institution

The Gospel according to Matthew quotes Jesus as saying to his disciples, "For you have the poor always with you." That may well indeed be true. But just like other groups, the poor change over time. Mass distribution of loaves and fishes was arguably an appropriate antipoverty strategy in 30 AD. Today, the needs of the poor, and our expectations for what antipoverty policy should achieve, are radically different.

As Alexander von Hoffman portrays earlier in this volume, community development gained currency over 40 years ago as a response to a particular set of challenges, affecting a particular set of people and places. From the Ford Foundation's Gray Areas programs in the early to mid-1960s, to President Johnson's Model Cities program, to grassroots community empowerment programs that grew out of the civil rights movement, community development focused the bulk of its early attention on inner-city, African American neighborhoods, particularly in the wake of urban riots in the late 1960s. While these new programs and community development corporations experimented with diverse tactics, the movement's early leaders gravitated toward afford-able housing and local economic development as key levers to attract private capital to help improve low-income neighbor-hoods, provide better opportunities for their residents, and reduce poverty.

Yet as this chapter documents, today's poverty differs in several fundamental ways from the poverty that reformers set out to address more than four decades ago. Community development has evolved significantly, too, but perhaps not at the same pace as the underlying problems it set out to address. The incidence, loca-tion, and socioeconomic characteristics of poverty have shifted dramatically in some cases. These changes highlight a series of challenges for the future of place-based initiatives that aim to alleviate poverty, enhance economic mobility, and ultimately ensure that no one is severely disadvantaged by where they live.

TRENDS IN THE U.S. POVERTY RATE AND POPULATION

Community development evolved as a response to a complex, interwoven set of issues affecting primarily inner-city minority communities: racism, redlining, and disinvestment in infra-structure and local economic activity. The movement's basic aim, however, was to attack the roots of poverty in inner-city America. Therefore, it is worth defining poverty en route to understanding changes in its incidence and character over time.

Since the late 1960s, the Census Bureau has tracked poverty in America using a measure developed by Social Security Administration researcher Mollie Orshansky in 1963. That measure was originally based on a family food budget and an estimate that families spent about one-third of their income on food. It provided a "poverty threshold" that varies by family size, and which has been updated annually for inflation ever since.[1]

---

1 Gordon M. Fisher, "Mollie Orshansky: Author of the Poverty Thresholds," Amstat News, September 2008, 15–18.

While the poverty measure provides a crucial barometer of changes in national economic well-being, it suffers from many flaws, some of which make it an even less useful measure today than it was in the early 1970s. Two shortcomings deserve special note. First, the measure does not account for differences in costs of living across the country, which have grown over time. The same thresholds apply to families in Sandusky, OH, as in San Francisco, CA, even though rents today are nearly three times as high in the latter market.[2] Second, it does not take into account key benefits and expenditures that alter resources available to families. These include child care expenditures, which rose as more women entered the workforce, and programs like the Earned Income Tax Credit (EITC), which greatly expanded income support for low-income working families. Under a new Supplemental Poverty Measure developed by the Census Bureau to correct for these deficiencies, 16.0 percent of the U.S. population would be considered poor in 2010, slightly higher than the 15.2 percent under the official measure.[3]

The official poverty measure, however, remains the best source of historical perspective on the changing population and profile of low-income individuals and families in the United States. And as the U.S. population grew over the past four decades, so too did the number of people living below the poverty line. In 1973, 23 million out of 208 million Americans lived in families with incomes below the applicable poverty threshold for their size, which at the time was $3,548 for a family of three.[4] By 2007, the U.S. population had expanded by about 100 million, and the below-poverty population rose to 37 million. In that year, families of three with incomes under $16,530 were considered poor.

---

2   In 2012, the two-bedroom fair market rent in the San Francisco metro area was 175 percent higher than in the Sandusky metro area. In 1983, the difference was 84 percent. Author's analysis of HUD Fair Market Rents, 2012.

3   Kathleen Short, "The Research Supplemental Poverty Measure: 2010" (Washington, DC: U.S. Census Bureau, 2011).

4   Unless otherwise noted, all statistics in this section derive from the author's analysis of Census Bureau data from the Current Population Survey, decennial censuses, and the American Community Survey.

The share of the U.S. population living in poverty has largely risen and fallen in line with the overall business cycle.[5] At the economy's peak in 1973, the U.S. poverty rate was 11.1 percent (Figure 1). This was well below the rates that prevailed a decade earlier, which fell rapidly in response to strong economic growth and increases in the generosity of welfare benefits.[6] Over the succeeding decades, the U.S. poverty rate rose to more than 15 percent following recessions in the early 1980s and 1990s, and approached its previous low in 2000, at the height of the economic boom that prevailed in the late 1990s. By 2007, the U.S. poverty rate reached 12.5 percent, before ballooning to 15.1 percent in 2010 in the wake of the Great Recession. Notably, the number of people below the poverty line dropped only marginally during the 2000s expansion, compared to steeper declines experienced in prior periods of economic growth. This reflected the relative weakness of labor demand during the recovery, especially for disadvantaged workers.

In this way, poverty reflects income inequality in the United States. Average living standards have improved greatly over the past few decades; from 1973 to 2007, inflation-adjusted per capita income rose from $18,164 to $28,186, a 55 percent jump. Yet the share of individuals with very low incomes has remained stagnant, between 11 and 15 percent. Indeed, the lack of progress in reducing the U.S. poverty rate exemplifies the relatively small gains that have accrued to families in the bottom parts of the income distribution over the past few decades.[7] Many other industrialized nations use relative measures of

---

5 Rebecca M. Blank, "Fighting Poverty: Lessons from Recent U.S. History," Journal of Economic Perspectives 14 (2) (2000): 3–19. For this reason, many of the comparisons over time in this chapter sensitive to business cycle conditions are made from "peak to peak," or between the years of 1973, 1980, 1990, 2001, and 2007.

6 Robert D. Plotnick et al., "The Twentieth Century Record of Inequality and Poverty in the United States" (Madison, WI: Institute for Research on Poverty, 1998).

7 From 1973 to 2007, average inflation-adjusted family income for the bottom 20 percent of families rose 2.7 percent, and it rose 13.0 percent for the second quintile of families. By contrast, families in the fourth and top quintiles enjoyed average gains of 35.0 and 60.0 percent, respectively. Economic Policy Institute, The State of Working America (Washington, DC: EPI), available at http://stateofworkingamerica.org.

FIGURE 1. U.S. Poor Population and Poverty Rate, 1973–2010
Source: U.S. Census Bureau, Current Population Survey Annual Social and Economic Supplements

············· U.S. Poverty Rate ———— U.S. Poverty Population

poverty that consider as poor anyone under 50 or 60 percent of median income.[8]

Incomes among the poor themselves have also shifted in troubling ways since the early 1970s. In 2007, the overall poverty rate (12.5 percent) was quite close to its 1975 level (12.3 percent). But in 2007, 5.2 percent of U.S. individuals were living in families with incomes under *half* the poverty threshold (equivalent that year to a family of three earning just $8,265), versus 3.7 percent in 1973. The Great Recession sent that rate of extreme poverty up to 6.7 percent by 2010, but even its heightened level at the previous business cycle peak represented cause for concern. This growth in deep poverty may partly reflect declines over time in the generosity of means-tested cash transfers such as Aid to Families with Dependent Children / Temporary Assistance for

8   OECD, *Divided We Stand: Why Inequality Keeps Rising* (Paris: OECD Publishing, 2011).

Needy Families (AFDC/TANF), Supplemental Security Income (SSI), and General Assistance, as well as in the earnings of poor families themselves.[9] Some research finds that welfare spending has become less effective in reducing the poverty rate since the 1970s, although this partly reflects that increases have been concentrated in programs like nutrition assistance and subsidized medical insurance, which do not factor into the poverty rate calculation.[10] Nonetheless, one of the chief problems that the community development movement set out to solve long ago remains very much with us today, and seems in many ways as permanent as the business cycle itself.

THE CHANGING DEMOGRAPHY OF U.S. POVERTY

Dramatic changes in the makeup of the U.S. population have transpired since the dawn of the community development movement. The aging of the baby boomers, immigration, and the continued evolution of family structure in America have transformed our society, influencing the incidence and the profile of U.S. poverty along the way.

Perhaps the single largest demographic shift affecting the United States since 1970 is a rapid increase in the Latino population. The Immigration and Nationality Act of 1965 paved the way for a new influx of workers and families from Mexico, Central America, and South America, among other world regions.[11] Successive waves of immigrants and their progeny have made Hispanics the nation's single largest racial/ethnic minority group. In 1970, U.S. residents of Hispanic or Latino origin stood at

---

9   John Karl Scholz, Robert Moffitt, and Benjamin Cowan, "Trends in Income Support," Focus 26 (2) (2009): 43–49; James P. Ziliak, "Filling the Poverty Gap: Then and Now." In Frontiers of Family Economics, vol. 1, edited by P. Rupert (Bingley, UK: Emerald Group, 2008).

10   Richard C. Fording and William D. Berry, "The Historical Impact of Welfare Programs on Poverty: Evidence from the American States," Policy Studies Journal 35 (1) (2007): 37–60.

11   James M. Lindsay and Audrey Singer, "Changing Faces: Immigrants and Diversity in the Twenty-First Century." In Agenda for the Nation, edited by Henry J. Aaron, James M. Lindsay, and Pietro S. Nivola (Washington, DC: Brookings Institution, 2003).

9.6 million, less than 5 percent of total U.S. population.[12] By 2010, their numbers had multiplied to 50.5 million, more than 16 percent of the population.[13] Over the same period, African Americans increased slightly from 11.1 to 12.6 percent of U.S. population, while Asian Americans' population share expanded from 0.8 to 4.8 percent.[14]

As a result, the U.S. poor population has become much more Latino in character over time, and consequently less white and black. In fact, Latinos now represent a larger share of the poor than African Americans (Figure 2). In 1973, 56 percent of poor Americans were white, 32 percent were black, and 10 percent were Hispanic. Today, 42 percent of the poor are white, 23 percent are black, and 29 percent are Hispanic. While poor Hispanics have overtaken poor blacks in number, members of these two groups were about equally likely to be poor in 2010 (27 percent), much more so than whites (10 percent). The Latino poor remain somewhat more regionally concentrated than their black counterparts, but nonetheless represent a much larger part of the poverty picture today than four decades ago.

Amid this diversifying population, the foreign born are more likely to live in poverty today than in 1970, although their poverty rates have stabilized and fallen somewhat since the early 1990s.[15] Immigrants represented about 16 percent of the nation's poor in 2010, up slightly from 13 percent in 1993.

A second demographic shift, one associated with aging, has also altered the nation's poverty profile. Poor people today are much more likely to be of working age than those in 1970. Fully

---

12 U.S. Census Bureau, "Hispanics in the United States" (Washington, DC: U.S. Census Bureau,, 2007). Numbers include those of any race who indicate Hispanic or Latino origin.

13 Sharon R. Ennis, Merays Ríos-Vargas, and Nora G. Albert, "The Hispanic Population: 2010" (Washington, DC: U.S. Census Bureau, 2011).

14 Karen R. Humes, Nicholas A. Jones, and Roberto Ramirez, "Overview of Race and Hispanic Origin: 2010" (Washington, DC: U.S. Census Bureau, 2011). Numbers include those of single-race groups, not of Hispanic or Latino ethnicity.

15 Steven Raphael and Eugene Smolensky, "Immigration and Poverty in the United States." In Changing Poverty, Changing Policies, edited by Maria Cancian and Sheldon Danziger (New York: Russell Sage Foundation, 2009).

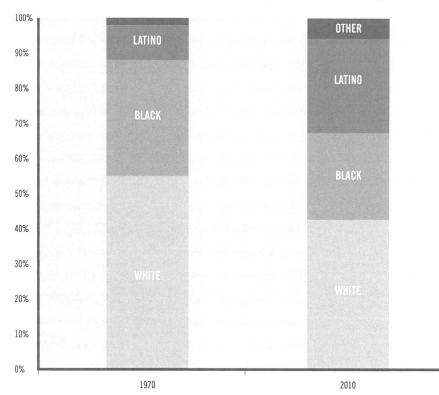

FIGURE 2. Racial / Ethnic Makeup of U.S. Poor Population, 1973 and 2010

Source: U.S. Census Bureau, Current Population Survey Annual Social and Economic Supplements

57 percent of individuals below the poverty line in 2010 were
between the ages of 18 and 64, up from 43 percent in 1970. This
results from the confluence of at least two trends. First, the aging
of the baby boom generation swelled the ranks of America's
working-age population generally, driving up their share of the
nation's poor as well. Second, increases in transfer programs such
as Social Security reduced the incidence of poverty among seniors
dramatically and cut their share of America's poor nearly in half
from 1973 to 2010.[16] Meanwhile, the under-18 share of the poor
increased from 36 to 42 percent. As the boomers enter retirement
age, the elderly share of the poor will undoubtedly increase once

---

16 Gary V. Engelhardt and Jonathan Gruber, "Social Security and the Evolution of Elderly
Poverty." NBER Working Paper 10466 (Cambridge, MA, 2004).

again, but working-age adults and their children seem likely to account for the vast majority of the poor in years to come.

A third demographic trend, the rise of single-parent households, also altered the picture of poverty in America during the past four decades. In 1970, 86 percent of children lived in married-couple families, a share that dropped to 61 percent by 2010.[17] Single-parent families have always represented a disproportionate share of the nation's poor; poverty rates for female-headed households were 38 percent in 1973 and 34 percent in 2010.[18] But the increasing share of all individuals, especially children, living in this type of household contributed to the long-term increase in the poverty rate. That increase was partially offset by the movement of single mothers into the labor force, which increased their earnings and reduced their poverty rate, especially in the mid- to late 1990s.[19] Still, the increasing prevalence of single-parent households over the past several decades has posed a series of new challenges for community development and related antipoverty efforts.

POVERTY AND THE LABOR MARKET

Poverty is often associated with unemployment and long-run detachment from the labor market. Scholars like William Julius Wilson and Charles Murray may disagree on the causes of that detachment, but both have vividly portrayed the relationship between a lack of work and poverty in America.[20]

Many poor people (46 percent in 2010) do live in households where the head of household works. In only a little more than one-third of those families, however, did that person work full-time, year-round. The poor also tend to cluster in industries that

---

17 Maria Cancian and Deborah Reed, "Family Structure, Childbearing, and Parental Employment: Implications for the Level and Trend in Poverty," Focus 26 (2) (2009): 21–26.

18 The share of the poor who were related children in female-headed households was roughly the same in 2010 as in 1970, at 18 percent.

19 Cancian and Reed, "Family Structure, Childbearing, and Parental Employment."

20 William Julius Wilson, When Work Disappears: The World of the New Urban Poor (New York: Vintage, 1997); Charles Murray, Losing Ground: American Social Policy, 1950–1980 (New York: Basic Books, 1984).

pay low wages or provide largely part-time or seasonal work, especially retail and personal/administrative services.[21] A significant share of poor, working-age adults cite illness, disability, or retirement as reasons for not working.[22] Work incentives and requirements in family-focused programs like TANF and the EITC have also encouraged work.

Yet in recent years, poverty in the United States has become more strongly associated with a lack of work. The share of poor adults who worked at least a portion of the year held steady through the 1990s at a little over 40 percent, declined during and after the 2001 recession, and never rose again during the recovery of the 2000s (Figure 3). Post Great Recession in 2010, about one-third of poor adults worked at any time during the year. A lack of stable employment is especially evident in extremely poor neighborhoods, where at least 40 percent of individuals live below the poverty line. From 2006 to 2010, only 47 percent of *all* working-age individuals (both poor and nonpoor) in those extreme-poverty neighborhoods worked full-time, year-round, versus 63 percent nationally.[23]

These labor market trends among the poor mask important differences by gender that can be viewed through the lens of worker skills. In 2010, about two-thirds of poor adults held no more than a high school diploma. Poverty scholar Rebecca Blank finds that among these individuals, the share of women in the labor force rose from 1979 to 2007, while the share of men declined. These trends coincided with policy changes that encouraged low-income single mothers to work and with long-run economic changes (primarily technological changes and globalization) that reduced the availability of jobs for less-skilled men in fields such as manufacturing. Less-educated men also faced

---

21 Marlene Kim, "Problems Facing the Working Poor" (Washington, DC: Bureau of Labor Statistics, 1999).

22 In 2010, about 5.9 million out of 17.2 million poor working-age adults (16 to 64)—34 percent—cited illness, disability, or retirement as reasons for not working at all during the year.

23 Alemayehu Bishaw, "Areas with Concentrated Poverty: 2006–2010" (Washington, DC: U.S. Census Bureau, 2011).

FIGURE 3. Share of Poor U.S. Adults Not In Work, 1987–2010
Source: U.S. Census Bureau, Current Population Survey Annual Social and Economic Supplements

declining economic incentives to work; adjusted for inflation, today's wages for men without some postsecondary education remain below their level in the 1970s.[24]

Labor market trends have been especially worrisome for young, less-educated black men. In 2010, 28 percent of black males aged 18 to 24 lived below the poverty line, up from just 20 percent in 2003. Georgetown economist Harry Holzer finds that the employment and labor force activity of 16-to-24-year-old black males deteriorated significantly after 1980. Even as young black females entered the labor force at record rates in the late 1990s, young black males continued to pour out.[25] High rates of incarceration, criminal records, and child support orders further complicate pathways to the labor market for these individuals.

24 Rebecca M. Blank, "Economic Change and the Structure of Opportunity for Less-Skilled Workers," Focus 26 (2) (2009): 14–20.

25 Harry J. Holzer, "The Labor Market and Young Black Men: Updating Moynihan's Perspective" (Washington, DC: Urban Institute, 2007).

As many of the above statistics indicate, the Great Recession and its aftermath plunged many more Americans below the poverty line and made stable work even less available to individuals and families already living in poverty. According to the Bureau of Labor Statistics, the number of "working poor" individuals—those whose incomes fell below the poverty line, but who worked for at least 27 weeks out of the year—increased by 1.5 million from 2008 to 2009. Meanwhile, unemployment rates in 2011 remained about 5 to 6 percentage points higher than their prerecession levels for workers with a high school diploma or less, versus only 2 percentage points higher for college graduates. Much of the growth in unemployment during the Great Recession was thus concentrated among less-skilled, lower-income, disproportionately minority individuals.[26] It may take some time before the U.S. economy can generate job and wage growth sufficient to connect very low-income families to work, and eventually pull them out of poverty.

SHIFTING GEOGRAPHY OF POVERTY

What defines community development as an antipoverty tool, above all else, is its focus on place. By concentrating on areas with high levels of poverty and disinvestment, community development aims not only to help disproportionate numbers of low-income individuals and families but also seeks to address the market failures that isolate people in very disadvantaged places from wider economic growth.

During the past four decades, however, the geography of poverty in America has shifted dramatically, challenging traditional place-based approaches for alleviating poverty and promoting growth. These changes are evident between urban and rural areas, across broad regions of the country, and within metropolitan areas themselves.

As metropolitan areas have grown in population and expanded in their geographic reach, they have accounted for an increasing

26 In 2011, blacks and Hispanics accounted for 47 percent of unemployed individuals with a high school diploma or less, versus 17 percent of the civilian labor force overall.

share of the nation's poor population. In 1970, there were slightly more individuals below the poverty line living inside (13.3 million) than outside (12.1 million) metropolitan areas. By 2010, the metropolitan poor population dwarfed the nonmetropolitan poor population, with four in five poor individuals living in metro areas. This reflected not only the reclassification of formerly rural places as part of metro areas but also the faster growth of poor populations within existing metropolitan territory.[27]

Much of the growth in metropolitan poverty over the last four decades occurred, not surprisingly, in the parts of the country that grew fastest overall. Most notably, the South and West, especially their fast-growing Sun Belt metropolitan areas, absorbed a growing share of America's poor. In 2010, those regions accounted for 66 percent of the U.S. poor population, up from 59 percent in 1969. Seven of the 10 metropolitan areas that added the most poor residents from 1970 to 2010 were in the South and West—Los Angeles, Houston, Dallas, Miami, Riverside, Phoenix, and Atlanta.[28] These increases reflected the in-migration of low-income residents from other parts of the country and the world, as well as economic and demographic changes occurring in these regions and metro areas that increased poverty among existing populations.

Suburbs, once bastions of the American middle class, are home to a large and growing share of America's poor. In 1970, major metro suburbs accounted for less than one-fourth of the nation's poor population. By 2010, they housed one-third of that population, a larger share than lived in big cities, smaller metro areas, or nonmetro areas (Figure 4). The pace of suburban poverty growth was particularly rapid in the 2000s, when the size of their poor

---

27 Counties classified as metropolitan in 1970 increased their share of the nation's poor population from 56 percent to 65 percent over the succeeding 40-year period. Counties that became metropolitan since 1970 contained an additional 14 percent of the poor in both 1970 and 2010.

28 Notably, among all four regions, only the South registered a long-run secular decline in poverty rate (from 15.3 percent in 1973 to 14.2 percent in 2007).

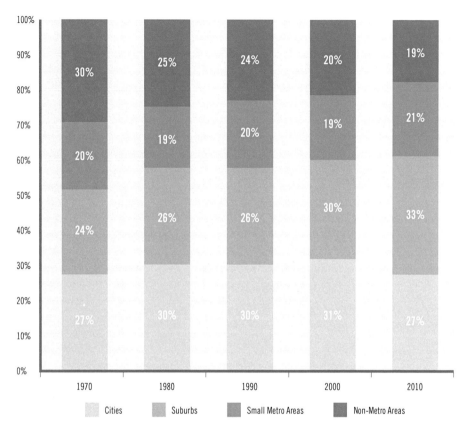

FIGURE 4. Share of U.S. Poor Populations by Community / Metro Type, 1970–2010

Source: U.S. Census Bureau decennial census data

population rose 53 percent, versus 23 percent in the large cities of these metro areas.[29]

The rapid growth of poor populations in suburbs largely mirrored their faster overall population growth. The poverty rate of suburban dwellers was higher in 2010 (11.4 percent) than in 1970 (8.7 percent), but this was also the case for city dwellers, and by an even greater margin (20.9 percent in 2010 versus 14.7 percent in 1970). Concentrated poverty, however, is still very much an inner-city phenomenon. Roughly four in five residents of extremely poor major metropolitan neighborhoods live in

29 These shares are calculated consistently across time using metropolitan area definitions effective in 2010.

cities. Nonetheless, growing shares of the suburban poor reside in communities of moderate to high poverty, where at least 20 or 30 percent of individuals live below the poverty line.[30]

Within suburban communities, poverty has grown unevenly. In many metro areas, it has spread along an axis that emerges from the traditionally segregated and impoverished communities in the urban core. Thus, poorer suburbs locate to the south of cities like Atlanta, Phoenix, and Seattle or to the east of cities like Cleveland, Pittsburgh, and Washington, DC. These communities are often located farther from jobs than neighborhoods in the urban core, or in other parts of the region, and lack convenient public transportation options to move workers to nodes of employment.[31] At the same time, so-called mature suburban communities built largely in the 1960s and 1970s are also home to a growing share of the suburban poor, even though their poverty rates remain lower than those affecting many older, inner metropolitan suburbs.

CONCLUSION

Community development didn't end poverty. As Jesus' quote suggests, that's probably an unfair yardstick for success.

Many of the fundamental problems that community development set out to address in the late 1960s are still present today. African Americans have higher poverty rates than other groups. A majority of poor individuals lack meaningful attachment to the labor market, while others toil in low-wage, low-mobility jobs. In the wake of the Great Recession, cities again exhibit rates of concentrated poverty that rival peaks from the early 1990s. And many of the older, northern, Rust Belt cities where community development originated still have among the highest poverty rates and the highest levels of disinvestment.

---

30 Elizabeth Kneebone, Carey Nadeau, and Alan Berube, "The Re-Emergence of Concentrated Poverty: Metropolitan Trends in the 2000s" (Washington, DC: Brookings Institution, 2011).

31 Michael Stoll and Steven Raphael, "Job Sprawl and the Suburbanization of Poverty" (Washington, DC: Brookings Institution, 2010); Adie Tomer et al., "Missed Opportunity: Transit and Jobs in Metropolitan America" (Washington, DC: Brookings Institution, 2011).

In this sense, the continued presence of community development primarily in historically disadvantaged locales, and serving historically disadvantaged populations, is neither unreasonable given the continued challenges they face nor altogether promising given the lack of progress against those challenges. In light of the massive changes that roiled the American and global economies over the last four decades, community development arguably brought a knife to what was always a gunfight.

The larger issue raised by this chapter, however, is whether community development—and place-based antipoverty policy more generally—can remain relevant to the national agenda if it is perceived as fighting the last war:

- Can it serve the needs of diverse communities in an ever-more pluralistic American society, where immigration and Latino growth are continuously transforming low-income populations and the issues they face?

- Can it shift its focus toward helping populations increasingly characterized by a lack of work in the post-recession economy, broadening activities well beyond housing and economic development to link people to much higher-quality skills than community-based job training has historically provided?

- Can it move well beyond inner-city communities in a world of majority-suburban poverty, where traditional place-based strategies may bump up against radically different physical, economic, and social environments?

With such substantial changes in the profile of U.S. poverty over the past four decades, does community development still have a role in addressing it? Brookings Institution scholars Isabel Sawhill and Ron Haskins find that adults who do three things—finish high school, work full-time, and wait until marriage to have children—have a poverty rate equivalent to one-sixth of the national average.[32] To be sure, these outcomes depend on one

---

32 Isabel Sawhill and Ron Haskins, Creating an Opportunity Society (Washington, DC: Brookings Institution Press, 2009).

another significantly (i.e., obtaining a high school diploma makes it much easier to find full-time work) and probably mask important differences between those who have achieved them and those who have not.

Nonetheless, the future success of community development as an antipoverty strategy may depend on whether it can help meaningfully increase the likelihood that children—black or brown, in working and nonworking families, in cities and in suburbs—achieve, at a minimum, those fundamental outcomes. In the following chapter, Eric Belsky and Jennifer Fauth highlight the growing prominence of multidimensional community development strategies that more aggressively addresses the human services needs of the poor, particularly the need to build human capital. That represents a hopeful trend amid a changing and challenging long-run picture of poverty in America, a picture that surely demands a flexible, multipronged public policy response to fulfill the promise of economic opportunity for all.

ALAN BERUBE *is a senior fellow at the Brookings Institution Metropolitan Policy Program in Washington, DC. In addition to coordinating the Metro Program's research agenda, Alan conducts research on the role and functions of U.S. metropolitan areas in a globalizing economy, poverty in neighborhoods and suburbs, and educational and skills of metropolitan workers. He has authored dozens of Brookings publications, including* State of Metropolitan America: On the Front Lines of Demographic Transformation, *and recent editions of the* Global MetroMonitor, *which tracks the economic performance of the world's 200 largest metro economies. Prior to joining Brookings in February 2001, Alan was a policy advisor in the Office of Community Development Policy at the U.S. Treasury Department, and a researcher at the Center on Budget and Policy Priorities.*

CROSSING OVER TO AN IMPROVED ERA OF COMMUNITY DEVELOPMENT

Eric S. Belsky
Harvard University

Jennifer Fauth
City of New York

T he field of community development is at an inflection point, poised to achieve scale, impact, and integration of the many lessons learned over the past 40 years. It is on the threshold of entering a new phase capable of meeting the twin goals of revitalizing low-income neighborhoods and narrowing achievement gaps of the poor. The field is well positioned to enter this more productive phase as a result of decades of capacity and network building, creating partnerships with private capital providers and public stakeholders, success in innovating with new programs and attracting private capital, and drawing on lessons learned about what approaches work best to produce the strongest outcomes. However, significant

The authors would like to thank Nancy Andrews, David Erickson, and Ellen Seidman for their thoughtful comments and their dedication to community development. They embody the best the field has to offer. We would also like to thank Mark Pinsky and David Wood for their review and comments.

challenges lie ahead. These challenges range from the battle for resources to the need to devise cost-effective ways of measuring social impact, from promoting greater cooperation among key private stakeholders to forging new public-private-philanthropic partnerships, and from nurturing smaller innovative community developers to consolidating organizations when it is in the best interest of the community.

THE OPPORTUNITY

There are significant opportunities for community builders, community capital providers, and their private capital partners to leverage public investment in low-income communities. For example, $16 billion in new social investment will be needed to support community health centers as an outgrowth of health care reform.[1] Annually, $1.5 billion in social capital investment will be needed to support high-performing, community-based charter schools, with community development financial institutions (CDFIs) likely to provide about $250 million of this each year.[2]

In addition, billions of dollars will be available to support transit systems over the next decade, and more may flow to transit-oriented development (TOD) as the value becomes more apparent of linking low-income people to jobs. TOD planning efforts are underway in cities from Seattle to Boston to Atlanta. Further, despite threats to the federal housing budget and tax incentives, billions of dollars of investment annually will likely be deployed to preserve and add to the nation's affordable housing stock. In short, the scale and opportunity for capital investment over the next decade is vast.

Such investment will create jobs and potentially serve as engines of economic vitality for distressed communities. Community developers, CDFIs, and private capital providers will need to

---

1 Ronda Kotelchuck, Daniel Lowenstein, and Jonathan N. Tobin, "Community Health Centers and Community Development Financial Institutions: Joining Forces to Address Determinants of Health," Health Affairs 30 (2011): 2090, 2093.

2 Annie Donovan, "Subsidy and the Charter School Facilities Finance Market." In Smart Subsidy for Community Development (Boston: Federal Reserve Bank of Boston, 2011), p. 57 n9.

work with public stakeholders to invest at scale in America's communities over the next decade. But budget constraints combined with the demands of resource providers will mean that investments will have to show impact and social return for the dollar.

CDFIs are playing a new and important role aggregating capital from private sources while leveraging philanthropic funding and government programs. Numbering nearly 1,000[3] and with well over $25 billion in assets,[4] CDFIs are deploying large sums of capital and in ways that are bringing the promise of integrated community development closer to hand. Many have demonstrated their capacity to generate operating surpluses while achieving meaningful social outcomes even in the midst of a severe economic downturn. As a result, the capitalization of CDFIs has been on a steep climb and may be on the threshold of even more dramatic increases.

Finally, and as we discuss below, promising new approaches are emerging with common elements that could lead toward more systemic and meaningful community impact. These approaches integrate place- and people-based strategies, aim for transformative neighborhood change, and work in creative partnerships to drive results and improve the ecosystem that supports community development.

---

3 Community Development Financial Institutions Fund, "Certified CDFIs as of June, 30 2012," available at http://www.cdfifund.gov/docs/certification/cdfi/CDFI%20List%20-%20 06-30-12.xls.

4 See CDP Publication Committee, "Fiscal Year 2007 Data." (Philadelphia: CDFI Data Project, 2007), available at http://opportunityfinance.net/store/downloads/cdp_fy2007.pdf. Just 508 CDFIs surveyed for the OFN's CDFI Data Project reported total asset of $25.5 billion in 2007. The capitalization of the CDFI has surely increased significantly since then and there are at least several hundred CDFIs that were not surveyed. A recent report by the CDFI Fund and the Carsey Institute found that loan funds they surveyed doubled their assets from 2006 to 2009, credit union CDFI median assets soared by 38 percent from 2005 to 2010, and bank CDFI median assets of 8 percent from 2006 to 2010. Michael Swack, Jack Northrup, and Eric Hangen, CDFI Industry Analysis: Summary Report (Durham, NH: Carsey Institute, Spring 2011), available at http://carseyinstitute.unh.edu/publications/ Report-Swack-CDFI-Industry-Analysis.pdf.

EMERGENCE OF PROMISING MODELS WITH COMMON ELEMENTS

Promising models are emerging that take a more integrated approach to community development and measure impact. These include the Building Sustainable Communities initiative, the activities of NEXT Award winners, and the Integration Initiative, as well as the Harlem Children's Zone and Purpose Built Communities being led by community developers. Other organizations historically focusing on people-based programs, like Neighborhood Centers, Inc. (NCI) in Houston, are in turn recognizing the importance of place-based investments and entering this sphere with large, concentrated, and quality investments. Many community developers, as well as housing authorities are also coming together with for-profit firms like McCormick Baron Salazar, Jonathan Rose Companies, and the Integral Group to deliver large-scale redevelopments.

All these examples share certain common elements:

- All leverage private capital in new and important ways.

- All are aimed at integrating people-based and place-based strategies within a master vision.

- All are directed toward closing the achievement gap in education.

- All are linked by a belief in measuring outcomes and directing resources toward what works.

- Most aim, in addition, to support small businesses and improve access to jobs that pay a living wage.

The field has made great strides but it is still striving to turn one-off successes into more replicable and scalable strategies to create systemic change.

Fortunately, the contours of effective strategies are coming into view as evidence mounts of the importance of combining interventions that develop human capital (through strategies

PEOPLE VERSUS PLACE

Although there are a number of ways to define people- versus placed-based interventions, we intend by the use of the term following categorization:

Place – real estate and infrastructure based activities, including affordable housing preservation and development, commercial development, green space set-asides and improvements, and community facilities including charter schools, health centers, day and eldercare centers, and community centers devoted to other community activities and gatherings; transit, communications, and energy improvements.

People – childcare and job training and placement to enable adults to work and improve their incomes, savings and homeownership programs to help people build assets (but not tied to housing development or rehabilitation), early child interventions and charter schools services intended to narrow educational achievement gaps, small business development and lending for economic develop-ment, community policing and safety, community organizing, and social case work to address special needs like addiction or disabili-ties or reentry after incarceration.

Research supports the importance of affordable and stable housing, access to strong community facilities and services, healthy real estate conditions, and the provision of neighborhood safety to human outcomes. It also supports the value of especially early child interventions and educational programs to closing lifetime achieve-ment gaps, among other important people-based interventions aimed at improving community life and wealth and employment among low-income adults.

such as early childhood interventions and social services) with placed-based interventions (such as developing and preserving affordable housing and developing commercial space, community centers, health clinics, child care centers, and charter schools). This more holistic approach holds out hope for closing the gaps in achievement and well-being that hurt the poor. At the same time, effective strategies will differ from place to place, as will the initial steps towards a holistic strategy.

THE CASE FOR INTEGRATED, RESULTS-BASED APPROACHES

As far back as the reform movement of the late 1800s and early 1900s, reformers working in poor communities understood that poverty had many causes and that meaningful progress demanded tackling several causes simultaneously. Beginning in the 1960s, the architects of the Model Cities program wanted to take a comprehensive approach to community development. Over the following decades other earnest efforts sought the same goals. Evaluations of these efforts, however, generally found them wanting.[5] They often foundered because one or more elements of an ambitious strategy failed to fall into place, funding for one or more elements was not secured, or organizations others depended on faltered.

But the field has never given up on the goal of a more holistic approach, or at least on the idea that it is important to place individual actions in a broader vision of what it takes to bring about meaningful community development. This impulse is increasingly finding expression in efforts to attend to human capital as well as the affordable housing needs of individuals and other real estate development needs of a community. Community-based organizations—from the Crittenton Women's Union and its effort to help lift women out of poverty through job training, child care, and housing, to the more well known Harlem Children's Zone (discussed below)—are striving to treat the multiple needs of their clients even as they try to improve the physical conditions and facilities in their neighborhoods.[6]

Foundations and national intermediaries have also been pushing to promote more holistic efforts to address the needs of poor communities and their residents through initiatives like Annie

---

5 See Alex von Hofmann's piece in this collection.

6 Crittenton Women's Union, available at http://liveworkthrive.org, and Harlem Children's Zone, available at http://hcz.org.

E. Casey Foundation's Rebuilding Communities Initiative, Enterprise Community Partners' Neighborhood Transformation Initiative, the Ford Foundation's Neighborhood and Family Initiative, Living Cities' Integration Initiative, and the Local Initiative Support Corporation's (LISC) Building Sustainable Communities Initiative. Indeed, a continued effort to bring about transformative change through multisectoral interventions is apparent.

The push to pay more attention to human outcomes while attending to physical and economic revitalization of communities has gathered momentum. Since the 1970s, many community developers have focused their attention on place-based housing strategies, working to transform vacant lots and abandoned properties by repairing and rehabilitating dilapidated housing and constructing new affordable units.[7] This remains important work: community developers have been willing to make investments in rundown, poverty-stricken neighborhoods and in housing for hard-to-serve residents that others might ignore. Without community developers and their continued efforts to not only revitalize this housing stock but prove the investment potential of these neighborhoods, the cycle of disinvestment in these areas would be harder to break.

Yet as the field has matured, those in it have increasingly recognized that substandard housing is only one of many problems facing the poor that community developers should address. Over time, CDC leaders have expanded their activities to include economic and commercial development and the provision of human services. While a full 92 percent of 163 community developers surveyed in 1999 developed housing, a solid 47 percent of them had workforce and youth programs. Furthermore, the same study found that an additional 17 percent of them planned to have workforce and youth programs in place within the following

---

7 For an excellent summary of the history of CDCs, spanning back to their inception with an effort led by Robert Kennedy to create and fund them through amendment of the Economic Opportunity Act, see Alex von Hoffman's piece in this volume.

two years alone.[8] Clearly, the trend leading into the 2000s was not to abandon a place-based housing strategy, but to complement it with a people-based one focused on social services.

The view that the community development field has to purposely pursue the development of human capital is the focus of Nancy Andrews's paper "Coming Out as a Human Capitalist."[9] David Erickson and Andrews take this argument further in a paper called "Partnerships among Community Development, Public Health, and Health Care Could Improve the Well-Being of Low-Income People."[10]

Failing to attend to the human development needs of poor and low-income individuals and families in addition to their housing and community needs can derail efforts to improve communities because it makes it harder for the residents to do well in school, find and keep jobs, and receive other supports they need. Conversely, failing to deal with place threatens to derail efforts to improve the lives of the poor because those lives are deeply affected by community conditions, including housing, schools, retail, access to jobs, and public safety.

Andrews recounts a growing body of scientific studies that plainly demonstrates that place matters to people's life chances, and conversely, that successful human development also affects place. Indeed, path-breaking research reported in 2011 by the *New England Journal of Medicine* demonstrates that living in better communities can lead to about a 20 percent reduction in obesity and diabetes, an impact as great as a medical intervention.[11] In

---

8   Christopher Walker, Community Development Corporations and their Changing Support Systems (Washington, DC: Urban Institute, 2002), available at http://urban.org/upload-edpdf/310638_changingsupportsystems.pdf.

9   Nancy Andrews and Chris Kramer, "Coming out as a Human Capitalist," Community Development Investment Review 5 (3) (2009): 47-65, available at http://frbsf.org/publications/community/review/vol5_issue3/andrews_kramer.pdf.

10 Health Affairs 30 (11) (November 2011), available at http://healthaffairs.org.

11 See Jens Ludwig et al., "Neighborhoods, Obesity, and Diabetes — A Randomized Social Experiment," New England Journal of Medicine 365 (2011):1509–1519. The study found about a reduction of about one-fifth among women with children with vouchers that moved to lower poverty communities under HUD's Moving to Opportunity program when compared to women who were not randomly assigned to this group.

addition, the stressful living environment that poverty all too often produces impedes cognitive development, as does the better known impact of certain toxins (like lead paint) often found in older, low-income housing.

Poverty is a multidimensional problem. Solutions must also be multipronged. Studies that have found a relationship between poor-quality housing, health problems, and educational attainment provide a clear and strong argument for the integration of housing with human services, including health, education, early childhood intervention, and daycare.[12] The most successful interventions are not limited to placed-based bricks-and-mortar strategies; rather, they include people-based services, especially early learning programs and health counseling.

In fact, early childhood interventions and health education have been found to outpace others in terms of the strength and reliability of their long-term effectiveness. A report by the MIT Workplace Center, for example, found that "every dollar invested in quality early care and education saves taxpayers up to $13.00 in future costs."[13] While the impact of job training programs has been less consistent and compelling, the most carefully controlled study done on the combination of housing and job training did show solid positive results on both employment rates and wage levels from bundling these two forms of assistance.[14]

---

12 In fact countless studies over the past several decades have demonstrated the correlation of poverty, housing instability, crime, low-performing schools, chronic health problems, environmental concerns, and limited access to nutritious foods. See S.C. Saegert et al., "Healthy Housing: A Structured Review of Published Evaluations of US Interventions to Improve Health by Modifying Housing in the U.S., 1990-2000," American Journal of Public Health 93 (2003): 1471–1477. See also Dolores Acevedo-Garcia, "Housing as a Platform for Health," paper presented at How Housing Matters Conference, November 2, 2011. See also Alice Park, "Change Your Neighborhood, Improve Your Health," Time, October 20, 2011. Available at http://healthland.time.com/2011/10/20/change-your-neighborhood-improve-your-health; Jens Ludwig et al., "Neighborhoods, Obesity, and Diabetes: A Randomized Social Experiment," New England Journal of Medicine 365: 1509–1519, available at http://nejm.org/doi/full/10.1056/NEJMsa1103216; MacArthur Foundation, "How Housing Matters," available at http://macfound.org/programs/how-housing-matters.

13 Leslie J. Calman and Linda Tarr-Whelan, Early Education for All: A Wise Investment (New York: April 2005), available at http://web.mit.edu/workplacecenter/docs/Full%20Report.pdf.

14 Howard S. Bloom et al., Public Housing: The Effectiveness of Jobs-Plus (New York: MDRC, March 2005), available at http://mdrc.org/publications/405/full.pdf.

Although effective, services are harder to fund because they do not provide solid financial returns to sponsors. Instead, sponsors must rely excessively on grants rather than fee or rental income to generate operating surpluses to provide the service. Furthermore, the social impacts of these programs may take decades to manifest fully.

Housing investment, on the other hand, generally produces a positive financial return, and multi-billion dollar federal programs exist to support it. Social impact investors, therefore, need to be convinced of the social worth of activities unrelated to real estate and be willing to accept lower financial returns for investing in them. And they need to find ways to lend to entities for the operation and expansion of schools and clinics not just to building the facilities.

STRIVING FOR—AND INVESTING IN—SOCIAL IMPACT

The emergence of social impact investment and pay for success programs are major developments in community development. Increasingly, socially motivated investors (including philanthropic organizations, financial institutions under regulatory incentives to serve poor and low-income communities, and funds that raise money from investors willing to accept below-market returns) are interested in channeling investment into activities that have social impacts that are large and measurable. They also are trying to understand how to best use their limited socially motivated capital to leverage private capital for maximum social impact.[15]

Linking impact and outcomes measurement to social investing has the potential to dramatically transform the landscape of funding for community development. If successful in attracting

---

15 A 2011 report sponsored by the Rockefeller Foundation, "Impact Investing: A Framework for Policy Design and Analysis," found that government and foundation support alone will be insufficient to fund all of the needed community programs in the future, but that "[p]olicy in impact investing catalyzes viable private markets for social goods."

endowment investment, this could produce a substantial amount of new capital.[16]

But it will take a coordinated effort, facilitated by policy and organizational infrastructure, to build an enduring and scaled social impact investing marketplace. Hopeful signs that this infrastructure is beginning to emerge include the formation and growth of organizations such as the U.S. Social Investment Fund, the Global Impact Investing Network, and Impact Reporting and Investment Standards.

BUILDING ON STRONG INSTITUTIONAL CAPACITY

The community development field is strong and well positioned to build on knowledge of what works and to prove the social, economic, and financial value of integrated programs.[17] Years of capacity building have paid off. There are now many financially strong community developers and CDFIs with track records of success. Several have succeeded in taking their operations to the regional and even national levels. Among community developers, these include Community Builders in the Northeast, BRIDGE in the Bay Area, and Mercy Housing and National Church Residences in states across the country. Among CDFIs, these include FAHE in the Appalachian region, the Low Income Investment Fund headquartered in the Bay Area, The Reinvestment Fund in the Mid-Atlantic region, IFF (formerly known as the Illinois Facilities Fund) in the Midwest, and LISC and Enterprise in states across the country. Although in some cities capacity is still weak, more and more places boast strong,

---

16 A 2009 Monitor Institute report estimates that even a 1 percent share of total investment by 2020 "would create a market of about $500 billion. Such scale would create an important supplement to philanthropy, nearly doubling the amount given away in the U.S. alone." Jessica Freireich and Katherine Fulton, Investing for Social and Environmental Impact: A Design for Catalyzing an Emerging Industry (New York: Monitor Institute, 2009), available at http://monitorinstitute.com/impactinvesting/documents/InvestingforSocialandEnvImpact_ExecSum_000.pdf.

17 See David Erickson, The Housing Policy Revolution: Networks and Neighborhoods (Washington, DC: Urban Institute Press, 2009), Chapter 2, and Alexander von Hofmann, House by House, Block by Block: The Rebirth of America's Urban Neighborhoods (New York: Oxford University Press, 2004).

local, community-based organizations or have strong regional or national players operating in their area.

Community developers and CDFIs are also bolstered by strong national intermediaries such as Enterprise Community Partners, the Housing Partnership Network, Living Cities, LISC, NeighborWorks, the Opportunity Finance Network, and Stewards of Affordable Housing (SAHF). These intermediaries are helping to capitalize the members in their networks, providing them with technical assistance, developing policy, and lobbying on their behalf. They also are working together in a number of field-building activities (such as Strength Matters, a consortium of NeighborWorks, the Housing Partnership Network, and the Stewards of Affordable Housing) that aim to improve the financial viability and standardize the financial reporting of affordable housing community developers.[18] National intermediaries are also banding together to solve common challenges such as the foreclosure crisis.[19]

These intermediaries are promoting more integrated community development as examples discussed below demonstrate. In addition, groups are devoted to promoting integrated community development specifically, such as Integrated Community Development International and the Institute for Comprehensive Community Development.

The maturation of the CDFI industry is an especially noteworthy and important development. The movement began with credit unions early in the twentieth century and expanded in the 1970s to include community banks and loan funds that sprang up in communities across the country in the 1970s to address unfulfilled capital needs in low-income and other disadvantaged areas. Working in all states and both rural and urban areas, there were 999 certified CDFIs as of June 2012, and additional opportunity

---

18 For more information see http://strengthmatters.net.

19 They are doing this, for example, by coordinating activities through the National Community Stabilization Trust and working together on the Mortgage Resolution Fund which is aimed a purchasing distressed notes and modifying loans to keep owners in their homes.

finance institutions including community development loan funds, private equity funds, community development credit unions, and community development banks that may not have sought certification.[20]

CDFIs have succeeded in attracting financing from large banks lacking the on-the-ground contacts or underwriting capabilities to identify bankable opportunities. They are able to aggregate capital from larger banks, individual donors, and foundations and can effectively channel it to multiple activities in pursuit of an integrated agenda. They have developed the expertise necessary to prudently lend to different types of activities—commercial development, residential development, small business, health provision, charter schools, and others. This enables other organizations, such as community developers, to concentrate on real estate development, property operation, and services they are best suited to provide.

Many CDFIs offer a full spectrum of lending to support community building. IFF, Low Income Investment Fund, Hope Enterprise Corporation, and The Reinvestment Fund are just a few examples. Among them, they lend to small businesses, charter school developers and operators, health clinic developers and operators, affordable housing developers and operators, and consumer financial products. In fact, many CDFIs now provide all or most of these lending services, and it is common for them also to provide technical assistance and to coordinate community building strategies that civic and city leaders are striving to launch. This capacity lends itself to driving and successfully supporting integrative community development.

BROADENING PARTNERSHIPS AND EXPANDING FEDERAL SUPPORTS

Although public-private partnerships have long been pursued as a way to leverage private capital and expertise, the partnerships

---

20 Community Development Financial Institutions Fund, "Certified CDFIs as of June, 30 2012," available at http://www.cdfifund.gov/docs/certification/cdfi/CDFI%20List%20-%20 06-30-12.xls.

that will drive social impact investing and integrated community development will extend these partnerships and engage more stakeholders both directly in funding and indirectly through the coordination of activities.[21]

Many partnerships are emerging that stretch beyond the familiar public-private model. There are a growing number of tripartite structures at the funding level, involving philanthropy, public funds, and private lenders. A good example of this is the New York Acquisition Fund (NYAF).[22] This initiative brings together multiple partners and the city to address housing preservation needs in New York City. NYAF provides low-cost loans to developers so that they can act quickly to acquire properties to prevent them from becoming unaffordable. Foundations and the city take the riskiest positions, covering the first-loss risks, while for-profit lenders supply the bulk of the capital and are in senior position. As a result, the initiative was able to attract more than $190 million in private bank capital that likely would not have been committed to housing preservation. Thus, the funding stream involved philanthropy, city, and private lenders and was coordinated and deployed through multiple nonprofits.

Another example is the work of the Atlanta Housing Authority and other housing authorities around HOPE VI public housing redevelopments. These local housing agencies worked with community developers and for-profit developers to create mixed-income communities, often supported by charter schools and other community facilities.[23]

Innovations such as these have ushered in new thinking around partnerships. They focus investors on understanding the "capital stack" needed to launch new approaches: how to best use the

---

21 As Living Cities argued "[w]hat [is] needed in the neighborhoods [to] marry national and local funding with technical competence and neighborhood enterprise and responsiveness— something that mount[s] a broad assault on the multiple interlocking problems of these neighborhoods." Living Cities: The National Community Development Initiative, 2001.

22 New York Acquisition Fund, available at http://www.nycacquisitionfund.com.

23 See for example John F. Sugg, "From Public Housing to Private Enterprise," Urban Land (March/April 2011): 90–93.

scarce foundation and government funds to leverage private capital. The highly structured nature of such partnerships brings foundations into new relations with government and private pools of capital. In addition, in the case of the NYAF, by taking a first-loss position, the fund also has the potential to demonstrate that lending for housing preservation can be profitable and to measure the risk of such lending.

Other sources of support for community development activities have come online during the last two decades that help facilitate more meaningful and integrated solutions to community development. In 1994, the CDFI Fund and in 2000 the New Markets Tax Credit (NMTC) program were added to the arsenal of tools available to spark community development. The CDFI Fund's mission is "to expand the capacity of financial institutions to provide credit, capital, and financial services to underserved populations and communities in the United States." By cultivating a network of CDFIs, the Fund has leveraged private investment and channeled it to organizations that can deploy capital across a wide range of investment types that spur community development. In so doing, it has also promoted and supported the diversification of CDFIs and positioned many to be able to press for and fund more integrated community development. The NMTC is allocated by the Treasury Department through a competitive process. Of a number of criteria used to rate applicants, one is community impact. These credits have been used to develop charter schools, health care centers, public markets, commercial space, industrial space, and a range of other community facilities. The program has been a major catalyst for more integrated community development. CDFIs and national intermediaries that have received NMTC allocations have used them to fund community facilities and business development, adding these activities to the housing activities many of them already funded.

INVESTING IN WHAT WORKS

To the extent that more integrative, impact-based approaches are now favored, several current initiatives show how these are being structured and how they can achieve impact. These include

LISC's Building Sustainable Communities Initiative, Living Cities' Integration Initiative, NEXT award program, Harlem Children's Zone, and Purpose Built Communities. All five examples demonstrate a movement toward integrated approaches and results-oriented interventions, as well as the potential of strong lead organizations to drive change and work closely with residents and cooperatively with multiple organizations.

Building Sustainable Communities

Launched in 2007, LISC's Building Sustainable Communities (BSC) project pursues more comprehensive community development. LISC is deploying capital, providing technical assistance, and evaluating results of efforts to invest in housing and other real estate. It is also promoting access to quality education, stimulating economic development, building incomes and wealth, and supporting healthy lifestyles.

LISC has established five goals for its BSC initiative: (1) expanding investment in housing and other real estate; (2) increasing family income and wealth; (3) stimulating economic development; (4) improving access to quality education; and (5) supporting healthy environments and lifestyles.[24]

Clearly, these goals express a commitment to integrated community development. Drawing on 25 years of experience, LISC has discovered ways to support all of these goals using what it views as time-tested approaches.

The approach "starts with a continued commitment to capital investment in a wide variety of new and renovated homes, community facilities, commercial and industrial property, and the public spaces that link all these elements together."[25] This is an area that LISC and other intermediaries have long focused on—leveraging private capital and public support through

---

24 LISC, "Our Work: Building Sustainable Communities." Available at http://lisc.org/section/ourwork/sc.

25 Building Sustainable Communities: A Progress Report on Meeting LISC's Next Generation of Challenges and Fulfilling the Promise of Community Development (Chicago: LISC, 2009), p. 3.

incentives and subsidies like the Low Income Housing Tax Credit, community development block grants, and NMTCs. To increase family income and wealth, LISC aspires to three other offerings: financial opportunity centers (pioneered by the Annie E. Casey Foundation and which have an established track record of success); individual development accounts, which studies show are effective in getting people to save; and job training and micro-enterprise development.

To stimulate economic development, LISC intends to augment its real estate investments (in commercial, retail, industrial, and residential development at qualities and densities intended to spur local demand) with marketing to attract local businesses. It also intends to work with anchor institutions to train and employ local residents, and press for government policies that promote business development.

To support access to education, in addition to aggregating capital to fund school facilities, LISC aims to use these schools to provide other afterschool community services and programs supportive of education, children, and parents. They can also help to organize parents into groups and support outside school programs. This is an approach that the two final examples below, Harlem Children's Zone and Purpose Built Communities, demonstrate can be highly effective in closing educational achievement gaps.

Finally, in addition to capitalizing health facilities like clinics and healthy food markets, LISC intends to support a range of other programs and facilities, such as partnerships with law enforcement, athletic fields and facilities, and better transportation options. Again, these are programs with proven track records of success when done properly.

Quad Communities in Chicago is the most advanced attempt to put the BSC approach into practice. LISC's efforts to build a sustainable community began with creating the Quad Communities Development Corporation to represent residents and bring multiple stakeholders together to develop a plan for the community's future. Plan in hand and with LISC and local government, civic, and business leaders' backing, the community has succeeded in redeveloping 3,000 public housing units, developing a charter elementary school, revitalizing the commercial core, developing an arts center, and establishing a financial opportunity center. The investments in facilities and services have been intentionally located in close proximity and in an area that had lacked investment of any sort for years. Quad Communities Development Corporation played a lead role in conceiving the plan. But it coordinated many other groups that have invested in and operate many of the newly developed facilities and services rather than doing so itself. Supported by LISC acting in the role of CDFI and capital aggregator, the Quad Communities initiative has laid the foundation for transformative change in the neighborhood.

Integration Initiative

The recently launched Living Cities Integration Initiative also aims to take a more integrative approach to community development and intends to bring a range of actors to the table (government, business, philanthropy, and community-based organizations). It uses an "ecosystem" approach to support policy and capacity, and is in the process of considering cultivating an investment-ready pipeline to ensure the range of functions is in place for sustainable and systemic community development.

Five cities will receive $80 million of investment from the initiative in the form of grants, loans, and program-related investments with the aim of leveraging significant amounts of private debt and venture capital. In all five, the initiative aims to overcome the fragmented nature of programs and interventions. Several of the strategies are centered on building on the capacities of anchor institutions like hospitals and universities to spur economic development and provide jobs to residents. Several also emphasize devising and testing ways to make adult education, job training, and job placement programs more responsive to local needs and opportunities. Along with service-based interventions aimed at supporting employment and economic development, most address affordable housing needs, infrastructure needs, and/ or abandoned properties. All designate a single lead coordinator and a single lead CDFI to work with local nonprofits, lenders, anchor institutions, and philanthropies.

This approach is similar to the one taken by BSC. Perhaps the city pilot that combines the most elements of this approach is the one now underway in Newark. This tests the idea of a "wellness economy" as a way to organize thinking about and planning investments. A central aim is to address the land and real estate needs for fresh foods, health care, and decent affordable housing. But it also features a municipal mechanism to align education, health, and social services planning with residential development.

Although the Integration Initiative does not focus as much on early childhood intervention and childhood education as others, it is clearly a place- and people-based strategy that emphasizes coordination, evaluation, and data-driven decisions about how to deploy resources over time.

NEXT Award Winners

The Wachovia Wells Fargo NEXT Awards for Opportunity Finance support innovative and effective CDFIs. Its winners underscore the growing number of CDFIs driving the kind of integrated, results-oriented approach to community development discussed in this paper as well as efforts to build capacity in areas where it is weaker.

The NEXT award program shows the extent to which the field is moving toward an integrative approach based on measurable impacts and results. The award winners underscore that the most important community issues and solutions vary from place to place but nevertheless offer models others can adapt and replicate. Take the Charter School Development Corporation in Michigan, which received an award for devising innovative ways to help charter schools fund their facilities in tough economic times, a model other communities in difficult economic straits can follow.

An award in 2011 also went to the Neighborhood Development Center in Minneapolis to recognize its important work in both bringing about economic development and measuring the results of its work. An award to the Progress Fund was made to support a regional partnership in Pennsylvania around small business development. And on the policy front, the Alternatives Federal Credit Union won an award for convincing the City of Ithaca and Tompkins County in New York to require any firm receiving funds from them to provide a living wage for all its employees. Like the work of the other awardees, their work establishes models others can follow.

Finally, Coastal Enterprises Inc. (CEI) won an award to support its national Working Partner Initiative aimed at partnering with organizations in rural regions to use NMTCs to fund projects with community benefit agreements. The latter are agreements that engage the community in determining the community outcomes that project sponsors must meet. CEI's award reflects the increased focus on local capacity through partnerships with stronger regional players and to extend community development activities to the schools, clinics, and other nonhousing activities that NMTCs support. CEI, like several past recipients, lends to a range of investments including in community facilities to support education and health, affordable housing, and business development.

Harlem Children's Zone

Harlem Children's Zone (HCZ) has helped improve the communities in which it operates while also closing residents' educational achievement and well-being gaps. It has measurable results to date. HCZ has been proclaimed as a "shining example of what is possible."[26] Credited with reducing the negative impacts of poverty in a part of Harlem, HCZ expanded from a purely educational program to a comprehensive community development strategy to address the deficiencies of a neighborhood block

---

26 Nicholas D. Kristof, "Escaping from Poverty," New York Times, March 24, 2010. Available at http://nytimes.com/2010/03/25/opinion/25kristof.html.

by block. Led by Geoffrey Canada since 1990, HCZ served more than 11,000 children and 10,000 adults in 2010.[27] With a focus on early intervention and breaking the cycle of poverty, HCZ started with a single-block focus but now works in a 97-block area in Harlem.

Although HCZ is clearly a place-based strategy focused on a part of Harlem, the program is really a marriage of a people-focused and place-based antipoverty strategy. As Canada explains:

> *What we're doing is not some kind of brilliant, eureka moment that we had when we figured out how to do this. We have been talking about these issues, providing comprehensive, integrated services to poor children since I was in graduate school.... So we just simply did it. We just decided that the time had come to actually put together all that the social scientists and the educators had been talking about for decades in approaching this problem.*[28]

The initiative involves charter schools and some physical redevelopment of dilapidated housing and provision of affordable housing but centers on prenatal education, parent education, early learning, and education.

HCZ's accomplishments are extensive and listed on its website, so we highlight only a few here.[29] Its Baby College for training parents was successful in getting 86 percent of parents who read to their children fewer than five times a week to read to them more often. All third graders in its Promise Academy tested at or above grade level on the math exam, and they outperformed peers throughout the state. In 2008, 93 percent of ninth graders in its Promise High School passed the statewide algebra exam. In 2010–11, all 284 students in its high school afterschool program stayed in school, and 254 (90 percent) of its high school seniors

---

27 Harlem Children's Zone, 2010-2011 Annual Report.

28 "Harlem Children's Zone Breaks Poverty Pattern," National Public Radio, July 28, 2009. Available at http://npr.org/templates/story/story.php?storyId=111193340.

29 Harlem Children's Zone, "Our Results." Available at http://hcz.org/our-results.

were accepted into college. And its asthma initiative, which has served nearly 1,500 children, showed striking improvements 42 months after enrollment, with the share of emergency room visits of enrollees with a prior three-month period dropping from 46 percent to 15 percent.

A major factor contributing to the success of the HCZ is its commitment to people and focus on outcomes. As one of the first major nonprofits to establish a 10-year business plan, it has demonstrated empirical results and has adjusted programming and funding as needed to maintain and improve outcomes for participants. From these proven results, HCZ has been able to solicit funding from major foundations such as Goldman Sachs Gives and Google to expand its agenda and increase its impact. As President Obama said, "It's an all-encompassing, all-hands-on-deck effort that's turning around the lives of New York City's children, block by block."[30] Moving beyond just a purely educational campaign, HCZ has expanded to include job training and computer workshops, nutrition classes and health clinics, and homeownership classes. Its current scope has many similarities with traditional community developers, despite very different roots.

Although acclaimed by many, HCZ is not without those who urge caution in interpreting its results. They have pointed out that the improvement in test scores in HCZ charter schools is only about average for other charter schools in New York City, even after adjusting for differences in student population. In addition, students attending HCZ charter schools but living outside the zone had test results that were on par with students living in the zone.[31] Although this suggests that the many other community services provided in the HCZ had little or no effect

30 Barack Obama, "Remarks by the President at Urban and Metropolitan Roundtable," July 13, 2009. Available at http://whitehouse.gov/the-press-office/remarks-president-urban-and-metropolitan-roundtable.

31 Grover J. Whitehurst and Michelle Croft, "The Harlem Children's Zone, Promise Neighborhoods, and the Broader, Bolder Approach to Education." (Washington, DC: Brookings Institution, 2010), available at http://brookings.edu/reports/2010/0720_hcz_whitehurst.aspx.

on educational attainment, these services have produced other benefits for residents.[32] Also, by trying to fight the systemic nature of poverty in Harlem, monitoring results, and adjusting its strategy, HCZ has shown that there is a different path than the status quo, giving the field a transformative example of how to approach community development.

Some have also questioned whether HCZ is too costly to be widely replicated and whether capital will be available to cover the costs of the high-touch approach part of its success. HCZ relied on a specialized source of capital (wealthy New York–based philanthropists) to pick up these costs. But pioneering efforts often are more costly than later replications because they involve much more trial and error. In addition, the social outcomes achieved in each case are impressive and just the sorts of outcomes social investors want to take to scale. On average, helping a child go on to college means hundreds of thousands of extra dollars earned over hers or his lifetime. In addition, it remains to be seen how much programs like these may save in the long run on other public expenditures like unemployment insurance payments, incarceration, remedial education, and health care for avoidable chronic disease. These public savings are bound to be substantial.

Purpose Built Communities

Similar to HCZ, Purpose Built Communities (PBC) envisions a "cradle-through-college" model that aims at closing the achievement gap in the East Lake neighborhood in Atlanta. Its aim is also to redevelop troubled real estate and offer community services and facilities to support the full range of needs of people in the community. Again, the data show it has succeeded in doing so. Originally started in 1995 as part of a HOPE VI public housing redevelopment project, PBC has expanded to eight cities and its network continues to grow. Its success suggests that a replicable model for closing the achievement gap is to redevelop rundown properties, mix moderate-income housing with

---

32 The report produced by the Brookings Institute also found that educational advantages of the HCZ end in middle school and that the complementary community services.

low-income housing, and provide high-quality education and early learning programs.

The public housing in East Lake was a notorious haven for crime, drugs, and underachievement. Of 650 units, only 260 were actually occupied, with the rest boarded up or uninhabitable. Only 5 percent of fifth graders met state math standards and the school was last out of 67 in the City of Atlanta. Violent crime was at an all time high, and 87 percent of East Lake's residents did not work. Fifteen years later, violent crime has dropped by 90 percent and 70 percent of the residents are now working. And kids are learning: 98 percent of fifth graders now meet or exceed state math standards, and the school now ranks fourth in the Atlanta public school system, despite the fact that nearly 80 percent of its students are sufficiently low-income to qualify for the free/reduced price lunch program. In 2009, more than 85 percent of eighth graders at the Drew Charter School in 2005 had graduated from high school.[33] By 2011, 99 percent of the local school's students met or exceeded state reading standards, and 94 percent met or exceeded math standards.

As of 2011, PBC has acted as advisors to eight different development groups across the country and continues to grow. Working in New Orleans after Hurricane Katrina, for example, PBC helped the Bayou District Foundation transform the dilapidated St. Bernard's public housing site into a mixed-use and mixed-income community. Using many of the lessons learned from the Villages at East Lake, the newly opened development has a new charter school, an early learning program and supportive services.[34]

PBC stresses open communication between the various groups in its network and hosts annual collaborative meetings so each organization can learn from one another's successes and challenges. Whereas each location is unique and needs a tailored

---

33 East Lake Foundation, "East Lake Then & Now." Available at http://eastlakefoundation. org/sites/courses/view.asp?id=346&page=8936.

34 Bayou District Foundation, "Education." Available at http://bayoudistrictfounda-tion.org/education.

solution, the collaborative model PBC has embraced has led to best practices and a basic framework. As Warren Buffett, one of PBC's cofounders, states, "I like to back success. I like things that change people's lives.... [PBC has] got the right mission. It's got a record of success. It's got the right leader and it's hard to find terrific leadership. And now it's been proven to be replicable."[35] Although still in its early stages, with sustained success only being able to be evaluated by future generations, PBC has provided a replicable model for communities to dramatically alter the achievement of low-income residents.

MEETING THE CHALLENGES AHEAD

Although the community development field has progressed, it still faces several challenges as it moves forward. Unless it successfully meets these challenges, the field will have a difficult time fulfilling the promise of an outcome-oriented, integrated approach to creating systemic change in low-income communities across the country.

First, integrated community development demands significant flows of capital into a community for diverse programs and activities. Finding ways to attract private capital to make such concentrated investments will remain an important challenge. Fortunately, the field can look to strong national intermediaries and CDFIs that have managed to aggregate private capital and leverage scarce government tax incentives and subsidies to fund integrative initiatives. It can also look to the growing number of strong community-based organizations and regional and national firms capable of launching and operating community development initiatives and activities at scale. Concentrated investment can spark additional investment and reduce risk to both community and investors because its benefits usually get capitalized into the value of real estate in the areas around it.

More specifically, to take integrated community development to scale it will be necessary to create a financial return on investment

---

35 Tim Evans, "Buffet Tackles Urban Redevelopment Challenge," USA Today, September 30, 2011. Available at http://usatoday.com/money/economy/story/2011-09-29/buffett-urban-development/50610124/1.

sufficient to attract private capital and sustain community developers and CDFIs. Moving beyond real estate investments to investments that promote human capital development will take special efforts to craft strategies that show people-based investments can enhance social return while generating financial returns.

Second, integrated community development places a premium on coordination and cooperation among community development organizations with different functions as well as among multiple other stakeholders, including business and civic leaders, philanthropic organizations, and government agencies. The field should support education that builds the skills of community development leaders to forge such partnerships and operate them effectively. In addition, innovative financial structures in which philanthropic and government capital work together to leverage private capital must be studied and efforts made to replicate successful ones. New government programs should learn from and build on these efforts.

Third, the structure of government programs and funding streams poses another set of challenges. Despite fledgling efforts at the federal level to coordinate sectors at the regional level (through the HUD-DOT-EPA Sustainable Communities Program) and to promote integrated solutions at the community level (through the Choice Neighborhood Program), funding and program innovations continue to take place at the federal level almost exclusively within silos that resist efforts to coordinate and meld them together in more flexible ways. Nevertheless, there are ample examples of the federal government giving states authority to experiment that have produced replicable approaches. Welfare reform, for example, was based on innovative programs piloted at the state level. Moving-to-Work public housing authorities, able to petition HUD to waive rules, have also become laboratories of invention.

Fourth, the Great Recession and its aftermath pose another set of challenges. Although some weaker community development organizations have failed, others are still teetering. Weak organizations often resist merging with or being acquired by stronger organizations until it is too late. Helping organizations know how and when to reach out to other organizations when they are in trouble—whether as an after-effect of the recession or for other future reasons—is important to sparing communities and the broader field from the ravages of failed organizations. The Great Recession has also resulted in massive disinvestment, foreclosures, and abandonment in communities across the country. Integrated investment in these communities will require dealing in new ways with housing distress, abandoned properties and the loss of jobs and civic services.

Fifth, the social impact investing movement brings its own set of trials to the field because it puts new responsibilities on community-based organizations to demonstrate social impacts to investors in measurable ways. Measuring social impact is not easy or cheap. The field would be well served by pooling its resources to generate efficient and transparent ways of evaluating community impact and facilitating the cross-organizational sharing of best practices for outcome measurement. Those leading this movement understand the importance of doing so and are already trying to sort out better ways to measure social impact and support quality local efforts to address poverty.[36]

Sixth, impact investment can place a greater burden on organizations that wrestle with causes of concentrated poverty with smaller or difficult-to-measure impacts but which are nevertheless important elements of a broader strategy. Socially motivated investors may have to accept that measurement of social impact of some activities, which have a logical place in improving the well-being and achievement of the poor, may be elusive or small and invest in them anyway.

---

36 See David Erickson, "Advancing Social Impact Investments through Measurement Conference: Summary and Themes," Community Development Investment Review 7 (2) (2011), available at http://www.frbsf.org/publications/community/review/vol6_issue1/index.html.

Seventh, although the success of strong CDFIs and community developers with regional or national reach has helped bring about better human and community outcomes, it has also made it a challenge for smaller organizations to grow even if they are financially strong and doing good and important work. Rural CDFIs and community developers and those in small cities also face special challenges finding capital because they fall outside of areas where large banks are assessed for Community Reinvestment Act (CRA) performance. It is therefore important for government agencies, national intermediaries, and large foundations to make extra efforts to identify and strengthen small but effective organizations, especially in rural areas. It could also be advantageous to give large banks CRA credit for certain forms of community investing even if outside of their traditional assessment areas.

Eighth, CDC capacity is constrained by a financing system (including most government incentives and subsidies, as well as equity and debt finance from the private market) that funds transactions (e.g., real estate development) rather than entities (such as capital provided to a CDC to strengthen its financial capacity). Efforts to apply lessons from European countries where investments are more often made to entities based on their balance sheet capacity—as well as to craft tailored approaches that work in the United States—could play an important part in strengthening CDC capacity.[37]

Ninth, and more broadly, the important work of building the capacity of community-based organizations and expanding their geographic coverage is far from done. Many communities are lacking in strong organizations or organizations that are able to work with nonprofits, for-profits, and governments in ways that are mutually beneficial and reinforcing. The CEI example discussed above, and IFF's efforts to branch to new markets, are attempts to close these gaps.

---

37 See Thomas A. Bledsoe and Paul Weech, "International Housing Partner Exchange," Community Development Investment Review, 7 (1) (2011), available at http://www.frbsf. org/publications/community/review/vol7_issue1/index.html.

Finally, fiscal austerity has added to the ever-present urgency of protecting but also expanding funding for critical but chronically underfunded government programs. The NMTC program could sunset at the end of 2012 if legislative action is not taken. The Sustainable Communities Program was not funded in fiscal year 2012 but managed to receive funding of $50 million in fiscal year 2013. All other programs are under pressure, and funding for several, such as the CDFI Fund, have been trimmed. Lastly, the potential for a broad overhaul of the tax code places at risk some of the cornerstones of community investing like the LIHTC and NMTC programs. The late Cushing Dolbeare, founder of the National Low Income Housing Coalition, would regularly remind groups that if they give up the battle to increase government funding for the poor, the War on Poverty would surely be lost.

THE WAY FORWARD

As active agents of social and economic change, CDFIs and community development organizations have successfully attracted large-scale support from private financial institutions, from banks to insurance companies to hedge funds. The opportunities that open for low-income communities and their residents because of these efforts include small business development, job training and creation, retail and commercial services, safe and affordable homes, improved education, new community health clinics, transit-oriented developments, green financing, and many successes in venture capital investing, the arts, recreational space, and an array of community facilities.

The community development field is ready to step into a period that will achieve scale, impact, and accountability for outcomes. The hints of the future lay in some of the innovative examples described above. Meeting the challenges ahead will help the community development field continue to mature and advance toward an integrated approach to community development informed by evaluation and proven tactics.

Still, community developers and CDFIs will have to continue to innovate and further develop, refine, and disseminate promising models like those discussed in this paper. Indeed, many of the most important sources of finance for community development emerged from successful experiments at the local level. Initiatives that sprung up spontaneously in local communities were later supported by the foundations, and several led to important federal policies, programs, or the emergence of national intermediaries. Examples include the CRA, which was modeled after ordinances in Chicago; the creation of NeighborWorks, which started with Federal Home Loan Bank officials taking notice on a field trip of the first Neighborhood Housing Services; the CDFI Fund, which was created to support CDFIs that sprung spontaneously in response to local problems; and Enterprise and LISC, which grew out of foundation support of successful local initiatives.

In all cases, the field can benefit from drawing on lessons learned from successful efforts. As detailed above, early childhood interventions can have dramatic impacts, and while the evidence of the value of job training and other employment-related services is less compelling, when it is combined with housing assistance, it seems to make a real difference. And daily we can see the value of improving schools, rehabilitating substandard housing, reducing housing costs, providing access to health care and job training, and improving public safety. Although it is less clear how much elements like these may work together to create synergies, there are reasons to believe that they do and the Integration Initiative and others are hunting to find and quantify them if they do.

Although the goal of comprehensive community development remains elusive, several organizations and initiatives have made significant progress in identifying the features most likely to lead to successful outcomes. In some cases, the successes have been spectacular, as in the rebuilding of the South Bronx and the turnarounds in East Lake and the Harlem Children's Zone. These successes demonstrate the value of concentrated public investment when administered by strong lead organizations and supported by national intermediaries, foundations, and state and local agencies. Success requires the very active participation of the community and coordination among multiple nonprofit service providers, community developers, government agencies, the business sector and financial institutions.

Nevertheless, launching truly multi-focused, integrative initiatives is costly, and the road map for doing it right does not yet exist. This is why LISC, Enterprise, Living Cities, and others are all investing now in pilot projects to understand what makes integration strategies effective and efficient.

Although actively pursuing and integrating both people- and place-based interventions is the aim, achieving it will usually require smaller first steps. It is impractical, and probably ultimately undesirable, to try to devise extensive plans initially rather than strategically make choices about initial areas of focus that can later serve as the foundation for other work. For example, Harlem's Children Zone started with a strong community center that was placed in a public school. It then branched to supporting the classroom experience of the school during the day and then launched a truly integrated approach but on a single block. As they gained experience and documented success, they were able to expand the zone beyond that block. Likewise, Purpose Built Communities started with a vision of what it takes to spark community development focused deliberately on both people and place.

It makes sense to take a page from these two playbooks and focus on two or three important initiatives first to anchor future efforts. Nonetheless, although community development can start from different entry points, ultimately it must attend to a broad range of community needs, from physical redevelopment to public safety, from community organizing to improving resident access to quality schools, child care, job training, health clinics, and elder care.

Finally, ensuring that the community's voice is heard and incorporated into plans and activities is critical. As holistic approaches increasingly emerge and as efforts to create replicable models gain momentum, there is a risk that the voice of the community itself will get lost in the cacophony of partners, as well as in an evolving confidence among practitioners that they have settled on the interventions that matter most. Although successes provide direction and guidance on tough issues, the field must avoid a one-size-fits-all approach to addressing poverty. Instead, it is critical not to lose sight of the importance of crafting strategies that address the political realities, institutional capacities, and specific needs and wants of widely varying communities.

ERIC BELSKY *is managing director of the Joint Center for Housing Studies of Harvard University and Lecturer in Urban Planning and Design at the Harvard Graduate School of Design. Prior to his Harvard appointments, Belsky held positions with Price Waterhouse LLP, Fannie Mae, the National Association of Home Builders, and the University of Massachusetts at Amherst. In 2001 and 2002, Belsky served as research director for the bipartisan Millennial Housing Commission established by the Congress of the United States. Belsky has co-edited five books and authored numerous articles and book chapters. Belsky currently serves on the editorial boards of the* Journal of Housing Research *and* Housing Policy Debate, *the board of the Opportunity Finance Network, the Affordable Housing Advisory Council of Fannie Mae, the National Community Advisory Council of Bank of America, and the National Advisory Council of CredAbility.*

JENNIFER FAUTH *currently works for the City of New York in the Department of Housing Preservation and Development. She works with private owners of subsidized housing developments to refinance and preserve the affordability of the projects. Prior to moving to New York, she graduated from Harvard's Graduate School of Design with a master's in Urban Planning. While at the GSD, Jenny focused her studies on transportation, affordable housing, and neighborhood development. She holds a BA in Architectural Studies from Brown University.*

II

OPEN FORUM

Voices and Opinions
From Leaders in Policy,
the Field, and Academia

From Leaders
in Policy

FIGHTING POVERTY THROUGH COMMUNITY DEVELOPMENT

Shaun Donovan
Secretary, U.S. Department of Housing and Urban Development

Arne Duncan
Secretary, U.S. Department of Education

Kathleen Sebelius
Secretary, U.S. Department of Health and Human Services

T he Great Recession forced families and communities to confront the worst economic collapse most of us had seen in our lifetimes. When President Obama took office, the economy was shedding 750,000 jobs per month, and foreclosures were rising to record levels. Since then, the economy has added over 4.5 million jobs, and the jobless rate has fallen—but work remains to repair the damage caused by the economic crisis.

As others in this book have noted, the shock of the economic crisis compounded a longer-term trend toward growing inequality and, over the last decade, higher poverty. As a result of the economic divergence since 1980, real median household income has grown four times faster for the top 10 percent of households as it has for middle-income households, making it harder for families to afford housing, transportation, health care, energy, and college.

The effects of the crisis were most severe for low-income Americans: 22 percent of all children in the United States are poor, and more than 10 million people now live in high-poverty neighborhoods. Poverty and social isolation not only make it hard for these individuals to succeed, but also affect the welfare of our country, and our economy, as a whole.

Recognizing these challenges, the Obama administration has adopted a multifaceted approach to reducing poverty and promoting opportunity in order to ensure that all Americans have the ability to reach their full potential. In addition to implementing broad efforts to improve job growth, this approach has focused on reducing immediate hardship owing to the recession while at the same time putting in place longer-term strategies to reduce poverty and put the American Dream in reach for all Americans.

THE IMPACT OF THE GREAT RECESSION

The Great Recession caused many middle-class families to confront unemployment and economic hardship, and even fall into poverty. Millions more families were struggling long before the recession began, and found themselves falling further after the recession took hold. The effects of the recession drove the typical (or median) household income to its lowest level since 1996, with the poverty rate increasing to 15.1 percent in 2010, with 46.2 million Americans living in poverty, which for a three-person family means earning less than $18,530 per year. Over 50 million more Americans are on the edge of poverty.

The poverty rate is highest among children, with nearly 16 million children growing up below the poverty line. More than 30 percent of minority children today live in poverty. And almost half of American children who are born to parents on the bottom rung of the income ladder remain at the bottom as adults. These children tend not to have the range of opportunities that have long characterized the American experience. For example, the aggregate impact of child poverty in the United States leads to reduced skills development and economic productivity, increased crime, and poorer health, all of which is conservatively estimated by recent research to cost the United States more than $620 billion per year.[1]

That one in five children in the richest nation in the world should live in poverty is a moral failing. But it also compromises our country's ability to compete in a global economy. A 22 percent poverty rate among our children not only costs Americans 5 percent of gross domestic product (GDP) every year, but it also sidelines huge pockets of untapped talent, creating barriers to the educational opportunities and skills development all children need to join an American economy built to last.

The impact of poverty is severe wherever it is felt but even as the spatial distribution of poverty changes, with higher increases in suburban communities, we recognize that its impact is particularly acute in America's highest-poverty neighborhoods, where poverty often spans generations. More than 10 million people live with the problems of concentrated neighborhood poverty—high unemployment rates, rampant crime, health disparities, inadequate early care and education, struggling schools, and disinvestment—up from 2.8 percent of the population in 2000 to 3.5 percent of the population in 2005–2009. This tells us that when it comes to addressing poverty in America, place matters. And locally based community developers are at the heart of an evolution in building the infrastructure necessary to provide support to families experiencing poverty, whether in suburbs

---

1 The economist Harry Holzer and colleagues have estimated that every percentage point of the child poverty rate costs the U.S. economy nearly $30 billion a year because of lost earnings and increased costs, particularly health and crime-related costs. In 2007, this meant there was a total annual cost of $500 billion per year from child poverty. By this estimation, the 4 percentage point increase in child poverty in the three years since the start of the Great Recession could cost the United States an additional $120 billion annually. Harry J. Holzer, Diane Schazenbach, Greg Duncan, and Jens Ludwig, "The Economic Costs of Poverty in the United States: Subsequent Effects of Children Growing Up Poor." Working Paper Series # 07-04 (Washington, DC: National Poverty Center, 2007).

first confronting these challenges or neighborhoods beset by distress over decades.[2]

As community developers have long recognized, the problems that contribute to poverty are very much interconnected. While poverty cannot be explained as merely a consequence of housing, education, and health, each poses unique challenges to low-income families at the community level—and none can be understood independently of one another.

THE WAY FORWARD

Since his first day in office, President Obama has taken important steps to combat the worst impacts of the economic crisis while putting in place long-term policy reforms to make sure everyone has a shot at the American Dream. For example, the American Reinvestment and Recovery Act (Recovery Act) kept nearly 7 million Americans out of poverty, and poverty was lessened for 32 million more in 2010 alone. Several of the administration's policies in the Recovery Act helped low-income Americans by providing tax relief and assistance with basic needs such as keeping food on the table, accessing health care, and maintaining a roof over families' heads. Well-timed and targeted tax credits, which included modest expansions in the Earned Income Tax Credit and Child Tax Credit as well as a Making Work Pay tax credit that offset payroll taxes, helped keep more than 3 million Americans, mostly those in families with children, out of poverty.[3] These tax credits, particularly the Making Work Pay credit, also reached middle-class families, providing help to those families and buttressing our economy. Modest expansions and

---

2 While suburban poverty is still lower than urban or rural poverty, it has since the Great Recession seen higher rates of growth (50 percent) from a lower base compared with increases of 25 percent in urban and rural areas. Further, just as suburbs are not immune from neighborhood poverty, children from middle-class families are not exempt from the effects either. Indeed, a federal evaluation of the reading and mathematics outcomes of elementary students in 71 schools in 18 districts and 7 states found that even when controlling for individual student poverty, there is a significant negative association between schools with high levels of poverty and student achievement.

3 Data drawn from tabulations of the U.S. Census and reported by the Center for Budget and Policy Priorities. See Arloc Sherman, "Poverty and Distress Would Have Been Substantially Worse in 2010 without Government Action, New Census Data Show" (Washington, DC: CBPP, November 7, 2011).

further outreach for Supplemental Nutrition Assistance Program (SNAP) benefits kept many families out of poverty and meant there was no increase in child hunger or food insecurity despite the severe economic downturn.

Indeed, during the past three years, the Obama administration has worked hard to put Americans back to work while building a foundation to address poverty and create ladders of opportunity for all Americans. The $7 billion invested through the Neighborhood Stabilization Program not only fought decline and blight in hard-hit communities, but it is also on track to create 90,000 jobs in the places that need them most. [4] More than 400,000 education-related jobs were created or saved by investments in the Recovery Act, ensuring that teachers remained in classrooms and children continued learning.[5] Through the Recovery Act, the Obama administration invested in summer and year-round jobs for disadvantaged youth, which placed more than 367,000 young people in jobs.[6] In addition, investments in the Recovery Act placed more than 260,000 low-income individuals in subsidized jobs.[7]

Recognizing that education is a key to success, the Obama administration has made historic investments to ensure that all children enter school ready to learn and all Americans have access to a complete and competitive education, from cradle-to-career. Typically, educational failure clusters in communities of need. Lack of school readiness among the youngest children, chronically poor-performing elementary and secondary schools, and limited postsecondary completion compound and sustain

---

4 This encompasses direct, indirect, and induced jobs that are likely supported by program expenditures, which was estimated by the Office of Policy Development and Research at the U.S. Department of Housing and Urban Development using the IMPLAN model. IMPLAN is a well-respected input-output model developed in collaboration between the University of Minnesota and the U.S. Forest Service: http://implan.com/V4/Index.php.

5 The White House, "Education and the American Jobs Act" (2011), available at http://www.whitehouse.gov/sites/default/files/aja_ed_state_by_state_report_final.pdf.

6 The White House, "Creating Pathways to Opportunity" (2011), available at http://www.whitehouse.gov/sites/default/files/revised_creating_pathways_to_opportunity_report_10_14_11.pdf.

7 Ibid.

intergenerational poverty. But integrated approaches can overcome these persistent challenges. Many of the lowest-achieving schools targeted for improvement under Race to the Top, an Obama administration competition to encourage and reward states that are creating the conditions for innovation and reform, are located in communities where local leaders are pursuing a range of neighborhood revitalization initiatives. So are many of the lowest-achieving schools targeted for significant reforms through School Improvement Grants that support their turnaround. In addition, our investments in improving access to high-quality early education have created opportunities for program alignment and the ability for community developers to leverage improvements in educational opportunity, as the administration has expanded Head Start, invested in efforts to expand evidence-based teaching methods, and required programs that do not meet quality benchmarks to compete against others for continued Head Start funding.

The Obama administration's new direction also includes efforts to improve health and health care. When families lack health insurance, they not only face limited access to care, but also a far greater risk of getting sick and incurring a mountain of health care bills that can lead to financial ruin. The Affordable Care Act will expand health insurance coverage to more than 30 million Americans. Many of those Americans have incomes well below the poverty line or that hover just above it but who remain ineligible for Medicaid today. Coverage means both access to care and protection against the financial risk that can come with illness. Access to affordable coverage is also critical to staying healthy and productive.

The Department of Health and Human Services is working closely with community groups and states to identify those neighborhoods and areas with the highest rates of uninsured individuals to help guarantee that the Affordable Care Act brings insurance coverage to those places with populations most in need. In addition to improving coverage, we have added to the health infrastructure in the most underserved areas. With investments made possible by the Recovery Act, more than 2,800 grants were awarded to health centers for construction, renovation, new equipment, and the implementation of health information technology; and 127 new health center sites were created, providing comprehensive, quality primary health care services to medically underserved communities and vulnerable populations with limited access to health care. The Affordable Care Act has continued this effort with almost 600 capital projects and the creation of nearly 300 new service delivery sites. Health centers' expansion into high-poverty neighborhoods recognizes these communities lack access to even basic preventive care, and it will change the mix of supports available to residents, providing an opportunity for coordination for developers serving high-need residents.

Under the President's leadership, the Obama administration has focused on expanding access to opportunity for all Americans. This focus has been accompanied by a new approach to governing, one that seeks to unlock individual and collective potential; that rewards results, evidence, and best practices over ideology; that puts people and places over programs; that rewards work and supports skill building; and that leverages the power unleashed when we join forces across all sectors—government, business, and nonprofits, both community-based and national—recognizing we are strongest when we work together.

The uniquely people- and place-based nature of the challenge of poverty in America requires people-based and place-based responses to expand access to opportunity. It is not enough to focus only on economic circumstances of individual families; we must also be clear-eyed about the opportunities and stressors that surround them where they live.

While we've discussed many of the Obama administration's most powerful efforts to expand opportunity in families' lives, the remainder of this chapter focuses on the place-based aspects of the Obama administration's larger strategies. To successfully revitalize high-poverty neighborhoods, change the trajectories of kids in those neighborhoods, and compete in the twenty-first century economy, we must follow the example that innovative local actors have set across the country—solving housing, education, safety, workforce, and health challenges concurrently, in partnerships built across government, business, and nonprofit sectors.

FOCUS ON PLACE-BASED STRATEGIES TO BUILD STRONG COMMUNITIES

As the first president to have worked in public housing, President Obama understands the need for this approach. The President is deeply familiar with how poverty connects to every aspect of a family's life and a neighborhood's success, as well as the innovations our community developers have forged to fight poverty and community distress. The President knows fighting poverty requires flexibility, adaptability, and above all, a comprehensive focus. That is why, in describing the Harlem Children's Zone, he noted that we need an "all-encompassing, all hands on deck" approach.

That's also why our three agencies have worked with one another and partners throughout state and local governments, businesses, and the community development field to attack poverty comprehensively—in the President's words, recognizing that "we cannot treat symptoms in isolation."

This shift may have been new for the federal government, but not for the "third sector" of nonprofits and philanthropies in the community development field, which long ago recognized that embracing educational, health, and other perspectives was critical to successful housing and to reducing concentrated poverty. Long before President Obama took office, community developers had recognized that rebuilding educational opportunities for children trapped in neighborhoods of concentrated poverty was just as important as rebuilding the neighborhoods themselves. They had seen how reducing homelessness was inextricably tied to our ability to provide behavioral health and other wrap-around services. And they understood that when the government does not act alone, but as a leader among private and nonprofit partners, these goals become achievable.

To take the innovative solutions developed at the neighborhood level across the entire country, we have focused on five fundamental principles:

1 Do what works. We have identified innovative policies that improve economic mobility, considered new ideas with a strong theoretical base, and scaled up promising approaches that have begun to show good evidence.

2 Use a clear set of measurable results. Successful community development requires a focus on a clear set of measurable results for children, families, and communities. Results allow stakeholders within and outside the administration to orient around common goals. A core set of desired results not only provides stakeholders with information about whether the discrete programs are making a difference, but also makes policymakers (and public and private funders) more willing to align with and invest in them.

3 Use existing resources more efficiently and effectively. At a moment when taxpayer resources are scarce at federal, state and local levels, we must focus on using our resources as effectively as possible based on the best available evidence. We must closely examine what works, being willing to challenge existing orthodoxy. That requires a reinvigorated research agenda that evaluates programs rigorously and provides evidence to facilitate continuous improvement.

4 Coordinate across partners. A comprehensive approach to transforming communities requires a strong partnership that includes the federal government, state and local government, and private and nonprofit partners. That includes improving government capital efficiency by leveraging private capital to maximize impact, reducing risk through credit enhancement, and creating conditions—in neighborhoods and regions—that are attractive for private capital investment.

5 Focus on people and places. In order to address barriers that arise from individual life circumstances as well as neighborhood and regional environments, efforts must be both people-based *and* place-based. This cannot be an "either/or" proposition; successful pursuit of this agenda demands a dual-track approach with complementary and mutually reinforcing efforts. This work must be centered on people-based policies and programs that increase economic mobility and break intergenerational cycles of poverty, including macro-level policies that ensure future economic growth is accompanied by real increases in wages and median incomes, as well as micro-level policies to support healthy child development, academic success, skills development, economic stability, geographic mobility, and work. They also must promote responsibility —to emphasize the importance of graduating from high school, making responsible parenting choices, and seeking and maintaining full-time work. And they must incorporate place-based access to opportunity, and counteract the place effects of concentrated poverty.

This approach is woven into three major administration place-based initiatives, each of which signals the direction that federal, state, and local governments can pursue to work as better partners across the community development sector, and build the foundation of America's twenty-first century economy.

TRANSFORMING NEIGHBORHOODS OF CONCENTRATED POVERTY: THE NEIGHBORHOOD REVITALIZATION INITIATIVE

Recognizing the disproportionate needs in America's highest-poverty neighborhoods, the Obama administration has pursued a groundbreaking, "all hands on deck" approach to neighborhood revitalization.

In the past, the federal approach toward neighborhoods of concentrated poverty was disconnected from new actors in the third sector. Rarely were efforts to transform public housing, invest in community health centers, or turn around local schools coordinated or aligned. It was not uncommon to see rebuilt public housing surrounded by failing schools or even other troubled housing, rife with lead hazards and asthma triggers.

In response to this history, the Obama administration formed the White House Neighborhood Revitalization Initiative (NRI), bringing together five agencies (Education, HHS, HUD, Treasury, and Justice) to support the work of local leaders from the public and private sectors to attract the private investment needed to transform distressed neighborhoods into sustainable, mixed-income neighborhoods with the affordable housing, safe streets, and good schools every family needs.

A centerpiece of the administration's initiative is a comprehensive neighborhood revitalization tool called Choice Neighborhoods, which builds on the HOPE VI public housing revitalization program that is planned to create more than 100,000 homes in healthy, mixed-income communities.[8] The program has already leveraged twice the federal investment in additional capital and raised the average median income of redevelopment sites by 75 percent or more.[9] Choice Neighborhoods provides local leaders with innovative, flexible tools to rebuild rundown housing in high-poverty neighborhoods, while expanding educational and economic opportunities for residents.

In San Francisco's Eastern Bayview neighborhood, where 40 percent of residents live in poverty and which suffers from high vacancies, poor schools, and inadequate access to job centers, we can see how the NRI is incorporating strategies designed by local leaders to meet the specific needs of unique, locally designated neighborhoods, creating the conditions for private capital to flow into disinvested communities.

---

8 Thomas Kingsley, "Taking Advantage of What We Have Learned." In From Despair to Hope: HOPE VI and the New Promise of Public Housing in America's Cities, edited by Henry Cisneros and Lora Engdahl (Washington, DC: Brookings Institution, 2009).

9 Ibid. Seventy-two percent of leveraged capital, an estimated $7.81 billion, came from private sources, which included private investments in the Low Income Housing Tax Credit; Abt Associates, "Interim Assessment of the HOPE VI Program, Cross Site Report." (Washington, DC: U.S. Department of Housing and Urban Development, 2003), available at http://www.huduser.org/Publications/pdf/HOPE_VI_Cross_Site.pdf.

There, a public-private nonprofit consortium composed of McCormack Baron Salazar (a private development company), the San Francisco Housing Authority, Lennar Homes (a publicly traded real estate development company), the city, school district, and Urban Strategies are using a Choice Neighborhoods implementation grant to build more than 1,200 mixed-income units, replacing 250 units of public housing and creating a new master-planned community with market-rate and workforce housing. The consortium has also identified a clear plan and goals to address their local needs, building on the School District's progress to improve the school quality and educational opportunities, setting employment targets, and working with the Job Readiness Initiative and the local Citybuild program to provide job training and placement. In addition, the team is bringing in needed everyday services and jobs by improving streetscapes to attract retail, removing blighted housing, and pursuing new commercial assets, fresh-food stores, and a new bus rapid transit with direct connections to key commuter rail lines.

Choice Neighborhoods recognizes that a healthy neighborhood depends on more than successful, stable housing and must ensure that children in newly built, mixed-income housing also have access to high-quality educational opportunities. That's why the administration has tied Choice Neighborhoods to another centerpiece of the Neighborhood Revitalization Initiative, the Department of Education's Promise Neighborhoods initiative, which emphasizes local, innovative partnerships to put education at the center of efforts to fight poverty.

Where Choice Neighborhoods' focus is on troubled housing, Promise Neighborhoods, inspired by the Harlem Children's Zone, works to significantly improve the educational and developmental outcomes of children and youth in our most distressed neighborhoods, and to transform those neighborhoods by building a complete continuum of cradle-through-college-to-career solutions of educational programs and family and community supports, with great schools at the center of each community. The continuum of solutions in Promise Neighborhoods includes high-quality early learning programs and services designed to improve outcomes across multiple domains of early learning; ambitious, rigorous, and comprehensive educational reforms; programs that prepare students to be college- and career-ready; and family and student support indicators. Promise Neighborhoods' success is measured by not only educational outcomes, but health and safety outcomes as well.

One of the five fiscal year 2011 Promise Neighborhoods implementation grantees, the Minneapolis Northside Achievement Zone (NAZ), operates as one integrated program across 50 organizational and school partners, with NAZ families and students at the center, and a shared goal to prepare all NAZ children to graduate from high school ready for college. NAZ helps parents to believe their children will succeed, and provides the right tools to improve their achievement in school and in life. NAZ families and children move through a cradle-to-career continuum of comprehensive supports from prenatal through adulthood, through three areas of impact: family engagement and opportunity alignment; an educational pipeline; and whole family support.

Since 2010, NAZ has shown promising results. Parents are setting and achieving education-focused goals (many for the first time); enrolling in and completing parent education classes at unprecedented rates; participating in high-quality early childhood education programs; stabilizing their housing; and setting their own improved career pathway plans.

As a Promise Neighborhood, NAZ is scaling up its successful strategies with a goal of reaching 1,200 families with 3,000 children all successfully on a path to college, and each experiencing a transformation in their lives. When Shira first met her NAZ Engagement Team "family coach," she had tears in her eyes.[10] She could not afford to keep the apartment she shared with her children and was becoming increasingly desperate. Shira's Engagement Team member connected her with the NAZ

---

10 Name has been changed.

"cradle-to-career" continuum of services, starting with the NAZ Housing Action Team.

With her home stabilized, Shira now focuses on supporting her children's academic success. She has graduated from both an eight-week parent empowerment training class and a twelve-week early childhood parent education class through the NAZ Family Academy—courses that provide a strong foundation to help her to build a culture of achievement in her home.

With the support of NAZ, Shira continually sets goals for herself and her family. She has returned to work and is taking college courses. Her daughter is enrolled in high-quality preschool, and her son attends a NAZ Anchor school, and he has been matched with a mentor through Big Brothers / Big Sisters.

Every child deserves the opportunities that NAZ is building in Minneapolis, and ensuring that all children have those opportunities requires innovative partnerships that stretch across government, private, and nonprofit sectors. At a time when federal funding is constrained, the Neighborhood Revitalization Initiative has been critical to stretching taxpayer dollars further, leveraging an array of untapped assets in those communities, from transit lines that connect housing to jobs, to nearby hospitals and universities. Indeed, the $122 million in Choice Neighborhoods implementation grants made thus far have already leveraged a combined $1.6 billion—more than 13 times their total grant award—with more to come as the redevelopment work accelerates. And Promise Neighborhoods has leveraged more than $36.5 million in local matching funds and resources through $38.5 million awarded.

OPENING DOORS: PREVENTING AND ENDING HOMELESSNESS

A decade ago, it was widely believed that the men and women who slept on our street corners, struggled with chemical dependency and mental illness, and often cycled from shelters to jails to emergency rooms would always be homeless and in some cases, even wanted to be.

But local leaders from rural Mankato, Minnesota, to urban San Francisco refused to believe the chronically ill, long-term homeless could not be helped. Partnering with local and state agencies and the private and nonprofit sectors, hundreds of communities committed themselves to proving otherwise.

In reducing chronic homelessness by more than one-third inside of five years by combining housing and supportive services, these communities proved what just a few years ago seemed nearly impossible: That we could actually end homelessness.

The tool these communities were using is known as permanent supportive housing, which recognizes that while every homeless person living on the street lacks affordable housing, just as often, they lack access to health and social services as well.

One study, reported in the *Journal of the American Medical Association*, centered on Seattle's 1811 Eastlake supportive housing project. Researchers examined 75 of the center's chronically homeless residents, one-half of whom had serious mental illness and all of whom struggled with alcohol addiction. In the year before participants in the program entered supportive housing, the 75 residents collectively spent more than 1,200 days in jail and visited the local medical center more than 1,100 times at a cost to Medicaid of more than $3.5 million. In the year after entering 1811 Eastlake, days spent in jail were cut almost in half. Medicaid costs dropped by more than 40 percent because hospital visits dropped by almost one-third.[11]

Another study in Chicago reached a similar conclusion. Housing assistance provided to homeless patients suffering from HIV/AIDS, or other chronic illnesses made medical services so much more effective that days in the hospital dropped 42 percent,

---

11 Mary E. Larimer et al., "Health Care and Public Service Use and Costs Before and After Provision of Housing for Chronically Homeless Persons With Severe Alcohol Problems," The Journal of the American Medical Association. 301 (13) (April 1, 2009).

days of required nursing home care dropped 45 percent, and most critically of all, the number of emergency room visits dropped 46 percent.

These examples remind us that using resources more effectively isn't only about doing more with less. Just as often, it is also about small investments that yield big savings.

Certainly the most ambitious partnership is Opening Doors, the first federal strategic plan to end homelessness, which was released by the Obama administration in 2010. Harnessing the talents and resources of 19 different federal agencies, Opening Doors provides a roadmap for ending chronic and veteran homelessness by 2015 and homelessness among families, youth, and children by 2020, while setting the country on a path to eradicate all types of homelessness. The plan proposes realignment of existing programs based on what we have learned and the best practices that are occurring at the local level, so that resources are focused on what works. From years of practice and research, the plan identifies successful approaches to end homelessness. Evidence points to the role housing plays as an essential platform for human and community development. Stable housing provides an ideal launching pad for the delivery of health care and other social services focused on improving life outcomes for individuals and families. It also redoubles our focus on expanding access to high-quality educational opportunities for homeless children and adults, helping to decrease financial vulnerability and the likelihood of homelessness later in life.

With the active participation of other cabinet secretaries and the White House, we have had unprecedented collaboration among federal agencies and with state and local governments and nonprofits.

Armed with this proven success, the number of beds for permanent supportive housing has increased by 34 percent since 2007. Building on these efforts, HUD, with support from President Obama and Congress, has made an unprecedented commitment to permanent supportive housing to end homelessness for people with severe disabilities and long histories of homelessness.

Another proven solution to ending homelessness that we have embraced is the combination of prevention and rapid re-housing. In 2009, the Recovery Act created the Homeless Prevention and Rapid Re-housing Program (HPRP), which has saved 1.2 million people from homelessness.

HPRP has helped homeless men and women transition into permanent supportive housing, often providing those at risk of homelessness with something as simple as a security deposit. For the majority of the people assisted by HPRP to date, it was the program's ability to help them find or stabilize housing arrangements quickly and effectively that made the difference.

Grantees report that fully 90 percent of people assisted by HPRP in its first year successfully found permanent housing. In a state like Michigan, 94 percent of homeless persons in rapid re-housing didn't fall back into homelessness.

We have seen similar successes across the country. These funds have helped speed progress in states like Utah, which in the last few years has invested in permanent supportive housing, helping to reduce chronic homelessness by nearly 70 percent since 2005. By targeting its HPRP resources to rapid re-housing, Utah was able to reduce chronic homelessness an astounding 26 percent over the last year alone.

While the lives of those who were homeless or at risk of homelessness have been helped dramatically by the HPRP approach, just as significant is how HPRP is "fundamentally changing" the way communities respond to homelessness, as the U.S. Conference of Mayors put it.[12]

For instance, Cleveland's Continuum of Care program is using HPRP funds to create a central intake system that provides

---

12 U.S. Conference of Mayors, "Hunger and Homelessness Survey: A Status Report on Hunger and Homelessness in America's Cities," (Washington, DC: Conference of Mayors, 2009), available at http://usmayors.org/pressreleases/uploads/USCMHungercompleteWEB2009.pdf.

customized services to those entering the shelter system. This helps the community not only manage beds and services more effectively but also ensures that households are transitioning to permanent housing as quickly as possible.

Cleveland provides a good example of how a federal program like HPRP is helping communities move from fragmented, duplicative programs to a comprehensive twenty-first century system that targets resources to those most in need—not with top-down rules, but with flexible tools from the ground up.

These successes have paved the way for critical reforms such as the HEARTH Act and helped several successful partnerships to emerge and flourish. In 2010, HUD partnered with the U.S. Department of Veterans Affairs (VA) to establish joint goals and monitor progress in the fight to end veterans' homelessness. Using the HUDStat performance system to identify promising practices and problems, the number of veterans housed under the "HUD-VASH" partnership increased by nearly 20 times in just two years. By June 2011, HUD and VA assisted nearly 30,000 veterans, surpassing the program's target by 50 percent. This progress is a big reason homelessness among veterans declined by 12 percent in 2011, and why we were able to secure another 10,000 vouchers for HUD-VASH in our FY2012 budget.

Another partnership, led by HHS, is improving services for people with disabilities. Using HHS' "Money Follows the Person" resources, HUD and HHS are working together on a significant capacity-building effort in five states to learn how to create a more seamless partnership between public housing authorities and state Medicaid agencies to help people with disabilities transition from institutional care to community living.

We know these sorts of partnerships work, as illustrated by the experience of Kay, from Cleveland, OH. Because of her psychiatric disability, Kay had gone between shelters and nursing homes for the majority of her life. She was discharged from a nursing facility to a temporary shelter, but could not afford a permanent home and was at risk of being re-institutionalized. With a

Housing Choice Voucher provided through HUD and the help of Ohio's Home Choice Program, funded by HHS, Kay got the support she needed to transition into her community.

New partnerships can be challenging at first, but communities have shown us they can be overcome and are leading the way. For example, the Greater Kansas City area is developing a Housing Sustainability Plan that integrates many of the strategies in Opening Doors—forging partnerships at the metropolitan level among governments, local businesses and nonprofits, philanthropies, and the investment community.

As Opening Doors highlights, the federal government—or government at any level—cannot end homelessness alone; it needs partners and community developers across the spectrum.

WORKING IN PARTNERSHIP WITH LOCAL LEADERS: STRONG CITIES, STRONG COMMUNITIES

If the economic crisis has taught us anything these last several years, it is that America needs strong cities and regions to create an economy built to last. And of all the elements that comprise a city, its leaders and institutions are the most fundamental; they impact the populace, the local economy, and all assets available in the region. But until now, Washington has not traditionally supported and partnered with local leaders and institutions to support their capacity and growth.

This administration recognizes that no city can succeed without strong local leadership and institutional capacity, no matter how big the federal grant or how well-crafted the federal policy. We have reflected that recognition through a customized pilot initiative called "Strong Cities, Strong Communities," which is providing on-the-ground technical assistance and resources to local leaders in six distressed cities and regions. Using no new federal dollars, SC2 recognizes that what distressed cities need from a federal partner is the flexibility to pursue their own visions—and the support to realize them.

While a federal partner that understands the importance of local capacity is important for every city and region in America, it is absolutely essential for those places that were facing long-term structural challenges long before the recession hit.

The six pilot cities and regions (Memphis, TN; Cleveland, OH; New Orleans, LA; Chester, PA; Fresno, CA; and Detroit, MI) were chosen not simply because they face common challenges —population loss and long-term economic challenges, high levels of poverty and unemployment, and low property values and deteriorating infrastructure—but also because of the assets they bring: anchor institutions; comprehensive visions for economic development; and political leadership and will of regional, city, and philanthropic leaders.

Modeled on the transformation of cities like Chicago, Seattle, and Pittsburgh, which successfully transitioned from one-industry powerhouses to the hubs of the dynamic, diverse, resilient, regional economies, SC2 is piloting several critical tools to the six economically and geographically diverse communities and regions.

The first tool consists of the Community Solutions Teams in each city, comprised of highly skilled federal officials who are working full-time on-site to help these cities navigate and harmonize existing federal programs. Together, they are identifying barriers to growth and helping these communities strategically put to work millions in federal dollars already awarded.

More than 90 percent of the members of Community Solutions Teams on the ground right now are not political appointees but career federal employees who will bring this knowledge and experience back to their agencies.

These cities also will benefit from the second tool: a Fellowship Placement Program, funded not by government but philanthropy, and "deepening the bench" of these pilot cities. The Fellowship Program makes sure there is capacity and strength within the local government not just to carry on when the federal teams depart, but to lead.

To ensure these lessons and tools can assist local governments across the nation, SC2 also created a National Resource Network that can act as a "one-stop-shop" for technical assistance. The Network will convene groups of national experts with wide-ranging skills that can provide the kind of cutting edge support and counsel cities need to maximize public and private dollars. And by ensuring this public-private partnership lives outside of government and is coordinated by philanthropy, our hope is that it can become the kind of critical capacity-building resource to communities that Living Cities is to the nonprofit sector.

Of course, many localities that have large deficits in their fiscal capacity are not as far along with respect to developing a compre-hensive strategy for their economic future. For these places, SC2 developed an Economic Challenge that will competitively award funding to six additional cities and regions so that they themselves can hold "X-prize style" competitions that challenge multidisciplinary teams of experts to help develop and imple-ment comprehensive, twenty-first century, globally competitive economic strategies for their regions.

The transformations underway in these cities will not happen overnight. But already, SC2 has made important progress.

In Memphis, our SC2 team is working in partnership with the Bloomberg team to create a CityStat performance management system that measures progress on the dozens of strategies already underway in the city.

In Cleveland, our SC2 team is working to align northeast Ohio's workforce delivery system with economic growth opportunities presented by efforts such as the Integration Initiative's Evergreen Cooperative green business development.

In New Orleans, our SC2 team is collaborating with city staff to improve access to primary care services and to develop a behavioral health strategy that establishes strong community partnerships to integrate behavioral health within the community.

In Detroit, we have seen that careful planning in places that have lost population and have high vacancy rates is essential, but not without challenges. There, our team has seen that capacity constraints within local government can affect the alignment with philanthropy. We are working to resolve these tensions, while understanding that some of them can be healthy.

We are also seeing how new partners can emerge. In Fresno, the General Services Administration worked with the Social Security Administration to help the latter sign a 15-year lease in downtown Fresno to bring more people into the heart of the city's historic district.

In all these cases, the work of SC2 is emblematic of the approach that this administration has taken with cities—engaging as a partner, focused on local visions, local leadership and local assets.

THE FOUNDATION FOR AN ECONOMY BUILT TO LAST

Even before the Great Recession, the middle class was under siege. But with median family net worth dropping nearly 40 percent, millions of families have been pushed even closer to the brink of poverty and far too many more are falling behind. The growing gap between the wealthiest Americans and those with the least makes the task of climbing into the middle class tougher than ever before.

Instead of economic growth fueled by speculation and phony profits, we need investment in the people and places that can prepare our communities for long-term economic success in a globally competitive economy. President Obama has called for putting in place long-term policy reforms for our nation to "out innovate, out educate, and out build the rest of the world," while taking important steps to combat the worst impacts of the economic crisis. We have focused on creating pathways to opportunity for all Americans, and the administration's approach to revitalizing neighborhoods of concentrated poverty, ending homelessness, and supporting city governments are but three examples of the kind of new thinking we need to strengthen communities and end the scourge of generational cycles of poverty.

The cost is too great to leave countless families on the sidelines as we compete in a global economy. We have an economic and moral imperative to ensure that all children grow up in places that prepare them for the twenty-first century economy. And we must recognize how far and wide that imperative stretches, from education reforms that ensure all Americans have access to a complete and affordable education, to tax policy that encourages and facilitates work, to transportation and telecommunications infrastructure that expands access to job opportunities, to a health care system where every American can get the care they need to get healthy and stay well.

The administration has developed an integrated approach to community development that supports locally-driven comprehensive strategies, invests in what works with a focus on data and results, leverages resources to maximize current and future federal investments, and lays a foundation for stronger urban, suburban, and rural communities.

Our focus must be to provide the kind of partnership that recognizes the importance of the federal role when it comes to community development but is humble enough to recognize the federal role is one of many. It's a partnership of families, neighborhoods, and governments that uses data to focus not simply on access and dollars, but on the outcomes that public investment produces, and understands the power not simply of federal investment in community development, but its ability to foster civic engagement and personal enrichment at the local level. With broad access to opportunity in an economy built to last, we can ensure that wherever Americans grow up, their hard work allows them to realize the American Dream.

SHAUN DONOVAN *was sworn in as the 15th U.S. Secretary for Housing and Urban Development on January 26, 2009. He has devoted his career to ensuring access to safe, decent, and affordable housing, and has continued that effort in the Obama administration. Secretary Donovan believes that America's homes are the foundation for family, safe neighborhoods, good schools, and job creation. His tenure as HUD Secretary has reflected his commitment to making quality housing possible for every American. Sworn in at a time when the foreclosure crisis had devastated American families, under Secretary Donovan's leadership HUD has helped stabilize the housing market and worked to keep responsible families in their homes. The agency has instituted reforms that have solidified the Federal Housing Administration's financial position and protected the taxpayer against risk, while still preserving FHA's mission of providing responsible access to homeownership. Prior to HUD, Secretary Donovan served as commissioner of the New York City Department of Housing Preservation and Development. Secretary Donovan previously served in the Clinton administration as Deputy Assistant Secretary for Multifamily Housing at HUD, where he was the primary federal official responsible for privately-owned multifamily housing. He also served as acting FHA Commissioner during the Clinton/Bush presidential transition. Prior to his first service at HUD, he worked at the Community Preservation Corporation (CPC) in New York City, a nonprofit lender and developer of afford-able housing. He also researched and wrote about housing policy at the Joint Center for Housing Studies at Harvard University and worked as an architect. Secretary Donovan holds a BA and masters' degrees in public administration and architecture from Harvard.*

ARNE DUNCAN *is the 9th U.S. Secretary of Education. He has served in this post since his confirmation by the U.S. Senate on Jan. 20, 2009, following his nomination by President Barack Obama. Secretary Duncan's tenure as secretary has been marked by a number of significant accomplishments on behalf of American students and teachers. He helped to secure congressional support for President Obama's investments in education, including the American Recovery and Reinvestment Act's $100 billion to fund 355,000 education jobs, increases in Pell grants, reform efforts such as Race to the Top and Investing in Innovation, and interventions in low-performing schools. Additionally, he has helped secure another $10 billion to support 65,000 additional education jobs; the elimination of student loan subsidies to banks; and an over $630 million national competi-tion for early learning programs. Before becoming Secretary of Education,*

Secretary Duncan served as the chief executive officer of the Chicago Public Schools (CPS), a position he held from June 2001 through December 2008. Prior to joining the Chicago Public Schools, from 1992 to 1998, Secretary Duncan ran the nonprofit education foundation Ariel Education Initiative, which helped fund a college education for a class of inner-city children under the I Have A Dream program. He was part of a team that later started a new public elementary school built around a financial literacy curriculum, the Ariel Community Academy, which today ranks among the top elementary schools in Chicago. From 1987 to 1991, Duncan played professional basketball in Australia, where he also worked with children who were wards of the state. Secretary Duncan graduated magna cum laude from Harvard University in 1987, after majoring in sociology. He was co-captain of Harvard's basketball team and was named a first team Academic All-American. Secretary Duncan is married to Karen Duncan, and they have two children who attend public school in Arlington, VA.

KATHLEEN SEBELIUS was sworn in as the 21st Secretary of the Department of Health and Human Services (HHS) on April 28, 2009. Since taking office, Secretary Sebelius has led ambitious efforts to improve America's health and enhance the delivery of human services to some of the nation's most vulnerable populations, including young children, those with disabilities, and the elderly. As part of the historic Affordable Care Act, she is implementing reforms that have ended many of the insurance industry's worst abuses and will help 34 million uninsured Americans get health coverage. She is also working with doctors, nurses, hospital leaders, employers, and patients to slow the growth in health care costs through better care and better health. Under Secretary Sebelius's leadership, HHS is committed to innovation, from promoting public- private collaboration to bring life-saving medicines to market, to building a 21st century food safety system that prevents outbreaks before they occur, to collaborating with the Department of Education, to help states increase the quality of early childhood education programs, and give parents more information to make the best choices for their children. Secretary Sebelius served as Governor of Kansas from 2003 until her Cabinet appointment in April, 2009, and was named one of America's Top Five Governors by Time magazine.

From Leaders
in the Field

AMERICA'S TOMORROW:
Race, Place, and the Equity Agenda

Angela Glover Blackwell
PolicyLink

T he quintessential promise of America is that through hard work, anyone born poor can succeed. The antipoverty movement grew out of recognition that this is a pipe dream for millions of people of color who are disproportionately saddled with failing schools, unemployment, poor health, and underinvested communities.

Those of us working to end poverty and racism used to make our case in moral terms: the nation must deliver on the promise of equal opportunity and shared prosperity because it is the right thing to do. But a demographic transformation more rapid and widespread than anyone had predicted has changed the conversation. By the middle of this century, the very same groups who have long been left behind will become America's majority population. By the end of this decade, most youth will be people of color. These shifts already have occurred in California, Texas,

New Mexico, and in metropolitan regions across the country. Equity—just and fair inclusion in a society in which all can participate and prosper—has become more than a moral issue. It is now an economic imperative.

We cannot afford to squander the talents and potential of so large a segment of our population. Yet we continue to do exactly that. The economic disaster beginning in 2008 hit communities of color first and worst, even as it also hurt many poor, working-class, and middle-class whites. In 2010, 27.4 percent of African Americans, 26.6 percent of Hispanics, 12.1 percent of Asians, and 9.9 percent of whites were poor.[1] More than one-fifth of the nation's children lived in poverty, the worst track record in the developed world. The reality in communities of color was even more abysmal: 38 percent of black children and 35 percent of Hispanic children were poor.[2]

How America produces such disparities is no mystery. Address is a proxy for opportunity. Where we live determines whether or not we have access to the requisite resources for success, including good schools, decently paid jobs, and transportation that connects to employment centers. It determines whether or not we have access to healthy living conditions—whether the air is reasonably clean or fouled by pollutants spewing from a freeway or rail line or bus depot in the neighborhood; whether we are likely to develop a long list of chronic illnesses and, if we do, whether we will survive them; whether we are likely to be killed during a crime, in a car crash, or simply when crossing the street. Any serious discussion of poverty inevitably turns to prevention and well-being—and that brings the conversation straight into the places where struggling people live.

However, we must not view these places simply as constructs of geography. In a nation where neighborhoods remain largely segregated by skin color and ethnicity, "place" can be understood only through the lens of race. Efforts to improve conditions in

---

1   National Poverty Center, available at http://npc.umich.edu/poverty.

2   Ibid.

low-income communities must address the systemic barriers to success and well-being—many of them erected on the structures of racism—that lie at the root of economic and social inequity.

Poverty is tied to educational attainment, and student outcomes reflect the effects of underinvestment. By the end of fourth grade, black and Hispanic students and poor students of all races trail two years behind their wealthier, predominantly white peers in reading and math. By eighth grade, the gap is three years; by 12th grade, it is four years.[3] Six of every 10 African American, Hispanic, and Native American students graduate high school, compared with eight in 10 white students and nine in 10 Asian and Pacific Islander students.[4] Nearly six million people ages 16–24—disproportionately young people of color—neither work nor attend school.[5]

The growing legion of disconnected youth forecasts bleak outcomes in terms of social stability and economic prospects for the youth themselves, for their families, for their communities, and for society at large. Youth without productive activities, options, or hope are more likely to be poor for the rest of their lives. They also are more likely to end up in the criminal justice system, leaving them with a stigma that will limit opportunities long after their release and imposing huge social and financial costs on all of us. The need for bold, comprehensive strategies to reverse this trajectory and open up possibilities for the young people who are America's future has never been more urgent. Policy change is key: policy created many of our problems, and it must advance and support solutions.

---

3   Campaign for Educational Equity, Teachers College, "Facts and Figures," http://tc.columbia.edu/equitycampaign/detail.asp?Id=Equity+Facts+and+Figures&Info=Facts+and+Figures (accessed April 30, 2011).

4   Robert Balfanz et al., Building a Grad Nation: Progress and Challenge in Ending the High School Dropout Epidemic (Washington, DC: America's Promise Alliance, 2010).

5   Andrew Sum et al., Still Young, Idle, and Jobless: The Continued Failure of the Nation's Teens to Benefit from Job Growth (Boston: Northeastern University Center for Labor Market Studies, 2006).

It is neither by accident nor by the force of the free market that society's most vulnerable groups generally live in its most distressed places, neighborhoods stripped of decently paid jobs and of investment in the infrastructure that fosters opportunity. In other words, poor people of color do not move into disinvested communities because that's all they can afford; rather, investment disappears when people of color move in. Neighborhoods and regions across the country bear the scars of government policies, real estate practices, and business strategies through much of the twentieth century that prevented African Americans and other targeted groups from obtaining loans or participating in government-sponsored housing programs while encouraging white residents to move to the ever-distant suburban edge.

While federal and state laws prohibit many overtly discriminatory policies, the nation's map remains carved into separate, shamefully unequal societies. More than half of Hispanics and nearly 65 percent of African Americans live in neighborhoods of color,[6] generally low-income ones. Two-thirds of black children live in high-poverty communities, compared with only 6 percent of white children—a percentage that has not changed in 30 years.[7]

Neighborhoods are working hard to address their challenges, often without policy support. In many of these communities, nonprofit organizations, places of worship, and residents come together to administer programs and services to help people in need and to provide venues for engagement with the issues they face. But in the absence of equity-driven policies and investments, programs struggle in isolation, grinding away for funding, recognition, and priority in reform agendas. Policies set the rules and parameters for all the factors that affect community

---

6   National Fair Housing Alliance, "Race, Religion, and Reconciliation in a
    Comparative Dialogue" (Powerpoint presentation, July 2008, to Summer 2008 Lott
    Leadership Exchange).

7   Patrick Sharkey, "Neighborhoods and the Black-White Mobility Gap." (Washington, DC:
    Pew Charitable Trusts, July 2009), available at http://economicmobility.org/assets/pdfs/
    PEW_NEIGHBORHOODS.pdf.

conditions and shape the lives of residents, from the types and locations of new schools, jobs, and services to the availability of fresh, nutritious foods and other health resources to the quality of teachers, the educational standards, and the physical state of school buildings.

Years of antipoverty work have revealed two things: community interventions achieve their greatest success when they are connected to policy, and policy solutions are most effective when they draw from what is working in communities.

These lessons lie at the heart of an equity agenda, which seeks to transform high-poverty communities into high-opportunity communities—places that provide all the resources people need to thrive, including employment, job training, good schools, safe streets, parks, healthy food retailers, transportation, and affordable high-quality housing. A successful equity agenda builds upon the wisdom, voice, and experience of local residents. It focuses on empowering people while strengthening the places where they live.

Research shows that communities, cities, and regions that pay attention to equity grow stronger, and that the effects of an equity agenda may be most pronounced in areas that have struggled most. If the nation is to have a bright future, the equity agenda must become America's agenda, and it must drive anti-poverty efforts. We can no longer stop at a singular economic or community development strategy; however worthy, it will prove insufficient to address growing inequality and increasing poverty at the necessary scale. Rather, we need to think differently about how broad policy agendas and legislation can incorporate equity-focused solutions that work. And we need robust alliances across fields—civil rights, environmental justice, education, health, community organizing, education, and economic development—to fight for investments to create communities of opportunity everywhere, and for all.

It is a big task, but it need not be daunting. Four principles can guide work to advance equity in tangible ways:

Focus on those left behind. By using data and community engagement, advocates and community developers can understand the structures and symptoms of exclusion. This is a good starting point for developing strategies, prioritizing outcomes, and measuring progress based on how effectively an initiative reaches the people who have been left behind.

Rebuild public infrastructure. High-quality roads, transit lines, bridges, sidewalks, schools, parks, water and sewer systems, and communications networks are fundamental to economic vitality. Infrastructure connects workers to jobs and educational opportunities, revitalizes distressed communities, increases business efficiency and productivity, and fosters growth and competitiveness.

Grow new businesses and new jobs. Small businesses employ half of all private-sector workers and create two out of every three jobs in this country. They also incubate many of the new innovations that contribute to growth. Enterprise development efforts can link local entrepreneurs to the larger-scale markets, financing sources, and growth strategies that are critical for long-term success.

Prepare workers for the jobs of tomorrow. Human capital was the key to national prosperity in the Industrial Era, and it will be even more important for competing effectively in this century. Education and workforce development systems must be retooled to equip the workers of tomorrow—and today—with the skills to succeed in an ever-changing, globalized, knowledge-based economy.

ANGELA GLOVER BLACKWELL *founded PolicyLink in 1999 and continues to drive its mission of advancing economic and social equity. Under Blackwell's leadership, PolicyLink has become a leading voice in the movement to use public policy to improve access and opportunity for all low-income people and communities of color, particularly in the areas of health, housing, transportation, education, and infrastructure. Blackwell is the co-author of the recently published* Uncommon Common Ground: Race and America's Future *(W.W. Norton & Co., 2010), and contributed to* Ending Poverty in America: How to Restore the American Dream *(The New Press, 2007) and* The Covenant with Black America *(Third World Press, 2006). Blackwell earned a bachelor's degree from Howard University and a law degree from the University of California, Berkeley. She serves on numerous boards and served as co-chair of the task force on poverty for the Center for American Progress.*

PEOPLE TRANSFORMING COMMUNITIES. FOR GOOD.

Angela Blanchard
Neighborhood Centers, Inc.

N eighborhood Centers, Inc., has a long and rich history in community development, beginning with our origin as a part of the Settlement House movement of the late 1800s and early 1900s, meant to welcome newcomers to the United States and designed to make sure people knew how to live in the new world in which they found themselves. When Alice Graham Baker founded the agency in 1907, she declared the intent to help every resident of Houston have an opportunity for an education, for health, for work with dignity, and to become an informed participant in democracy. Today, everything old is new again as Houston has become the nation's new Ellis Island. The most diverse city in the country, Houston relies on organizations like Neighborhood Centers to build the first rung of the ladder so that people who come here can take advantage of the opportunities in Houston.

We are very clear at Neighborhood Centers about why we exist and the principles by which we intend to operate. Although many organizations like ours have come to identify closely with one or two services or distinct programmatic efforts, Neighborhood Centers is different. We define ourselves in terms of our purpose. That leaves us free to change what we do and how we do it, and we have done so for more than a hundred years. Quite simply, as Houston grows, we grow. As new issues emerge, we evolve.

At Neighborhood Centers, we believe that what makes Houston, and all great metro regions, dynamic and vibrant engines of recovery are our neighborhoods. Neighborhoods are the bridges between individuals and the regional economy, and when we take a targeted and thoughtful approach we can create real and lasting change. Strengthening underserved neighborhoods raises the quality of life for everyone in the region. If we are to transform our economy and our country, we must start out person to person, door to door, neighborhood to neighborhood building bridges to opportunities. Neighborhood Centers exists to keep our region a place of opportunity for everyone who is working for a better life.

WHAT IS UNIQUE ABOUT HOUSTON?

In Houston, we have a flat social structure. If you come here and work, you belong. Well over half the people who live in the region came from somewhere else. We don't share a past, we share a future. It keeps us looking forward. This is a fertile place for the growth of people willing to work for a life better than the one they were born to. Here, there is a new immigrant formula. In the early days, immigrants came to this country and hurried to set aside their old ways of life. They often sacrificed language and culture in the interest of belonging. The new immigrant formula is economic and political assimilation, and cultural independence. So Houston is fed by a rich source of cultural alternatives. It also is as close to a meritocracy as you can get. This is not just about immigrants. We like to say whether your journey takes you across the tracks, the river, or the ocean, we want you if you are ready to work for a better future.

WHAT ARE THE VALUES AND PRINCIPLES OF COMMUNITY DEVELOPMENT?

The first principle of community development is that the people are not the problem, people are the asset. The second principle is that the leadership needed in every neighborhood is already there. Community development is about unlocking that asset, releasing people's potential to move forward together.

Every person needs community. Families are not strong all alone; they are strong together, supporting and reinforcing one another, helping and connecting so that they can all move forward. Researchers have tried to put a dollar amount on the value of community. What is the value of a neighbor who will give you a ride when you need one, or sit with your child while you take another one to the clinic, or lend you a truck to help you move? How do you price someone who shows you how to use the public transportation system or guides you to the best school? People connected in communities have priceless assets in one another. They work together day by day to get ahead.

We believe that the people who have found their way to Houston, no matter how they came—whether from some small town in Texas or from overseas, displaced by a storm, forced by political oppression, or driven by economic desperation—already have the most important ingredient for success when they arrive. At Neighborhood Centers, our job then is not to fix them. It's not to define goals for them so that they might live according to our expectations. Instead, we must listen deeply, study rigorously, document faithfully what motivates them, and build on that. We build on strengths and skills. You can't build on broken. In the past, many communities were demoralized by formulas that forced them to show up on the bread lines of government assistance, proving first that they were sufficiently broken to require help. It did not work. It will not work. We have to capture instead the deep longing of people to better themselves, to nurture their children, to learn and to contribute—that is what fuels a sustainable approach to community development.

HOW DOES THE WORK BEGIN IN A NEW NEIGHBORHOOD?

We operate in many locations, and people in struggling neighborhoods often approach us asking for a community center. We believe in putting a roof over community. But when we are asked to build a center, we say "first you build the community, then you build the center." So we engage communities wherever we work—and yes, we knock on doors. Repeatedly. We go from door to door, house to house, business to business. And we ask questions. Not the old, worn-out "needs assessment" questions that demoralize even the interviewer—a brand-new set of questions, because we believe the change begins with the first new question. What works here? Who really cares about this community? What are the sights, sounds, and smells that make this neighborhood feel like home? Who do you go to when you want advice? Who knows the history of why this street, this building, this school matters so much? What is your most treasured hope for your child?

These are powerful questions, and it is challenging to ask them over and over. Many communities have already been so well trained to think of themselves as broken that they automatically answer with what is wrong even when you are asking what is right about the place they call home.

When you think as we do—that there are strengths and assets in every community—it can sound like people are on their own, that they shouldn't need any help. But that's not how it works. Everyone wants to live in a neighborhood where they can be connected, where there is a good school, where there is a financial institution they can trust, and a clinic, and a grocery market. Poor people are not different, and any approach to community and neighborhood development premised on an idea that they are somehow distinct as a group—a group lacking in some respect—is doomed to failure. Under that model, you may provide a service, but you will never achieve a transformation.

We don't ignore the problems. In fact, we are only interested in those neighborhoods with the biggest challenges. We fulfill our mission to bring resources, education, and connection by working side by side with people in neighborhoods. Simply put, we go where we are invited and we do what we are asked to do.

HOW DO YOU DECIDE WHERE AND HOW TO WORK?

When a small community group from Gulfton/Sharpstown came to us eight years ago asking for a community center—asking for a Ripley House—they did so because they knew what we had accomplished in several other Houston neighborhoods. They had seen Ripley House in the East End. They knew children went to school there. They knew residents took their children to a clinic at Ripley House instead of to the emergency room. They knew that if you were struggling and at the end of your rope, someone there would help you. They had witnessed the rebuilding of that center, after 70 years, into a new 75,000 square foot building on eight acres. They wanted a Ripley house, too. Many of them were already our neighbors—clients, if you will—in Head Start or one of the other many programs we offered in 60 locations. But they wanted a place of their own.

Gulfton/Sharpstown is Houston's most diverse, most densely populated neighborhood. Everyone outside of the community knew only the stories they had heard: the highest juvenile crime ZIP code in the nation; police didn't want to go there; non-English-speaking immigrants; overrun with the uninsured, the undocumented, and gangs; absentee landlords; unbooked and unbanked; and on and on. These were the only Gulfton/Sharpstown stories told in the larger region. Home to more than 55,000 people from more than 40 countries, Gulfton/Sharpstown was both the biggest challenge and most important opportunity.

Using our appreciative, asset-based approach, we changed the story of the neighborhood. We took the dreams, hopes, and aspirations of hardworking people and put them up on a big screen. We published their stories and held them up as examples of what is best about our country. We told all of Houston how much the Gulfton residents were like the people who built Houston—hardworking, ambitious, entrepreneurial, passionate about their children.

While we were reintroducing Gulfton as a place of opportunity, a community worthy of investment, we began dreaming more specifically about what should be in the center. Working with residents, we outlined a plan and a campaign. It was clear that local check-cashing booths and payday lenders were ripping off residents. It was obvious that tax preparers who took 50 percent of the returns for the "service" of filing a 1040 had to be replaced. It was clear that the hunger to learn English, especially "vocational English" you could use in your job, was a priority for families.

People spoke passionately about their children's education as the motivation for all that they did. They showed us their entrepreneurial efforts and told us about their desire to remember the old ways and celebrations of their cultures. And most important of all, they said, "We don't want just a place where we get help. We want a place where we can give to others, as well." So we began a plan for Baker Ripley, to create a village center for this precious community. One of my favorite memories is of a meeting with 300 people from more than a dozen countries conducted in eight languages, all planning their future together. Inspired by them, Neighborhood Centers staff and volunteers took the show on the road to funders, many of whom had heard only the old stories of Gulfton/Sharpstown. We went out with the new story to raise the money and put together the resources to invest in our neighbors.

We are convinced that real transformation comes from an integrated, focused approach to neighborhood transformation, not from an "either/or" set of choices like housing or school, health or financial, infrastructure or immigration. *All* elements of what makes a neighborhood a great place to live, grow, and raise children are necessary. Although we do not believe that one organization has to do all of it for every neighborhood, we do believe that organizations, funding, and communities can come together for powerful integrated approaches.

HOW DO WE SECURE INVESTMENT FOR A FOCUSED, INTEGRATED APPROACH?

Let's be very clear. There is nothing simple about securing investment for this work. It is not fast. No single funder will write the check for what will need to be done. When we answer the call of a community for transformation, we must have the courage to make a commitment well beyond what any funder will make to us. We will gain and lose grants, partners, and collaborators over the course of the work. All along the way we will be told that it is impossible, that the neighborhood is too broken, that the people are the problem. We will be urged to set our sights lower, even as we are chastised for failing to produce more results more quickly.

Each of the deep governmental silos—federal, state, and local, covering housing, health, education, economic matters, and more—has its own requirements. Every funder has a different theory of change. Every paradigm has different reporting demands. Different definitions of accountability abound. We must build very strong organizations and make internal investments in infrastructure so that we can meet those differing demands where we cannot change them. This cannot be ignored. It is absolutely critical to create effective organizations, with a firm platform of processes and tools to secure and manage resources and information. Passion is insufficient to the task, and all the knowledge about neighborhoods will not be a substitute for good fiscal management. It is essential to address the old nonprofit dilemma of choosing between more investment in programs or more investment in overhead: *both* are necessary. Nonprofits must anticipate and plan for growth, considering the "new and the next" in every budget year. As difficult as this is, disciplined efforts year after year to strengthen infrastructure will ensure the organization can deal with the complexity inherent in community development work, and enable it to tackle the challenge of integration.

Every day we witness the need for integrated efforts and investments that work together to tackle housing, education, economic opportunity, health, and infrastructure. If we want to see true transformation, we must find a way to bring all the disparate investments together. When we look back, we see many failed attempts to revitalize and transform neighborhoods on the back of just one element—the siloed school, heroic housing, a transformational clinic. These attempts fall short. If we imagine we are "setting the community development table," we must imagine it as a giant potluck where the dishes, plates, and morsels are contributed from many sources. It becomes the job of a community development organization to create an artful arrangement that feeds the hunger of the community.

We cannot afford to leave any dollar on the table, and the best and most sustainable efforts take advantage of public, private, and nonprofit elements. Although we cannot underestimate the difficulty of crafting integrated approaches in a siloed world, the return is worth any amount of effort.

WHAT DOES SUCCESS LOOK LIKE?

With Gulfton/Sharpstown, we were successful. Funders responded to the new story, and they responded in a big way. In the most difficult of fundraising environments, in the midst of an ugly national debate on immigration, despite the complexities of an integrated approach, people in our region came together to invest. When Baker Ripley was completed, our celebration crossed all boundaries—political, social, economic, and cultural—to bring together the true face of the Houston region. It was extraordinary, and we love to watch our many visitors from around the country discover Houston through the lens of Baker Ripley Neighborhood Center.

Today Baker Ripley—five buildings, 75,000 square feet, on four acres in the heart of Gulfton/Sharpstown—stands as a monument to the dreams and aspirations of 55,000 hardworking residents. These are people who reached beyond the safety and certainty of what they knew and sought a better future—people who in every way represented the values and strengths that built the rest of Houston. The philanthropic dollars that built this village center, and the public and private dollars that keep the doors open on a credit union, charter elementary school, immigration services, reunion hall and indoor/outdoor stage, tax center, art shop, and playground, are a modest investment with an unlimited return in realized potential and fulfilled promises.

In our first year and half of operation, 23,000 people passed through the doors. More powerful than the beautiful, accessible, colorful, joyful structures themselves is the incredible power of integrating education, financial opportunity, health services, and performing and visual arts into one site. Despite all the complexity, neighbors coming to the site see only the place they helped to build, one place with many doors, all of which are open to them. But we know about the dollars returned to the community, the improvement in graduation rates, the reduction in juvenile crime, and the number of new citizens. These are priceless accomplishments. While our visitors comment on the absence of fences and security, we are proud of the number of partners that work out of the center and are inspired by the sheer energy of the place. We recognize that the future leaders of Houston will come out of Baker Ripley and know they will remember the investment made in their families.

Side by side with the community, supported by Houston philanthropy, using public dollars and private investment, nurtured by a strong agency built to last, we changed the story of Gulfton from a problem place to a place of promise. For good.

ANGELA BLANCHARD *is the president and CEO of Neighborhood Centers, Inc. Through her more than 25 years of experience, Ms. Blanchard has reached an epiphany: a community should be defined by its strengths, resources, achievements, and hopes, not its degree of "brokenness." By focusing on strengths, Ms. Blanchard has found success with her work at Neighborhood Centers, Inc., and giving speeches around the world on the power of the human spirit, community development, and overcoming personal and communal tragedy. Ms. Blanchard has been honored by a number of organizations for her advocacy on behalf of working immigrants as well as her excellence in nonprofit leadership and community service initiatives, including being named as the ARAMARK Building Community 2011 National Innovation Award Leadership Honoree.*

FUTURE OF COMMUNITY DEVELOPMENT:
How CDFIs Can Best Ride the Impact Investing Wave

Antony Bugg-Levine
Nonprofit Finance Fund

T hink of the community development finance industry as a small boat with an outboard motor. For four decades, pioneering leaders have helped to build this boat, take it out of port, and chart new waters. This boat has served as a lifeline, bringing essential resources to previously cut-off communities. But you don't have to be a soothsayer to see that this boating life is unlikely to continue. Even if the economy and the capital markets stabilize, three fundamental forces will prevent us continuing with business as usual:

- Our boat may still be solid, but we are running out of fuel: With the 30-year wave of retail bank consolidation largely behind us, there are fewer institutions remaining for which Community Reinvestment Act (CRA) credit represent a major driver of institutional community development investments.[1] Looking ahead, as regulators remain focused on the safety and soundness of the banking system, CRA will likely diminish in importance there as well.

- **Our investees are running out of fuel too:** Many of our borrowers have relied on direct or indirect government reimbursements and subsidies to repay our investments. These government reimbursements are eroding and unlikely to recover soon. Therefore, even if we can mobilize capital to lend, it's not clear that our traditional borrowers will be in a solid position to pay us back.

- **We have not been building everything the communities need:** Crucially, safe housing and adequate facilities are increasingly recognized as insufficient to create the just and vibrant communities we aspire to support. These communities also need health care, educational opportunities, viable social service agencies, and decent job opportunities. Many community development finance institutions have worked on these issues, but our individual successes have not combined effectively to support neighborhoods with sufficient durability to withstand the current "perfect storm" of high unemployment, frozen credit, and declining real estate values.

None of these realities threaten to sink our sector in the short term. But they will become increasingly undeniable and problematic in the next decade. We should work together to find more fuel that works in our current engines. We should also look to the horizon for other boats out there, and entirely new ways to navigate these waters.

---

1 The Community Reinvestment Act of 1977 is intended to encourage depository institutions to help meet the credit needs of the communities in which they operate, including low- and moderate-income neighborhoods, consistent with safe and sound operations. It was enacted by the Congress in 1977 (12 USC 2901) and is implemented by Regulation BB (12 CFR 228). The regulation was substantially revised in May 1995 and updated again in August 2005. More information is available at http://federalreserve.gov/communitydev/cra_about.htm.

The emerging impact investing industry looms on the horizon and has been coming into clearer view in the past few years. Is it a lifeline, bringing the promise of new supplies to allow us to continue our current operations? Is it an oceangoing vessel that we can climb aboard to sail more deeply into the multitrillion dollar mainstream capital markets? Or is it a Spanish galleon on the sixteenth-century South American shore, poised to disrupt the world we have so carefully cultivated?

Leaving these metaphorical waters behind, this essay considers sources of impact investing capital and what it will take to tap them. But even if impact investing flourishes, it may not prove a lifeline to all existing community finance intermediaries. The organizations that flourish in an impact investing world must provide value in new ways to new partners, and they must create new disciplines and practices. Ultimately, impact investing's greatest contribution may not be what it does or does not bring to community finance, but rather that it could prompt us to reexamine why we do what we do and to reaffirm "community development" as the organizing force of community development finance.

THE PROMISE OF IMPACT INVESTING

Impact investments seek to generate a "blended value" of both financial and social return. This concept is not new. In Europe, seventeenth-century Quaker communities aligned investments with spiritual practice, capitalizing worker-owned communities and community housing schemes. In the United States, private companies were the original "community development" investors, building housing and facilities for workers, and taking stewardship in the cultural development of their towns. And certainly any American reading a book like this one on community development finance has likely made or supported impact investments through a community development finance institution (CDFI) or socially responsible investment account.

But the rather simple idea that for-profit investment is both a morally legitimate and economically effective way to address social and environmental challenges is making its way out of the niche in which it has grown up. Its emergence is fomenting demand for private capital and talent to be put to work. Increasingly, influential capital owners and capital markets participants are developing creative mechanisms to tap this demand.

The stakes are enormous. Even with the successes of the CDFI sector, we still leave $999 in the U.S. capital markets untapped for every $1 we have mobilized directly for socially motivated finance. Impact investing offers potential to unlock a portion of the other 99.9 percent. Obviously, most of that money is locked away in vaults unlikely to be opened for impact investments. It will remain beyond our reach. But even a small share of that treasure could transform the capital available to community development finance.

CDFIs are poised to be an important partner for impact investors, bringing their decades of knowledge in financing the organizations that tackle social issues. We bring to the table structuring expertise, as well as a pipeline of high-quality, high-social-impact investments. And the "complete capital" approach we will explain later in this article outlines a structure by which we can bring together these players and their capital, which to-date have approached social problem-solving separately.

WHERE WILL WE FIND THE MONEY?

Today the U.S. capital market is valued in the tens of trillions of dollars. This is an eye-catching number, but it is still more of an abstraction than a concrete market. Instead of one "market," this capital sits in discrete pools with varying relevance for community finance investors. Most of this capital is not poised to flow into impact investments. But four areas are particularly interesting to explore.

Private Foundations

Given that they are formally constituted (and tax privileged) to contribute to social good, private foundations are an obvious place to start. Pioneers such as the John D. and Catherine T. MacArthur and Ford Foundations helped fund some of the early models of community development finance. But historically the private foundation sector as a whole has focused only a tiny portion of its grant-making budgets on program-related investments (PRIs).[2]

The impact investing movement is spurring rapid growth of PRIs from this tiny base. More important, perhaps, it is galvanizing attention on the approximately $590 billion in total endowment assets these foundations currently hold.[3] The twin forces of wealth concentration and the aging baby boom generation are set to precipitate a second great era of private foundation capitalization in the coming decade. If we are able to unlock even 5 percent for impact investment, this could provide nearly $30 billion, an amount equal to the balance sheets of all CDFIs today.

Private Banks and Family Offices

Private banks and family offices represent a potential sweet spot for impact investing. Their clients typically hold tens of millions of dollars in their accounts and can influence directly where their money goes. Various private banks are beginning to build impact investing products. These are funds-of-funds channeling money into emerging market impact fund managers and even platforms for direct investment into CDFIs such as the Calvert Foundation. Family offices are also making direct investments in deals as well as through intermediaries.

Donor-Advised Funds

Donor-advised funds—another opportunity for impact investing—are investment vehicles that give their owners immediate tax write-offs for future charitable donations. While

---

2 PRIs are investments that further the mission of the foundation and also earn a return. According to the IRS, "To be program-related, the investments must significantly further the foundation's exempt activities. They must be investments that would not have been made except for their relationship to the exempt purposes." A PRI may count as part of the 5 percent of assets that a foundation must deploy every year. More information is available at http://irs.gov/charities/foundations/article/0,,id=137793,00.html.

3 Foundation Center. Aggregate Fiscal Data by Foundation Type, 2009, FCStats, available at www.foundationcenter.org/findfunders/statistics/pdf/01_found_fin_data/2009/02_09.pdf.

they await donation placement, funds reside in profit-seeking investments. Major investment firms have mobilized billions of dollars into this increasingly popular product. With the capital pre-allocated to charity, these tools could be particularly well poised for impact investing. In one pioneering example, the Schwab Charitable Fund used donor-advised fund assets as a guarantee to secure a cheaper loan for the Grameen Foundation. This approach could be replicated widely for community development finance. Community foundations are also waking up to the opportunity to enhance impact and marketing by putting their clients' donor-advised assets to work in the local community.

The Person on the Street

So where does that leave the "regular investor"? Impact investing has until now largely been inaccessible to them. But that is starting to change. The economic crisis and backlash against large banks have led many to explore community banks and credit unions. Internet-enabled peer-to-peer lending platforms are also emerging and challenging regulatory practice. With Kiva.org, a website that enables the public to make very small loans globally for socially valuable purposes, now making investments in the United States, and Calvert Foundation working through MicroPlace, which offers a similar way to make small, online investments to help alleviate poverty, retail investors can make U.S. impact investments over the internet for as little as $20.

POTENTIAL BARRIERS TO TAPPING NEW CAPITAL

Together, these are not the largest pools of the capital markets (those are assets managed by pension funds and insurance companies). However, they add up to a capital pool far deeper than we have mobilized to date for community finance. As businesses begin to develop products and services for impact investors, and more deals demonstrate the viability of this approach, impact investing could take off.

Yet impact investors operate in an inhospitable set of systems. Chief among them is a regulatory and policy system built on the twin assumptions that only charity and government can address social issues and that the only purpose of investment is to make money. Relatively small changes to existing policy mandates and structures could make a significant positive difference. The Treasury Department's ongoing review of decades-old guidance for PRIs could stimulate more private foundation impact investments. The Small Business Administration's creation of a $500 million impact investing mandate for Small Business Investment Corporations is yet another promising development.

Government can also build on impact investing momentum with bolder action. As the premise of impact investing is to unlock private capital for social purpose, it would be self-defeating to demand substantial public money to make this work. Government, however, can seed the industry with risk-taking capital and by offering coordination to a highly fragmented market. The United Kingdom's launch last year of a $1 billion impact investment wholesale bank, Big Society Capital, with investment from major banks, is one model. Government can also play a coordinating and legitimizing role, as the White House has done in bringing together states, cities, and potential investors in Social Impact Bonds.

WHAT DOES MOMENTUM AROUND IMPACT INVESTING MEAN FOR THE CDFI INDUSTRY?

CDFIs were making impact investments long before the current buzz about them surfaced. As such, they should be well poised to reap the benefits of these increased private capital flows. Yet there is a real danger that CDFIs will be left on the sideline as impact investing takes off. To understand why, and what we can do about it, we first must recognize that the new wave of impact investing creates fundamentally different strategic dynamics for intermediaries. To navigate successfully, CDFIs must orient themselves to new clients with new demands, using new practices.

The fundamental differences between the new approach and the old are the source of capital and its motivation. CDFIs have largely been capitalized by government and by retail banks seeking to fulfill CRA mandates. Impact investors are increasingly mobilized through private capital pools seeking to meet private social motivations. The CRA bankers sought intermediaries that could provide the most efficient conversion of capital into reliable CRA credit. The private impact investors are seeking intermediaries that can most effectively convert capital into compelling social solutions. These motivations may seem similar but have important, distinct implications. Successful intermediaries in this new world will offer their lenders and investors:

- Sector diversification: Although the efficiency imperative of CRA bankers has led most CRA capital to flow to capital-intensive real estate deals (the easiest way to put the most capital to work), the social imperative of impact investors will require greater diversification. Impact investors want to affect health care, education, social services, and the arts, not just housing.

- National capacity to invest locally: To serve private investors with strong local ties, intermediaries will need to put capital to work in local communities. The aggregators of impact investing assets in private banks and national donor-advised funds, however, will seek the efficiency gains from working with national-scale partners. They will look to work with intermediaries who can offer local investment expertise and capabilities across a national or at least regional footprint. Few existing intermediaries have the products, practices, and presence to pull this off.

- Off-balance-sheet capabilities (and beyond): The new client will focus on connecting capital to specific projects. Growing the balance sheet of an intermediary to make general investments will not be as compelling. Therefore, successful intermediaries will be nimble in setting up off-balance-sheet vehicles to pool capital for specific projects with tailored underwriting standards. Going one step further, some impact investors will keep their assets on book and seek advisors and deal brokers who can advise on direct transactions. Depending on how we respond, this is either a disintermediation threat or a new business opportunity.

- Enhanced capabilities to measure and report our impact: The new impact investor will want to know how CDFIs manage our social impact beyond our ability to comply with government mandates. Especially as we move toward the retail investor, communicating our social impact in ways that resonate with laypeople rather than insiders will be crucial. We will need to come to terms with "marketing" and find an appropriate balance between simplicity and substance in our impact measurement.

Some CDFIs are already quite innovative and are working with these new capital sources to provide these capabilities. But few of us have strategically reoriented our work to thrive in this new world. Other innovators are not waiting for CDFIs to move. New firms are springing up to offer off-balance-sheet structuring and advice. Mainstream financial services institutions like JPMorgan Chase and MorganStanley have set up impact investing units, and new investment firms are offering donor-advised funds and other more widely available products. Many of the new entrants, however, lack the experience and skills required to make the best impact investments. The CDFI sector's decades of experience and community links enable us to provide powerful solutions for communities; we need to become the partner of choice for the new impact investors. Beyond these institutional-level responses, as a sector CDFIs must engage more fully in expanding the political and social acceptance of impact investing. Rather than narrowly lobbying government for subsidies and regulatory mandates, we need to advocate widely for the legitimacy and effectiveness of for-profit approaches. Recent history shows how failure to proactively address the skepticism most people have about investors can torpedo otherwise thriving industries. The Indian microfinance industry's inattention to proving its social value set it up for a disastrous backlash in 2010.

REINFORCING THE "COMMUNITY DEVELOPMENT" IN COMMUNITY DEVELOPMENT FINANCE

Some existing community finance institutions will likely build new services and approaches that enable them to tap into private impact investing capital as a new source of sustenance. Private impact investing could, however, be more than just a source of new capital to continue to do old things. Instead, it could spur the field to put investment in its appropriate place. Impact investing is a tool, not an end in itself. So is community finance. If you approach the world asking, "Where can I invest?" you will end up doing far less interesting work than if you ask, "What social challenges need addressing, and how can investing be one of the tools I use to address them?"

This may sound like mere semantics, but in our work at Nonprofit Finance Fund, this reframing has opened up great opportunities. In New York City in 2010, we set up a fund to provide working capital loans to frontline agencies such as soup kitchens and homeless shelters. They were too financially shaky to take on debt, however. If we were only looking for places to invest, we would have moved on to find other less risky borrowers, but because preserving New York's safety net was crucial, we structured a new initiative, the Community Resilience Fund. The fund aims to support up to 100 agencies seeking to transition to a more sustainable business model. This fund would not be possible without impact investors offering millions of dollars of loans. It also requires credit enhancement from city government and substantial grant support from private donors. No one piece would work alone. The most interesting impact investing in the next few years will involve similar collaboration, as impact investors work with governments and donors to tackle challenges that cannot be addressed with any one tool.

As poor communities continue to suffer the aftershocks of the economic crisis, more essential organizations will become riskier and riskier borrowers. If we want to make a difference in these organizations, we will have to work alongside philanthropic and government support, with each part made more powerful and useful because of its complementarity. We call this approach "complete capital." Complete capital weaves together financial capital (grants and impact investments), intellectual capital (the ideas about what we need to do and how to do it), human capital (the ability to support organizations to implement bold strategies), and social capital (which allows collaboration among people and institutions that don't typically work together).

Complete capital approaches require those of us who seek to address fundamental social challenges in the field to reorient our work around development as the end goal, with investment as only one tool. Complete capital practitioners will need to become accustomed to working with different organizations. This sounds banal, but it will be difficult to pull off, especially as economic pressures spur an instinct to retreat into defending narrowly claimed territory for "our organization" or "our sector." CDFIs will need to develop enhanced cultures of innovation that build on but are not constrained by our historic experiences as primarily relatively conservative lenders. We will need new approaches to mitigating risk by mobilizing impact investing capital into mezzanine finance structures. We must better understand how grants can be used not just to mitigate the risk to investors *when* investments fail but also to reduce the likelihood that investments *will* fail with timely and efficient technical assistance to investees.

Many of the easy problems that can be solved with singular, siloed approaches are already being tackled. The increasingly complex and accelerating challenges that remain will require complete capital approaches to solve them. Impact investing capital from private sources will be an important part of these solutions. But they will not work alone. It will take collaborative, creative energy and problem-solving to deepen the community development impact of community development finance.

ANTONY BUGG-LEVINE *is the CEO of Nonprofit Finance Fund, a national nonprofit and financial intermediary dedicated to mobilizing and deploying resources effectively to build a just and vibrant society. In this role, he oversees more than*

$265 million in loans, New Markets Tax Credits and grant funds and a national consulting practice, and works with a range of philanthropic, private sector, and government partners to develop and implement innovative approaches to financing social change. Bugg-Levine writes and speaks regularly on the evolution of the social sector and the emergence of the global impact investing industry. He is the coauthor of Impact Investing: Transforming How We Make Money While Making a Difference *(Wiley, 2011).*

COMMUNITY DEVELOPMENT IN RURAL AMERICA:
Collaborative, Regional, and Comprehensive

Cynthia M. Duncan
AGree

More than 59 million people live in rural America, and nearly 9 million, or 18 percent, are living in poverty. This compares with 12 percent poor in the suburbs and 20 percent in central cities. One-fourth of all rural children are growing up poor, and in some chronically poor areas, child poverty is nearly 50 percent. While this is an improvement from the 1960s, many parts of rural America still have lagging or seasonal economies where families piece together a livelihood, making wreaths in one season, picking blueberries in another, or fishing in another.

Rural poverty has been high for decades, but not all rural areas face the same challenges or opportunities. Some, like Appalachia, the Mississippi Delta, and Native American reservations, remain chronically poor. In contrast, the rural Midwest, vibrant for many years, is suffering from loss of jobs and depopulation brought on by technological and other changes in the economy. Many of these same changes, however, such as the focus on the environment and the spread of broadband, have created opportunities in other parts of rural America, especially in locales rich in natural resources, such as parts of the Northeast, Pacific Northwest, and Michigan's Upper Peninsula. And many conservation groups are now cooperating with rural community development finance groups to invest in working landscapes, forests, and sustainable fisheries.

In the 1960s, in some chronically distressed areas like Appalachia and the Delta, 50–75 percent of the population lived in poverty. Conditions in these areas were appalling, with substandard housing, one-room school houses with underprepared teachers, and limited access to health care for the poor. Families struggled to put food on the table.[1] Rural poverty still goes hand in hand with low educational attainment. In chronic poverty areas, one-fourth or more of working aged adults have not completed high school. Fully one-half of rural Americans live in these high-poverty areas.

In recent years traditional rural economic sectors, from mining to manufacturing to forestry and agriculture, have become increasingly capital-intensive. This means fewer jobs overall, fewer low-skilled jobs that provide employment to those who dropped out of school, and greater demand for skilled and specialized workers. The result is a skills mismatch in many rural communities, and the traditional education and training institutions often have not adapted to employers' new needs.

In preparing this short piece, I talked with a number of rural development practitioners to get their perspective on the challenges and opportunities their organizations encounter. What

---

1 Cynthia M. Duncan, Worlds Apart: Why Poverty Persists in Rural America (New Haven, CT: Yale University Press, 1999).

follows is my distillation of their experience and reflections.[2] Like their urban counterparts, community development groups in rural America are lending to and investing in businesses, housing, and community institutions, providing technical assistance and working to build capacity in distressed or struggling communities. However, the challenges they face, and the strategies they employ, differ from those in urban areas. Rural community development practitioners are working in communities that are geographically isolated, with long distances between relatively sparsely populated communities. Human capital is much more limited, and often the same key leaders play multiple roles. Financial capital and supporting institutions are also much more scarce. For these reasons, rural developers are less likely to be operating in a specialized niche and concentrating solely on financial transactions. They are more likely to approach development comprehensively, and they increasingly are working on a regional scale.

CHALLENGES

The physical characteristics of a rural landscape create challenges for rural community developers. Communities are isolated and lack the population density and infrastructure that can support economic development. Distances between communities are great, and everyone relies on cars for transportation. These physical and geographical characteristics have institutional consequences as well. Fewer basic institutions make up the ecology of development investment, and rural development practitioners often must play multiple roles to make up for the lack of supporting organizations.

These physical factors have "people" implications. Far and away the biggest challenge rural development practitioners face

---

2   Ron Phillips, working in northern New England with Coastal Enterprises, Inc.; Keith Bisson, also with Coastal Enterprises, Inc.; Dennis West, with Northern Initiative in Michigan's Upper Peninsula; John Berdes, working in the Pacific Northwest with Craft3, formerly Enterprise Cascadia; Nancy Straw with West Central Initiative in Minnesota; Bill Bynum, working in the rural South and Mississippi Delta at the Enterprise Corporation; Justin Maxson, with the Mountain Association for Community Economic Development in Appalachia; Dee Davis, president of the Center for Rural Strategies; and Sandra Rosenblith, founder of Rural LISC.

is the need for greater human capital—for more leaders, more entrepreneurs, more skilled workers, and even more economic development professionals to work in their own organizations. Because leaders in rural communities play multiple roles, the loss of one "spark plug" can devastate a small community. The crunch for people also means that organizational capacity is often thin. There are fewer banks and fewer specialized lenders in those banks. Equally important, there are few, if any, corporate partners. Moreover, community development practitioners often must help local leaders move from the old, more stable economy they once relied on to new, more dynamic and less predictable economies of the future.

Indeed, many development practitioners find that long-term residents' nostalgia for the "good times" in rural America can be another barrier to moving forward. People long for the economy and the vibrancy that "used to be," when the retail sector was strong and stores stayed open on Thursday nights, when every community had a local school, and sons followed their fathers into the mine or woods, onto the farm, or onto the fishing boats. The fiscal systems, local institutions, and public infrastructure were forged for those old economies, with different needs and different distribution of responsibility. Habits change slowly, and governance systems are rigid. These challenges are exacerbated by the current fiscal crisis, as towns and cities and states cut back on public investment.

The challenges and opportunities vary by the nature of the local economy, demographic trends, and the natural amenities and resources in a rural community. Areas rich in natural amenities such as lakes and forests, mountains, and seashores are in many ways like urban areas with strong markets. They have been attracting second-home buyers and retirees, and sometimes young professionals with ties to the area, and communities are changing with these newcomers. These places, such as in the Northwest, Northeast, Upper Peninsula of Michigan, and Rocky Mountain West, have long relied on extracting or processing natural resources. Today their populations are growing, and energetic young people and retirees are building on the potential for "heritage economies," transforming old natural resource economies into new, more sustainable enterprises.

On the other hand, large areas of the agricultural heartland of the Midwest and Great Plains have seen protracted population decline, leaving a broad swath through the heart of the country witnessing population loss and an aging population. Yet, the community spirit and trust in these traditionally agricultural communities reflect the ideal of small-town America, where people know and look after one another, even as they struggle with a demographic crisis of deaths outnumbering births and young people leaving in droves.[3]

Finally, half the rural population lives in areas plagued by chronic poverty, places where adequate resources have never been invested in education or community infrastructure. Whole communities stand broken. Chronically poor rural areas, mostly in the South and on reservations, have much in common with inner-city neighborhoods: poor people are concentrated and community institutions are weak and lack resources, trust is low, patronage and bad politics are prevalent, drug problems are widespread, education lags and high school graduation rates are dismal, and unemployment and disability are high. Families struggle in these communities, and many of those who could leave did so long ago, leaving remaining residents with even fewer social, economic, and human resources with which to build stronger, resilient communities.

OPPORTUNITIES AND STRATEGIES

The rural landscape and a reliance on natural resources present challenges, but according to the development practitioners with whom I spoke, they also offer significant opportunity for future development, and for more deliberate integration of rural

---

3   Cynthia M. Duncan, "Demographic Trends and Challenges in Rural America," Carsey Institute, Meridian IFAP Roundtable (December 8, 2010), available at http://carseyinstitute. unh.edu/docs/Duncan-Meridian-Roundtable-12-2010.pdf.

and urban economies. They see five primary opportunities for rural economies.

- First, there are opportunities to create and deliver energy, through wind farms, biomass plants, and other alternative fuels.

- Second, there are opportunities to provide "ecosystem services" such as carbon sequestration and watershed protection, in part through collaboration with environmental groups that increasingly see the value of working landscapes as a way to conserve and enhance the natural environment and habitat in rural America.

- Third, there are growing efforts to link ecotourism with cultural heritage in a higher wage tourism strategy.

- Fourth, the growing interest in local fresh food offers opportunities for a return to regional food systems that can bolster local regional economies, particularly when larger stores are buying local products.

- Finally, e-commerce and telework offer multiple business and development opportunities, from enabling laptop professionals to work from a rural home to provide services, creating new e-commerce businesses that can link to global markets, and even data centers.

However, to make any of these strategies work, logistics have to work. Access to fast and reliable broadband and to shipping are key, for example.

Rural developers are increasingly approaching development as a regional undertaking, promoting a whole region, linking urban and rural places in the region, and providing regional goods in regional markets. They are also looking for opportunities to collaborate with anchor institutions and advocates, environmental organizations, policy developers, and public sector state and regional development actors.

In every case, the biggest challenge to rural community development success is human capital: finding the people with the talents, skills, and energy needed to bring about comprehensive development in rural communities. Rural community developers provide regional leadership and collaborate with a wide range of players to achieve this comprehensive development. What they need from policymakers in their state capitals and Washington, DC, are committed resources and basic investment in education and infrastructure, including broadband. Because they take a comprehensive approach to development, they also need support from foundations to fund their innovations in leadership and capacity development, and their work on policy. Foundation investment is at an all-time low in rural communities, and rural developers struggle to maintain their comprehensive programs.

Development economist Albert Hirschman liked to point out that people in underdeveloped economies have three choices: exit, loyalty, or voice.[4] By exit he meant people who leave for opportunities elsewhere, in the case of rural migrants, often to cities. By loyalty he meant those who accept conditions as they are, upholding the status quo in a faltering or exploitative economy. By voice he meant that those who stay and speak up and act for change. Rural community developers are part of those raising their voices and working for change. Doing so helps make change possible for others who also have chosen to make their communities more resilient.

Rural community development organizations provide critical leadership in communities that are hard pressed. They bring resources, financial and technical assistance, and they bring innovation that is rooted in local history and culture. They are "classic" economic developers, looking for collaboration, building institutional capacity, and taking a comprehensive approach that recognizes politics and long-standing relationships but that also pushes community leaders and entrepreneurs toward positive social change.

---

4   Albert Hirschman Exit, Loyalty or Voice: Responses to Decline in Firms, Organizations and States (Cambridge: Harvard University Press, 1972).

CYNTHIA "MIL" DUNCAN *is research director of AGree. From 2004-2011 she was professor of sociology and founding director of the University of New Hampshire's Carsey Institute, an interdisciplinary research center focused on vulnerable families and sustainable development in rural America. From 2000-2004 she served as the Ford Foundation's director of community and resource development; from 1989-2000 she was a professor of sociology at the University of New Hampshire. Duncan wrote* Worlds Apart: Why Poverty Persists in Rural America *(Yale University Press 1999), which won the American Sociological Association's Robert E. Park Award, numerous articles on poverty and development, and edited* Rural Poverty in America. *She serves on several regional and national boards related to poverty and development. Mil Duncan received her BA in English from Stanford University, and her MA and PhD from the University of Kentucky.*

IT TAKES A NEIGHBORHOOD:
Purpose Built Communities and Neighborhood Transformation

Shirley Franklin
Purpose Built Communities

David Edwards
IBM Corporation

> *About 70 percent of prisoners in New York State come from eight neighborhoods in New York City. These neighborhoods suffer profound poverty, exclusion, marginalization and despair. All these things nourish crime.*[1]

I n December 1993, Atlanta developer and philanthropist Tom Cousins came across the above passage in the *New York Times*. Like most of us, Cousins understood that all cities have "good" neighborhoods and "bad" neighborhoods. He was nevertheless surprised to be confronted with statistics that illustrate how inadequate the bad and good labels are for characterizing the differences among regions in a single city. It's not that some neighborhoods are simply bad; they are, in many ways, catastrophic.

---

1 Todd Clear, "Tougher Is Dumber," New York Times, December 4, 1993.

These neighborhoods serve as the centers of dysfunction in a city. Although crime is generally a leading metric, most other dreary social indicators are attached to these areas as well, including rampant school truancy, elevated high school dropout rates, low employment, little if any private investment, a transient residential population, and, of course, entrenched poverty.

The truly negative outcomes of poverty flow directly from its concentration in a small number of isolated city neighborhoods. To successfully address the issue of poverty in American cities, governments must organize around this geographic dimension of the problem. Poverty, and its many negative outcomes, can only be solved on a neighborhood basis. Transforming these neighborhoods should be our highest priority.

The challenge is that the public mechanisms and resources available to transform neighborhoods are not organized around this goal. Large local, state, and federal bureaucracies and funding streams are focused on "silos" such as housing, education, public safety, and nutrition. None are focused on neighborhood health. As a result, government agencies attack poverty by applying solutions within these functional silos rather than using solutions tailored to neighborhood-specific needs. If the problem of concentrated poverty is to be effectively addressed, government— local, state and federal—needs to develop approaches that are *geographic, holistic, and specific* to the unique set of assets and deficits that exist within neighborhoods.

Purpose Built Communities offers one such model. The Purpose Built model can serve as one component among a family of solutions for transforming distressed neighborhoods and eradicating concentrated poverty in our urban centers.

"SHAKING UP" YOUR CITY

Poverty is an elusive concept, almost too abstract to be of much use to those running municipal governments. Although poverty intuitively sounds like something city managers should care about, a cursory review of performance management systems around the country found no reference to "poverty rate" as a metric that mayors or city managers use to measure their performance. Although some cities do deploy measures related to poverty—NYCStat, for example, tracks "persons receiving food stamps"—they are typically used to characterize the state of the city or neighborhood. They are generally not measures that city services are expected to directly affect.

In that sense, the poverty rate as a measurement of urban health lacks practical value even after setting aside the challenges associated with measuring it in a meaningful way. What does the poverty rate tell us? Although it certainly conveys how many individuals or families are living at a certain income level, it does not describe the conditions under which they are living. Are they safe? Can they easily travel to their jobs? Are their children being educated? In other words, does their neighborhood and accessible public services put them in a position to improve their lives?

If the answer is no, then the problem is not so much impoverished families as it is impoverished neighborhoods. It is not the absolute level of poverty that matters, but how it is distributed. Impoverished neighborhoods lead to truancy, unsafe streets, low employment rates and opportunities, underperforming schools, gang and youth violence, and deteriorating public and private infrastructure. These are problems that arise not from poor individuals and families, but from their geographic concentration.

This geographic concentration of poverty generates the social pathologies that concern all of us. Consider your own city. If it is like the typical American city in the 2010s, it is socially and economically segregated. Family incomes between the wealthiest region and the poorest likely differ by a factor of 10, perhaps even higher. In the worst performing elementary schools more than 70 percent of students will be receiving federally subsidized school lunches, which serve children from low-income families. High school dropout rates in those neighborhoods will exceed 40 percent. More than 60 percent of 911 emergency calls will originate within 10 percent of the local geography, all of which will be in ZIP codes with the highest poverty rates. Foreclosures, vacant housing, and code enforcement complaints will also be disproportionately concentrated in these neighborhoods.

Consider Atlanta. Five of the 1,700 U.S. high schools labeled "dropout factories" are located in Atlanta. These schools are 99 percent minority and 76 percent of students receive free or reduced school lunch. More than one-half of freshmen in these schools will drop out before graduation. All five of these schools serve neighborhoods with average annual household incomes below $25,000. In fact, there are 20 census tracts in Atlanta with household incomes below that level, whereas there are eight with incomes of more than $100,000. The city's poorest neighborhood—with an average household income of $14,051—has less than 8 percent of the income of the city's wealthiest neighborhood ($168,411).

Now let's suppose that we all go to sleep tonight in our divided cities and some maniacal ogre appears. The ogre picks up the city and shakes it like a snow globe. When the ogre stops shaking, all of the building and roads, parks and parking lots, hospitals and schools gently settle to the ground, but this time they are randomly dispersed. Everyone wakes up safe in their bed, but living in a radically reorganized city.

What changed? In short, everything. Rich, poor, and middle-class people now find themselves living side-by-side, sending their kids to the same schools, relying on the same roads and transit systems. Poor families are evenly distributed, living on safe streets, playing in clean parks, and learning shoulder-to-shoulder with kids from privileged backgrounds in high-functioning schools.

In effect, our maniacal ogre reversed a century of bad public policy. The impact of zoning laws that pushed affordable housing options out of high-income neighborhoods is no longer evident. The legacy of urban renewal and redlining that tore apart mixed-income urban neighborhoods is eradicated. The unforeseen consequences of busing policies that drove the middle class to the suburbs are extinguished. And the highways, designed (apparently) for the express purpose of hollowing out the urban core of our cities, no longer serve that purpose. In short, our ogre has erased all evidence of the policies that impoverished our urban neighborhoods in the first place.

"I REALLY DIDN'T KNOW WHETHER THIS WAS GOING TO WORK"[2]

Unfortunately, relying on crazed ogres to fix our cities is not a viable policy option. Tom Cousins understood this. After years of directing his family's philanthropic dollars toward traditional national, regional, and urban issues and seeing no change in generational poverty and educational outcomes for low-income students, he decided to focus on a problem that he thought he could directly affect. He decided to take on the challenge of transforming and revitalizing a single neighborhood, the southeast Atlanta neighborhood of East Lake.

East Lake was a disaster. Known locally as "Little Vietnam," it was neighborhood dysfunction writ large. Crime in the neighborhood was 18 times higher than the national average. Nearly 60 percent of adults were receiving public assistance, and only 13 percent were employed. A mere 5 percent of fifth graders were hitting state academic performance targets. "Can we believe this is America? If I was born here," Cousins later speculated, "I would probably be one of those kids in jail."[3]

With the East Lake Meadows public housing project at its center, this once prosperous region of the city was essentially ungovernable. The housing complex proved to be conveniently located for the gangs peddling drugs and arms in eastern Atlanta. Politicians stayed away. No one could look at the condition of this neighborhood and have any reasonable hope that it could be turned around.

---

2   "Miracle at East Lake," CNBC Business Nation, March 2007.

3   Ibid.

Cousins thought otherwise. He decided to embark on a neighborhood transformation project that was, as it turned out, largely of his own invention. It centered on the idea that to thrive, an area of concentrated poverty had to change to a neighborhood where families across a range of incomes, from the very poor to the upper middle class, were willing to live.

The first thing Cousins realized was that he could not tackle this problem one issue at a time. Replacing housing would not attract families if the schools were in poor shape. Schools could not be expected to perform well in neighborhoods where children feared for their safety and showed up hungry and unprepared. And it is hard to reduce crime in neighborhoods full of unemployed high school dropouts.

All of these issues needed to be addressed simultaneously. The neighborhood basically needed to be reconstituted with functioning families, safe streets, and high-performing schools. But how?

Cousins's plan was to partner with the Atlanta Housing Authority to replace the East Lake Meadows housing project. Simultaneously, he would secure the rights to build an independently operated public charter school. He would also attract nonprofit organizations to invest in community facilities and programs. This approach—pieced together though it was over several years—now constitutes the "Purpose Built model" (see Figure 1). At the core of the model is a new neighborhood with several key features:

- Quality mixed-income housing that ensures low-income residents can afford to remain in the neighborhood but that also draws new residents from across the income spectrum (effectively deconcentrating poverty);

- An effective, independently run cradle-to-college educational approach that ensures low-income children start school ahead of grade level, but that also attracts middle-income families and eradicates educational performance gaps;

FIGURE 1
Adapted from Bridgespan Group

THE PURPOSE BUILT MODEL

If a neighborhood...

creates high quality mixed-income housing

develops cradle-to-college education with local control

delivers workforce development and other social services

offers infrastructure and services that enhance quality of life

is directed by a community-based organization

Then the neighborhood becomes...

a community that is safe and economically sustainable with rising incomes and property values that can attract middle income families to its high performing schools

- Community facilities and services that not only support low-income families who may need extra help to break the cycle of poverty, but that also tie the neighborhood together and create a sense of community.

These attributes result from a planning and implementation process coordinated across a variety of strategic partners, including: a public housing authority in control of core residential real estate with access to redevelopment funding (in the East Lake case the Department of Housing and Urban Development provided some capital funding); a public school district willing to authorize a charter school; and nonprofit organizations willing to build and operate facilities and implement a set of social services central to the success of the project (in East Lake, the YMCA). And, of course, all of these partners must be engaged with the neighborhood's residents, without whom none of this transformation can occur.

"I really didn't know whether this was going to work" Cousins later said.[4] Arguably the most important decision Cousins made was to establish an organization focused exclusively on managing this effort. The East Lake Foundation's sole purpose was to facilitate all of the initiatives needed to move the neighborhood from distress to health. The Foundation created the forum for engaging residents in the planning process, financed one-third of the infrastructure investment, and, perhaps most important, coordinated all of the public, nonprofit, and private initiatives so that the project unfolded at the right pace and in the appropriate sequence.

In the end, the Foundation replaced 650 public housing project units with a 542-unit, mixed-income development. One-half of the housing units are subsidized and the remaining are market rate.[5] The Foundation also launched the Drew Charter School, with programs that emphasize early childhood education. It also partnered with Sheltering Arms, a premier early childhood learning provider, to build an early learning center serving 135 children. With the YMCA, it built and operates a state-of-the-art health and fitness community center in the heart of the neighborhood. Finally, the Foundation has worked to attract local commercial investments, including a grocery store, bank, and restaurants.

This was not a short-term endeavor. Creating a plan, aligning the public and private interests, and executing the specific projects was a 10-year undertaking. And yet the results are remarkable:

- The residential population of the Villages of East Lake increased from 1,400 to 2,100.

- Crime in the neighborhood declined by 73 percent and violent crime is down 90 percent.

---

4 Ibid.

5 Because many of the existing units were vacant and uninhabitable, there was no net loss of affordable units. The Atlanta Housing Authority (AHA) replaced all of the 650 units demolished at East Lake Meadows through a combination on the new onsite replacement housing, offsite replacement housing (also delivered in a mixed-income setting), and by the acquisition by AHA of new section 8 tenant-based vouchers.

- The percentage of low-income adults employed increased from 13 percent to 70 percent.

- The Drew Charter School moved from last place in performance in its first year of operation among the 69 schools in the Atlanta Public Schools system to fourth place in 2011. Even with a 74 percent free and reduced lunch student population, Drew performs at the same level as Atlanta's schools with just 10 percent free and reduced lunch or less.

CLOSING THE ACHIEVEMENT GAP

The success of Drew Charter School is particularly important because it demonstrates that it is possible to eliminate the achievement gap—quite possibly the single most powerful result of the Purpose Built model. Drew students outperform their peers in the Atlanta Public Schools and in the State of Georgia in every single subject at every single grade level. Drew, where at one point only 5 percent of fifth graders could pass the state math test, now ranks 53rd of 1,219 elementary schools in the state. Among schools in the state with more than 60 percent African American students and 60 percent economically disadvantaged students, no school outperforms Drew.

Society pays a high cost for failing to graduate students from high school. A study by Columbia University argues that the net present value of one high school graduate yields a public benefit of $209,000.[6] The introduction of a school like Drew into a neighborhood like East Lake is arguably as much of an economic investment, and as important to America's continued prosperity, as any new factory or employment center.

The bottom line is that East Lake is now a healthy, functional neighborhood. More than $200 million of private investment has poured into the neighborhood.[7] By any measure, Cousins' plan for transforming a neighborhood has worked.

---

6 "The Costs and Benefits of an Excellent Education for All of America's Children," Teachers College, Columbia University, October 2006.

7 Selig Center for Economic Growth, Terry College of Business, University of Georgia, June 2008.

ONE COMPONENT OF A LARGER STRATEGY

In 2009, Cousins launched Purpose Built Communities to replicate the East Lake experience in cities across the country. Warren Buffett and Julian Robertson have made substantial funding commitments. As Buffett said, "Purpose Built Communities works... There is really no limit to how far this can go."[8]

Projects in New Orleans and Indianapolis are already underway and the plan is to have 25 projects in progress by 2015. The challenge is that although the framework is indeed replicable, it does require a specific set of conditions, including:

- A housing development of concentrated poverty that, when replaced with quality mixed-income housing, has sufficient scale to transform the neighborhood from a housing and income perspective;

- The opportunity to create a neighborhood public charter or contract school accountable to the surrounding community;

- Strong civic and business leadership willing to create a new entity that will ensure the long-term success and sustainability of the community.

The economics of the Purpose Built model are not particularly daunting. The affordable housing component of the mixed-income investment can be financed with Low Income Housing Tax Credits, Choice Neighborhood or HUD project-based rental assistance, community development block grant funding, or other capital funds generated by development agencies. The experience of the past 20 years shows that the market-rate component of mixed-income housing can be financed through traditional commercial sources.

Much the same can be said for financing charter schools. When the East Lake effort began, charter schools were relatively new and finding viable financing was a challenge. Since then,

---

8 Warren Buffet interview, Purpose Built Communities 2011 Conference, Indianapolis, September 2011.

a variety of financial intermediaries have emerged willing to provide capital financing for charter schools. And given that nearly all charter schools are able to operate on their public state or local funding, no philanthropic operating subsidies are generally required.

The only component in the Purpose Built model that requires direct philanthropic participation is the community-based supportive programming—recreation, afterschool programs, financial literacy classes, job training, and the like. Many times, lead organizations can find existing groups to provide these programs with little extra effort. It is not unreasonable to ask local funders to pick up the cost of these traditional programs. As a practical matter, this funding does not have to be new. Given that similar programs already exist in cities, they simply need to be coordinated and focused on the Purpose Built neighborhood initiative. Convincing these providers that their efforts will be more effective by being leveraged with the Purpose Built model is not hard.

Of course, the Purpose Built model is not the complete answer to neighborhood transformation. Not all distressed neighborhoods in our cities have the required conditions to apply it successfully. It is therefore critical that other approaches be pursued in tandem.

What the East Lake experience does suggest, however, is that all neighborhood transformation efforts need to be geographic, holistic, and specific (see Figure 2). They should:

- Focus on a well-defined geography and a single community of interest;

- Orchestrate change across multiple dimensions, primarily housing, education, private investment, and social services; and

- Be specifically designed to leverage the unique assets of the target neighborhood.

Public authorities, in particular city governments, housing authorities, and public school systems, must find a means to

FIGURE 2

NEIGHBORHOOD TRANSFORMATION FRAMEWORK

Geographic
Focused on a specific geography

Holistic
Addresses housing, education, social services, and economic development simultaneously

Specific
Tailored to the unique geographic, housing, community and economic assets

collaborate across their operating silos such that neighborhood transformation becomes a central strategic imperative. Organizations like Purpose Built Communities can strike strategically in key neighborhoods, but they cannot push change across entire cities. To truly transform all distressed neighborhoods, there must be public-sector leadership.

This is hard. Although cities are an aggregation of neighborhoods, city governments are not organized around them. School boards, housing authorities, and transit systems have unique missions and generally operate independently of city governments. City governments themselves are organized in functional areas that do not have neighborhood health as a central strategic goal. This functional division of labor is mirrored in state and federal agencies, further compounding the problem. Although programs such as Choice Neighborhoods, Promise Neighborhoods, and Race to the Top are worthy attempts to increase collaboration across federal agencies, the vast majority of federal and state resources continue to be channeled through traditional, functional programs that do not have a geographic or neighborhood dimension. This must change.

IT TAKES A NEIGHBORHOOD

In some respects, we, the public, are victims of our own unrealistic expectations governing the silos we have created. Schools systems cannot change educational outcomes on their own. Housing authorities cannot make up for the lack of affordable housing on their own. Police cannot on their own make streets safe. It takes a healthy, functioning neighborhood for these systems to stand a chance of delivering the outcomes we expect.

As a result, neighborhood transformation is not a complementary strategy in the fight on poverty: it is the central one. A specific, tailored plan is needed for every distressed neighborhood in the country. Alternative models must be developed for success, measuring results, and replicating them as rapidly as possible.

What East Lake has proven is that although neighborhood transformation is possible, it is tough work. It needs to be easier. When it is all said and done, the health of a city is inextricably linked to the health of its neighborhoods. They are in fact one in the same. Our nation cannot hope to advance the goal of improving educational outcomes and reducing poverty if there is not an appreciation and response to the geographic dimension of these problems. A vibrant and prosperous future for our cities can be created, but it needs to be created one neighborhood at a time.

SHIRLEY FRANKLIN *currently serves as the chairman of the Board of Directors and CEO of Purpose Built Communities and president of Clarke-Franklin and Associates, Inc. She was elected the first African American woman mayor of Atlanta in 2002 and served two terms. After leaving office, she was appointed to the William and Camille Cosby Endowed Chair at Spelman College and served in this capacity until June 2011. She co-chairs the United Way of Atlanta's Regional Commission on Homelessness, is chair of the National Center of Civil and Human Rights, and serves on the boards of the United Nations Institute for Training and Research (UNITAR), United Way of Atlanta, Mueller Water Products, and Delta Air Lines.*

DAVID EDWARDS *leads the Smarter Cities Campaign for IBM's Strategy and Innovation Public Sector Consulting Practice, providing strategic and financial advisory services to cities around the world. Before joining IBM, he served for eight years as the chief policy advisor to Mayor Shirley Franklin in the City of Atlanta. He has over 10 years of private-sector management consulting experience with both Coopers & Lybrand and The Boston Consulting Group. He began his career as an analyst in the federal Office of Management and Budget.*

THE FUTURE OF COMMUNITY DEVELOPMENT

Paul Grogan
The Boston Foundation

This volume offers a series of views on the future of community development. The future entails developing effective ways to increase human development. Over the last three decades, our industry has made dramatic strides in rebuilding the physical fabric of neighborhoods. It has mobilized people and resources, attracting millions of dollars of investments in affordable housing, urban supermarkets, daycare centers, community centers, and school buildings. New community-police partnerships linked to revitalization strategies have restored a basic sense of safety in urban neighborhoods. In many strong-market cities, we witnessed the virtual elimination of physical blight—trash-strewn vacant lots, abandoned buildings, and crumbling streets and sidewalks are things of the past.

Yet despite great successes in reversing disinvestment, we face persistent poverty and the prevalence of fragile families. In an economy with shrinking opportunity for low-skilled workers, low- and middle-income families struggle in an increasingly difficult landscape. A "back-to-the-city movement" intensifies competition for land and drives up rents, schools continue to fail students, and globalization undermines wide swaths of employment that formerly provided a decent living and a ladder of opportunity for workers without college or advanced degrees.

The combined cost of housing and transportation consumes a large and growing share of household budgets. In my home state of Massachusetts, more than a quarter of working households now pay more than half of their income for rent alone. Food and energy prices rise faster than incomes. And the soaring cost of health care crowds out both vital public spending on safety net issues and productive investments at the city and state levels. Federal and state budget deficits those who advocate for reducing welfare benefits, and increase pressure to cut aid to the poor and investments in upward mobility. These failing ladders of opportunity force attention to systems and structures that create and destroy opportunity.

The central challenge for community developers and their partners is to deploy effective strategies to promote human development. Meeting this challenge requires confronting major systems such as urban education, probation, criminal justice, workforce development, and community colleges. These systems must realign to prepare today's residents to meet tomorrow's workforce needs.

The architecture of community development has much to recommend it. It relied on local initiative, a diverse support base consisting of state and local government, financial institutions, philanthropy, and a focus on real results that could be highly leveraged. As I look back, I see a spirit of localism—local solutions at a workable scale—as the engine that brought cities back block by block. The movement was born at a time when cities were in peril, wracked by rampant crime, "arson for profit," disinvestment, white flight, and a sense of hopelessness. Feeding an organic process of housing development were innovations designed and created as part of a well-integrated infrastructure that brought together public, private, and nonprofit sectors. They offered flexible tools that helped fund market-rate and affordable apartments, homes for purchase, or housing for the homeless. Innovative leaders and national institutions leveraged private financing to the greatest extent practicable to increase the reach of public dollars in different market contexts.

We need to redirect this dynamic, flexible model and capitalize on research and new models in child development, health, education, and employment support. Moreover, problem-solvers need to look beyond the neighborhood, linking to regional economies, regional labor markets, and education and training resources located outside of cities. Community development will continue to find practical solutions to connect communities and capital. Intermediaries like the Local Initiatives Support Corporation (LISC) and Enterprise Community Partners will need to diversify the skill sets and tactics that have successfully created pathways for productive investment in housing and commercial development.

In *Comeback Cities*, Tony Proscio and I described the dramatic changes that had come to the Bronx. We noted with pride that "from having lived as virtual captives in a neighborhood that everyone fled when they could, residents of the South Bronx had become citizens again, participants in the forces that had restored their community to a livable place. This is significant not only in itself, but even more in light of what was *not* achieved in the Bronx, and in some places was never even attempted: The poverty rate did not decline.... Participation in the labor force is mostly unchanged.... The South Bronx has not become a middle-class neighborhood.... But it has become something that, in the midst of New York's stratospheric rents and high-skills job market, is more needed and more valuable:

It is a place where lower-income people can live affordably, in tranquility and safety."[1]

Financial innovation has been at the core of building this infrastructure. The community development industry grew out of a desire to promote equity and racial justice, and also a recognition that urban disinvestment could be turned around given smart public investments and new tools to seed local initiatives.

Community developers crafted a series of tools to link national pools of capital with local investment opportunities. The Low Income Housing Tax Credit created a channel for private investment in low-income housing projects. The New Markets Tax Credit created a vehicle for private investment in businesses, daycare centers, charter schools, and other community facilities that bring vital services to low-income neighborhoods. Affordable housing goals for government-sponsored entities such as Fannie Mae and Freddie Mac ensured that low-income communities and creditworthy low-income borrowers enjoyed similar access to low-cost mortgage capital as the rest of the homeownership market. The federal HOME program offered critical capital subsidies dedicated to affordable housing.

Together, these tools formed a system that allowed public-private partnerships to create real change on the ground in neighborhoods. National intermediaries like LISC and Enterprise provided two critical ingredients: first, access to capital and the technical assistance necessary for community development corporations and community-based development organizations to become capable strategic actors and investment-ready partners; and second, the ability to engage state and federal policymakers to promote tweaks in program structures that would enable capital to flow from national pools to targeted local investments.

This effort has been wildly successful. It has financed innovations such as the Low Income Housing Tax Credit, which have provided the bulk of housing and revenues for community

---

1 Paul Grogan and Tony Proscio, Comeback Cities: A Blueprint for Urban Neighborhood Revival (New York: Basic Books, 2000), p. 29.

development corporations (CDCs). In Massachusetts, CDCs have developed more than 25,000 housing units. Since the early 1990s, LISC's Retail Initiative (TRI) invested more than $100 million in 59 supermarkets and food markets around the country. That success spurred the creation of the New Markets Tax Credit, which has channeled $30 billion in investments in projects and businesses in low-income communities in all 50 states since 2000.

By engaging the corporate, philanthropic, and government sectors in strong public-private partnerships, the community development industry succeeded in creating a remarkably durable financing system. Its diversified funding base—government, philanthropy, and private-sector investment—and broad constituency are key to this success. In this way, we have built a national infrastructure for improving the poorest neighborhoods. David Erickson aptly chronicles this development in *The Housing Policy Revolution: Networks and Neighborhoods*.[2]

What, then, is the future of community development? It lies in turning the architecture we have created to meet urgent challenges of human development. How can we turn a successful community organizing and real estate development system toward the goal of increasing educational outcomes, employment success, family asset building, and individual and community resilience to weather setbacks? As an industry, we need new strategies to face these challenges.

We need to develop potent national intermediaries, like LISC and Enterprise have been for community development, to connect local efforts in education, employment, health promotion, and family asset building with public and philanthropic resources and social-sector investors. For instance, a national intermediary to help cities build cradle-to-career education training structures— like Strive in Cincinnati or the Opportunity Agenda in Boston— could perform some of the essential functions that community development intermediaries have performed, such as providing

---

2 David J. Erickson, The Housing Policy Revolution: Networks and Neighborhoods (Washington, DC: Urban Institute, 2009).

incentives for additional cities to start programs, elevating best practices, connecting local efforts to national sources of support, and exerting influence over public policy at the national level.

Intermediaries working with local partnerships could identify ways to deploy investment capital to promote effective schools, transit-oriented development, walkable communities, fresh food access, and physical activity. National- and state-level experiments with pay for success contracts and Social Impact Bonds are promising mechanisms to mobilize social-sector capital for investments to scale up effective prevention practices in reducing recidivism, ending chronic homelessness, and providing alternatives to nursing home care.

It is unclear how such an effort will ultimately be financed, but philanthropic seed capital will be crucial, as it has been for many social innovations. Keep in mind that the community development movement got underway with only philanthropic support, but ended up building a highly diverse funding base sufficient to keep the movement productive for more than three decades. The role, then, of community development will again be to find practical solutions to connect communities and capital.

It is equally important that the movement step up its game in telling the stories of what works for communities, making it clear that these investments have real impact on real lives. Too often, our political conversation drifts into abstractions. Effective storytelling and community mobilization remain vital to protecting the infrastructure that builds communities. For instance, LISC conducted a multiyear campaign during the Clinton administration to entice first Secretary of the Treasury Robert Rubin, then subsequently the President himself, to visit the South Bronx. Given the well-established reputation of the South Bronx as the ultimate urban wasteland, the eminent visitors were absolutely stunned and deeply affected by the scale of revitalization that was underway, and they confirmed strong support for the movement. In fact, Robert Rubin became chairman of the Board of LISC after leaving the Treasury, an office he still holds.

In closing, I must underscore the need to address an urgent threat to all the work we do to strengthen cities and improve the life chances of low-income Americans. The basic capacity of cities, states, and the federal government to invest in the future of this country is under assault. Without exaggeration, the United States faces a pivotal moment. A financial crisis wiped out trillions of dollars of real (and imagined) wealth created during a cycle of real estate speculation, the middle class faces stagnant wage growth, and our public school system fails to equip students to meet the demands of the 21st-century labor market. Yet while the crisis cries out for urgent action, our national politics remains gridlocked. Calls for smart public investment are drowned out by demands for budget cutting in the name of deficit reduction and assertions that government "is too big" or "does too much." In this budget and political climate, there is an urgent need to fight to preserve the basic capacity of city, state, and federal government to invest in America's future.

The current debate about public spending tends to lump all expenses together and call for their reduction. It fails to distinguish between maintenance investments, like Social Security or Medicare, and those investments intended to improve society for the future, like education, housing, infrastructure, the environment, energy conservation, and so on. My read of United States history is that such forward-looking investments have been crucial to the nation's development at every stage. If we deprive ourselves of the ability to make these investments in our future, the consequences will be dire.

PAUL S. GROGAN *is president and CEO of The Boston Foundation, one of the nation's oldest and largest community foundations. Mr. Grogan joined The Boston Foundation from Harvard University. From 1986 through 1998, he served as president and CEO of the nonprofit Local Initiatives Support Corporation, the nation's largest community development intermediary. During his term, LISC raised and invested more than $3 billion of private capital in inner-city revitalization efforts and contributed to the creation of the Low Income Housing Tax Credit, the HOME program, and the New Markets Tax Credit. Mr. Grogan served Boston Mayors Kevin H. White and Raymond L. Flynn and headed Boston's* *neighborhood revitalization efforts, pioneering a series of public-private ventures that have been widely emulated by other cities.*

FROM COMMUNITY TO PROSPERITY

Ben Hecht
Living Cities

> *"Past performance should not be seen as an indicator of future success."*

A nyone who has ever had to decide among investment options, whether for retirement, an endowment, or savings, should be familiar with this warning. Just because a certain investment achieved a 20 percent return over the past 10 years does not mean it will perform anywhere close to that over the next 10. No admonition is more appropriate for the community development industry today.

Since the 1960s, this sector has grown and produced staggering returns: billions of dollars in private capital invested; millions of affordable housing units built; the development of an extraordinary number of high-performing local, regional, and national nonprofit organizations; and the creation of the most successful private-public partnership the nation has ever seen, the Low Income Housing Tax Credit.

These successes were largely achieved in a different era, before community was redefined by revolutionary forces of change—primarily, globalization and the internet—that have reshaped not only America but also the world and America's place in it. Despite the heady successes in this sector, our work has not had the effect that many of us intended: a material impact on the number of Americans living in poverty.

Our long-held assumptions about the levers required to address poverty in a globalized world, and the appropriate role of place in that effort, are being challenged. Community development must move from an industry viewed by many as focused on managing decline—think older industrial cities—to one that is ushering change in new collaborative ways, disrupting obsolete and fragmented systems, keeping an eye on underinvested places, and connecting low-income people to economic opportunities wherever they exist in this hyperconnected world.

WHAT HAS CHANGED

Since its inception in the decades after World War II, the community development sector in the United States has emphasized the *primacy of place*. It has championed place-based revitalization strategies aimed at alleviating poverty by improving the physical environment and increasing access to wraparound services in a contained geographic area. According to this theory, poverty was largely considered to be a side effect of geographic isolation and disinvestment. It could therefore be alleviated through a strategy of concentration: by targeting energy and resources to defined geographies, or disadvantaged subsections of cities, material improvements in physical places would lead to corresponding improvements in lives and livelihoods.

But a lot has changed. Once-in-a-lifetime developments such as the internet and globalization, fundamentally have transformed the way people live and how the world works. An increasingly global trading system accelerated the globalization of the U.S. economy with profound impacts on neighborhoods and low-income people. It further reduced the role that low-income neighborhoods could play in the economic lives of their residents by moving jobs not just out of the neighborhood to the suburbs, as had happened in the 1970s and 1980s, but out of the country. It disrupted almost 40 years of steady increases to the economic well-being of America as a whole. As a direct result, the geography of opportunity today stretches far beyond neighborhood and city boundaries. Jobs are not limited to the small business opening up on the corner or the factory that closed downtown, or even the nearby suburbs. New York City does not only compete with Newark for employers and jobs; instead, both cities compete with Bangalore, Rio de Janeiro, and Beijing.

Similarly, the internet has profoundly reshaped notions of connection and community. The definition of "community" has, in many instances, lost a geographic, placed-based character as smart phones, text messaging, and social networks like Facebook have become ubiquitous. Today people identify and interact with their online communities, social networks comprising self-selected individuals who share interests, values, family ties, and more.

Political and societal changes such as the development of school vouchers, charter schools, and mega-churches have also accelerated the displacement of place. People have increasingly chosen to disconnect themselves from local institutions. In short, the primacy of place has lost out to mobility.

Finally, poverty is no longer limited to the disadvantaged subsections of our cities. Issues once thought to be unique to isolated geographies, such as bad schools and underemployment, are now ubiquitous. High-performing public systems that since World War II have helped to build our country's middle class and create broadly shared economic prosperity are broken and no longer produce such results. In most cities today, for example, we do not need to fix the elementary school in only one neighborhood, we need to fix most of the elementary, middle, and high schools in regional school systems.

The community development industry, and the United States as a whole, has failed to adequately adapt to these seismic changes. As the United States transitioned from the center of the world's economy to being a player in a truly global one, income inequality and stagnation has increased. Economic opportunity and prosperity declined for most Americans over the past 30 years, as highlighted by the recent Occupy Wall Street movement. Not surprisingly, the economic conditions of low-income people in the neighborhoods targeted by community developers were also negatively affected over this time. Very local community-based strategies that were disconnected from the quickly changing mainstream global economy simply had no hope of helping people overcome the economic forces at play.

In a twenty-first century world, how do we define "community" and what role should it play in our work? Can strategies that concentrate on narrowly defined places create broadly shared economic prosperity? If connectivity is key and systems need to be changed at a city or regional level, what is the role for traditional community development practitioners? Can an industry largely built on real estate transactions pivot to be influential in approaches where those transactions are important but insufficient? If transformational changes have occurred, why are so many of the very poor still trapped, symbolically and literally?

These questions are uncomfortable. They challenge our long-held assumptions about community development and urban revitalization. They also demand a fundamentally redefined notion of social change and an innovative approach to implementing it. Such an approach would require unprecedented collective action; a focus on reengineering long-broken systems such as education, workforce development, and transportation that addresses people and not just real estate; and a commitment to connecting low-income individuals to opportunities and private markets. As community development practitioners and citizens we are not simply fitting the last pieces—underserved neighborhoods—into an otherwise healthy puzzle of the American city. Instead, we are facing fundamental challenges to post–World War II ways of life.

FIXING THE METHOD

Our problem is not that we do not know what we want to achieve. Instead, it involves "fixing the method by which these goals are attained," as management legend Edward Deming said.[1] The community development sector must change the way it works and with whom it works. We need a method that is commensurate with the scope and nature of the problem. We have gone "all in" on local strategies, ignoring global realities. We have become technical experts on transactions when we need to lead a new way of adaptive problem-solving.[2] Our focus has been on a singular strategy and unit of change, the community, but we must integrate geography, connectivity, and systems innovation. We have become very influential to those involved at the neighborhood level, yet we remain largely unknown beyond that sphere. Our new method must accomplish four things:

Invest in Dynamic Collaboration.

Unfortunately, our ability to come together and solve important and complex problems is broken, as evidenced regularly in the U.S. Congress and many state houses. Problems such as stunted economic growth and an unprepared workforce are complex and demand long-term solutions. They will require a new civic problem-solving infrastructure that is resilient and able to adapt to changing conditions—an infrastructure that is not commonly found in the United States.

This civic infrastructure must be founded on the same model that is being adopted by businesses around the world: dynamic

---

1 Eric Reis, The Lean Startup: How Today's Entrepreneurs Use Continuous Innovation to Create Radically Successful Businesses (New York: Random House, 2011), ebook location 3911–13.

2 Technical challenges can be solved through the knowledge of experts and those in positions of authority. Adaptive challenges require changing people's values, beliefs, and habits. See Ron Heifetz, Leadership without Easy Answers (Cambridge, MA: Harvard University Press, 1994).

collaboration or distributed leadership. In the words of Dow Chemical CEO Andrew Liveris, "collaboration is the new competition."[3] New realities mean that old-line institutions must break out of old paradigms. In order to effect long-term solutions, what is required is the right pool of talent and entities (both public and private), participants who bring formal and informal authority to the table, and the setting aside of old mental models of organization. In the words of Unsectored's Laura Tomasko, collaborative leaders must be "infrapreneurs," or people who create change by developing and connecting systems.[4]

At Living Cities, we have been supporting cities to create "one table," where government, philanthropy, the nonprofit sector, and the business community can come together. The results so far have been encouraging. For example, as a part of our five-city Integration Initiative, which began in 2010, leaders in Minneapolis–St. Paul are using this approach to consolidate the governance of multiple transit-oriented development efforts, coordinate precious financial and human resources, and ensure that region-wide transportation efforts create broadly shared economic opportunities. In Detroit, the inclusion of lenders at "the table" has resulted in progress toward $20 million of new community-enhancing transactions.

End Workarounds.

Our systems are failing us, largely because they were built for different times and on now-outdated assumptions, such as an entire K–12 education system designed around the imperative of a nine-month school year to accommodate summer harvests. Yet, overhauling systems has proven to be very difficult given entrenched interests and the sheer force of inertia. As such, the nonprofit sector has responded largely with "carve-outs" and workarounds. We have been astonishingly innovative, but this

---

3 Ben Hecht, "Revitalizing Struggling American Cities," Stanford Social Innovation Review (Fall 2011), available at http://ssireview.org/articles/entry/revitalizing_struggling_american_cities. Andrew Liveris' comments were made at IBM 100 Anniversary Conference, New York, New York, September, 2011.

4 For more infomration see http://www.unsectored.net/tag/infrapreneur.

innovation has remained on the periphery: the one good school in a failing system, the one successful job training program serving a small number of people. We have accepted that we are program rich but systems poor, to borrow a phrase often stated by Cincinnati's civic leaders.

We must commit to long-term systems innovation, not another new program. A vastly restructured system is needed to serve as a lasting platform for wealth building and well-being of low-income Americans. To paraphrase Jon Gertner in *The Idea Factory: Bell Labs and the Great Age of American Innovation*, systems innovation is a new process that does the job with consistently better results, is deployed on a large scale, becomes the new normal or mainstream way of doing business, and has a significant impact on both society and the economy. It is this impact on both society and the economy on which we must focus.[5]

Systems work is necessary, and it is possible. As a supporter of the viral Strive Network, in the past two years alone we have seen dozens of cities take on this challenge with education. Each city has not only built a multisector table, it has also adopted a shared vision for how to fix education from cradle-to-career. They use a combination of data-driven decision making and public accountability to drive results and move funding to programs that work.

Engage Private Markets.

If the community development sector has learned anything in four decades, it is how to innovate using the tools and the language of the private sector. Community development financial institutions (CDFIs) and Low Income Housing and New Markets Tax Credits engage markets at scale; other parts of the nonprofit sector look on this with envy. We must implement this distinct competitive advantage, but in even more ambitious ways. We need to be the bridge that helps to bring private-sector discipline and resources, especially for those who seek financial and social returns, to public-purpose activities. And we must help the

---

5   Jon Gertner, The Idea Factory: Bell Labs and the Great Age of American Innovation (New York: Penguin Books, 2012).

private sector to see how it can use its investments and practices for greater social results.

On the capital side, we need to build a practice of domestic-impact investment that is at least as robust in the United States as it is abroad. This means continuing to innovate in ways to deploy capital into health centers, making fresh food more available, and other parts of the social safety net. At Living Cities, we are looking closely at how we might help bring private-sector capital into public-sector infrastructure investments, primarily at the local level. Foreign sovereign wealth funds and international financial institutions are innovating in this area; we should be able to so in the United States as well. With our Catalyst Fund, we are investing in the nation's leading energy efficiency effort in Portland, OR, and the future-looking multicounty transit-oriented development fund in the San Francisco Bay Area.

Our sector's efforts should not be limited to capital. We have to build more relationships with the private sector that are driven by the creation of what Michael Porter terms "shared value."[6] We should imagine new ways for our industry to help the private sector bring its other assets, including jobs and mainstream products and services, to low-income people and communities. For example, recent research shows that 3–5 million jobs will be "reshored" from abroad to the United States by 2020, and the addition of fresh food to local Target and Wal-Mart stores has significantly affected urban food deserts.[7]

Use Accelerators.

There is no way to avoid the difficult, multisector work required to change long-broken systems, but there are powerful ways to accelerate those efforts. Technology has the greatest potential to do that when it is intelligently combined with the public sector,

---

6 Michael Porter and Mark Kramer, "Creating Shared Value," Harvard Business Review (January 2011), available at http://hbr.org/2011/01/the-big-idea-creating-shared-value.

7 Harold Sirkin and Michael Zinser, "New Math Will Drive a U.S. Manufacturing Comeback," Harvard Business Review Blog, March 6, 2012, available at http://blogs.hbr.org/cs/2012/03/new_math_will_drive_a_us_manuf.html.

for example, through social networks to connect people and organizations to opportunity and to each other.

Big Data. Technology is increasingly being deployed for social change. No area has more promise than Big Data, which a recent *New York Times* article[8] described as "shorthand for advancing trends in technology that open the door to a new approach to understanding the world and making decisions." The great promise of Big Data is that it can help us to build "humanity's dashboard," a phrase coined by Rick Smolan: it can provide us with information about where our public dollars are actually working and where our human and financial resources should be concentrated to make the biggest difference.[9]

With more government data becoming publicly available, an explosion of innovation has occurred that is redefining how citizens participate in and interact with their government. To date, "civic tech," or the building of apps based on public data, has focused on civic life, from real-time bus schedules to virtual land-use planning. However, it is not hard to imagine how civic tech could be transformational when applied to the lives of low-income people and communities, from changing the relationship between police and neighborhoods to enabling online appointment scheduling and enrollment for public benefits.

Social Media. Another application of technology with great promise for accelerating change is social media. Whether via crowd-based funding of a startup or local business, using sites such as Kickstarter and Smallknot, or microloans made available through organizations such as Kiva, social media has the capacity to make accessible previously inaccessible resources. It also enables citizens to voice their opinions on matters that are critically important to them. Just recently, within hours of announcing it, Verizon cancelled a $2 "convenience fee" it planned to implement when more than 130,000 people signed

---

8 Steve Lohr, "The Age of Big Data," New York Times, February 11, 2012, available at http://nytimes.com/2012/02/12/sunday-review/big-datas-impact-in-the-world.html.

9 Ibid.

an online petition against it on Change.org. The power today to organize and be heard is unprecedented. Social media can also hasten the adoption of dynamic collaboration. Increasingly, private- and public-sector organizations whose success is tied to that of others are using social media to share intelligence and ideas, get real-time feedback, and broadcast knowledge.[10]

At Living Cities, we see these accelerators in action every day. We are working with organizations such as Code for America and TechNet to bring the technology community together, to build applications using openly available public data to improve municipal operations, innovate to discover Big Data's predictive powers, and increase the delivery of government products and services to low-income people. We are partnering with NBA Hall of Famer David Robinson and other celebrities to reach their large numbers of social media followers. As a leader in a network of problem-solving organizations, we are prioritizing rapid prototyping and the distribution of knowledge, and we are changing the way in which we communicate in order to accelerate innovation in our field.

THE ROAD TO THE FUTURE

Bruce Katz of the Brookings Institution said that "successful organizations cannot stand still in times of disruptive change. They maintain their core goals and values but readjust their strategies and tactics to reflect new realities."[11] This same tenet must be applied to the community development sector. The road to the future requires that we move from a geographically bounded and named strategy, *community development*, to one that reflects the needs and realities of the twenty-first century, *prosperity development*.

Prosperity development focuses on people, place, and opportunity. Its goal is the convergence of vibrant places, effective

---

10 See the archive of Living Cities' webinar "Leading in a Hyperconnected World" (https://video.webcasts.com/events/pmny001/viewer/index.jsp?eventid=42685), where more than 1,000 leaders across the country came together to discuss how they need to change how they work to achieve this goal.

11 Living Cities, 2011 Annual Report, p. 24.

systems, rich networks, and quality jobs. The commitment to vibrant places will build most directly on the sector's legacy work in neighborhoods. It will seek to insure that a person's quality of life is not predetermined by ZIP code. Vibrant places will be healthy, safe, and affordable and have access to education, jobs, and mainstream products and services.

Efforts to build effective systems will require a new, resilient civic infrastructure and an intolerance of the workaround. Civic leaders from multiple sectors will be held accountable to rebuild systems so that they provide consistently better results over time for all Americans, restoring the expectation that our children's lives will be better than our own. Rich networks will facilitate the ability of low-income people to benefit from technology, social media, and the internet. Ubiquitous broadband connectivity and active participation in social networks will enable everyone, regardless of where they live, to access the economic and political potential of these media and connect to opportunities anywhere in the world.

Ultimately, prosperity is possible only if we dramatically increase the number of Americans who have quality jobs, that is, jobs that offer economic security and wealth-building potential. We will have to improve our access to those jobs already tethered to geography, such as at universities and hospitals. We must pay attention to how we can apply our services to help small, ambitious businesses grow and larger existing enterprises translate shared value into quality jobs.

The past performance of the community development sector could be an indicator of future success, but not unless we change. We need a wider aperture than the one we are using. Community development has half a century worth of experience in building unprecedented partnerships, harnessing market forces, and generating innovative solutions. In this time of distributed leadership, no other sector has a more relevant perspective and set of skills; this should allow us to have significant influence on the shaping of our nation's future. We must commit ourselves to working in new ways, making new friends, taking different risks, and challenging orthodoxies believed to be unchallengeable. Nothing less than the economic future of our country and the values undergirding our democracy are at stake.

BEN HECHT has been president and CEO of Living Cities since July 2007. Since that time, the organization has adopted a broad, integrative agenda that harnesses the collective knowledge of its 22 member foundations and financial institutions to benefit low-income people and the cities where they live. Living Cities deploys a unique blend of grants, loans and influence to reengineer obsolete public and private systems and connect low-income people and underinvested places to opportunity.

OWNING YOUR OWN JOB IS A BEAUTIFUL THING:
Community Wealth Building in Cleveland, Ohio

Ted Howard
Democracy Collaborative

n September 2011, the U.S. Census Bureau released new statistics about poverty in the United States. According to the Bureau's analysis, fully 25 percent of very young children (below the age of five) in America are now living in poverty. Further, 46.2 million Americans lived in poverty in 2010, the highest number since the agency began tracking poverty levels in the 1950s.[1]

Accompanying this growth in poverty has been the escalating concentration of wealth in American society. As frequently cited,

- The top 5 percent of Americans own 70 percent of all financial wealth.

---

1 Carmen DeNovas-Walt et al., Income, Poverty, and Health Insurance Coverage in the United States: 2010. (Washington, DC: Sept. 2011). Available at http://census.gov/prod/2011pubs/p60-239.pdf.

- The top 1 percent of Americans now claim more income per year than the bottom 100 million Americans taken together. This growing inequality is particularly notable between racial-ethnic groups. The average family of color owns less than 10 cents for every dollar held by a white family.

- Two in five American children are raised in asset-poor households, including one-half of Latino and African American children.

The Census Bureau reports that even before the Great Recession hit, in 2007 Detroit had a poverty rate of 33.8 percent, Cleveland 29.5 percent, and Buffalo 28.7 percent. The level of pain in our smaller cities is even greater: in 2007, Bloomington, IN, led the list with a poverty rate of 41.6 percent. Dealing with the challenge of concentrated urban poverty necessitates, at bottom, a serious strategy to provide stable, living wage employment in every community and every neighborhood in the country.

Some of the most exciting and dynamic experimentation is occurring across America at the community level, as cities and residents beset by pain and decades of failed promises and disinvestment begin charting innovative new approaches to rebuilding their communities.

Even in economically struggling cities, "anchor institutions" such as hospitals and universities can be leveraged to generate support for community-based enterprise. An important example is taking place in Cleveland, OH, where a network of worker-owned businesses called the Evergreen Cooperatives has been launched in low-income, inner-city neighborhoods. The cooperatives will initially provide services to anchor institutions, particularly local hospitals and universities. Rather than allowing vast streams of money to leak out of the community or be captured by distant companies, local anchor institutions can agree to make their purchases locally. Already the "Cleveland model" has spread beyond Cleveland, with efforts now gathering early momentum in places as diverse as Amarillo, TX; Atlanta;

Milwaukee; Pittsburgh; Richmond, CA; Springfield, MA; and Washington, DC.

During the past few decades there has been a steady build-up of new forms of community-supportive economic enterprises. These ideas, now being implemented in communities across the country, are beginning to define the underlying structural building blocks of a democratic political-economic system—a new model that is different in fundamental ways from both traditional capitalism and socialism.

This approach is commonly known as "community wealth-building." It is a form of development that puts wealth in the hands of locally rooted forms of business enterprise (with ownership vested in community stakeholders), not just investor-driven corporations. These anchored businesses (both for-profit and nonprofit) in turn reinvest in their local neighborhoods, building wealth in asset-poor communities. As such, they contribute to local economic stability and stop the leakage of dollars from communities, which in turn reinforces environmental sustainability and equitable development.

Community wealth-building strategies spread the benefits of business ownership widely, thus improving the ability of communities and their residents to own assets, anchor jobs, expand public services, and ensure local economic stability. The field is composed of a broad array of locally anchored institutions, such as hospitals and educational institutions that have the potential to be powerful agents to build both individual and commonly held assets. Their activities range along a continuum from efforts focused solely on building modest levels of assets for low-income individuals to establishing urban land trusts, community-benefiting businesses, municipal enterprises, nonprofit financial institutions, cooperatives, social enterprises, and employee-owned companies. Also included in the mix is a range of new asset-development policy proposals that are winning support in city and state governments.

These institutional forms of community wealth-building help a community build on its own assets. They make asset accumulation and community-shared ownership central to local economic development. In so doing, community wealth-building provides a new way to begin to heal the economic opportunity divide between haves and have-nots at its source: providing low- and moderate-income communities with the tools necessary to build their own wealth.

Although a strategy to scale up community wealth-building strategies will face many challenges, a pair of unusual openings exist that, if seized on, can greatly strengthen the effort. In particular, momentum and scale can be achieved by: (1) aligning wealth-building efforts with the growing movement among anchor institutions to participate in community-building and economic development, and (2) capitalizing on the growing interest in building local green economies and green jobs.

Anchor institutions are firmly rooted in their locales. In addition to universities and hospitals (often referred to as "eds and meds"), anchors may include cultural institutions, health care facilities, community foundations, faith-based institutions, public utilities, and municipal governments. Typically, anchors tend to be nonprofit corporations. Because they are rooted in place (unlike for-profit corporations, which may relocate for a variety of reasons), anchors have, at least in principle, an economic self-interest in helping to ensure that the communities in which they are based are safe, vibrant, healthy, and stable.

A key strategic issue is how to leverage the vast resources that flow through these institutions to build community wealth by such means as targeted local purchasing, hiring, real estate development, and investment. Importantly, within both the higher education and health care sectors, institutions are increasingly committed to defined and measurable environmental goals, such as shrinking their carbon footprints, that help reinforce a focus on localizing their procurement, investment, and other business practices.

Over the past decade a great deal of momentum has been built around engaging anchor institutions in local community and economic development. It is now widely recognized that anchor institutions are important economic engines in many cities and regions, including their role as significant employers. For example, a 1999 Brookings Institution report found that in the 20 largest U.S. cities, universities and hospitals accounted for 35 percent of the workforce employed by the top 10 private employers.[2]

The potential for anchor institutions to generate local jobs is substantial. The most straightforward way to create jobs is to shift a portion of their purchase of food, energy, supplies, and services to local businesses. Targeted procurement can create jobs directly and have multiplier effects in regional economies.

The University of Pennsylvania is a good example. In fiscal year 2008 alone, Penn purchased approximately $89.6 million (approximately 11 percent of its total purchase order spending) from West Philadelphia suppliers. When Penn began its effort in 1986, its local spending was only $1.3 million. Determining economic impact is an inexact science, but given that Penn has shifted nearly $90 million of its spending to West Philadelphia, a very conservative estimate would suggest that minimally Penn's effort has generated 160 additional local jobs and $5 million more in local wages than if old spending patterns had stayed in place.

Another innovative example of an anchor institution using its economic power to directly benefit the community is in Cleveland and its surrounding counties in northeast Ohio. In 2005, University Hospitals announced a path-breaking, five-year strategic growth plan called Vision 2010. The most visible feature of Vision 2010 was new construction of five major facilities, as well as outpatient health centers and expansion of a number of

---

2 Ira Harkavy and Harmon Zuckerman, "Eds and Meds: Cities' Hidden Assets." (Washington, DC: Brookings Institution, 1999). Available at http://community-wealth. org/_pdfs/articles-publications/anchors/report-harkavy.pdf.

other facilities. Total cost of the plan was $1.2 billion, of which about $750 million was in construction.

In implementing Vision 2010, University Hospitals made a decision to intentionally target and leverage its expenditures to directly benefit the residents of Cleveland and the overall economy of northeast Ohio. For example, Vision 2010 included diversity goals (minority and female business targets were set and monitored), procurement of products and services offered by local companies, hiring of local residents, and other targeted initiatives. These goals were linked both to the construction phase and the ongoing operation of the new facilities once opened. By the conclusion of the project, more than 100 minority- or female-owned businesses were engaged through University Hospitals' efforts, and more than 90 percent of all businesses that participated in Vision 2010 were locally based, far exceeding the target. To realize its objectives, the hospital instituted internal administrative changes to its traditional business practices to give preference to local residents and vendors, and to ensure that its "spend" would be leveraged to produce a multiplier effect in the region. These changes have recently been implemented throughout the hospital's annual supply chain (beyond construction projects), with local purchasing targets now set for all purchases over $50,000. Given that University Hospitals' annual "spend" is in excess of $800 million, this should produce considerable local economic value and job creation in the region.

Another Cleveland effort—the Greater University Circle Initiative—involves the Cleveland Foundation, anchor institutions, the municipal government, community-based organizations, and other civic leaders. Over time, the Initiative has become a comprehensive community-building and development strategy designed to transform Greater University Circle by breaking down barriers between institutions and neighborhoods. The goal of this anchor-based effort is to stabilize and revitalize the neighborhoods of Greater University Circle and similar areas of Cleveland.

The Initiative works on a number of fronts: new transportation projects and transit-oriented commercial development; an employer-assisted housing program is encouraging employees of area nonprofits to move back into the city's neighborhoods; an education transformation plan designed in partnership with the city government; and community engagement and outreach efforts that promote resident involvement. The most recent strategic development was the launch in 2007 of an economic inclusion program known as the Evergreen Cooperative Initiative.

The Evergreen Initiative's audacious goal is to spur an economic breakthrough in Cleveland by creating living wage jobs and asset-building opportunities in six low-income neighborhoods with 43,000 residents. Rather than a trickle-down strategy, Evergreen focuses on economic inclusion and building a local economy from the ground up. Rather than offering public subsidy to induce corporations to bring what are often low-wage jobs into the city, the Evergreen strategy is catalyzing new businesses that are owned by their employees. And rather than concentrate on workforce training for jobs that are largely unavailable to low-skilled and low-income workers, the Evergreen Initiative first creates the jobs and then recruits and trains local residents to take them.

Evergreen represents a powerful mechanism to bring together anchor institutions' economic power to create widely shared and owned assets and capital in low-income neighborhoods. It creates green jobs that not only pay a decent wage and benefits, but also, unlike most green efforts, builds assets and wealth for employees through ownership mechanisms.

The initiative is built on five strategic pillars: (1) leveraging a portion of the multi-billion-dollar annual business expenditures of anchor institutions into the surrounding neighborhoods; (2) establishing a robust network of Evergreen Cooperative enterprises based on community wealth building and ownership models designed to service these institutional needs; (3) building on the growing momentum to create environmentally sustainable energy and green-collar jobs (and, concurrently, support area anchor institutions in achieving their own environmental goals to shrink their carbon footprints); (4) linking the entire effort to expanding sectors of the economy (e.g., health and sustainable energy) that are recipients of large-scale public investment; and (5) developing the financing and management capacities that can take this effort to scale, that is, to move beyond a few boutique projects or models to have significant municipal impact.

Although still in its early stages, the Evergreen Cooperative Initiative is already drawing substantial support, including multi-million-dollar financial investments from the federal government (particularly U.S. Department of Housing and Urban Development) and from major institutional actors in Cleveland.

The near-term goal (over the next 3–5 years) is to spark the creation of up to 10 new for-profit, worker-owned cooperatives based in the Greater University Circle area of Cleveland. Together, these 10 businesses could employ approximately 500 low-income residents. Each business is designed as the greenest within its sector in northeast Ohio. Financial projections indicate that after approximately eight years, a typical Evergreen worker-owner could possess an equity stake in their company of about $65,000. The longer-term objective of the Evergreen Initiative is to stabilize and revitalize Greater University Circle's neighborhoods.

The first two businesses—the Evergreen Cooperative Laundry (ECL) and Evergreen Energy Solutions (E2S, formerly Ohio Cooperative Solar)—today employ about 50 worker-owners between them. Furthermore:

- ECL is the greenest commercial-scale health care bed linen laundry in Ohio. When working at full capacity, it will clean 10–12 million pounds of health care linen a year, and will employ 50 residents of Greater University Circle neighborhoods. The laundry is the greenest in northeast Ohio; it is based in a LEED Gold building, requires less than one-quarter of the amount of water used by competitors to clean each pound of bed linen, and produces considerable carbon emission savings through reduced energy consumption.

- E2S is a community-based clean energy and weatherization company that will ultimately employ as many as 50 residents. In addition to home weatherization, E2S installs, owns, and maintains large-scale solar generators (panels) on the roofs of the city's biggest nonprofit health and education buildings. The institutions, in turn, purchase the generated electricity over a 15-year period. Within three years, E2S likely will have more than doubled the total installed solar in the entire state of Ohio.

A third business, Green City Growers (GCG), will be open for business later this year. GCG will be a year-round, large-scale, hydroponic greenhouse employing approximately 40 people year-round. The greenhouse, which is now under construction, will be located on 10 acres in the heart of Cleveland, with 3.25 acres under glass (making it the largest urban food production facility in America). GCG will produce approximately three million heads of lettuce per year, along with several hundred thousand pounds of basil and other herbs. Virtually every head of lettuce consumed in northeast Ohio is currently trucked from California and Arizona. By growing its product locally, GCG will save more than 2,000 miles of transportation, and the resulting carbon emissions, for each head of lettuce it sells. The region's produce wholesalers are enthusiastic because they will gain seven days more shelf life for the product.

Beyond these three specific businesses, the Evergreen Cooperative Corporation acts as a research-and-development vehicle for new business creation tied to specific needs of area anchor institutions. Through this process, a pipeline of next-generation businesses is being developed.

Virtually all of the financing of Evergreen is in the form of debt—a combination of long-term, low-interest loans from the federal government (such as HUD108) that focus on job creation targeted at low-income census tracts; tax credits (in particular, New Markets Tax Credit and federal solar tax credits); and grant funds from the Cleveland Foundation and others that have capitalized a revolving loan fund (the Evergreen Cooperative Development Fund). The fund invests in individual Evergreen companies as deeply subordinated debt at a 1 percent interest rate. Recently, Evergreen has secured five-year below-market rate loans from "impact investors" who are willing to make a lower return in order to put their money to work to improve the Cleveland community. Evergreen has also succeeded in attracting some local bank participation, particularly for its solar company.

An anchor institution strategy like the one in Cleveland can be a powerful job creation engine, not simply by localizing production, but also by forging a local business development strategy that effectively meets many of the anchor institutions' own needs, which the existing market may not be equipped to handle. Or, put more succinctly, anchor institutions have the potential to not only support local job creation, but also to shape local markets.

Ultimately, of course, the success of Evergreen will depend not only on Cleveland's anchor institutions, its local philanthropy, and the support of the city government. The men and women who have become Evergreen's worker-owners will determine the viability of the strategy. Keith Parkham, the first neighborhood resident hired in 2009, is now the managing supervisor of the Evergreen Cooperative Laundry. Says Parkham, "Because this is an employee-owned business, it's all up to us if we want the company to grow and succeed. This is not just an eight-hour job. This is our business." His colleague, Medrick Addison, speaks for many Evergreen worker-owners when he says, "I never thought I could become an owner of a major corporation. Maybe through Evergreen things that I always thought would be out of reach for me might become possible. Owning your own job is a beautiful thing."

TED HOWARD *is the executive director of the Democracy Collaborative at the University of Maryland and the Steven Minter Senior Fellow for Social Justice at the Cleveland Foundation. This paper draws in part on work previously* *published by the Democracy Collaborative and authored by Gar Alperovitz, Steve Dubb, and Ted Howard.*

WHY HEALTH, POVERTY, AND COMMUNITY DEVELOPMENT ARE INSEPARABLE

Risa Lavizzo-Mourey
Robert Wood Johnson Foundation

F or 40 years, the Robert Wood Johnson Foundation has worked to improve health and health care for all Americans. Our mission demands that we confront head-on inequalities in access to high-quality health care and other factors that contribute to health and longevity, especially for populations that are most vulnerable. As we define vulnerable children and families, poverty weighs in no matter what criteria we use.

Health status trends have paralleled the patterns of poverty over the years. Who is affected, where they live, and what their backstory is all contribute to explaining changes in health as well as wealth. Although in the United States we can claim many advances and improvements, in comparison with the rest of the developed world we are not in good health. According to the most recent United Nations data, the United States ranks 36th in life expectancy among industrialized nations.

For decades, policymakers, scholars, public health workers, community development leaders, advocates, and others have worked to address the problems of poverty *or* poor health. To effectively reduce poverty *and* poor health, however, we now know that we must address both, as well as the contributing factors they share. We have learned that factors that are integral to poverty, such as insufficient education, inadequate housing, racism, and food insecurity, are also indicators of poor health. We know that a child's life expectancy is predicted more by his ZIP code than his genetic code.

Although it is essential, increasing access to health care is not sufficient to improve health. There is more to health than health care. In fact, health care plays a surprisingly small role among the factors that contribute to premature death, just 10 percent; in contrast, social circumstances (15 percent), environmental exposures, genetic predisposition, and personal behavior combined contribute to 90 percent of preventable deaths.[1] With this in mind, we have broadened our foundation's strategies to embrace improving health where it starts: in the places where people live, learn, work, and play.

A large and growing body of research evidence shows that the complex arrays of factors that are intrinsically linked with poverty make up the "social determinants" of health. As we documented in our *Overcoming Obstacles to Health* report,

- The higher a person's educational attainment and income, the more likely that person is to have a longer life expectancy. In fact, those in the highest income group can expect to live at least six and a half years longer than those living in poverty.[2]

---

1 J. Michael McGinnis, Pamela Williams-Russo, and James R. Knickman, "The Case For More Active Policy Attention to Health Promotion," Health Affairs 21 (2) (2002): 78–93.

2 Paula Braveman and Susan Egerter, "Overcoming Obstacles to Health: Report from the Robert Wood Johnson Foundation to the Commission to Build a Healthier America," Robert Wood Johnson Foundation (2008), available at http://commissiononhealth.org/PDF/ObstaclesToHealth-Report.pdf.

- Compared with adults in the highest income group, poor adults are nearly five times as likely to be in poor or fair health.[3]

Why is this? A few explanations exist that are both evidence based and logical: Adults with higher incomes or more education are more likely to be physically active; as a family's income rises, their children are also less likely to be sedentary. Additionally, as a family's income rises, the quality of their diet improves and the likelihood of smoking cigarettes decreases. And the higher the family income, the healthier their children are likely to be.

The cross-generational ties to poverty are also ties to poorer health. Here are a few examples: Babies born to mothers who did not finish high school are nearly twice as likely to die before their first birthdays as babies born to college graduates. Children in poor families are about seven times as likely to be in poor or fair health as children in the highest income families. Children whose parents did not finish high school are more than six times as likely to be in poor or fair health as children of parents who earned a college degree.

Because of the need to address these "social factors" in the most strategic way, four years ago we convened the Commission to Build a Healthier America to explore those factors *outside* the health care system that affect health. We charged the commissioners to craft actionable recommendations for change. The commission, led by economists Alice Rivlin and Mark McClellan and comprising leading experts from a broad range of sectors, came back with 10 recommendations that focused largely on communities rather than health or disease prevention. As they reminded us, the economic and social vitality of the neighborhood or community contributes to residents' health and longevity. From ensuring that children have access to early childhood education, to creating public-private partnerships to open and sustain full-service grocery stores, to developing cross-sector healthy community demonstration projects, to making sure that housing and infrastructure projects consider the health impacts

---

3 Ibid.

of their work, the commission made clear points about how we should shape our foundation's work.

As stated in *Overcoming Obstacles to Health*, our background report to commissioners, "the greatest potential lies in solutions that will help people choose health. That means both strengthening individuals' ability to make healthy choices and removing obstacles to choosing health."[4] What does this tell us? In order to improve health in this country, the health sector must work closely with those who plan and build communities, especially the community development and finance organizations that work in low-income neighborhoods to build child care centers, schools, grocery stores, community health clinics, and affordable housing. From the health perspective, our interest is less about the buildings and more about what happens in them. Are the schools providing healthful food and eliminating empty-calorie snacks? Is there daily physical activity during and after school? Are grocery stores providing and promoting healthful foods? Are health clinics providing "prescriptions" of healthy lifestyles and services such as the Supplemental Nutrition Assistance Program, in addition to medications? Is affordable housing situated in proximity to safe places to play and be physically active? Is the neighborhood walkable, with well-lighted sidewalks that lead to public transportation, jobs, and services?

Health care providers also are well aware of this need. As a physician, I generally cannot discuss health with a patient who lives in poverty without talking about the areas where community development works: affordable housing, access to nutritious food, and safe places to play and exercise. I can attest that it is important for us to ensure that health and community development work together. In fact, a recent national survey by our grantee HealthLeads[5] (a program that provides to patients "prescriptions" for community services) found that four in five

---

4 Ibid.

5 Harris Interactive, "2011 Physicians' Daily Life Report." Survey findings presented for the Robert Wood Johnson Foundation, November 15, 2011, available at http://rwjf.org/files/research/73646rwjfphysicianssurveyrev.pdf.

physicians believe that unmet social needs—lack of access to nutritious food, transportation assistance, and housing assistance—are leading to worse health among Americans. These findings send a clear message: the health care system cannot overlook social needs if we want to improve health in this country.

We have seen that despite a person's personal motivation to practice healthy behaviors, the barriers to change are often too great. Consider, for example, a woman with diabetes. In addition to the health care she receives, she also will be counseled to modify her diet to include more fruit and vegetables, or to exercise more. But if this woman is poor, there is no accessible supermarket, and her neighborhood is unsafe, she will be much less likely to follow these recommendations. Her diabetes will likely not be abated, her health will deteriorate faster, hospitalizations will be required sooner and more often, and complications will come earlier. All of these are affected by factors outside the medical care system.

Improving America's health requires leadership and action from every sector, public, private, and nonprofit, including people who work in public health and health care, education, transportation, community planning, business, and other areas. As Opportunity Finance Network President and CEO Mark Pinsky and I wrote in a joint column in early 2012, "building new collaborations also makes fiscal sense since improving low-income communities yields both health and economic benefits."[6]

OUR PERSPECTIVE ON THE ROLE OF PHILANTHROPY

Let me be clear: the work of the Robert Wood Johnson Foundation is laser-focused on improving health and health care. But we know that to do so, we must expand the scope of our vision and work. We understand that neither improving health nor reducing poverty is the endgame. Our vision is to create opportunities for all Americans to lead long, healthy, and productive lives. At the foundation, this outlook has led to evolution in

6   Risa Lavizzo-Mourey and Mark Pinsky, "A Win-Win: Job Creation Will Grow the Economy and Improve Health," The Health Care Blog, January 16, 2012, available at http://thehealth careblog.com/blog/2012/01/16/a-win-win-job-creation-will-grow-the-economy-and-improve-health.

how we work: changes in grant making, how we use our assets, and how we work with others.

First, the focus of grant making is evolving: we are investing in research and data, policy advocacy, and infrastructure building that strengthens communities. A recent example of this involves our County Health Rankings,[7] which rank the health of every county in the United States, in part on the basis of social factors. These rankings have inspired change. Two years ago, Wyandotte County, KS, was ranked last in the state because of factors including high levels of violent crime and unemployment, deteriorating neighborhoods, and a high percentage of families living below the poverty line. When he saw how badly the county was doing, Kansas City Mayor Joe Reardon tapped county officials and stakeholders to address the social problems that were at the root of the health problems. This community is now cited as a national example of partners working together on social determinants of health to create effective change.

A related project and another grantee of our foundation, Roadmaps to Health,[8] funds community partners to address the impact of social factors identified in the County Health Rankings, such as employment or education. In Alameda County, CA, for example, the project will make consumer-focused banking services available to residents of low-income neighborhoods and educate them about the benefits of these services, such as using bank accounts without minimum balance requirements instead of check-cashing or bill-payment services with fees. In New Mexico, they will advocate for policies that create, fund, and sustain a high-quality, universally accessible continuum of early childhood care, health, and education services.

---

7 "County Health Rankings," Robert Wood Johnson Foundation, available at http://www.countyhealthrankings.org.

8 "County Health Roadmaps," Robert Wood Johnson Foundation, available at http://www.countyhealthrankings.org/roadmaps.

The foundation also funds the Health Impact Project,[9] which promotes the use of health impact assessments to help local decision makers to identify and address the health impacts of a policy decision or project such as building a major roadway or planning community improvements. In Minnesota, an assessment[10] of the possible health impacts of changing public transportation lines indicated "serious potential threats" to more than 1,000 small businesses as well as to health, housing, and job access for the large low-income and minority communities in the affected area.

The foundation was also an early supporter of work to build grocery stores in "food deserts" that helped to shape the Healthy Food Financing Initiative (HFFI), which will improve access to healthful foods in similar food deserts across the country. A partnership between the Community Development Financial Institutions Fund in the U.S. Treasury Department and the U.S. Departments of Agriculture and Health and Human Services, HFFI is investing $500 million annually to subsidize grocery stores in low-income neighborhoods. This increases access to healthy foods and creates jobs, and these stores are profitable.

Our Healthy Kids, Healthy Communities[11] program supports local action to increase opportunities for physical activity and access to healthful, affordable foods for children and families. The goal is to catalyze policy and environmental changes that can make a lasting difference and be replicated across the country. The program is part of the foundation's $500 million commitment to help reverse the childhood obesity epidemic in the United States by 2015.

---

9   "HIA in the United States," Health Impact Project, A Collaboration of the Robert Wood Johnson Foundation and The Pew Charitable Trusts, available at http://healthimpactproject.org/hia/us.

10 Shireen Malekafzali and Danielle Bergstrom, "Healthy Corridor for All: A Community Health Impact Assessment of Transit-Oriented Development Policy in Saint Paul, Minnesota," PolicyLink (2011), available at http://healthimpactproject.org/news/project/body/Healthy-Corridor-Technical-Report_FINAL.pdf.

11 "Healthy Kids, Healthy Communities: Supporting Community Action to Prevent Childhood Obesity," Robert Wood Johnson Foundation, available at http://healthykidshealthycommunities.org.

We are also broadening the ways that we use our financial assets. In 2011, we announced a $100 million capital impact fund to leverage funding and nonfinancial resources from other foundations, government, and nontraditional funding partners, including private capital from individual and institutional investors. By building on growing interest in using investments to address issues such as economic development, education, housing, and the environment, we intend to be among the foundations leading the way, sending a market signal that health is the new frontier for impact investing.

However, we know that to increase the effects of our investments, we need to work with others whose expertise, resources, and missions add strength to our own so that together we can add health metrics to financial and other bottom-line indicators of success. This is where the finance and community development sectors come in.

The finance and community development sectors have traditionally joined together to improve neighborhoods, developing safe, affordable housing, child care centers, community health centers, and grocery stores. The health sector can help. We can provide the tools, evaluation research, and data to show what works: for example, the impact of developing a new transit line or building a grocery store in a food desert. Public health can provide a nationwide network of health departments, public health workers, and insights to increase support for on-the-ground community improvements. And philanthropies can serve as conveners, bringing together leaders from diverse fields and funding innovative approaches. Together, these partnerships can lead to smarter investments and new evidence-based solutions.

Each of these sectors has had the same goal for decades: improving the lives of low-income families. Together we spend billions of dollars each year. Joining forces is not about spending more money but about better targeting our efforts, sharing tools and data, and learning what is working and then replicating those programs and investments. There are promising examples sprinkled in communities across the country:

- In Seattle, public health and housing leaders are working together to reduce the allergens in low-income homes that can cause asthma, a scourge of low-income children that results in an estimated 13 million missed school days and $3.2 billion in treatment costs.[12]

- Mercy Housing, a nonprofit affordable housing developer, has created with its San Francisco Mission Creek Apartments a healthier environment for seniors and is saving the city nearly $1.5 million a year.[13]

- In San Diego, Market Creek Plaza, a $23.5 million real estate development project located in what was once one of the most distressed and dangerous communities in the city, has brought together affordable housing, healthful food, a community center, and jobs for community residents that include living wages, health insurance, and pension plans.[14]

We are energized by such examples. What is missing, however, is the pervasive will, momentum, infrastructure, and framework to take these efforts to a nationwide scale.

WORKING TOGETHER TO ACCELERATE CHANGE

To make working together the routine rather than the exception, we have recognized that we need better measures of the health outcomes of community development work. One response is the changes we are making to our annual County Health Rankings

---

12 James K. Krieger et al. "The Seattle-King County Healthy Homes Project: Implementation of a Comprehensive Approach to Improving Indoor Environmental Quality for Low-Income Children with Asthma," Environmental Health Perspectives 110 (suppl. 2) (2002): 311–322.

13 The $1.45 million is a rough calculation based on the 50 residents who were shifted from higher cost facilities to Mission Creek, multiplied by per-person savings of $29,000 per year. This annual savings was estimated by the San Francisco Public Health Department and communicated to Mercy Housing in a letter titled "Cost and Housing Stability at Mission Creek Senior Supportive Housing," dated July 14, 2009.

14 Judith Bell and Marion Standish, "Building Healthy Communities Through Equitable Food Access," Community Development Investment Review 5 (3) (2009): 75–83.

to better translate the value of improved health into economic terms, such as greater productivity and lower health care costs for businesses.

Another challenge is that whereas the community development sector is quite good at finding ways to attract all types of capital (government subsidy and below-market-rate and market-rate capital) to projects with good business fundamentals, the health sector has struggled with how to capture and explain returns on investments in health. This is another near-term goal. We believe we can create a powerful partnership, marrying public health's ability to measure health outcomes with community development's business acumen to make a stronger financial case for community-building work as a way to improve people's lives and save on health expenditures down the road.

This work has begun, and it has been met with enormous response and interest across the health and community development sectors. It has gained federal attention as well, including from the Federal Reserve System and the U.S. Department of Housing and Urban Development. However, we need to do more to ensure that these cross-sector collaborations become the acceptable way to work.

I envision a time in the near future when our fields and the people who work in them do not need to make a special effort to develop partnerships because we will be working side by side in communities, in states, and nationally, with common aims, combining our best assets and skills to improve the lives of all Americans. In fact, we are likely to look back at this time and wonder why community development and health were ever separate industries.

RISA LAVIZZO-MOUREY, MD, MBA, *is president and CEO of the Robert Wood Johnson Foundation, the nation's largest philanthropic organization dedicated to improving health and health care. She joined RWJF in 2001 as senior vice president and director of the Health Care group. Previously, she was the Sylvan Eisman professor of medicine and health care systems at the University of*

Pennsylvania and director of Penn's Institute on Aging. In Washington, DC, she was deputy administrator of what is now the Agency for Health Care Research and Quality. Lavizzo-Mourey is a member of the Institute of Medicine of the National Academy of Sciences, the President's Council for Fitness, Sports and Nutrition, and several boards of directors.

THE WORLD HAS CHANGED AND SO MUST WE

Clara Miller
F. B. Heron Foundation[1]

A RUDE AWAKENING

Like other American foundations, the F. B. Heron Foundation has for years focused on helping families at the bottom of the economic and social scale—inheritors of persistent poverty, racial and ethnic discrimination, social and geographic isolation, and various failures in markets, social policies, and safety nets. The goal has been to equip them to join what progressive reformers confidently called "the mainstream." As have others, we have concentrated on helping lower-income families purchase homes and acquire assets, the cornerstones of the "ownership society" that was one of few values on which the American left and right could generally agree. We also sought to help disadvantaged families develop the financial skills necessary to save, borrow wisely, manage budgets and assets, and survive periods of economic stress. These were all useful, often successful efforts. But they were based on a

---

1 This article is based on the writing of several contributors and excerpts from F. B. Heron's Strategy Document. Miller was a contributing writer and served as editor of this piece. Other contributors, reviewers, and editors included the Foundation's board of directors; staff members Kate Starr, Dana Pancrazi, John Weiler, and Jim Metzinger; and consultant Tony Proscio.

view of social need that presumed the existence of a healthy and growing labor market—a reliable mainstream that, if it could be entered, would flow steadily toward prosperity, or at least toward fair opportunity that provided employment and with it, steady income.

That view had become comfortable for foundations and government alike, for two reasons. First, for a few decades it was true, and many families and communities were made materially better off by the opportunities that this approach helped to open up for them. But second, this view was soothing because we had grown *used to it*, and it carried the reassuring promise of a happy ending—a persuasive connection between philanthropic, for-profit, and government initiatives and expanding economic and social opportunity on which a generation of orderly logic models and theories of change relied.

This calm contentment has been shattered: more Americans experience poverty today than at any time in the 53 years the Census Bureau has published such figures, and in 2010 the percentage of Americans living below the poverty line (a household income of $22,314 for a family of four) was at its highest level since 1993.[2] We have come to conclude that unfortunately, our comfortable habit appears to have outlasted the accuracy of the premises on which it was founded, and in the process has grown less useful year by year. The world has changed, and so must we. It's time for a new approach.

The premises on which most of the economic access and opportunity strategies were based were in many ways drawn from a post–World War II story. This story featured steady expansion in industrial employment, mass upward mobility (or at least opportunity) across the social ladder, ever-broadening homeownership and accumulation of assets, escalating rewards for education and hard work, and a concentration of economic hardship and social disadvantage in a small but persistent "underclass."

---

2 Sabrina Tavernise, "Poverty Rate Soars to Highest Level Since 1993," New York Times, September 14, 2011, page A1.

That blend of widespread opportunity and marginal poverty is plainly over. For the great bulk of the U.S. population, social and economic mobility have been stagnant for decades. Industrial and technological advances now lead as often to reductions in employment as to increases. Loyalty, diligence, and a history of regular promotions no longer inoculate most workers from the risk of sudden, enduring unemployment that raises the odds of lasting poverty. Employment at a living wage is neither reliable nor commonplace. Poverty is structural, not marginal.

In its current state, our economy isn't likely to reverse these trends. A particularly hair-raising study, "An Economy that Works: Job Creation and America's Future," issued by the McKinsey Global Institute in June 2011, intones a litany of daunting statistics: "7 million decline in the number of US jobs since December 2007… 60 months projected length of 'jobless recovery'… 20 percent of men in the population not working today, up from 7 percent in 1970 … 23 percent drop in rate of new business creation since 2007, resulting in as many as 1.8 million fewer jobs, and 58 percent of employers say that they will hire more temporary and part-time workers." The executive summary goes on to say, "only in the most optimistic scenario will the United States return to full employment (5 percent unemployment) before 2020." Possibly the most worrisome findings are that we have experienced lengthening "jobless recoveries" from recessions in the past two decades, coupled with a documented mismatch of predicted opportunities with the available skills and education levels of U.S. workers.[3]

An economy capable of offering a job to every willing worker, or at least to every household—as well as a workforce capable of seizing the available opportunities—is a fundamental prerequisite to achieve most other societal aspirations. Conversely, lack of

---

3 "It took roughly 6 months for employment to recover to its prerecession level after each postwar recession throughout the 1980s, but it took 15 months after the 1990–91 recession and 39 months after the 2001 recession. At the recent pace of job creation it will take more than 60 months after GDP reached its prerecession level in December 2010 for employment to recover" (James Manyika et al., Executive Summary, An Economy that Works: Job Creation and America's Future, McKinsey Global Institute, June 2011).

work invites in a witches' brew of health, educational, and social problems that accelerate one's spiral into poverty.

Indeed, beyond the mere availability of work, the nature of work itself is changing, with temporary, contingent, or episodic employment dominating the working years of more and more people. And, as I noted above, jobs in some industries are more complex and demanding. By itself, a high school diploma—the great goal of social reformers for half a century—is now more a guarantor of severely limited opportunity than of possible advancement. The extranational job flight, now driven primarily by lower labor costs abroad, will likely be further accelerated and accentuated by U.S. workers' lagging skills and education levels.

And yet, in much of American philanthropy and social policy, the old narrative and its familiar assumptions linger on, sometimes questioned but rarely discarded. One result is that despite the widespread structural change transforming the economy, the assumptions behind most antipoverty policy and programs, both in government and in civil society, remain fundamentally unaltered: poverty is an outlier, a temporary condition brought on by temporary conditions in a fundamentally sound system.

IT'S THE ECONOMY...!

A course change in our economic vision, antipoverty strategy, and day-to-day tactics must overcome two limiting narratives. The first is that access strategies alone—appropriate to marginal but not to structural poverty—are adequate. They are not. The second claims that we must tolerate expanded poverty and income inequality as the price of economic globalization, coupled with the equally dour view that government programs for the poor are the only route out of poverty. Neither narrative acknowledges the need to rebalance the economy *itself* so it can fulfill three fundamental American promises: full livelihood, democracy, and opportunity for all. To invest in the building blocks of that economy and to ensure the basics of entry are critical responsibilities not only of philanthropic institutions and government but also of banks and businesses. We plan to engage accordingly.

The notion that our society must move backward economically and socially to compete in a global economy is mistaken. Technological and social innovation—from information to biotech to enterprise evolution—will change the nature of work, community, opportunity, and philanthropy. As the mainstream evolves, we must invest in models of innovation that share future value with those now excluded or unserved, and at the center of this proposition is work. The first and most fundamental prerequisite to helping people help themselves out of poverty is reliable work for adequate pay. A corollary to this belief is that economic and technological innovation must include and enrich people and communities in poverty.

Delivering on this promise is not beyond our reach. We believe that we can realize an economic vision for a more universally prosperous society, one that supports democratic pluralism and civic vibrancy, provides dependable work for adequate pay, protects the most vulnerable, and successfully competes in the global market. This approach emphasizes investment in small and midsized enterprises, a strengthening of the direct connection of local and regional economies with global as well as local and regional markets, and the primacy of reliable revenue (as opposed to a default position favoring investment in fixed assets, such as real estate) in economic development strategies. In a sense, this pragmatic middle represents nothing more than a revitalization of America's traditional vision of an economy that delivers value and opportunity to a larger rather than a smaller number of workers and stakeholders.

"BUSINESS AS USUAL" MUST CHANGE

If our field is to address a more fundamental set of issues, our tactics must change, broadening our approach to go beyond a traditional set of activities. Admittedly, this emerging approach lacks some of the theoretical certainty of the dominant view, which sees access and ownership strategies as reliable steps into mainstream opportunity. Yet given the reality that access strategies have been helpful but not adequate, we must be intentionally experimental. Only by rigorously questioning and transcending our own cherished assumptions will we progress. Our path at F. B. Heron represents an effort to do so.

How might philanthropy realistically contribute? We know that neither the F. B. Heron Foundation, nor philanthropy, nor the nonprofit sector, nor government can take on these issues alone. Furthermore, we believe that these problems and their solutions are interconnected. Not only is "changing the economy" unattainable by one actor, the dominant context for our work is a range of mega-problems in the environment, health, global security, and civil society (to name just a few) that expands and accelerates the challenge. Business as usual—with respect to both strategy and the way we operate as a foundation—is no longer an option.

The urgency and size of the problems we face require that we work differently. Everything at our disposal is now a mission-critical resource. Grants are one tool but not the only tool we have at our disposal, and to define ourselves primarily as a grantmaking foundation is limiting. Endowments have always been a source of investable capital for fostering businesses, industries, and nonprofit organizations that may be able to help in overcoming the new economic challenges. This foundation along with others has made such investments for years, but we must do more. Philanthropy's financial toolkit should include every investment instrument, all asset classes, and all enterprise types.

The *way* we deploy capital and the assumptions and approaches we use to do so can in themselves make a difference. We plan to invest 100 percent of our endowment, as well as other forms of capital, for mission. Beyond money, we are obligated to deploy all of the resources at our disposal—capital, revenue, ideas, talents, influence, and natural allies—toward the broad, multi-sector approach which will be necessary for the pursuit of goals that are, admittedly, much bigger than those we have pursued in the past. Philanthropy's collective talents and influence provide valuable intellectual and social capital alongside its money. We will not only wield all our capital to the fullest, we will affirmatively and reflexively seek opportunities to influence and be influenced by others through co-investment, advocacy, and example.

Beyond the scope and scale of our financial capital investment, we will operate differently as a foundation, a prerequisite to the broader market engagement we seek. Here are some of the actions we are taking:

- We will invest through a single capital deployment department, removing the traditional foundation's separation of investment and grantmaking. In our current operations, we have combined them into a single, dedicated activity: to deploy capital for mission. Essentially, the "foundation as enterprise" will have as its sole purpose the effective deployment of philanthropic capital to achieve our mission.

- As I noted above, we will engage with both social and business enterprises as a capital investor dedicated to the viability and mission productivity of organizations and their business engines, regardless of legal form of business or tax status. By taking on the role of capital provider, we will seek to stabilize, make more effective, and build sustainability in the sector's key enterprises, whatever their tax status or legal form of business.

- We will routinely look outside our foundation, sector, and industry for opportunities to become a joint investor, working with individuals, banks, government, foundations, and businesses.

- Our grants will be concentrated on providing philanthropic equity and building this capacity within Heron and more generally in the sector.

- We will renew our determination to promote the simplified sharing of data, methods, underwriting, and research with others to reduce transaction costs, improve efficiency for our investees, and generally promote better functioning, more efficient, and more productive enterprise investing relevant to our mission.

- We will scrupulously avoid rebuilding, undermining, or creating redundant infrastructure where institutions such as community development financial institutions exist to retail our funds or partner with us.

REBALANCE TO A FOCUS ON WORK AND INCOME

Our belief, at this stage, is that our financial capital investment will focus first on opportunities that, above all, add jobs to the economy and help combat persistent poverty and unemployment. Other investments would focus on influence through public companies and partnerships and on innovation/effectiveness in work and opportunity for low income people through nonprofits, cooperatives, hybrids, and for-profits with "mission first" orientations. We are encouraged that progress along these lines is already underway: we are seeing a diverse universe of opportunity in proven industries refreshed by new technology; place-based commercial "supply chains" powered by institutions and businesses; and experimentation with reimagined community economies, business types, technologies, and forms of employment. Companies along the spectrum of size and tax status are paying attention to a broader value proposition.

We see no reason to target investment to a particular industry, subsector, or tax status, although not every financial investment tool is relevant to every organization. For example, it is highly unlikely we will make a program-related investment (PRI)[4] to a public company or buy tradable stock of a nonprofit without significant regulatory changes, and we don't think we need such changes to have a full spectrum of tools or opportunities.

---

4 "Program-related investments (PRIs) are investments made by foundations to support charitable activities that involve the potential return of capital within an established time frame. PRIs include financing methods commonly associated with banks or other private investors, such as loans, loan guarantees, linked deposits, and even equity investments in charitable organizations or in commercial ventures for charitable purposes." The Foundation Center, Grantspace, available at http://grantspace.org/Tools/Knowledge-Base/Grantmakers/PRIs.

Our enterprise framework will continue to be the private foundation, and we assume we will exist as long as we can add value to society. We also assume that there will be investment opportunities in the full spectrum of enterprises, regardless of industry or sector, and that those we pursue can help produce vitality, job growth, and economic activity fully inclusive of low-income people.

We expect that although our portfolio has for years emphasized opportunities for low- and moderate-income people to invest in real estate and own homes, this emphasis will change as time passes, and we will seek a more tactical balance. In much of the community development world, lenders' business exigencies—the need to secure transactions through leveraged real estate coupled with the interaction of transaction size, tenure, and profitability, and the resulting industry-wide focus on dedicated streams of federal subsidy—have driven antipoverty investment and strategy to become overly narrow. As bankers and developers, community development organizations have tended to overinvest in real estate assets and underinvest in other assets such as enterprise innovation, technology, and human capital. We are looking for ways to diversify.

Diversification in our portfolio is likely to emphasize investment that improves lower-income people's access to reliable income and opportunity. From our point of view, owning fixed assets is important to an individual's longer term prosperity only insofar as jobs and income are steady and reliable, and cash is obtainable. Noncash assets such as real estate, securities, and even education derive their *financial* value largely from the income they attract and embody. When borrowers acquire these assets with debt, revenue reliability is even more important to protect acquirers from risk. Our strategy puts reliable income and cash first, and illiquid assets, especially those acquired with debt, second.

For the F. B. Heron Foundation, all financial investing is a *direct* means to enact strategy, so our fundamental question for deployment of *all* capital will be, "what is the highest and best use of this asset for furthering our mission?" Financial returns to our own portfolio will be a necessary part of answering that question, but so will returns to society, to the organizations in which we invest, and to the fields of social endeavor on which we focus. We include grants among the investments we think of in this way, and we will deploy them as a primarily financial tool. The protective "equity holders' ethic," so central to successful commerce, is relevant to other investment tools, including grants.

MAKING COMMON CAUSE

We harbor no illusion of being a unique, prophetic voice in American philanthropic or financial markets. In fact, success requires a chorus rather than a soloist. It is an unavoidable reality that with assets of roughly a quarter billion dollars as of 2011, the F. B. Heron Foundation is not in a position, purely on its own, to make much of an aggregate difference in the way investors, enterprises, and labor markets function. Neither, for that matter, is any other single philanthropic actor, even much larger ones. Ultimately, we will succeed by influencing the attitudes and behavior of *many* other investors, perhaps beginning with philanthropy but extending well beyond. Forming networks of thought, communication, and action with other investors will become a central priority.

Some of what we are attempting may not work. We have much to learn about the possibilities of success, failure, reinvention, co-investment, and "the foundation as enterprise" with this approach. Yet, we are determined to contribute, by advocacy, by example, and, just as powerfully, by joining our colleagues in their efforts, to the development of an increasingly expansive, dynamic, and effective philanthropic response to poverty. The pathway of out of poverty for many Americans in the twenty-first century requires economic reinvention, not only marginal access to assets and service. The work of philanthropic organizations can be a full-spectrum contributor to that end, both through enterprise reinvention and by guiding the full deployment of capital in the mainstream to promote a more inclusive, just, and productive society.

CLARA MILLER *is president of the F. B. Heron Foundation in New York City, a private foundation dedicated to helping low-income people and communities help themselves. Miller founded and spent 27 years as President and CEO of the Nonprofit Finance Fund, a national CDFI that provides direct financing and financial counsel to social sector organizations. She was appointed by President Clinton to the U.S. Treasury Department's first Community Development Advisory Board for the then-newly-created Community Development Financial Institutions Fund in 1996. She also chaired the Opportunity Finance Network board for six years and was a member of the Federal Reserve Bank of New York's Community Advisory Council. Miller serves on the boards of GuideStar, PopTech, and the Robert Sterling Clark Foundation and is a member of the Social Investment Committee of the Kresge Foundation. She is a member of Bank of America's National Community Advisory Council, the Aspen Philanthropy Group, and the first Nonprofit Advisory Committee of the Financial Accounting Standards Board.*

GETTING TO SCALE:
The Need for a New Model in Housing and Community Development

Sister Lillian Murphy and Janet Falk
Mercy Housing

Housing is a key component in the history of community development. Although there are many calls to focus on other important aspects of building sustainable communities, providing quality, affordable housing is still a crucial part of the equation. For children to be able to learn, for families to be healthy, and for the elderly to be safe, a supply of stable, affordable housing must be available.

The recent Great Recession has highlighted the importance of housing in the United States. As foreclosures have increased and credit has waned, new housing starts (which are a major source of jobs) have plummeted. The recession has also challenged the assumption that the American Dream of owning a home is attainable by many. Although many households will continue to be able to afford a home, for one-quarter to one-third of the population there will always be a need for quality rental housing. Affordable rental housing must be available to all populations, particularly those with the lowest incomes. Federal housing policy must redefine the American Dream to include a supply of good rental housing in addition to the promotion of homeownership.

In the United States there is a major gap between the demand for affordable rental housing and the available supply. Foreclosures and changes in the ability to purchase a home have had an impact on the rental market. As previous homeowners flooded the rental market, vacancy rates in 2011 dropped to their lowest levels since 2001. This demand has caused rental costs to increase, which has affected those with the lowest incomes the most.

The National Low Income Housing Coalition, in its "Out of Reach 2012" report, observed a significant gap in housing affordability throughout the country.[1] The report measured the housing wage, which is "an estimate of the full-time hourly wage a household must earn in order to afford a decent apartment at the HUD estimated Fair Market Rent (FMR) while spending no more than 30% of income on housing costs."[2] With an average FMR for a two-bedroom apartment in the United States of $949 per month, the 2012 housing wage is $18.25. This is significantly higher than the average hourly wage of $14.15 that renters actually earn nationally (the "earned wage"). The housing wage exceeded the earned wage in 86 percent of the counties studied in the report. This gap between the wage required and the wage actually earned indicates a need for more affordable rental units.

MORE THAN JUST HOUSING

Affordable housing has always been about more than just bricks and mortar. The building of stable, vital, healthy communities that include services such as child care, health care, and educational opportunities has been the vision for changing the nature of poverty. It is a holistic approach that includes the promotion

---

1 Elina Bravve et al., Out of Reach 2012 (Washington, DC: National Low Income Housing Coalition).

2 Ibid, p. 2.

of stability and long-term homeownership and the provision of services to meet the needs of community residents.

Housing development organizations, particularly nonprofit developers, have a history of providing such services with the housing they have built. Their mission is long term, as they understand that it is necessary to have long-term ownership in order to preserve the affordability of what they have built. These developers now need a sustainable business model to continue to survive and thrive.

NEED FOR A SUSTAINABLE MODEL

Since the Tax Reform Act of 1986, affordable housing in the United States has primarily been developed for lower-income households, using a financing model that combines public subsidies, conventional debt, and private equity (using the Low Income Housing Tax Credit). At Mercy Housing, we provide a successful example of this model. We have built, acquired, and financed more than 41,000 apartments that house more than 139,000 people; in doing so we have proven that we are capable business partners who can produce and operate housing while providing support services. We know how to do complex deals in difficult markets, and we are committed to serving those communities most in need. However, this financing model is unsustainable, for many reasons:

1 At precisely the time when more rental housing is needed to serve a widening segment of the population, the traditional resources to provide it are dwindling rapidly. Following substantial cutbacks in government programs, we have fewer resources available to continue to meet the increasing demand for affordable rental housing.

2 Traditional funding provides only limited support to organizations at the operations level. Nonprofit developers in particular have been chronically undercapitalized. Their primary source of support has been the developer fee, which has increased little in the past 25 years. (Some government programs,

such as HUD Section 202 for the elderly, have only recently permitted organizations to recoup a developer fee to pay for their organizational costs.) Without significant assistance from support organizations, it is difficult to provide and retain the infrastructure necessary to develop or rehabilitate housing for lower-income people, let alone take the risks of developing new models and programs.

3 The current model does not permit or encourage organizations to go to a larger scale, funding each project individually. Going to scale is the only way to narrow the gap between supply and demand.

4 Projects take too long (three to five years is not uncommon) to reach completion. Each project is subject to regulation by every funding source involved, and it is typical to have four to six funding sources. What results is a very inefficient system. Although we do not have accurate measurements of the costs of these time delays, we know that land costs, interest carry costs, staff time, required changes in design, and other factors make projects more expensive. As well, the multiple levels of compliance that are required increase operational and asset management costs. These increases mean that developments are either less affordable or require more subsidy.

5 Because it is so risk averse, the current model does not permit innovation. Cautiousness on the part of government programs (at federal, state, and local levels) has led to separate regulations and rules that are designed for the one percent (or fewer) who might abuse the system, rather than the 99 percent who are in compliance. This model may be a good system to manage risk, but it is not a good system for getting to scale.

GETTING TO SCALE

A new approach is necessary if we are to continue to progress toward meeting the country's housing and community development needs. Government programs, capital markets, and philanthropic foundations must change the way they perceive affordable housing production, in order to create new models that will be sustainable over the long term. The primary paradigm shift necessary will involve developing a system that allows housing developers with a holistic, community approach to housing, including the commitment to long-term ownership, to get to scale.

To achieve this shift, any new model should have the following characteristics/features:

Allow for Flexibility and Diversification. Currently, most government programs at all levels (federal, state, and local) have defined a narrow range of who can be served: those at the lowest level of income, which is generally defined as 60 percent or less of area median income.[3] Although it is good public policy to target resources to those most in need, this focus solely on the lowest income population is not sustainable for the organizations that provide housing. The compliance costs to operate properties and provide services, along with strict limitations on rent, mean that there is little or no cash flow for organizations to be able to sustain or grow. In fact, to serve those most in need—the homeless, the frail elderly, and those with disabilities—requires an effort that is diversified enough to allow for some organizational income to be generated from other activities. Having multiple "business lines" that are not all tied to the same resource cycles also allows organizations to be able to deal with any disruptions that may occur in funding sources.

Encourage Innovation. All of the players in the housing industry—developers, private capital providers, the philanthropic sector, and government agencies—must be encouraged to innovate if new models are going to emerge. The current system focuses on avoidance of risk by encumbering government programs with rules and regulations. Banks and other lenders are also very risk averse. We must build in some tolerance for failure, as all new ideas are not going to be successful. Venture

---

3 Area median income is determined at the county level and is published periodically by the U.S. Department of Housing and Urban Development.

capital firms have recognized this as they take risks with emerging companies.

Fund at the Enterprise Level. Low-cost funding at the enterprise level—that is, providing debt and equity capital to an organization rather than project by project—is necessary to allow provider organizations to innovate, diversify, and become sustainable. It enables the developer to build reserves to be able to quickly take advantage of opportunities in rapidly changing markets. Access to funds for predevelopment without individual project application requirements can expedite the development process and reduce costs. A source of operating capital allows an organization to invest in infrastructure and other organizational needs to position it for future growth.

Enterprise-level funding assumes that the enterprise knows what it must do to develop what is appropriate for the market and the local community. One size does not fit all markets, resident needs, or project types, and yet the current system creates a fairly narrow set of rules with which all must comply. A major shift from a focus on compliance with rules to a focus on outcomes must occur. Goals should be set through public policy, and then development organizations should be allowed to propose ways to achieve these goals. Accountability should be through the outcome rather than unwavering compliance with a large set of very specific rules and regulations.

Encourage Collaborations across Sectors. A major goal of scale is creating a road to sustainability that is nimble and flexible enough to weather the current economic storm and other disruptions that may occur, such as natural disasters, loss of public subsidies, and health epidemics. The major elements of community stability—housing, health care, transportation, education, and jobs—must be united to solve the problems of community development and poverty. To date, although there is nascent recognition at the federal level that such linkages are needed, the governmental infrastructure to facilitate such partnerships and collaborations across the urban and rural landscape has not been created.

Promote Public-Private-Nonprofit Partnerships. Part of the problem in getting to scale is that most organizations are not big enough or do not have expertise in enough areas to undertake the necessary level of effort to attack the magnitude of the problems we are facing. However, by working together, organizations with different competencies can undertake much larger efforts than they could alone. This allows them to have the flexibility to move quickly rather than wait to hire or train staff in order to develop additional expertise.

Develop Comprehensive Impact Measurement. The housing and community development sector is late to the party in measuring the impact of what we do. Investors are looking for social, economic, and environmental impacts. The public wants to know that its tax dollars are well spent. Resources must be invested in systems that measure the outcomes of the work that is done. Such systems will also make it easier to develop programs on the basis of outcomes rather than on compliance with the rules.

HOW IT CAN WORK: A CURRENT EXAMPLE

When the elements above are combined, a new model emerges to move to scale and address today's acute problems. One such example is the Mortgage Resolution Fund (MRF), a public-private partnership established to preserve affordable homeownership by keeping in their homes those families at risk of foreclosure. MRF purchases nonperforming mortgages from banks and loan servicers at a discount, modifies the mortgages to align with the properties' current market values and the families' abilities to pay, provides intensive educational and debt management support, and eventually recapitalizes the mortgages. MRF is a joint venture of the Enterprise Foundation, the Housing Partnership Network, the National Community Stabilization Trust, and Mercy Housing.

MRF is funded at the enterprise level by the Hardest Hit Funds program, which was established in 2010 to provide targeted aid to families in states hit hard by the economic and housing market downturn. Funds were distributed to 19 state housing agencies on the basis of high unemployment rates or steep home price declines. Each state determines how to use the money it receives, for example, for mortgage payment assistance, principal reduction, elimination of second lien loans, or assistance for those moving to more affordable places to live. Allowing states to determine how best to implement their goals permits flexibility and innovation.

In addition to the partnership among its four members, MRF has leveraged private-sector capacity. It has service agreements with several private firms for mortgage due diligence and valuation, which enable it to negotiate with global capital market desks that specialize in nonperforming mortgages. MRF also works with a large special servicer with a responsibility to work in conjunction with local housing counselors, as well as a debt manager that services the loans and supports mortgage reperformance. These partnerships have permitted MRF to get to scale quickly.

Although it is still in its early stages (its first fund closed in November 2011 and the first pool of mortgages was purchased in March 2012), MRF is an example of how four national nonprofit organizations can join forces to form an innovative new venture that will have an impact on a major national housing problem at a scale large enough to be meaningful. At the same time, MRF has enabled each of its component organizations to diversify into new territory. If it is successful, MRF will provide income to these organizations, which will increase their sustainability.

MOVING FORWARD

The future of community development depends on developing new responses to the current problems of poverty, income inequality, and lack of affordable housing. In an era of deficits and government cutbacks, organizations must get to scale to become sustainable.

All sectors of the housing industry will have to step up in several ways. The public sector must become more flexible in its regulations and provide funding at the enterprise level on the basis of outcomes rather than just compliance. Private financial institutions will have to provide funds at lower costs (particularly equity) and be willing to tolerate greater risk. Intermediaries and foundations must seek out creative and nontraditional solutions and then fund them. Developer organizations must create partnerships that will enhance their strengths, and then these organizations must be accountable for the outcomes. The challenge is for everyone to think outside of the box.

SISTER LILLIAN MURPHY *has been chief executive officer of Mercy Housing since 1987. Under her leadership, Mercy Housing has grown to become an award-winning national not-for-profit housing organization operating in 41 states and the District of Columbia and serving over 139,000 people in more than 41,000 units of quality affordable homes. She holds a master's in public health from the University of California, Berkeley and an undergraduate degree in social science from the University of San Francisco.*

JANET FALK *was vice president for real estate development for Mercy Housing California until she retired in 2011. She has extensive experience in the development and financing of nonprofit housing after nearly 40 years in the field. She is particularly knowledgeable in using the Low Income Housing Tax Credit and tax-exempt bonds for nonprofit projects. She holds a master's in city and regional planning from University of California, Berkeley and an undergraduate degree in political science from Stanford University.*

WHAT PROBLEM ARE WE TRYING TO SOLVE?

Mark A. Pinsky
Opportunity Finance Network

hat is the problem that community development was created to solve? What is the problem it is solving today? And will it be able to solve the problems of tomorrow?

I think I know the answer to the first question. Community development emerged as a product of the War on Poverty to give disadvantaged people, neighborhoods, and communities a chance to lift themselves up by their bootstraps. It put resources directly in their control and circumvented the historical reliance on local and state governments. Even now, it is easy to understand how important this was in the Deep South in the 1960s. The creation of community action programs, community action agencies, and community development corporations in the same era introduced a new type of public-private partnership embedded in locally controlled private and quasi-public institutions caring for communities.

These innovations spurred a movement that worked better than its proponents dreamed possible and served more purposes than its original supporters envisioned. Federal spending, often in partnership with states, municipalities, public foundations, and—much later—banks, leveraged the unique market knowledge and community dedication of local corporations—almost all nonprofits—to create jobs, build affordable housing, and provide vital community services.

But I don't think anyone knows the answer to the second question—or perhaps, everyone knows *an* answer, and everyone's answer is different.

Community development long ago became an ever-expanding big tent that morphed almost magically as if out of Harry Potter, to cover everyone making a claim to the name. Today, as an unfortunate result, that tent is occupied not only by people and organizations committed to serving underserved communities but also by those interested primarily in profiting from those same communities. Community development today is no longer focused solely on benefitting low-income and low-wealth people.

It seems easy to see that predatory mortgage and payday lenders do not belong in that tent, but people such as Angelo Mozilo, the one-time king of the predatory lending hill while running Countrywide Mortgage company, seem to see it another way. Mozilo claimed his intent was to help disadvantaged people gain access to the American Dream of owning a home. He was investing for a particular kind of impact.

If Mozilo seems an outlier, ask yourself if you can differentiate the values intrinsic to three different community-improving investment strategies: program-related investments, mission-related investments, and impact investments. They all serve important but different purposes. Most important to me is the various extents to which each benefits low-income, low-wealth, and other disadvantaged people and places. That is what community development does. Or did.

Our best intentions and our willingness to be inclusive have produced a community development "brand" that is unmoored from its history, practice, and purpose. Community development is sliding down a slippery slope because of our unwillingness to delineate clearly the differences among strategies and, perhaps more important, the markets that those strategies target. The ride is exhilarating but sooner rather than later we will hit bottom and have to pick up the pieces. As a result, the answer to the third question—Will community development be able to solve the problems of tomorrow?—rests heavily on our ability to move quickly from amorphous ideas of community development to something more concrete, and to which we hold ourselves, our investors, and our partners more accountable.

We need to step past the community development paradigm, for all its successes and struggles, and into an approach that better suits what we have learned, what we have accomplished, and where we are going. One way to think of this needed change is for the community development industry to better understand and market its "brand." Brand is more than just selling consumer products; it defines who we are as an industry, organizes and aligns the efforts of multiple players in a disciplined way, and effectively communicates with a larger world. At its best, your brand connects you to the right people in the right way and makes you more efficient and effective, which is the critical challenge in a time of scarce resources.

WHAT DOES IT MEAN TO BUILD A BRAND?

If we intend to transform our movement to meet the challenges before us, we need to double down on the core purpose and core values that spurred community development in the first place. That requires that we differentiate clearly what must never change—what is core—and what *must* change to ensure that our efforts are relevant and influential in the future.

Few things seem more important to me now. We must do this work first. It is the only way to answer, in more than a self-serving way, the third question: Will we be able to solve the problems of tomorrow? The last 20 years have revealed challenges and tantalizing opportunities that demand innovative responses. The last years have demonstrated convincingly that our nation needs a disruptive break in our financial, economic, and fiscal habits if we are going to better serve low-income, low-wealth, and other disadvantaged people and places. For people and institutions dedicated to that end, we need to think less about "community development" and more about what comes after community development.[1] I would suggest that what comes after community development—that is, what emerges to connect low-income, low-wealth communities to economic and social opportunities—will be shaped substantially by four factors, which also point to a promising role for community development finance institutions (CDFIs):

- Distressed markets have grown substantially (and unfortunately), and these markets will not shrink as rapidly as they expanded.

- CDFIs bring unique expertise and experience in serving distressed markets that translates into value for policymakers, banks, and nonbank corporations.

- Mainstream private and government leaders are beginning to recognize that high-performing CDFIs offer good, perhaps the best, options for extending economic growth and opportunity to distressed markets.

- CDFIs, in particular, are reaping benefits from a 25-year commitment to disciplined practice, innovation, pragmatic idealism, and patience and as such are well-positioned to help

---

1 The emerging meme among impact investing leaders is that impact investing will supplant and replace community development finance. Impact investing has the potential to play an important role, but that role will have little to do with benefitting low-income, low-wealth, and other disadvantaged people and places. Mission-related investing followed a similar arc over the past decade or so; it is important but its value to the target markets that CDFIs serve is structurally limited.

lead an economic resurgence in a growing number of markets and communities.

That final factor also should increase the field's collective ability to advance the purposes that underlay community development from its birth: opportunity for all and better alignment of capital (and capitalism) with justice.

Brand reflects underlying assumptions and values. It tells other people who you are, what you believe in, and what you stand for. Done well, it captures and conveys what is at your core. It also amplifies how to act on your core—in these four instances, through proven efficacy; market relevance; a clear value proposition; and mature practices, policies, and systems. These are the founding principles of what comes after community development.

OUTWARD-IN THINKING

In 2003, Nic Retsinas, who then served on the Opportunity Finance Network board of directors, observed that working in community development finance was like working in a hall of mirrors. What we needed to do was learn to work in a hall of windows—to look outward to understand what others see when they look in at us.

One result of that observation was that Opportunity Finance Network commissioned a market study of how others, the majority of Americans, viewed community development and CDFIs. The results shocked and saddened me; to paraphrase the immemorial words of Pogo, "We had met the enemy and they is us."

Our market research found again and again that the prevailing and consistent view of "community development" was, and no doubt still is, that it is government-driven, broken, ineffective, and often corrupt.

Still, we resisted fully accepting this perception until a final market research study put a price tag on our stubborn adherence to the community development brand. Working with a group of financial market executives and high-net-worth investors, we learned two seemingly conflicting things.

First, as a group they liked and would consider investing in what we do: financing quality affordable housing, supporting small businesses, backing community facilities and services, creating jobs. When we asked them what financial yield they would expect on their theoretical investments, they offered rates that generally grouped at the high end of market-rate fixed-income yields. We were stunned. We did not expect to hear that we were market-rate investment grade.

Second, when we later reminded them what we do, using the list from the previous paragraph but slipping in the words "and community development," pretty much every person said they would not invest. Why not? Community development, they believed, is ineffective and often corrupt. They might donate a little money but they would *not* invest.

We pushed them to name a price at which they would invest. With reluctance, they named yields that were about 600 basis points higher than what they had said they expected earlier. I consider 600 basis points the "community development premium."

The bad brand caused problems in the policy realm, as well. When President George W. Bush proposed in 2005 to consolidate a wide swath of federal antipoverty and community development programs into a single block grant program, I thought it was popcorn policy—a kernel of truth surrounded by a lot of hot air. While the community development movement defeated that effort, we missed the opportunity to embrace the brutally honest, and long overdue conversation about that kernel of truth: Not all programs work well and not all merit ongoing federal, state, socially responsible, and philanthropic support. The truth is that community development, like so many other things, is imperfect. Some is effective, but some is not. Some is a wise use of limited resources, some is not. Some approaches worked well once but no longer do.

BUILDING A BETTER BRAND

Opportunity Finance Network embraced "opportunity" in its name and brand in part because our research told us that people liked that we finance opportunities. Many of the several thousand career community development professionals in and around our membership were upset by the proposed change, though most now understand why it was necessary.

A brand that is associated with opportunity has a value that can be monetized, leveraged, and grown. It can make an organization (or an industry) more attractive to partners, investors, funders, and policymakers. The corollary, of course, is that brand value can decline, taking resources and opportunities with it.

Since last summer, Opportunity Finance Network has partnered with Starbucks on the "Create Jobs for USA" movement.[2] This experience has taught me many things, but I am struck most by the extent to which the senior management at Starbucks focuses at every moment on brand—brand for Create Jobs, brand for Opportunity Finance Network, and brand for Starbucks. It is a very precise metric against which they size up decisions. For Starbucks, the metric is "coffee": does a decision lead to a better coffee experience for its customers? For Create Jobs, the metric is "jobs": will a decision help create or retain jobs?

Before Create Jobs for USA, I would have said that the defining CDFI brand characteristic was "opportunity." It seemed to capture the essence of what CDFIs offer. Create Jobs for USA has changed my mind. I now think that the CDFI brand is something much more powerful and important—"solutions."

Community development is an intervention strategy, a set of programs, a movement, a dynamic list of outcomes, a career, and more. We need to get specific, and particular, about which elements are core. From that, we can begin to drive a strategy and a brand that is built for enduring success at providing

---

2 For more information see www.createjobsforusa.org.

solutions for low-income, low-wealth, and other disadvantaged people and places.

I would suggest four key attributes of the CDFI brand:

1 We build and operate organizations and approaches that are profitable but not profit-maximizing. Although there are many important things that are not profitable (public goods), these are not what CDFIs can provide—government and philanthropy must take the lead role.

2 We operate as private-sector enterprises and not as byproducts or extensions of government programs or foundations; we retain the ability to make independent choices and to put mission before self-interest.

3 We measure success by both financial results and impact—quality jobs, quality affordable housing, quality facilities and services—that produce opportunities for low-income, low-wealth, and other disadvantaged individuals, communities, and investors. We must sustain ourselves *and* our beneficiaries now and in the future.

4 We hold ourselves accountable to our customers and our funders, our beneficiaries and our investors, and our communities and our nation. Our success or failure is collective, as each of our institutions alone lacks the resources and scale to provide relevant solutions proportional to the challenges our nation faces.

Put another way: Our solutions must be authentic, sound, sustainable, and scalable.

These attributes may be enough to build a movement brand that both maintains discipline internally and inspires confidence to a larger audience. When the rubber meets the road, brand is not just what you want to believe about yourself. It is what you do and how you do it. If your actions, services, products, and decisions are not true in an obvious way to your idea about your organization, your brand is inauthentic and worth very little.

When you fall back on an inauthentic brand in a tough moment, it does not support the weight of your good intentions.

OUR FUTURE

Will our work be relevant to the problems of tomorrow—the challenges that low-income, low-wealth, and other disadvantaged people and communities will face?

I spoke recently at a graduate school to an audience of students passionate about community development. One young woman spoke of her frustration as an intern in the federal government, witnessing the passion for cutting discretionary government spending and the lack of passion for community development. When, she asked, can we turn the debate on its head to focus on the good things that community development does?

I stumbled to reassure her by explaining the progress I believe CDFIs are making: the increasing number of federal agencies reaching out to CDFIs, steady funding for 2012 for the U.S. Treasury's CDFI Fund, the potential of the Small Business Administration's Community Advantage program, and more. But I could not leave my answer there. I wanted to be honest about my hope that she and her peers will lead us beyond community development. "As long as we are talking about 'community development,'" I told her, "we are going to lose."

MARK PINSKY *is president and CEO of Opportunity Finance Network (opportunityfinance.net), the leading U.S. CDFI network, where he is responsible for vision and strategy. He chairs the boards of the CDFI Assessment and Ratings Service (CARS, available at CDFIratingsystem.org) and Net Impact (netimpact.org) and sits on multiple other advisory and governing boards.*

TRANSIT-ORIENTED DEVELOPMENT IS GOOD COMMUNITY DEVELOPMENT

John Robert Smith and Allison Brooks
Reconnecting America

The steady dispersion of people and jobs across core cities, suburbs, and exurbs has contributed to more fragmented lifestyles, with people often living in one neighborhood, working in another, and shopping and recreating in another. There are myriad reasons for this fragmentation of land use. They include the initial drivers of suburbanization, such as the GI Bill, which made mortgages cheaper in the suburbs (at least for those who weren't redlined out), the separation of land uses in response to contamination by industry in the mid-20th century, the expansion of the highway system and the attendant white flight to the suburbs, and the relative ease of building on greenfields versus more complicated infill development in existing urbanized areas. Today, the quality of people's lives is increasingly influenced by the time and resources it takes to get where they need to go throughout the day and their ability to access the jobs, educational opportunities, and other life essentials that are located throughout the region where they live and interact.

This reality is particularly true for people living on the economic margins, many of whom are finding access to gainful employment literally out of reach. Well-paying jobs that were once available for employees with a high school diploma or less are much harder to come by. Furthermore, a growing spatial mismatch has occurred between where people live and where jobs of any skill level are located. When one-half or fewer of the jobs in a region are located near transit, workers who cannot afford a car are further challenged in accessing economic opportunity. As many of the contributing authors of this book have expressed, it has become clear that neighborhood- or county-based approaches to poverty alleviation have not effectively addressed the systemic challenges poor people face when trying to improve their quality of life.

We are necessarily entering a new era of community development that embraces the role of transportation and mobility options in connecting people to opportunity, as well as the role of policy at the local, regional, state, and federal levels in supporting comprehensive approaches that address the problematic underpinnings of the new and dispersed landscape of poverty and opportunity. Taking into account the major demographic shifts underway across the country—the aging baby boom population, which will begin to experience limited mobility; the rise in single-person households; a 23 percent drop in miles driven for the 16- to 34-year-old age group in the last decade; and the fact that the majority of youth in America are children of color—the community development field must in turn undergo its own shifts, refocusing efforts to recognize that our cities and regions must accommodate the changing needs of all Americans.[1]

---

1 U.S. Public Interest Research Group Education Fund and the Frontier Group, "Transportation and the New Generation: Why Young People are Driving Less and What it Means for Transportation Policy," April 5, 2012, available at http://www.uspirg.org/reports/ usp/transportation-and-new-generation.

Location matters when considering successful community and economic development strategies in both a local and a regional context. The term "transit-oriented development" (TOD) is most often used to describe this integration of transportation and land use and the improved social, economic, health, and environmental outcomes that can result by locating housing, jobs, and other activities near quality transit. We think TOD is just good community development.

INFLUENCING REGIONAL ACTION

There is little dispute that growth patterns in American communities during the past 60 years have not served the poor well. As Alan Berube discusses in this volume, sprawl and the growing inequality between the haves and have-nots have led to more intense concentrations of poverty among the very poor, with poverty becoming more "equal opportunity" through growth in suburban and rural communities. Many of the low- and moderate-income individuals and families who have moved to the suburbs in search of home ownership opportunities and improved amenities are now spending more of their limited income on transportation—a much more volatile expense—than they are on housing.[2] In many cases, people are finding themselves living in isolated conditions, dependent on their car, family members, or infrequent public transportation to access services and meet daily needs.

The fragmentation of the core elements of our day-to-day lives requires people to make lifestyle choices on the basis of what are now competing factors, including housing, quality education, and employment. Increasingly, individuals and families are finding they must choose one over the others because many of our communities no longer have that combination of elements that make them "complete," including affordable housing, good schools, safe streets, low crime, parks and recreation, quality transportation, amenities and services, and jobs for people of

---

2 American Public Transportation Association, Public Transportation Protects Americans from Gas Price Volatility (Washington, DC: APTA Policy Development and Research Department, May 2012).

different skill levels. Of course, it's always been difficult to ensure that complete communities are accessible to people of all incomes, but the trends in zoning, disinvestment, economic polarization, and an auto-oriented culture have made successful community development a truly uphill battle. The result is that for the transit-dependent, largely made up of the poor, the elderly, and the disabled, just getting to their jobs, doctor's appointments, or the grocery store can be exhausting.

Turning the tide on the growth of poverty and rising inequalities will require interdisciplinary approaches to community and economic development that better connect people and places, and in the process make their lives easier and more affordable, reduce congestion, improve air quality, and make our regions more economically competitive, socially equitable, and environmentally sustainable. To accomplish this requires the diverse parties involved in community development to understand the connection of local conditions and needs to regional actions and investment. Although the community development field has often defined success as the ability to pool capital and build an affordable housing development or an on-site day care center, this new paradigm requires that every place-based effort or project be tied to a broader regional framework that understands where people need to go and how they get there. This approach requires working with local and regional stakeholders involved in transportation and land use planning, economic development, health, and other disciplines.

CHANGING THE RULES OF THE GAME

The old rules of the game did not encourage interdisciplinary approaches among practitioners of community and economic development, transportation, workforce development, education, and health and business, among others. When Shaun Donovan, Secretary of the U.S. Department of Housing and Urban Development (HUD), stated he was going to "put the UD back in HUD," he was referring to the separation of housing departments and housing developers from broader urban planning activities. The housing community has been focused on generating the much-needed resources and entitlements to build housing projects, but it has disengaged as a result from broader strategies that could comprehensively improve the livelihoods of their constituents, which includes affordable living, not just affordable housing. Not only have the existing rules of the game served to partition disciplines and the financial tools to alleviate poverty, but they have also served to distort and thwart people's perspectives on what is possible.

Successful TOD by its very nature requires active collaboration among elected officials, transit planners, housing department professionals, private developers, philanthropic leaders, community development financial institutions, and community advocates, to name a few. TOD is operationalized at all levels, including through federal and state policy, through regional guidance and incentives, and through local station-area planning and project delivery. Community development professionals can reach better outcomes when they understand the role of each stakeholder and their varying emphasis on policy and investments at these different scales. The game only changes when we align and coordinate processes that operate on different timelines and scales, such as transportation planning (long-term and regional scale) and housing development (short-term and project scale).

This is especially true in the transportation arena, not traditionally a focus area of community development activities. A strong case can be made that shoring up our existing transit systems with supportive infrastructure and dependable operating budgets can positively affect the quality of life for the poor and the transit-dependent, the most vulnerable to changes in transit service. Supportive TOD that includes affordable housing and a mix of services and amenities, and links up to important destinations can be a linchpin in helping the working poor improve their quality of life. New transit corridors and existing transit services need to be provided where equitable outcomes associated with TOD can best be realized. With that in mind, community development practitioners can play a critical role in influencing decision-making at the front end to better serve the transit-dependent, the transit user by choice, and people of low- and moderate-incomes. This could include influencing the location decisions of major employers, facilities investments by school districts and hospitals, and strategic for-profit and nonprofit housing development. Ideally, these types of resources would be located in transit-rich locations or along future transit corridors to address the regional spatial mismatch discussed above.

BUILDING FROM STRENGTH

In an era of constrained resources, communities stand a better chance of serving their residents over the long term by playing to community strengths. Critical leaders such as mayors are increasingly realizing that they can no longer support the infrastructure costs of further far-flung fringe development and instead are reinforcing use of existing infrastructure (water, sewage, utilities) wherever possible. Community leaders are considering investments in transportation and TOD to bring new energy and vitality to their downtown and surrounding neighborhoods by leveraging market forces. Using data analysis and mapping to show how a city and its neighborhoods relate and connect to the larger regional economy allows community stakeholders to develop realistic and feasible strategies that build from strength and promote economic resiliency. Asking questions is part of getting to the appropriate solutions: Is our community well positioned to attract new jobs, and is there a way for people to get to them? Are our residents susceptible to displacement once a new transit line comes in? As a bedroom community, what can we do to accommodate more walking and biking? Where should that new grocery store really go to maximize fresh food access for our residents? This analysis and strategy development can also foster education, collaboration, and capacity building—the types of activities that community development leaders can support in addition to capital formation and project delivery.

Some stakeholders may characterize a strategy of focusing and prioritizing investments as choosing winners and losers, but the more politically palatable "spreading the peanut butter" approach most often results in short-term bandages and little longer term, systemic improvements to poverty. Economically, communities that focus on their strengths also can achieve that hard-to-find critical mass of new investment that spurs revitalization. The truth is that every city and community needs to start somewhere, and in a risk-averse economic climate, a strong case can be made to focus initially on neighborhoods that already have good infrastructure in place to support the development of complete communities, ultimately resulting in increased investment in neighborhoods throughout a city.

Reconnecting America calls places that already have much of the foundation in place to build complete communities "opportunity areas." Walkable blocks, compact development, and a mix of land uses are important building blocks in the foundation of a complete community. Opportunity areas can be found in the hearts of cities, suburbs, and small towns, and occasionally in outlying centers of economic activity. Reinvesting in opportunity areas is a great community development strategy because it is much more challenging to add the bones of a walkable community to a more auto-oriented neighborhood, although that too is a strategy community development professionals must embrace. In our research, Reconnecting America has identified opportunity areas in just about every one of the 366 Metropolitan Statistical Areas in the United States. This means that just about every metropolitan region has a place to start.

Decades of transportation research have shown that places we have identified as opportunity areas are more likely to support walking, bicycling, and transit use than other, more conventional suburban neighborhoods. Although the elements that make these vibrant places—major employers, retail, services, and entertainment choices—may have declined or disappeared over the years owing to disinvestment or the siren call of cheap "big-box" stores at the fringe, these places offer the potential for regeneration because the bones of a walkable, mixed-use community remain. Such regeneration is particularly feasible if their connection to the regional economy is strengthened through good transit.

CONCLUSION

Despite the polarized politics that have stymied progressive action in our nation's capital, unprecedented innovation and collaboration are underway in regions across the country that support TOD, transit investment, and development patterns that better serve the poor, the environment, and the economy over the long term. Given the economic downtown and housing crises, changes underway in entire industries and employment sectors, the elimination of redevelopment agencies in California and potentially other states, and the demographic shifts transforming our communities, it is clearly time to step out of our comfort zones and standard ways of doing business, whether a housing developer, a transit planner, or a community advocate. In this new era of community development, we need to forge partnerships with unlikely allies, build collaborations that will stand the test of time and the vagaries of the political environment. In this new era we have the opportunity to redefine and build communities that are well supported by quality transportation systems and that will serve the life needs of today's grandparents and tomorrow's grandchildren.

JOHN ROBERT SMITH *is the president and CEO of Reconnecting America. Reconnecting America is a national nonprofit organization that helps transform promising ideas into thriving communities, where transportation choices make it easy to get from place to place, where businesses flourish and where people from all walks of life can afford to live, work and visit. Reconnecting America not only conducts research and public policy, but also builds on-the-ground partnerships and convenes the players necessary to accelerate decision-making. He is the former Mayor of Meridian, Mississippi, and a long-time leader on behalf of passenger rail. He is co-chairman of Transportation for America, a former Chairman of Amtrak's board, and a former member of the transportation committees of the National League of Cities and the U.S. Conference of Mayors, as well as former co-chairman of the National Forum on the Future of Passenger Rail. He is a veteran of the station-centered community development movement, and led the drive to renovate the City of Meridian's Union Station, a $7 million historic restoration project that created a new multimodal transportation center, dramatically increased use of the station, raised property values and* *city tax receipts, and lowered crime in the station's neighborhood. He served on Reconnecting America's board for five years, and was a founding partner and board member of Reconnecting America's predecessor organization, the Great American Station Foundation.*

ALLISON BROOKS *is chief of staff at Reconnecting America where she helps guide the strategic direction of the organization, overseeing RA's programs and partnerships across the United States. In her role, Allison leads national and regional efforts on a range of issues including fostering multi-sector collaborative partnerships across the fields of transportation, housing, and community and economic development to support more equitable and sustainable outcomes. Prior to joining RA, Allison served for over six years as a program officer for the Livable Communities Program at the East Bay Community Foundation where she spearheaded a number of innovative transit-oriented and community development initiatives in the San Francisco Bay Area. She was one of the founders of a collaboration of nonprofits and community foundations called the Great Communities Collaborative—geared towards influencing regional planning and investment in transit-oriented development across the 9-county Bay Area. Allison holds a BA in Political Science from the University of California, San Diego and a master's in sustainable international development from the Heller School for Social Policy and Management at Brandeis University.*

HOUSEHOLD AND COMMUNITY FINANCIAL STABILITY:
Essential and Interconnected

Jennifer Tescher
Center for Financial Services Innovation

F inancial services are the plumbing of our financial lives. They are the critical infrastructure that enable and support financial stability. Consumer finance practitioners often speak of the "pipes" or "rails" that move money, extend credit, and keep savings and investments safe. Just as communities struggle without access to credit for homeowners and small businesses, consumers struggle to save and build assets without institutional mechanisms.[1]

---

1 For a discussion about the constructs thought to be important aspects of institutions designed to promote saving and asset accumulation, see Michael S. Barr and Michael W. Sherraden, "Institutions and Inclusion in Saving Policy." In Building Assets, Building Wealth; Creating Wealth In Low-Income Communities, edited by N. Retsinas and E. Belsky (Washington, DC: Brookings Institution Press, 2005).

An estimated 30 million American households—one out of every four—lack this plumbing.[2] They lack access to the kinds of high-quality financial products and services that enable them to save, build assets, and achieve financial prosperity. Roughly one-third of these households are unbanked, meaning they have no checking or savings account with a bank or credit union. The remaining two-thirds are underbanked. They may have an account, but they are not using it to its fullest, and instead rely on a broad array of money-service businesses to meet their short-term needs.

Further, an estimated 42 percent of financially underserved households also face challenges in accessing traditional forms of credit because they have insufficient credit history.[3] Access to credit overall has become more limited since the Great Recession. As of 2010, an estimated 52 percent of the U.S. population had a FICO score below 600, representing a shift of 16 million people from "average" to damaged credit in just four years.[4]

Although unbanked and underbanked consumers are a large group representing a variety of behavioral and attitudinal segments, they are more likely to have lower incomes, be ethnic minorities, and have less education.[5] Yet this is not just a problem of the poor. The financial crisis and resulting foreclosure, unemployment, and financial deleveraging have exacerbated financial dislocation, affecting a wide range of households whose incomes masked weak balance sheets.[6] For instance, a recent study showed that nearly one-half of the households surveyed

---

2 Federal Deposit Insurance Corporation, "National Survey of Unbanked and Underbanked Households" (Washington, DC: FDIC, December 2009).

3 Center for Financial Services Innovation, "CFSI Underbanked Consumer Study" (Chicago: CFSI, June 2008).

4 KPMG, "Serving the Underserved Market" (New York: KPMG, 2011).

5 FDIC, "National Survey."

6 My thinking has been heavily influenced by the Household Financial Stability Project, a new effort led by Ray Boshara, senior advisor at the Federal Reserve Bank of St. Louis, to better understand and improve household balance sheets.

could not come up with $2,000 in 30 days, including 25 percent of the households earning $100,000 to $150,000 a year.[7]

Although financial exclusion and the resulting financial fragility appear to be an increasingly broad-based problem, it is a plight that continues to fall most heavily on lower-income and minority families with children. They are more at risk financially because they disproportionally lack steady income, savings and assets, and financial capability. Moreover, they are more likely to live in communities that offer less access to high-quality financial products and providers.

Participating in the financial mainstream and having the information and tools to manage money effectively in the short-term is a prerequisite for longer term saving and asset-building. Financially healthy households in turn yield healthy communities and vibrant economies. Consumers who rely primarily on cash spend extra time and money conducting basic financial transactions, creating friction and inefficiencies. Without appropriate incentives to encourage savings and a safe place to store funds, consumers lack a financial cushion to weather crises. Lack of access to formal financial networks also makes it more difficult to build a strong credit history, increasing the cost of credit and, for some, putting it out of reach entirely.

Despite the importance of financial services to household and community stability, basic financial products are often designed, marketed, and delivered in ways that fail to meet the needs, interests, and abilities of average consumers. They have requirements and minimums that are out of reach for those with lower incomes. They lack transparent pricing and terms and are increasingly complicated to use and understand. They often fail to provide consumers living paycheck to paycheck with immediate and convenient access to their money. They are marketed with poorly tailored messages and sold in locations that are intimidating, with operating hours that are inconvenient for

---

7 Annamaria Lusardi, Daniel Schneider, and Peter Tufano, "Financially Fragile Households: Evidence and Implications." Working paper no. 17072 (Cambridge, MA: National Bureau of Economic Research, May 2011).

many working families. They are underwritten with tools that cannot properly evaluate consumers with thin or nonexistent credit histories. Small mistakes can have enormous consequences, with consumers being shut out the system completely.

FINANCIAL SERVICES AS A COMMUNITY DEVELOPMENT IMPERATIVE

The emergence of the individual development account (IDA) is often credited as the moment when the community development field widened its focus beyond "place" to "people" by demonstrating the importance of individual assets in alleviating poverty. IDAs also had a different, unintended consequence: They demonstrated the importance of financial services in the asset-building equation. Research by Michael Sherraden, the grandfather of the IDA movement, showed the importance of formal financial mechanisms in facilitating savings. Simultaneously, grassroots efforts showed just how difficult it could be for some consumers to qualify for, open, and manage a basic bank account. Local nonprofit organizations had experience working with local banks on mortgage and small business lending; IDAs led them to the other side of the bank's balance sheet. The hundreds of grassroots organizations around the country that went on to launch IDA programs found themselves negotiating with local banks over the structure and price of bank accounts and learning about the systems and processes banks use to open and manage those accounts. Through financial education and one-on-one counseling with clients, they also learned just how financially fragile many were.

As IDAs were gaining in popularity in the mid-1990s, the federal government stumbled on the problem of the unbanked when it sought to deliver all federal benefits through direct deposit, only to discover that millions of benefit recipients had no account. To develop a strategy for dealing with this problem, the U.S. Treasury Department commissioned research that led to a better understanding of why people did not have bank accounts. Despite this increased recognition of the unbanked, the

Treasury's ultimate solution, the Electronic Transfer Account, did little to move significant numbers of benefit recipients to direct deposit. But because of the importance of basic bank accounts to the IDA model, a broader constituency became interested in the problem.

At the same time, the nonbank financial services sector was growing rapidly. For example, the number of payday lending stores grew from a few hundred outlets in the mid-1990s to more than 10,000 by 2000. The number of pawnshops increased from about 4,800 in 1986 to more than 11,600 in 2003.[8] Check-cashing outlets proliferated. This shadow banking system demonstrated that lower-income consumers had pent-up demand for financial services, and that they had money to spend. Unfortunately, it also became clear that predatory providers were stripping wealth from consumers and communities.

The 2000 and 2010 U.S. Census showed significant growth in the size of the Latino population, helping banks and credit unions recognize unbanked consumers as an untapped opportunity. The Latino population has more than doubled since 1990 and now totals 50.5 million, or 16 percent of the U.S. population, and as many as 43 percent are financially underserved.[9] These changes, coupled with the fact that nonbank providers were serving the market profitably, caused banks to focus more attention and resources on Latinos and other minority communities. A few banks and credit unions sought to leverage the growing distribution channel offered by alternative players by buying nonbank companies, partnering with them, or adding alternative products to their traditional product lines. Numerous banks began accepting government identification from Mexico and other Latin American countries in order to authenticate new customers, while the largest banks rolled out new remittance products. Underlying all these trends was the technology boom, which continues unabated today.

---

8   Annie E. Casey Foundation, "Double Jeopardy: AdvoCacey Explores The High Cost of Being Poor" (Baltimore, MD: AECF, 2005).

9   FDIC, "National Survey."

THE TECHNOLOGY REVOLUTION: OPPORTUNITIES AND ISSUES

It is difficult to overstate the changes and opportunities wrought by the technology revolution in financial services of the last 15 years. Technology-led innovation has yielded new products, marketing methods, underwriting mechanisms, and communication tools. The expansion of automated teller machines, the introduction of debit cards and point-of-sale terminals, and the emergence of online banking all offer new access points and reduced delivery costs that hold promise for reaching lower-income consumers. Technology can eliminate the barriers of time and distance, enabling people to move their money anytime, anywhere.

As the pace of development in financial technology has increased, so too has access to technology among the underserved. In 2000, a Pew Research Center survey found that 30 percent of adults with annual household incomes under $30,000 reported going online to access the internet or send email. By 2012, this number had more than doubled.[10] But the real story is the penetration of mobile phones, and in particular smartphones, which are becoming the device of choice for online access for the underserved and people of color. Today, nearly 90 percent of Americans own a mobile phone; 78 percent of financially underserved consumers have one. In 2012, smartphone users outnumbered users of more basic mobile phones. As a part of the overall trend, 38 percent of the underserved now own smartphones, compared to nearly 45 percent for Americans as a whole. Among African Americans and Hispanics, smartphone ownership rates are slightly higher than for the general population.[11]

---

10 Pew Internet and American Life Project, "Tracking Survey," available at http://pewinternet.org/Shared-Content/Data-Sets/2000/March-2000-Survey-Data.aspx (March 2000). Also see, Pew Internet and American Life Project, "Demographics of Internet Users," available at http://pewinternet.org/Static-Pages/Trend-Data/Whos-Online.aspx.

11 Board of Governors of the Federal Reserve System, "Consumers and Mobile Financial Services" (Washington, DC: Board of Governors of the Federal Reserve System, March 2012).

Financial services providers are capitalizing on the trend, with traditional depositories and their nonbank competitors introducing a bevy of mobile banking interfaces and payment platforms that can be accessed on all types of phones. While mobile financial services are designed to appeal to consumers across the income spectrum, the channel has considerable potential to provide services to underserved and lower-income consumers to encourage saving, debt reduction, and improved financial decision-making.

Technology also has expanded the playing field beyond banks and credit unions. Retailers, technology companies, and others have entered the market with new and innovative business models aimed at the underbanked market, thus increasing competition. Companies once considered financial services vendors, providing products for banks to use, are now marketing their products directly to consumers or using other nonbank firms, such as retailers or employers, to market them. More nonprofit organizations are exploring links between the services they provide and the financial health and capability of their clients, and some are beginning to form product marketing and distribution partnerships with financial providers. In addition, a new category of technology "enablers" has emerged, providing enhanced platforms for reaching consumers and moving funds. Companies like Google, PayPal, and Facebook are moving into financial services, largely as payment facilitators, but with the potential for far broader roles. There is also tremendous energy among financial technology entrepreneurs to combine mobile technology and social media to tap into the "power of the crowd" to provide peer support and incentives and make money management fun.

Banks are adopting many of these same technologies, but their ability and willingness to reach and serve financially underserved consumers, at least directly, remains in question. Although the technology by itself can reduce transaction costs, banks are piling that technology onto legacy systems and branch networks that are expensive and inefficient, resulting in costs-to-serve that far exceed the likely revenue they can generate in the short term from lower-income customers. Moreover, underserved consumers are not well understood by most banks and are often assumed to be "subprime," which has become a dirty word in the wake of the mortgage meltdown.

The emergence of new providers and distribution channels does not mean that banks and credit unions are no longer important partners. At a minimum, their "plumbing" is critical. One positive scenario would be for more banks to manufacture products for underserved consumers that can be distributed by other businesses and organizations, serving as the "back end" and letting someone else be the front door.

The question is what role banks should play in these relationships. Technology is shifting financial services from an institution-centric model to a customer-centric model. Do consumers need a financial "hub" to knit together the various products and services into a coherent quilt? Banks have always been the intermediary, and they still will be for many consumers. Today, however, many others are vying for the role. Understanding what models work best for linking basic transactions with high-quality saving and borrowing opportunities will be critical to effectively answering this question.

THE SEARCH FOR QUALITY

The most important question may not be *who* is best positioned to serve the underserved, but *what* products are they selling, and are they any good? The financial crisis was a crisis of quality. While some categories of providers behaved better than others, financial services providers of all kinds behaved badly. They sold harmful products in deceptive ways to unqualified borrowers, in many cases pushing households and communities off a financial cliff.

We now have an access problem, especially for credit, but we still are not clear about what high-quality financial products and services look like. Financial services providers are largely waiting for guidance from their regulators, fearful that any misstep will be seized on by both the media and consumer advocates. Regulators do not have a unified definition of high-quality financial products, and the Consumer Financial Protection Bureau, which has the greatest responsibility for figuring out the answer, will need to move more slowly and piecemeal than is ideal given its nascence and the nature of the rule-writing process. Consumer advocates are clear on the specific practices they think are harmful, but they generally lack a holistic perspective on what would be both beneficial for consumers and financially sustainable for providers.

Frustrated by this state of affairs and determined to continue moving the market forward, my organization, the Center for Financial Services Innovation, published a framing document in 2012 describing our vision of quality financial services and articulating a set of Compass Principles to guide product design and delivery: embrace inclusion to responsibly expand access; build trust to develop mutually beneficial products that deliver clear and consistent value; promote success to drive positive consumer behavior through smart design and communication; and create opportunity to provide options for upward mobility.

The principles are grounded in a broader view of how to make markets work. Financial services offerings must be profitable and scalable from a business standpoint if they are to offer lasting solutions for consumers. They must be based on knowledge of consumer needs and demand, as well as the desire to meet those needs safely and responsibly over the long term. No single provider can meet all consumer needs; there is value to variation and choice in the marketplace. Finally, providers and consumers must both act responsibly for healthy financial relationships to flourish.

Regulation is critical, but not sufficient, for restoring credibility to the idea that financial services can be a force for good in people's lives. Banks must demonstrate that they can self-regulate their worst impulses if they are to regain the trust of consumers and policymakers. Nonbank providers have long suffered from the perception that they are either second-class institutions or predators, or both. Some indeed are, but many represent potentially positive alternatives. They, too, need a way to demonstrate a commitment to quality products and practices if they are to be viewed as trustworthy. Technology-led providers may be today's darlings, but they are the most lightly regulated in the financial services marketplace, and they have lost points over their recent handling of customer privacy and security issues.

Trust is essential for positive innovation to flourish. We need innovation to replace the corroded pipes of the financial services system with an infrastructure that is modern, high quality, and inclusive. Only then will underserved consumers have the tools they need to shore up their own finances.

JENNIFER TESCHER *is the president and CEO for the Center for Financial Services Innovation, which aims to transform the financial services experience in America in order to better serve underbanked consumers and help them achieve prosperity. Ms. Tescher founded CFSI in 2004 and has since achieved notable success in raising the profile of underbanked access and asset-building as an objective for the industry. Ms. Tescher serves as a member of the Board of Directors for Credit Builders Alliance and is a member of Bank of America's National Community Advisory Council. A recipient of the Crain's Chicago Business "40 Under 40" Award for 2006, Ms. Tescher received undergraduate and graduate degrees in journalism from Northwestern University and a public policy degree from the University of Chicago.*

From Leaders
in Academia

ASSESSING HEALTH EFFECTS OF COMMUNITY DEVELOPMENT

Nancy E. Adler
University of California, San Francisco

A lthough health is a major topic of U.S. policy debates, the focus has not been on *health* policy but rather on *health care* policy. The emphasis in such discussions on the organization and financing of health care is understandable given that health care consumes 17.6 percent of our gross domestic product, and projections are that it could constitute almost 20 percent within eight years.[1] This single-minded perspective ignores the fact that health care is only one input to health, and among the various determinants, it accounts for a relatively small proportion of differences in overall health and longevity. Access to and quality of health care has been estimated to account for only about 10–20 percent of premature

---

1 Centers for Medicare and Medicaid Services. National Health Expenditure Data (2012). Available at http://cms.gov/Research-Statistics-Data-and-Systems/Statistics-Trends-and-Reports/NationalHealthExpendData/index.html?redirect=/NationalHealthExpendData/25_NHE_Fact_Sheet.asp.

mortality in the United States. Genetic vulnerabilities account for another 30–40 percent. The remaining determinants, accounting for the largest proportion of lost years of life, involve behavioral and social factors and environmental exposures.[2]

Our lack of attention to determinants of health other than health care may be one reason that we incur the highest per capita health care costs of any nation by far, but have relatively poor health status. The Organization for Economic Co-operation and Development (OECD) is a helpful source of cross-national health and spending comparisons. It provides evidence-based analysis and data on a wide range of the social and economic character-istics of its 34 member nations. According to the OECD, U.S. per capita spending on health care (over $8,000) is more than one-third higher than that of the next highest spending country. Despite this, of the 34 OECD nations, the United States ranked 31st in infant mortality, 25th in male life expectancy, and 27th in female life expectancy.[3] These international comparisons illustrate that we are not getting as much health benefit per dollar spent on health care as are other countries.

Even setting aside problems of inefficient, unnecessary, and/or poor quality services, investing solely in health care as our vehicle for assuring health is unlikely to succeed. A recent study of 30 OECD countries examined the association of five different health indicators with expenditures on both health care and social services (including housing). Higher per capita expendi-tures on both health services and social services were related to longer life expectancy, but, independent of the level of health expenditures in a country, the greater the ratio of its spending on social services relative to health services, the better the country's health outcomes.[4] Compared with other OECD countries, our

---

2 J.M. McGinnis, P. Williams-Russo, and J.R. Knickman, "The Case for More Active Policy Attention to Health Promotion." Health Affairs 21 (2) (2002): 78–93.

3 OECD. "Statistics from A to Z." Available at http://oecd.org/document/0,374 6,en_2649_201185_46462759_1_1_1_1,00.html.

4 E.H. Bradley, B.R. Elkins, J. Herrin, & and B. Ibel, "Health and Social Services Expenditures: Associations with Health Outcomes," BMJ Quality and Safety 20 (10) (2011): 826–831.

relatively greater investment in health care services is accompanied by relatively poorer investment in social services. Given the comparatively greater contribution to health of behavioral and social conditions than of health care, it is not surprising that expenditures on social programs appear to yield better health returns than do equivalent expenditures on medical care.

WHY SHOULD THIS BE OF INTEREST TO THE COMMUNITY DEVELOPMENT INDUSTRY?

The analysis of spending by OECD countries suggests that investments in housing along with other social spending are associated with improvements in health. This interpretation is consistent with findings from a number of U.S. studies linking specific aspects of housing and other community factors with health outcomes. However, although it follows that community development investments should yield health benefits, this has not yet been well established.

Empirical demonstrations of the health impact of community development would be helpful for a number of reasons. Such demonstrations could provide added impetus for future projects and garner greater public and governmental support. In addition to these indirect benefits, empirical evidence of health care savings resulting from community development could potentially help fund these projects. Given the unsustainability of today's health care costs, as well as anticipated cost increases, both public and private payers are looking for creative ways to reward interventions that will reduce health expenditures.

In new payment arrangements such as Accountable Care Organizations (ACOs), a group of health care providers agrees to share risk for the health care costs incurred by a designated population for which they have taken responsibility. In return, they are offered a chance to share in the savings on expected costs for that population. Health systems operating as ACOs benefit financially if their designated populations stay healthier and require fewer services. If a developer can show that some of an ACO's cost savings are the result of a community development project, there would be a legitimate call on the profits enjoyed by the ACO as a result of the population's changed health care use.

HOW SHOULD HEALTH EFFECTS BE QUANTIFIED?

The ability to reward community developers for savings in health care costs will depend on the ability to quantify such savings. It is too early to provide an explicit formula for doing this, but not too early to begin the conversation on how to do so.

Research Design

The debate will likely be about what evidence is sufficient to conclude that there has been a health benefit from a given project. Among health researchers, the gold standard for demonstrating causality is the randomized clinical trial (RCT), but many feel that reliance on RCTs is too limiting.

In an RCT, volunteers are randomly assigned to an experimental condition in which they receive a "treatment" designed to effect change, or to a control condition that is identical to the experimental group but with no intervention. When individuals are assigned at random to an experimental or control condition, there is less worry that the differences following treatment are due to preexisting differences among individuals or to aspects of the research experience unrelated to the treatment itself. The most rigorous RCTs are "double-blind," meaning that neither the participants nor those providing treatment know which group an individual is in until the end of the study period.

RCTs are expensive and challenging. A double-blind RCT at the social level is impossible; even randomization to group has formidable barriers. Despite this, randomized trials of social programs have been done. One example is Oportunidades, which involved the most impoverished segment of the entire Mexican population. Families below an income cut-off were randomized by community to participate in an income supplement program tied to incentives for health-promoting behaviors or to a control condition that delayed the start of the program.[5] An evaluation of the program found that children in families that received the cash transfers achieved greater height and showed better motor, cognitive, and language development than did controls.

Another example is Moving to Opportunity, which randomly assigned residents of housing projects in several U.S. communities to one of three conditions: residents received vouchers to move to another community of their choice; residents were given vouchers that restricted their move to a community with low poverty rates; and the control group.[6] The program resulted in significant health benefits for those in the treated condition versus controls up to 10 years later. Specifically, moving to a better neighborhood led to lower rates of extreme obesity and diabetes, psychological distress, and major depression.

When randomization is impossible, researchers rely on "quasi-experimental" designs. The strongest quasi-experimental designs use a well-matched comparison group, measured along with the treated group before and after a treatment. This design helps rule out preexisting differences in the treatment and comparison groups as a reason for different outcomes following the inter-vention. Weaker designs examine change from pre- to post-intervention only in the treated group or obtain measures on both groups only after the intervention. There are obvious trade-offs in the difficulty and cost of implementing these designs versus the value of the resulting data.

Health Measures

Beyond the designs for evaluation, it is critical to consider when and how health effects should be measured. Unless the outcome measures are well matched to the expected benefits, evaluators may fail to detect positive results. A community development

---

5   L.C. Fernald, P.J. Gertler, and L.M. Neufeld, "10-year Effect of Oportunidades, Mexico's Conditional Cash Transfer Programme, on Child Growth, Cognition, Language, and Behavior: A Longitudinal Follow-up Study." The Lancet 374 (9706) (2009): 1997–2005.

6   J.R. Kling, J. Ludwig, and L.F. Katz, "Neighborhood Effects on Crime for Female and Male Youth: Evidence from a Randomized Housing Voucher Experiment." Quarterly Journal of Economics 120 (2005): 87–130.

project could, for example, help delay or prevent the onset of cancer, cardiovascular disease, or diabetes, but these conditions take a number of years to develop, and benefits of the project may not be immediately measureable. This may lead to an erroneous conclusion that the project had no effect on health. Several strategies can address this problem. One is to focus on conditions (e.g., injury, birth outcomes, depression, or asthma) that are more immediately sensitive to current environmental conditions. A second strategy is to look at subpopulations that already have a condition and compare the disease course and complications of those in the "exposed" and "control" populations. A third option is to look for risk factors that may appear before actual disease emerges and that can capture effects within a more reasonable time frame.

In addition to considering how a project may affect a specific disease or condition, global assessment of health status may provide a more sensitive indicator of benefits and better capture cumulative effects of community improvement. Community development projects are likely to affect a range of health problems, whereas their effects on any one disease may be relatively rare in a given time period and hard to detect. Therefore an overall measure of health will be more informative.

One of the simplest measures of global health status is the question, "How would you rate your health relative to others your age?" Responses to this question predict future mortality even when controlling for objective measures of health.[7] Other self-report questions can be used to assess functional status, ability to perform activities of daily living, or depression. Each of these conditions not only has implications for health care costs but also translates into costs associated with lack of productivity in the workplace and with need for care at home.

Data Sources
Although some measures of the health effects of community development will require new, targeted data collection, evidence

---

7 E.L. Idler and Y. Benyamini, "Self-rated Health and Mortality: A Review of Twenty-seven Community studies." Journal of Health and Social Behavior 38 (1) (1997): 21–37.

of health impact may also be found in existing data. Many surveys include self-reported health status, including ongoing national and state-level health surveys. Some local public health departments also conduct surveys of their communities. Linking to such publicly available data may reduce the need for additional data collection.

Administrative records are another source of existing data that may be informative. Medical claims data provide direct evidence of health care costs, reflecting use of services and expenditures. For example, relative costs incurred per capita for a population served by a community development project could be compared to those of another community (ideally both before and after the project was implemented), or benchmarked against national trends in per capita health care costs during the same period.

Biological changes that indicate risk for subsequent disease can provide earlier evidence of health effects from community development than will disease diagnosis or progression. Substantial advances in identifying "biomarkers" or surrogate end points for disease now make it possible to collect such information outside of the doctor's office or laboratory. For example, it is possible to assay a number of biological indicators either from saliva or from a blood spot obtained from a small finger prick.[8] Some biomarkers are disease-specific (e.g., glucose tolerance for diabetes, HDL [high-density lipoprotein] and LDL [low-density lipoprotein cholesterol] for cardiovascular disease). Others assess risk factors associated with dysregulation of metabolic function and immune function, and cellular aging. Biomarkers indicating more general risk of disease and mortality include BMI (body mass index, which is a ratio of weight to height), waist-to-hip ratio (which assesses fat deposition in the abdominal area), interleukin 6 (IL-6, a protein secreted by the body to fight infection which provides a measure of chronic inflammation), and telomere

---

8   T.W. McDade, S. Williams, and J.J. Snodgrass, "What a Drop Can Do: Dried Blood Spots as a Minimally Invasive Method for Integrating Biomarkers into Population-based Research." Demography 44 (4) (2007): 889–925.

length (the length of the protein sequences that cap the tips of chromosomes and maintain their structural integrity).

In the coming years, more information is likely to become available through advances in remote monitoring of health status and use of biomarkers to track disease risk. Similarly, innovative approaches to measuring fitness are coming on the market. Advances in collecting and analyzing biological specimens are reducing the cost and burden of obtaining biomarkers that reflect early stages of disease or predict later onset. Increasingly, biomarkers are being added to population surveys and may provide community-wide indicators of risk that can be linked to community development efforts.

Any discussion of data collection to evaluate health effects of community development must include consideration of ethical issues. Individual privacy must be maintained and procedures must be in place to ensure that no one in the study can be individually identified.

Opportunities to Collect and Use Quality Data

Choosing the best health measure will depend on the nature of the community development project and the characteristics of the population it will serve. Special attention should be given to possible confounders that could bias the findings or random factors that add "noise" and make it harder to detect the effect of the project. The more thinking that goes into such challenges in advance, the greater the chance that the designs can guard against "false positives" (finding a health benefit of a project when, in fact, no real benefit occurred) as well as "false negatives" (failing to find a benefit that does, in fact, exist).

At this early stage in linking community development and health, it would be helpful if all projects would use a core set of common measures (e.g., self-rated health). The resulting data would allow for comparisons across projects and populations and facilitate establishment of a national database that could reduce the need for original data collection by each project.

Data collection is expensive, but it may be possible to leverage an initial investment in well-designed research to lower the demands on subsequent projects. The National Institutes of Health, the U.S. Department of Housing and Urban Development, other government agency funders, and private foundations may be willing to support an initial demonstration of the health effects and health care savings of a few community development projects. As groups collect data, the findings could be amassed in a publicly accessible archive that would allow future projects to model potential savings and collect information on targeted outcomes to confirm that national trends are reflected in their populations. Data that are being generated in the context of health impact assessments could also be entered into such an archive, and, conversely, investigators could draw on it to conduct their analyses.

CONCLUSION

Attention to the health effects of community development is consistent with a movement toward "health in all policy." The time is ripe to move beyond a general discussion of the value of linking health and development to creating an action plan for directly testing the link and determining the magnitude of the effects. Although each development project will have unique characteristics that will affect the research design and measures needed to assess its health impacts, evaluation of any one project will be less costly and more effective if there is agreement on minimal standards for evidence, use of common measures, and development of a data archive that can be used as a basis for comparison for a given population and project. This argues for a roadmap designed collaboratively by community development and health professionals. The Federal Reserve meetings that have occurred over the past two years have set the goal and direction for such efforts. We now need to draw the map and construct the roads that will get us there.

NANCY E. ADLER, PHD, *is the vice-chair of the Department of Psychiatry, and director of the Center for Health and Community. She is also the Lisa and*

John Pritzker Professor of Medical Psychology in the Departments of Psychiatry and Pediatrics at the University of California, San Francisco. She received a bachelor's degree from Wellesley College and a PhD in Psychology from Harvard University. After serving as assistant and associate professor at University of California, Santa Cruz, she came to University of California, San Francisco, to initiate a graduate program in health psychology, and now directs two postdoctoral training programs and conducts research on socioeconomic determinants of health.

DEEP DEMOCRACY IS NOT MEETINGS THAT LAST FOREVER:
Community Development Next

Xavier de Souza Briggs and J. Phillip Thompson
Massachusetts Institute of Technology

Community development has long been part industry, part social movement. At its core is an idea that American educator and philosopher John Dewey would have recognized but that many of today's activists, entrepreneurs, and change agents sadly do not. It is the idea of deep democracy. For Dewey, this meant, first and foremost, the essence of community life—the public inventing and deploying the collective means to solve its problems. "Regarded as an idea," he wrote in *The Public and Its Problems* (1927), "democracy is not an alternative to other principles of associated life. It is the idea of community life itself."

This is not what most of us learned about democracy in grade school civics. Dewey's conception is not primarily about the machinery of government, although reimagining and revitalizing government for each age is a critical part of "inventing and deploying"; government cannot simply shrink or become a gladiatorial arena. It is not primarily about adhering to a specific decision-making procedure, although procedural rules, forums for both learning and bargaining with each other, and meaningful checks and balances matter. Dewey's view of democracy is not even about ever-broader "participation," although the extremes of exclusion and the norm of top-down decision making are not, we hope, in for a great revival any time soon.

As important as these things are for the infrastructure of democracy and indicators of its "vital signs," Dewey's view reminds us that a narrow focus on these definitions confuses ends with means and loses the thread. For this century, for the material and institutional tools at our disposal, democracy is two things, which together should define the future of community development and win our full commitment. First, democracy is the craft of collective problem solving, which hinges on developing and using "civic capacity" with and beyond the government. This demands radically different conceptions of citizenship, leadership, and mobilization, all for a different kind of future. Extant conceptions of "working in partnership" barely scratch the surface of what it is possible and required. Second, democracy is giving the greatest number of people—regardless of background, inherited privilege, address, or creed—control over, not just access to, capital as a vital part of control over their own lives and fortunes. As a recipe, we might call these twin ideas "empowerment 2.0."

DEMOCRACY AS EFFECTIVE GOVERNANCE

Voting for government officials is only one avenue for citizen participation, political development, and governance. Direct and sustained participation in civic institutions and organizations is equally important. Democracy is defined as much by the democratic practices of civic institutions and organizations as it is by open government elections and procedures. America's historical practice of "private" (de facto) racial segregation, for example, undermines the essence of democracy—the building of community. Segregation has often turned elections intended to promote fairness into opportunities for racial majorities to tyrannize racial minorities.

Conversely, democratic civic organizations help develop citizens' capacity to play active roles in problem solving, including the problem of getting past racial and ethnic prejudices through regular civil interaction with those who are different; or more to the point, for discovering that those who are different from us in one respect or another are much like us in other respects. We care about the health and safety of children and elders, we face higher costs of living and struggle to save, we want there to be a planet for our children to inherit and thrive in. This kind of "bridging" is crucial in a society that has rapidly become both more racially and ethnically diverse and more economically unequal.

Local 1199, a health care worker's union in New York, for example, brings its racially and ethnically diverse members together to guide its highly popular program (funded through collective bargaining agreements) that builds and operates day care facilities for its members' children. Unions like this that have multiple venues for member engagement and interaction—and do not merely focus on bosses negotiating on behalf of members for wages and benefits—promote a democratic culture and develop democratic leadership capacities among their members. These habits and capacities spill over into other areas of society. The same goes for churches, schools, and other civic institutions—if they work to *be* civic. Civicness is not an artifact of nonprofit status and therefore cannot be claimed, mechanically, like a tax exemption. Civicness is a question of how an institution operates.

As Dewey recognized long before there was a modern movement called community development, addressing our biggest and toughest social problems requires sustained effort, trust among multiple groups, and the creative exchange of ideas. In vibrant democracies, the processes by which organized groups are brought together to work on social and economic problems cannot be limited to optional, occasional "initiatives," dependent on philanthropy for funding. They are the *sine qua non* of conducting our public life, the standard operating approach.

The Emerald Cities Collaborative is a good example of this in action. The collaboration is an intermediary organization established to bring together often-warring community, business, and labor union organizations to work out cooperative approaches to retrofitting the nation's building stock to improve energy efficiency. The data clearly show that the most job-intensive sector of the "green economy"—and therefore a key pathway to better jobs and economic security—is the building trades. Yet there has been much conflict between community and labor groups, stemming from high unemployment among predominantly white, unionized construction workers and high unemployment among minority workers. The latter contend that they have been historically excluded from membership in construction unions. The question is, who should get priority access to energy retrofitting jobs, particularly those jobs that include taxpayer subsidies?

The proposed Emerald Cities solution, hammered out over a year of emotionally intense and also information-rich exchanges, is that unionized workers—half of whom are near retirement—should claim the commercial market and train more minorities to fill the shoes of their retiring members. Meanwhile, minorities recruited into union apprenticeship and pre-apprenticeship programs should, for now, focus on residential retrofits, primarily single-family home projects that are, for now, almost all nonunionized.

Intermediaries such as the Emerald Cities Collaborative only partially address the need for go-between functions even in the narrow area of energy efficiency. Many landlords of large multifamily properties have been unable to introduce cost-saving energy improvements, such as installing submeters to monitor and reward individual household energy savings, because many tenants do not believe that landlords will fairly allocate energy savings or provide accurate accounting of energy data. Another intermediary organization, perhaps one funded from energy cost savings, is needed to bring landlords and tenants together to work on allocation issues and provide both parties accurate and verifiable data on building performance.

DEMOCRATIC CONTROL AND DEVELOPMENT OF CAPITAL

Despite the near-universal characterization of the U.S. economy as "private," to distinguish it from economies driven by state-owned enterprises and state-centralized planning, advanced economies are social, arguably the most social, of all institutions. Investment firms compete to manage the combined savings of hundreds of millions of citizens; firm managers receive commissions but do not own the funds. The evidence is that investors govern managers so poorly that the latter often form a type of autocracy, but the funds nonetheless belong to "the community," mainly workers and retirees. Most large companies are publicly traded on Wall Street by investment firms or citizens. Large companies are themselves social organizations (some firms have more employees than midsized cities have residents) managed by salaried professionals. In most companies, workers have little say in decision making despite the social and public nature of the corporation, defined by law. Most technological innovation, the primary driver of productivity and therefore economic growth, is funded initially through taxpayer-funded grants to research institutions and then through socially funded firms. Markets of exchange are also highly social in their function. They are forums for the exchange of ideas, products and services, and civil competition for investment in promising organizations. What gives all of these institutions the appearance of being "private" is not their ownership structure, but the weakness of accountability structures between management and owners.

Yet most citizens lack a basic literacy of economic governance. It is a nontopic even at the university level. Where and how citizens invest their money is arguably as important, and as relevant for democratic engagement, as voting in government elections.

Viewed democratically, for example, investment priorities should be the subject of active debate and decision among the full range of owners and investors, that is, the public—conscious of itself *as* a public, as Dewey put it. It should not be an exclusive domain for elite professionals or financial and legal jargon. There is no *ex ante* reason, for example, why investment and purchasing decisions should prioritize financial return on investment above other social concerns such as environmental sustainability, the health and welfare of workers and consumers, or full employment (measurable social returns).

The failure to democratize economic institutions is as corrosive to government in this century as racial segregation was in the last century. Throughout world history, elite economic control has produced elite political control, as the recently published study *Why Nations Fail* shows persuasively, and ultimately led to economic and social stagnation.

Workplaces can and should be prime sites for democratic problem solving and citizen capacity-building. In March 2012, the United Steel Workers of America and the U.S. branch of Mondragon International—a network of industrial cooperatives headquartered in Spain—took a step in this direction when they announced a new union-coop agreement structured to enhance workers' roles as investors, owners, and active directors of newly created manufacturing firms.

In the next five years, we predict that more community-based organizations will likewise partner with major health care organizations to deliver better health outcomes at lower cost. It is hard to imagine progress on our ailing health care system that does not include a "market" for wellness that employs and deploys street-level innovation of many kinds. In this regard, community development can become a much bigger contributor to effective *care* (which connotes protection in the broad sense) even as it works more boldly to advance *opportunity* (which demands expanded capability and access to livelihoods).

An ongoing process of creative destruction is reshaping the competitive landscape. As the digital revolution moves from social media to physical science, manufacturing, and design, the infrastructure needed for production of many goods and services will *shrink* from large factories to small buildings or even garages (think of the space once required for mainframe computing versus mobile iPads and smartphones today). Meanwhile, access to tools, education, and information needed for research, production, and distribution of goods and services will *expand* exponentially. The effectiveness of traditional hierarchical corporate management, established to plan and manage large-scale production, will diminish, even if centralized authority retains key functions and firms that are run hierarchically fight to dominate. Smaller, highly creative, energetic, and flexible companies will have new advantages.

With greater access to education and tools for production and distribution, and greater worker participation in the creation and use of those tools, economic productivity could advance substantially. But our larger point is that a deeper and more meaningful democracy could advance too, as a result. Those countries and sectors that promote open source—enabling the broadest learning, the most rapid discussions, and socially diverse and inclusive feedback loops—and that provide the best incentives and structures for active participation will develop fastest and most sustainably. In short, economic democracy is imperative for economic success.

COMMUNITY DEVELOPMENT NEXT
Community development faces linked challenges in the realms of civics and equitable economic development. We have argued that both of these factors promise, and indeed require, a deeper democracy—democracy reimagined, retaught, practiced often. Community development can once again become an arena for practicing what we have outlined as economic democracy, for partnering in creative new ways, and for outgrowing a survivalist dependence on philanthropic grants and government contracts and subsidies. These sources of funding are not the problem, and

they do much good. It is the narrow reliance on these sources, along with resignation to narrow control of the "private" market that obscures the big stakes and opportunities at hand.

XAVIER DE SOUZA BRIGGS *is associate professor of sociology and planning and head of the Housing, Community, and Economic Development Group in the Department of Urban Studies and Planning at the Massachusetts Institute of Technology. During 2009-11, Xav served as associate director of the Office of Management and Budget in the Obama White House. A former community planner, his research and teaching are about economic opportunity, effective democracy and governance, and racial and ethnic diversity in cities and metropolitan regions. His books include* The Geography of Opportunity *(2005),* Democracy as Problem-Solving: Civic Capacity in Communities across the Globe *(2008), and* Moving to Opportunity: The Story of an American Experiment to Fight Ghetto Poverty *(2010). A former faculty member in public policy at Harvard, he has designed and led major leadership development, strategy, and other training programs for change agents in the public, private, and nonprofit/ nongovernmental sectors. Xav is a member of the Aspen Institute's Roundtable on Community Change and other advisory groups and serves on the board of The Community Builders. His views have appeared in* The New York Times, *Salon.com,* National Public Radio, *and other major media.*

J. PHILLIP THOMPSON *is an associate professor of urban politics, Department of Urban Studies and Planning, Massachusetts Institute of Technology. Before entering academic life, Thompson worked as deputy general manager of the New York Housing Authority and as Director of the Mayor's Office of Housing Coordination. Thompson is the author of* Double Trouble: Black Mayors, Black Communities, and the Struggle for a Deep Democracy *(Oxford University Press, 2005).*

RULES, NOT RESOURCES

Mark Calabria
Cato Institute

C ommunity development policy, at least at the federal level, has continued to approach poverty as if it were the result of a lack of resources: if communities are poor, give them income, and if infrastructure is lacking, have higher levels of government fund more of it. Here, by contrast, I take the approach that the fundamental problem facing poor communities in America is poor governance and not a lack of resources. In other words, the existing resources available to community development would be more than enough to revitalize struggling communities across the country if local governments were run better, allowing the market to work more efficiently to provide the goods and services communities need.

The existing framework of community development programs focuses more on the redistribution of wealth, rather than wealth creation. Yet we have examples of some cities that have shifted their emphasis toward responsible management and away from redistribution. These cities have witnessed some renaissance, while those that have continued to function largely as transfer states have fallen behind.

There is a tendency in American politics to associate governmental redistribution of wealth with transfers from the wealthy to the poor. That happens sometimes (e.g., the Earned Income Tax Credit), but too often temporary majorities transfer wealth to themselves from temporary minorities. In the parlance of economics and political science, the concern of this essay is with redistribution that is "rent-seeking" rather than the provision of a social safety net.[1] Not to be confused with "rents" in the housing sense, rent-seeking is comprised of expending resources to capture wealth rather than create wealth. Examples could include activities intended to influence government officials (lobbying) or limiting the access of occupations or other lines of business in order to create monopoly "rents." And the sums of government funds that are subject to rent-seeking are massive. Consider that the budget of the U.S. Department of Housing and Urban Development (HUD) has totaled more than $1 trillion over the nearly 50-year life of the agency (nominal dollars). That's enough to have purchased outright more than one-third of the existing rental stock in the country.

The point of the preceding is not to argue that federal community development and housing funding have been well-spent or that such subsidies have even flowed thorough to their ultimate intended recipients, but to show that we have expended a tremendous amount of resources toward this effort with, at best, questionable results. Given these staggering amounts, the burden of proof should rest on those who advocate for even more spending.

---

1   The seminal works on rent-seeking are Anne Krueger, "The Political Economy of the Rent-Seeking Society," American Economic Review 64 (3) (1974): 291–303; and Gordon Tullock, "The Welfare Costs of Tariffs, Monopolies, and Theft," Western Economic Journal 5 (3) (1967): 224–232.

BEYOND MAJORITARIAN POLITICS

Despite a long history of urban scandals and corruption,[2] community development continues as largely an engineering exercise to some. Once the right answer is properly formulated, good government only need implement it, the argument goes. What I claim here is that policy on the ground is rarely that clean and neat. It often involves political coalitions and special interests, jockeying for advantage.

To illuminate, one can conceive of local government as individuals, or coalitions, coming together to provide a basket of public goods, which could include a social safety net. The game matrix below, although highly stylized, displays the choice environment.

		Coalition I	
		A	B
Coalition II	A	10, 10	3, 12
	B	12, 3	5,5

If both coalitions cooperate and choose action A, then social welfare is maximized. Collective action will have improved social well-being. In the context of local government, this would represent a situation in which public officials provide a high-quality bundle of services in a nondiscriminatory manner at a reasonable cost. All citizens, or in the game matrix members of both coalitions I and II, have equal and fair access to locally provided public goods.

The problem is that the outcome of both coalitions choosing action A is not a stable situation (or "Nash" equilibrium).[3] One can think of each coalition taking a set turn at governing.

---

2 For a recent example, see Abby Sewell and Jessica Garrison, "Corruption Can Leave Cities with Enormous Legal Bills," Los Angeles Times, April 18, 2012, available at http://latimes.com/news/local/la-me-city-attorney-spending-20120418,0,1261390.story.

3 John F. Nash, "Equilibrium Points in N-Person Games," Proceedings of the National Academy of Sciences 36 (1) (1950): 48–49. See more generally Martin Osborne and Ariel Rubinstein, A Course in Game Theory (Cambridge, MA: MIT Press, 1994).

Coalition I governs for one period, then coalition II governs the next, and so on. If both coalitions choose A, which we can call the "broader public interest" position, then social welfare is again maximized over time. The temptation, however, for a coalition to instead choose action B dominates the choice of action A. Think of B as using their term at governance to enrich members of their coalition at the expense of the public good. The out-of-power, or minority, coalition may still receive positive benefits, as illustrated in the payoff matrix, but now the distribution of public benefits is grossly unequal. When the other coalition gains control, its incentives are also to choose action B. Whereas action A was called the "broader public interest" choice, we can think of B as the "Tammany Hall" choice, where governing coalitions use power to enrich themselves at the expense of the out-coalitions.[4]

The above results could continue to hold even in the face of entrenched coalitions without turnover. For instance, throughout much of U.S. history, southern cities and states were governed for the benefit of white citizens, while African Americans were largely exploited in order to benefit the governing coalitions. If African Americans had not attained the ability to move out of the South or if external pressure had not been placed on the governing coalitions of the South, the off-diagonal outcome of (A, B) would likely have lasted considerably longer. Therefore, to generalize the game matrix, action B could be seen as either exit or exploit. One could also envision the opening up of governance in southern cities to African Americans as a belated recognition by the governing coalition that they were stuck in a (B, B) situation.

While all parties recognize that (A, A) is superior choice to (B, B), the incentives facing governing coalitions make (B, B) the only stable outcome. It is my contention that many declining or depressed American cities are essentially stuck in (B, B). The question facing citizens is how to move from (B, B) to (A, A) or

---

4 The classic text on Tammany Hall is William Riordan, Plunkitt of Tammany Hall: A Series of Plain Talks on Very Practical Politics (New York: E.P. Dutton, 1963). See also Alfred Connable and Edward Silberfarb, Tigers of Tammany: Nine Men Who Ran New York (New York: Holt, Rinehart and Winston, 1967).

in the parlance of Buchanan and Congleton, how to "eliminate the off-diagonals."[5] This is where the need for "rules" comes in.

CREATING A RULES-BASED GOVERNANCE THAT ALLOWS FOR GREATER EFFICIENCY AND LESS RENT-SEEKING

Rules can take a variety of forms, not all of which are embedded in written laws or constitutions. Attitudes, for example, can reflect the rules of social norms. While certainly changes in federal and state laws pushed the governance of southern cities to be more inclusive, attitudes also changed, which have also helped local governments move from (B, B) to something more closely resembling (A, A). Several northeastern cities, in particular New York, have moved away from coalitional redistribution and toward a more technocratic city manager model of governance. Examples such as New York's Rudy Giuliani or Philadelphia's Ed Rendell illustrate the trend. While such cities continue to engage in some degree of insider-outsider redistribution, greater emphasis toward providing broadly available and quality public goods has helped such cities move to a superior position.

Attitudes can and do change. The question becomes how to institute durable mechanisms that focus government toward the common good while reducing its use for coalitional advantage. In a general sense, one solution is to move toward reducing the scope of discretion on the part of local government. Consider real estate construction permits. Although most urban land is zoned for one use or another, such use is rarely by right. That is, even if land is zoned "multifamily," a proposed apartment complex still must run a maze of regulatory approvals, most of which are characterized by considerable discretion. Such discretion, besides adding considerable cost to developments, also opens up government to the coalitional redistribution discussed above. Approvals may only come after political donations or payoffs to various constituencies of the governing coalition. To increase the

---

5 James Buchanan and Roger Congleton, Politics by Principle, Not Interest: Toward Nondiscriminatory Democracy (Cambridge, UK: Cambridge University Press, 1998).

value of such regulatory discretion, governments would rationally choose to limit the supply of such approvals as well. In addition to leading to greater levels of corruption, such a structure also reduces the supply of goods and services available to residents of the community. Similar schemes are evident in other locally licensed businesses, from taxicabs to hair salons.

Reducing discriminatory treatment of businesses and potential businesses would be a significant first step in moving local government away from the Tammany Hall outcome. Governments should also embrace a variety of mechanisms that would reduce coalitional redistribution in the domain of individual citizens. In regard to taxation, and regardless of the base rate, local governments can institute single flat taxes with few, if any, exemptions or deductions. The same would hold for property taxes. For instance, property taxes on rentals tend to be higher than for single-family homes in many cities, with little evidence that renters consume a greater share of public goods. The likely rationale lies in homeowners' greater propensity to vote and the varying transparency in taxation between rental and owner-occupied units.[6] Similar uniformity would hold across property types, whether residential, industrial, or commercial.

No discrimination is likely easier to achieve on both the taxation and regulatory sides of government than on the benefits side only. Issuance of permits and differences in tax rates are generally observable and verifiable, whereas differences in the provision of public goods may be more subjective. Nevertheless, provisions should be implemented that minimize varied public good provision among residents. This would minimize the ability to use public goods as hidden transfers to members of the governing coalition. Local public goods should be available to all members of the community, even if such goods are provided neighborhood by neighborhood. Separate will never be equal. Public goods should also be limited to those goods that actually are public in

---

6 See William Fischel, The Homevoter Hypothesis: How Home Values Influence Local Government Taxation, School Finance, and Land-Use Policies (Cambridge, MA: Harvard University Press 2005).

nature. As a general rule, keeping government out of the provision of purely private goods would greatly reduce the potential for coalitional redistribution.

While few American cities truly embrace market delivery for public services and while every city likely suffers from some amount of public corruption, some of the biggest innovators have been cities that were once the poster-children for corruption. One of the biggest surprises has been Chicago under Mayor Rahm Emanuel.[7] One of Mayor Emanuel's steps in the direction of market-based delivery has been changing the city's Blue Cart recycling program into one of "managed competition." Under this system, the city is divided into six service areas. Private companies manage four of those areas while public employees manage the other two. By injecting some degree of competition into the provision of public services, Chicago can reduce costs while also minimizing the temptation to use public services as a hidden transfer to specific interests, such as city employees. While monitoring these contracts will be critical, the differing contract pricing of numerous providers offers an important benchmark of cost. These efforts build on earlier steps by Mayor Emanuel's immediate predecessor, such as the privatization of Chicago's parking meters.

Reducing discriminatory and discretionary provision of local public goods also helps to increase both a community's wealth and level of innovation. Instead of resources, including human capital, being used simply for the capture of existing wealth, those resources can be used to create new wealth. Not having to run the maze at City Hall in order to get a building permit or business license is time that can instead be spent on running a business. Money not spent on lawyers and lobbyists is money that is invested back into the community, and done in a way that increases the productivity of workers in the community, ultimately increasing wealth. Reducing political discretion also

---

7 Harris Kenny and Adam Summers, "Privatization and Public-Private Partnership Trends in Local Government." Annual Privatization Report 2011 (Washington, DC: Reason Foundation, 2012).

allows workers and entrepreneurs to devote their efforts to activities where they have a comparative advantage. It is a sad reflection of the residential construction industry that so many developers are lawyers by training, the result of the highly politicized atmosphere surrounding real estate.

Minimizing opportunities for corruption at the local level can also increase the level of investment and ultimately wealth in the community. Researchers have found, unsurprisingly, that greater corruption reduces investment, partly by acting as a tax on investment but also by increasing uncertainty.[8] One of the most important areas of local government regulation is the entry of new business, particularly via the issuance of new business licensing. The more difficult it is for new businesses to start, the lower will be both wealth and employment in a community. When looking at data across countries, researchers from Harvard, Yale, and the World Bank found that countries with greater regulation of new business entry have higher corruption but do not have better quality of public or private goods.[9] Countries with more democratic and limited governments have less regulation of entry and accordingly higher quality public and private goods. The same is expected to hold across American cities. Places that make it easier to start a business, particularly by removing the political discretion surrounding the granting of new business licenses, are likely to see greater growth, more opportunity, and less corruption. Areas such as taxicab licenses, restaurants, and beauty salons can offer tremendous opportunities for entrepreneurship by low- and moderate-income individuals if those industries had lower barriers to entry.

WHY CAN'T POLITICS SOLVE DISCRIMINATORY GOVERNMENT?

The general approach to limiting coalitional redistribution, at least in the community development context, has been to institute

---

8 See Paolo Mauro, "Corruption and Growth," Quarterly Journal of Economics 110 (3) (1995): 681–712.

9 Simeon Djankov et al., "The Regulation of Entry," Quarterly Journal of Economics 117 (1) (2002): 1–37.

mechanisms that include a greater share of the community in political decision making. Initial efforts also focused on reducing the influence of "politics" and instead having "experts" drive urban policy. Whatever the direction taken, urban reformers have long recognized that coalitional redistribution, or "machine politics," came at a considerable cost to the community.[10]

Federal housing and community development statutes are littered with various requirements for community input into how state and local governments will use federal dollars. For instance, Section 104 of the Housing and Community Development Act of 1974, which governs the community development block grant (CDBG) program, requires grantees to prepare "a final statement of community development objectives and projected use of funds" and to make that statement available to the public. In addition, grantees are required to hold public hearings and take public comment on the statement. Grantees, in some instances, must also develop a "detailed citizen participant plan," which may provide technical assistance to "groups representative of persons of low and moderate income" so that said groups are able to participate. Clearly, there are multiple opportunities for "citizen participation" in federal housing and community development programs.

Despite these multiple opportunities to offer input, there is little evidence of widespread participation. Of course, participation increases when there is a reasonable probability that government will be responsive. Otherwise, the citizen investment required is likely to be prohibitive.[11]

Regardless of the desired impact of the regulatory language and requirements for greater participation and accountability,

---

10 Early examples include Lincoln Steffens, The Shame of the Cities (Dover, UK: Dover Publications, 1904) and Harold Zink, City Bosses in the United States: A Study of Twenty Municipal Bosses (Durham, NC: Duke University Press, 1930). For more recent work in context of replacing politics with experts, see Kenneth Finegold, Experts and Politicians: Reform Challenges to Machine Politics in New York, Cleveland, and Chicago (Princeton, NJ: Princeton University Press, 1995).

11 Samuel Paul, "Accountability in Public Services: Exit, Voice and Control," World Development 20 (7) (1992): 1047–1060.

it is likely that those with the largest financial interests in the proposed projects will dominate community participation. A review of community participation efforts in economic development conducted by the World Bank found that:

> *Projects that rely on community participation have not been particularly effective at targeting the poor. There is some evidence that such projects create effective community infrastructure, but not a single study establishes a causal relationship between any outcome and participatory elements of a community-based development project. Most such projects are dominated by elites, and both targeting and project quality tend to be markedly worse in more unequal communities.*[12]

Early research on the impact of the CDBG program has also found that the "elite" drove community participation in the planning process.[13] In fact, there is some evidence that urban governments in the United States have reduced the quality of public services in order to encourage specific segments of the population to move out of the city, with the intent of solidifying political control.[14] Even when local elites feel they have the best interests of the local community in mind, those trade-offs might not reflect the desires of those most in need. For instance, Matthew Kahn has found that California cities that are more liberal approve fewer housing permits, all else equal, including income.[15] While elites may place more value on an additional dog park or open spaces in which to play Frisbee golf, it is far from obvious that these uses of space are more valuable than, say, the provision of additional market-rate housing.

---

12 Ghazala Mansuri and Vijayendra Rao, "Community-Based and -Driven Development: A Critical Review," World Bank Research Observer 19 (1) (Spring 2004): 1–39.

13 Donald E. Voth, "An Evaluation of Community Development Programs in Illinois," Social Forces 53 (4) (1975): 635–647.

14 Edward Glaeser and Andrei Schleifer, "The Curley Effect: The Economics of Shaping the Electorate," Journal of Law, Economics, and Organizations 21 (2005): 1–19.

15 Matthew Kahn, "Do Liberal Cities Limit New Housing Development? Evidence from California," Journal of Urban Economics 69 (2) (March 2011): 223–228.

INFORMATION, THE MARKET, AND PUBLIC POLICY

While determining who benefits is certainly critical with any public policy, and federal development programs have had, at best, mixed results, a more important question with respect to the long-run health of a community is how is knowledge incorporated into policy.

From the 1930s until the 1970s, community development was largely top-down and expert-driven. Perhaps the best-known and worst-case example is Robert Moses' remaking of New York City and the surrounding environs. Robert Caro's masterful narrative of Moses in *The Power Broker* leaves one both impressed at the feats accomplished and horrified at the lack of accountability and transparency, not to mention the destruction of vibrant neighborhoods in the name of urban renewal. Such was the horror that Jane Jacobs was motivated both to protect her own neighborhood from Moses's path and to start writing what eventually became *The Death and Life of Great American Cities*.

Popular writers and community activists were not the only ones to spot the failure of this top-down model of community development. Academics began to argue for "collaborative planning"[16] and "communicative action"[17] to correct the imbalance between the experts and the communities affected. The emphasis of these theorists was the use of citizen participation as a method to convey information to professional planners. Their proposed method was public discourse and debate, hence the increased calls for public hearings, along with the requirement that comprehensive plans be subject to notice and comment.

The limit of increased citizen participation is, however, that some knowledge cannot be communicated via testimony, comment, and debate.[18] As Nobel laureate F.A. Hayek observed, it is

---

16 See generally Patsy Healy, Collaborative Planning (London: Macmillian, 1997).

17 Jurgen Habermas, The Theory of Communicative Action (Boston: Beacon Press, 1984).

18 See generally Mark Pennington, "Citizen Participation, the 'Knowledge Problem' and Urban Land Use Planning: An Austrian Perspective on Institutional Choice," Review of Austrian Economics 17 (2/3) (2004): 213–231.

only the price system, embedded in a general system of private property, that is able to convey the subjective value judgments of numerous individuals into a simple and easy-to-understand measure.[19] Without the guidance of market prices based on relative scarcity, a community that must allocate its available resources to competing demands has little guidance, other than politics, on what it should prioritize. Determining which public goods should be produced—for example, a park versus a pool—is an arbitrary decision without knowing what the community values more. Given the evidence that the citizen participation process is often captured by elites, or the governing coalition, we clearly need market-based mechanisms instead. These would allow all community members to make their subjective value judgments count as well as reduce the ability to discriminate in providing public goods.

Even if citizen participation could functionally convey all relevant information, such a process depends on all necessary knowledge actually being known ahead of the decision. As Hayek[20] and fellow Nobel laureate James Buchanan[21] have emphasized, the market process is not simply one of allocation, but also of discovery. Economic development is not an engineering problem, where one just adds more investment to X or allocates more capital to Y. The appropriate variables and their optimal quantities and combinations are simply not knowable ahead of time and must be discovered via trial and error, a process not particularly amenable to any sort of government intervention.

While it is difficult (if not impossible) to know the optimal amount of community development funding that should be spent annually on new activities, such an amount could serve as a useful proxy for the ability of local governments to respond

---

19 F.A. Hayek, "The Use of Knowledge in Society," American Economic Review 35 (4) (1945): 519–530.

20 F.A. Hayek, "Competition as a Discovery Procedure." In New Studies in Politics, Economics and the History of Ideas, edited by F.A. Hayek (London: Routledge, 1978).

21 James Buchanan and G. Vanberg, "The Market as a Creative Process," Economics and Philosophy 7 (1991): 167–186.

to changing community circumstances. It is unlikely that a community faces the exact same set of needs from one year to the next, and this is even more unlikely over the course of several years. Even if this were the case, it is more unlikely still that a community would place the exact same relative priorities on these needs over time. Despite all these facts, what little evidence we have suggests a high degree of rigidity in spending over time. Typically, how a city spends its community development funds bears a strong resemblance to how it spent funds in the previous year, all the way down to the same projects. A group of researchers in Michigan examined the CDBG expenditures for a handful of Michigan communities over a five-year period and found it was quite rare for those subsidies to be used for new projects.[22] Cities like Pontiac were representative, which spent 9 percent of its CDBG funding on new activities over five years. Some cities, such as Saginaw, spent even smaller shares, at 5 percent. Although these data are not conclusive, they do suggest that, even with extensive community participation requirements, local government community spending doesn't adjust well to changing community needs or preferences.

It could be tempting to respond to such concerns with "so what?" Even if policies do not reflect the preferences of the overall community, assist members most in need, or accurately reflect the community's relative needs, at least some good is being done, right? Community development and urban renewal programs of the 1950s and 1960s most likely did more harm than good, eliminating far more affordable housing than they created and destroying vibrant working-class neighborhoods. One could argue we have since learned our lesson: we include the communities in question, hold public hearings and, in general, no longer demolish large tracts of housing. Without a doubt, current community development programs are a major improvement over their predecessors.

---

22 Raymond Rosenfeld et al., "Community Development Block Grant Spending Revisited: Patterns of Benefit and Program Institutionalization," Publius 25 (4) (1995): 55–72.

That said, moving from truly harmful to perhaps less harmful public policy is hardly inspiring. Despite our having spent hundreds of billions (in excess of $120 billion for CDBG alone)— and as Eileen Norcross reminds us, "CDBG [having] awarded funds to the most depressed cities for over thirty years"—many of these same cities remain depressed. Norcross raises the possibility that "the steady and expected infusion of federal dollars may act as a 'signal buffer' in city governments, encouraging less efficient management of public dollars, or forestalling more significant policy reforms that might stimulate economic development."[23] This, I believe, is the real harm from federal community development programs: they insulate local governments from local accountability and hence reduce the pace of community learning and adaptation.

Some scholars have argued that earlier urban renewal and developments plans failed because they were actually too inclusive. Jon Teaford, for instance, claims that "the inclusiveness of urban renewal proved a weakness."[24] Teaford argues that, because the program goals were "ambiguous and ill-defined," each interest could see the goals in its own desired light. Residents could demand more affordable housing, commercial developers and business leaders could envision new hotels and conference centers, while mayors and city council members could savor the prospect of new property tax revenues. While Teaford sees this broad inclusiveness as a fatal flaw, believing that a strong, centralized figure (such as Robert Moses) is needed, the true flaw is that a participatory process based on debate has no way of reconciling and comparing these competing demands. Even Teaford's claimed successes were less than effective: Detroit's Lafayette Park did not turn around Detroit's population loss, as he himself recognizes.

---

23 Eileen Norcross, The Community Development Block Grant: Does It Work? (Fairfax, VA: Mercatus Center, George Mason University, November 2007), available at http://mercatus. org/publication/community-development-block-grant-does-it-work.

24 Jon Teaford, "Urban Renewal and Its Aftermath," Housing Policy Debate 11 (2) (2000): 443–466.

Although the available evidence can be characterized as mixed, there is sufficient support for concluding that federal participatory requirements may have changed the composition of the governing coalition but have done little to change the nature of the game. In fact, the shift away from coalitional redistribution and toward an emphasis on the general welfare has occurred in an environment of both reduced federal support for cities and a reduced share of city expenditures on redistribution. In addition, the use of community participation, regardless of the composition of the governing coalition, still suffers from knowledge problems that plague any system of nonmarket allocation.

BEHIND THE GAME THEORY MATRIX

Although models by their nature are a simplification of reality, they do need to bear some resemblance to provide useful analysis. Is it realistic to believe that losses from rent-seeking can be so large as to push cities into decline? The late Mancur Olson provided substantial theoretical and empirical evidence that rent-seeking drives national decline.[25] Several researchers have found fairly large negative effects on economic growth from rent-seeking activities. Estimates have been as high as 45 percent of economic output, certainly large enough to push communities into decline.[26] Similar results have been found across U.S. states. For instance both the raw number of interest groups in a state and the number compared to the size of a state's economy have large negative effects on state economic growth.[27]

Empirical results, however strong they may be, can fail to convince in the absence of a theory. The theory here is that community members invest resources into capturing existing

---

25 Mancur Olson, The Rise and Decline of Nations: Economic Growth, Stagflation, and Social Rigidities (New Haven, CT: Yale University Press, 1982).

26 David N. Laband and John P. Sophocleus, "The Social Cost of Rent-Seeking: First Estimates," Public Choice 58 (3) (1988): 269–275; see also William Dougan, "The Cost of Rent Seeking: Is GNP Negative?" Journal of Political Economy 99 (3) (1991): 660–664; Kevin Murphy, Andrei Shleifer, and Robert W. Vishny, "Why Is Rent-Seeking So Costly to Growth?" American Economic Review 83 (2) (1993): 409–414.

27 Ismail Cole and M. Arshad Chawdhry, "Rent Seeking and Economic Growth: Evidence from a Panel of U.S. States," Cato Journal 22 (2) (2002).

resources from others, rather than investing in productive activities that would spur economic growth. In addition to rent-seeking representing a loss of community resources, it can also drive community members on the losing end to exit the community, further reducing the productive capacity of the community. Rent-seeking can also divert government resources away from physical capital investment and public services that could potentially boost long-term growth, and toward short-term consumption on the part of governing coalitions. Rent-seeking can also reduce growth by skewing the career choices of talented and creative individuals.[28] Much has been made recently about the graduates seeking jobs on Wall Street rather than pursuing other activities that might contribute more to economic growth and community development. Similar patterns can be expected at the local level.

CONCLUSION

This essay has argued that many cities are essentially stuck in a bad political trap, where coalitional politics have reduced the overall pie. Moving toward a situation in which local governance fosters the general welfare will not be easy, but implementing rules that minimize, if not eliminate, discrimination across citizens, on both the tax and benefit sides of government, could help shift communities to a position that increases the total welfare of community members.

MARK A. CALABRIA *is director of financial regulation studies at the Cato Institute. Before joining Cato in 2009, he spent seven years as a member of the senior professional staff of the U.S. Senate Committee on Banking, Housing and Urban Affairs. Prior to his service on Capitol Hill, Calabria served as Deputy Assistant Secretary for Regulatory Affairs at the U.S. Department of Housing and Urban Development, and also held a variety of positions at Harvard University's Joint Center for Housing Studies, the National Association of Home Builders' and the National Association of Realtors. Calabria has also been a research associate with the U.S. Census Bureau's Center for Economic Studies. He holds a doctorate in economics from George Mason University.*

---

28 Kevin Murphy, Andrei Shleifer, and Robert W. Vishny, "The Allocation of Talent: Implications for Growth," Quarterly Journal of Economics 106 (2) (1991): 503–530.

OUR HISTORY WITH CONCENTRATED POVERTY

Peter Edelman
Georgetown University Law Center

merican poverty has many faces. The poor are elderly and young, families and single individuals, men and women, with and without disabilities. They are of all races and ethnicities. They work in restaurants, on farms, in packinghouses, in day-labor settings, and at many more workplaces that do not pay enough to get them out of poverty. Their work is often part-time, intermittent, or largely nonexistent. They live in inner cities, suburbs, and rural areas that range from Appalachia to the Mississippi delta and from the *colonias* of South Texas to the Pine Ridge Reservation of South Dakota.

We declared a "war" on poverty almost half a century ago, and we have taken major steps forward, but poverty is still with us. Some have even said we fought a war on poverty and poverty won. That's quite wrong. Considering the low-wage economy of the past 40 years, we've actually done pretty well. Things would be much worse if we had not acted. We have far too much poverty still, but our policy achievements now keep some 40 million people from becoming poor, according to analysis by the Center on Budget and Policy Priorities. Poverty did not win. Social Security, Medicare, Medicaid, food stamps, Supplemental Security Income (SSI), the Earned Income Tax Credit (EITC), the Child Tax Credit, public housing, housing vouchers, and Pell grants have made a huge difference. The civil rights laws of the 1960s have played a significant role as well.

Nonetheless, we have a long way to go, and that is especially the case with concentrated poverty, which is of course one of the subjects of this book.

Most people who experience poverty have a short stint of it. We need to do much better at cushioning their fall and helping them get back on their feet, but, as troubling as poverty of any duration is, the far more vexing problem is that of those who are persistently poor and whose children tend to be poor as well. Persistent and intergenerational poverty sorts itself by race and gender, too, but it is particularly a feature of concentrated poverty, both urban and rural.

We have had far less success in attacking the hard core of poverty that persists from year to year and generation to generation and is often associated with where people live, especially when a disproportionate number of residents of a neighborhood, town, or rural area are poor.

Why have we had less success? Both experience and research tell us that when too many people in a place are poor, their situation produces "concentration effects." All of us have our individual strengths and weaknesses, and almost all of us are also part of some kind of community. The community of which we are a part is both influenced by and influences our individual strengths and weaknesses. The economic health of a community has a reverberative effect on its social capital that in turn has a multiplier effect on numerous behaviors and outcomes for people who live there. Once the concentration of poverty takes hold, we have seen that it is tough to root out.

My focus here is urban concentrated poverty and the history of efforts to ameliorate it. Many Americans see urban concentrated poverty, or to be more precise, African American urban concentrated poverty, as the face of American poverty generally. That is untrue in two respects. People who live in places of concentrated poverty are a minority of the poor, and people of color are not the only residents of such places. White Appalachia is a longstanding example of persistent poverty with devastating effects that carry on from generation to generation. And with the economic decline of predominantly white small towns around the country, we see many places where the social fabric is wearing thin, a phenomenon appearing more frequently as the current recession drags on. And, sad to say, Indian reservations are another pertinent example.

Nevertheless, African Americans make up a disproportionate number of the people who live in such circumstances, constituting about half of the inner-city poor. It is important to understand why this is, as well as to be aware of the history of efforts to confront it. The answer to why this especially difficult set of issues came to pass in the first place and why it is so hard to root out involves a complexly intertwined set of forces and factors: racism, economic trends, demographic changes, politics, and policy failures.

I think it is fair to say that inner-city poverty, like poverty generally in post–World War II America, was on few people's radar screens before the 1960s. Urban "ghettos" began to make their way into public consciousness with the civil rights movement in the early part of the decade and forced their way onto national television with the civil unrest of the mid-decade. The police dogs in Alabama and the murders in Mississippi had shocked the nation into positive action to end state-mandated segregation, but the violence and burnings in South Central Los Angeles and elsewhere shortly thereafter evoked a more negative response to the widespread injustices in the North and West.

The history of significant inner-city segregation and poverty goes back to the Great Migration. Beginning with World War I and continuing for a half century and beyond, black Americans moved northward and westward by the millions from the South. Comparatively speaking, the cities of the North and West constituted liberation from sharecropping and backbreaking work in the fields for bare subsistence wages, and from a constant danger of violent reprisal for invented transgressions against whites. That the migrants were required to live in segregated neighborhoods when they moved North and West was degrading but in fact an improvement over what they had left behind.

The generation that migrated saw their new life as a step forward on the whole and accommodated themselves to the (hardly insubstantial) barriers they encountered. Their children saw things very differently, eventuating in the violence that ripped away the veneer of normalcy.

The civil unrest of the 1960s changed everything. Until then, racially segregated inner-city neighborhoods were economically integrated and, at least in the later telling, had a strong sense of community. With expectations raised by the legal fruits of civil rights activism, younger residents—frustrated by the failure of the movement to make a difference for them—exploded in anger. The proximate cause was police misconduct. The real point, though, was palpable discrimination in the world of work, exacerbated by inferior educational opportunities and daily reminders of de facto second-class citizenship. To a new generation coming of age, going along to get along was no longer acceptable.

Visionaries like Ted Watkins in Los Angeles and Arthur Brazier in Chicago were already at work on inner-city organizing and community economic development when the cities began to burn, as were farsighted people like Dick Boone at the Ford Foundation and Mike Sviridoff in New Haven. Robert Kennedy, for whom I worked, found himself challenged by leaders in the Bedford-Stuyvesant neighborhood of Brooklyn to help them revitalize the neighborhood, and started a process that led to the founding of what became the Bedford-Stuyvesant Restoration Corporation.

Importantly, Kennedy and his Senate colleague Jacob Javits successfully attached an amendment to the legislation reauthorizing the War on Poverty that made federal funding available for multidimensional inner-city revitalization initiatives. Via this funding and significant financial support made available by the Ford Foundation, community development corporations (CDCs) sprouted in many communities, as did the community action agencies that were at the heart of the War on Poverty. Even with the violence and the burning, there was a sense of purpose and movement and a new activism that transformed politics in city after city.

Kennedy and others who came after him—notably, George Romney as Secretary of Housing and Urban Development in the Nixon administration—had a dual vision of policies relating to place. Improving life chances for inner-city residents was one objective, but it was nested in a framework of metropolitan desegregation that would promote genuine choice for people of color to live and work outside the inner city. Romney's insistence about this ultimately wore out his welcome with the Nixon administration.

Kennedy's interest in the question of place began with three speeches that he delivered in January 1966. The speeches made two major points. The first was a call for metropolitan residential desegregation that would include people of all income levels. The second was his idea for an inner-city revitalization initiative, which turned out to be the cornerstone for what became the Bedford-Stuyvesant Restoration Corporation.

Kennedy and Romney notwithstanding, the part of the vision that called for metropolitan desegregation regardless of income disappeared from the table. Inner-city strategies, which in Kennedy's view would have included both revitalization in the inner-city areas themselves and the wherewithal for people to move out if they wanted to, focused solely on revitalizing the neighborhoods themselves.

So the story after 1968 was not what some of us had envisioned. Of course history often surprises us. Robert Kennedy was murdered, and Richard Nixon was elected. But this is just the beginning of the story.

To start with, the premises on which neighborhood revitalization efforts operated were at best too narrow. The fundamental operational idea was that the neighborhood could be lifted up within its four corners—that enough new jobs could be created inside of or just adjacent to the neighborhood to turn things around. Improved housing, neighborhood amenities, and community safety were also important aims, but they, too, focused within the neighborhood. And the all-important economic strategy—to attract enough manufacturing plants and small businesses to close the employment gap—was deeply flawed. For the most part, CDCs did not pursue strategies of helping people find jobs in the regional economy, let alone pursue the vital transit facilities necessary for people to get to those jobs once found. In retrospect, it is obvious that the only way to maximize employment was to pursue jobs wherever they were available. But that was not the strategy chosen.

To some extent this was an effort to make a virtue out of a necessity. If metropolitan housing desegregation and even access to jobs were unavailable to low-income inner-city residents, the only avenue for change was to transform the inner city. But the mistake also had an ideological driver. CDCs came into being during the era of black power, and many of their leaders' political views matured at that time. Their vision was one of political power grounded in economic strength. If new jobs could be situated in the immediate area, the economic success for the residents would become the building block for political power. And there was a third point, in my view. I have always thought as well that some of the white establishment's support for CDCs was driven by its comfort with a strategy of self-segregation.

If the premises were flawed, the demographic, economic, and political trends were toxic. With large sections of inner cities resembling bombed-out European cities after World War II, many residents of inner-city neighborhoods wanted to get out if they possibly could. The striking expansion of the black middle class and the enactment of the Fair Housing Act of 1968 gave some people the economic and legal basis for doing so. Not everyone who had the economic capacity to leave did so, but the exodus was big enough to destabilize the preexisting economic and community mix, and the descent into concentrated poverty was underway. Efforts at inner-city neighborhood development, already facing tough odds, became even more challenging. Whether greater mobility for lower-income people in inner cities to disperse would have helped or made matters worse is of course impossible to say. The larger point is that economic trends, racial attitudes, and political factors converged in the 1970s and 1980s to push things in the wrong direction.

Trends in the larger economy exacerbated the process. The industrial jobs that had brought impressive gains to black men along with others began disappearing in large numbers—to other parts of the country, to other parts of the world, and to technological change. The income of the lower half of earners of all races declined, and income in inner cities dropped even more.

The war on crime and the war on drugs began—in my view, in large measure as a conservative strategy to help attract white votes. The effect was devastating for inner cities. Black men, already hit hardest by the economic changes, ended up behind bars in large numbers, with major negative effects on family formation. The percentage of births to unmarried women, which was growing all over the world and among all races and ethnicities, grew disproportionately among African American women. With available jobs increasingly so low wage that a one-worker family with children could not make enough to escape poverty, unmarried women in inner cities were hit the hardest. And welfare benefits, never an avenue out of poverty, lost more ground to inflation every year. In the 1980s crack cocaine made everything even worse.

Not surprisingly, as all of this was going on, comprehensive inner-city neighborhood initiatives lost momentum. Federal and foundation funding decreased, and the problems they were trying to attack were worsening day by day and year by year.

With so many forces influencing things, it's difficult to isolate the significance of any one variable. What we do know is that urban concentrated poverty rose dramatically from 1970 to 1990, essentially doubling over the two decades. CDCs and other community economic development initiatives expanded over that period and made a tangible difference in limited ways. But the bigger picture overshadowed these achievements. Inner cities were caught in a pincers. On the one side was a national economy that was deteriorating for all lower-income people and disproportionately for people of color. On the other side were public policies that, if anything, made matters even worse. The 1990s saw a significant improvement, largely because of the hot economy of the last half of the decade, but things slipped badly between 2000 and 2010.

Can we do better? I think so. Despite the slippage in recent years, I think we know more now about what we should do if we can command the necessary resources and political support.

Most important, we need to clarify the premises of our policies. I believe the operative word is "choice," as Robert Kennedy said in 1966. Everything we do should empower the choice of people to live where they want to live. They should have the economic wherewithal, supported by strong enforcement of antidiscrimination laws and housing vouchers as necessary, to make a real choice of where to live in any metropolitan area. At the same time, they should have a realistic possibility of staying where they live in the inner city, but in a revitalized inner-city community that offers decent housing; good early childhood programs;

high-quality schools; safe streets, parks, and playgrounds; and healthy food sold at nationally advertised prices. This would be new. I do not believe there has ever been a time when we could say with any honesty that we really offered a genuine choice for people to be able to move out or stay in their current neighborhood, with both options being to live in healthy communities.

What are the elements of such a policy?

First, every element of good antipoverty policy that is applicable to people everywhere is relevant to people who live in concentrated poverty. Jobs that pay enough to live on, based as much as possible on wages and supplemented as needed by policies like the EITC, will make it easier for people to move if that is their choice and will collectively raise the quality of life in the neighborhood for those who stay. The same is true for public benefits such as health care, child care, housing, and others.

Second, jobs in the regional economy should be a real policy instead of a bumper sticker. The legacy of the myopia of the early neighborhood revitalization enthusiasts persists despite the lip service of too many who should be doing more. Job training and placement strategies should be simultaneously aggressive in partnering with employers and recruiting inner-city residents for jobs. Transit access is a crucial component of a more robust policy that needs to be pursued at every level of government. Jobs in the regional economy are a key building block in strategies to help people take steps toward moving out and to help them stay in place if that is what they prefer.

Third, housing strategies to facilitate mobility must be pursued in new and improved form. The experience of HOPE VI—a program begun in 1992 at the end of the first Bush administration to demolish rundown public housing and replace it with mixed-income housing—offers lessons in how to avoid moving people to unfamiliar neighborhoods without adequate support services. As operated over the past two decades, it includes excellent examples of creating new mixed-income neighborhoods, but also resulted in a net loss of housing stock for low-income people.

The Obama administration reconceptualized the program in the form of Choice Neighborhoods but was unable to obtain funding to move forward on an adequate scale. Fully implemented, it would promote choice for those who wish to move out, but care must be taken to couple it with strategies to vindicate the choices of those who wish to stay where they are.

Fourth, education must become a central strategy for transforming inner-city neighborhoods into healthy communities. One of the most serious failings of neighborhood revitalization strategies until quite recently has been their lack of attention to the schools attended by the children of the area, including emphasis in the all-important area of early childhood development. Although not the first effort in regard to education, the work of Geoffrey Canada and the Harlem Children's Zone (HCZ) has brought the issue to national prominence and resulted in President Obama's Promise Neighborhoods program.

HCZ teaches a number of important lessons, in addition to the basic fact that quality schools are a key to opportunity for children in low-income neighborhoods. One lesson is that the 1960s mythology that one meta-initiative can transform a neighborhood is just that—a myth—and that multiple actors doing multiple tasks in a collaboratively strategic way is crucial. The second is that charter schools make projects like HCZ substantially more viable. It is not impossible to mount an effort like HCZ in collaboration with a traditional public school or schools—such examples exist in a number of cities—but charters have a flexibility that local schools, controlled as they are from "downtown," are unlikely to have. And the third lesson is that school reform cannot succeed to the maximum degree possible if it occurs in a vacuum. Good schools will make a difference and will be the reason why some children will make it when they otherwise would not have done so, but they will make a much greater difference if they are part of a broader antipoverty strategy.

This point is worthy of extra emphasis. There is a bogus debate going on that pits school reform against antipoverty advocates.

School reformers, wanting to squelch teachers and others who have said over the years that they cannot teach children who come to school with multiple problems that stem from poverty, say (correctly) that there are no valid excuses for failing to teach low-income children. They point (as they could not until quite recently) to multiple examples of schools that excel in teaching low-income children. But to the extent they say or imply that reducing poverty now is somehow less important than school reform, they overstate their point. Antipoverty advocates, for their part, in some instances downplay the independent efficacy of school reform.

The real answer, quite obviously, is that both school reform and serious antipoverty policies are vital. Better schools in inner cities, both charters and traditional public schools, are crucial to children's possibilities of having a better life. But far more inner-city children will succeed in school if their parents have better jobs and higher incomes and if the communities in which they are growing up are healthy. There is no either-or here. Good schools are a must for inner-city children, but they cannot achieve maximum effect unless the schools strategy is part of a larger antipoverty approach.

The fifth element of a productive policy is that for some but not all inner-city neighborhoods, attracting people with somewhat higher incomes will be possible and can be a stepping-stone toward neighborhood improvement. For this to be a possibility at all, we must talk about a neighborhood that is accessible to the city's center, not one that is located miles away, which is frequently the case. But the strategy is hardly without risk. Cities like Washington, DC, have seen neighborhoods gentrified and transformed to the point where the previous residents are pushed out by rising property taxes and rents. On the other hand, HOPE VI provides numerous examples of mixed-income developments located in low-income neighborhoods, with the consequent effect of raising incomes in adjacent blocks.

Sixth, and finally, explicit attention to the behavioral patterns—crime, nonmarital childbearing, denigration of the value of education, and more—that have been associated with concentrated poverty is essential. Sad to say, they have become embedded and, in effect, intergenerational. The structural frameworks and continuing racial discrimination have to be addressed, but so do the issues of personal and parental responsibility. Much of what is needed has to happen on the ground, in the community, carried out as a matter of civic action. Personal and parental responsibility is an indispensable part of building a healthy community.

Issues of concentrated poverty and place are not inherently racial, either in the United States or around the world. Yet we need at the same time to confront the racial facts that are disproportionately present in America's version of concentrated poverty: the official as well as attitudinal racism that created inner-city segregation in the first place and the structural and institutional (and sometimes illegal) racism of inferior schooling, the criminal justice system, the housing market, and employer behavior that perpetuates it.

If we are to make progress in this century toward ending urban concentrated poverty, we must understand what caused it, what perpetuates it, and the plethora of remedies that must be applied to bring about changes of the necessary magnitude.

PETER EDELMAN *is a professor of law at Georgetown Law Center and faculty co-director of the Georgetown Center on Poverty, Inequality, and Public Policy. He served as a legislative assistant to Senator Robert F. Kennedy and as an assistant secretary in the Department of Health and Human Services in the Clinton administration. His latest book is* So Rich So Poor: Why It's So Hard to End Poverty in America.

CRIME AND COMMUNITY DEVELOPMENT

Ingrid Gould Ellen
New York University

C ommunity development has traditionally focused on investments in housing, commercial revitalization, and physical improvements. Although all three are clearly critical to communities, the field has largely ignored (or paid too little attention to) one of the key factors that shape the quality of the everyday life: public safety.

Yet there is growing evidence that families care a great deal about safety and prioritize it above many other community attributes. Concern about safety and crime was one of the main reasons why families participating in the Moving to Opportunity (MTO) demonstration program accepted the option to move out of their high-poverty neighborhoods. Moreover, participating families who received vouchers and assistance to move to lower-poverty environments relocated to safer neighborhoods. At the outset of the study, nearly half of all of the participating households in Boston reported feeling unsafe or very unsafe. Among those offered vouchers to move to lower poverty areas, that share fell to only 24 percent several years later.[1] (Crime was falling during this period, so control group members who received no mobility assistance also reported feeling more safe in their neighborhoods at the time of the follow-up survey; however, the improvement for these individuals was far smaller.)

A recent New York University study of 91 cities found suggestive evidence that housing voucher holders weighted crime and safety more heavily than poverty levels when choosing a neighborhood in which to live.[2] As of 2000, the average voucher household lived in a significantly lower-crime neighborhood than the average tenant participating in the Low Income Housing Tax Credit program, although members of both sets lived in communities with nearly identical poverty rates and minority population shares. In other words, individuals with greater residential choice—that is, voucher recipients—chose to live in neighborhoods with markedly lower crime rates but not lower poverty rates or different racial compositions.

Recent research shows that families have good reason to worry about the safety of their environment. Most directly, people who live in high-crime neighborhoods are more likely to be victims of crime. In addition, there is strong evidence to indicate that such unsafe environments affect families and children in other ways. People who live in high-crime environments are more likely to witness a violent crime or know someone who has been victimized; this can profoundly shape one's outlook on the world and level of ambition. Fear of crime can lead individuals to withdraw from their communities and live more sheltered and isolated lives. Finally, a growing number of studies are finding that exposure to crime, and especially violence, can heighten stress in children

---

1 Lawrence F. Katz, Jeffrey R. Kling, and Jeffrey B. Liebman, "Moving to Opportunity in Boston: Early Results of a Randomized Mobility Experiment," Quarterly Journal of Economics 116 (2) (2001): 607–654.

2 Michael C. Lens, Ingrid Gould Ellen, and Katherine O'Regan, "Neighborhood Crime Exposure among Housing Choice Voucher Households," Cityscape: A Journal of Policy Development and Research 13 (3) (2011): 135–159.

and lead to lower cognitive test scores and diminished performance in school.[3]

In addition to causing fear and stress, which can shape individual outcomes, crime may also profoundly affect the social structures of communities through high levels of incarceration. In neighborhoods where violence and crime are particularly prevalent, incarceration removes large numbers of young adults—fathers, in particular—from the community, disrupting social networks, breaking up families, and weakening local institutions.[4]

In short, the evidence is strong that community development practitioners should increase the attention paid to safety and crime. The more difficult question, of course, is how: what tools do community development practitioners and policymakers have to fight crime? Most obviously, they can and should work with law enforcement to ensure that police are responsive to local calls and maintain a presence in problem areas. In addition, there are at least three other strategies community development practitioners and policymakers might adopt. The first and perhaps easiest is to combat physical blight. The "broken windows" theory of George Kelling and James Q. Wilson argues that signs of physical disorder, such as uncollected garbage, graffiti, and broken windows, signal to potential offenders that local residents are not invested in the community and would be unlikely to intervene

3 Anna Aizer, "Neighborhood Violence and Urban Youth: Working Paper" no. 13773 (Cambridge, MA: National Bureau of Economic Research, 2008). Available at nber.org/papers/w13773.pdf; Patrick Sharkey, "The Acute Effect of Local Homicides on Children's Cognitive Performance," proceedings of the National Academy of Sciences of the USA 107 (26) (2010): 11733–11738; Mai Stafford, Tarani Chandola, and Michael Marmot, "Association between Fear of Crime and Mental Health and Physical Functioning," American Journal of Public Health 97 (11) (2007): 2076–2081.

4 Dina R. Rose and Todd Clear, "Incarceration, Reentry, and Social Capital: Social Networks in the Balance," prepared for the conference From Prison to Home: The Effect of Incarceration and Reentry on Children, Families and Communities (Washington, DC: U.S. Department of Health and Human Services, 2001). Available at http://aspe.hhs.gov/hsp/prison2home02/Rose.htm.

in or report any crime.[5] Although few studies have been able to pinpoint the direction of causality, there is strong evidence that physical disorder is at least associated with higher levels of crime; thus, community members should act quickly to address such signs of disorder.

A second and arguably more fundamental approach is to develop the collective efficacy of a community, which is the willingness of residents to monitor public spaces, intervene when those spaces are threatened, and help neighbors in need. Robert Sampson and his colleagues showed that collective efficacy is highly predictive of crime, and they argue that building collective efficacy is far more important to controlling crime than fixing signs of physical blight.[6] Their study recommends strategies to organize community residents and encourage collective work on social control. A partnership with local law enforcement may be useful when implementing this strategy, but the residents of a community must drive this effort.

Finally, while impacts of such programs have not yet been rigorously evaluated, community courts such as the Red Hook Community Justice Center in Brooklyn appear to be a promising way to engage communities and address low-level crime.[7] These courts bring the justice system closer to citizens and aim to make it more responsive to everyday concerns. Community residents are involved in identifying public safety concerns and priorities, and they help to determine community service assignments for convicted offenders that both reconnect these individuals to

---

5 George Kelling and James Q. Wilson, "Broken Windows: The Police and Neighborhood Safety," The Atlantic, March 1982. Available at theatlantic.com/magazine/archive/1982/03/broken-windows/4465; Bernard Harcourt and Jens Ludwig, "Broken Windows: New Evidence from New York City and a Five-City Social Experiment," University of Chicago Law Review 73 (2006). Available at http://home.uchicago.edu/%7Eludwigj/papers/Broken_windows_2006.pdf.

6 Robert Sampson, Stephen Raudenbush, and Felton Earls. "Neighborhoods and Violent Crime: A Multilevel Study of Collective Efficacy 1997," Science 277 (5328) (1997): 918–924.

7 See Jeffrey Fagan and Victoria Malkin. "Theorizing Community Justice Through Community Courts" Fordham Urban Law Journal, 2003 (30): 857–953; and Eric Lee, Community Courts: An Evolving Model. Bureau of Justice Statistics Monograph 183452 (2000). United States Department of Justice.

the community and help to address neighborhood problems. Many community courts also house a variety of social service programs (such as job training and placement, drug treatment, and tutoring) to address the root causes of criminal behavior. Although each community court employs a different approach, they all seek to promptly administer punishments for nonserious offenses that can serve to benefit the community, provide services to address some of the root problems that contribute to crime, and forge meaningful partnerships with the neighborhoods they serve.

We are only just beginning to understand the costs that crime—and fear of crime—can impose on communities and their residents. Crime can lead to social isolation, encourage unhealthy behaviors by changing perceived risks, and heighten stress levels. Such elevated stress may make it difficult for children to focus in school and to learn, and in the long-run it may compromise their immune systems and increase vulnerability to disease. The latest findings from the MTO demonstration indicate that providing an opportunity for very poor families to move to neighborhoods with lower levels of poverty can lead to improvements in physical and mental health.[8] Although the mechanism of this effect is unclear, the opportunity to live in a safer neighborhood may be the critical ingredient in ending the cycle of poverty for many families.

INGRID GOULD ELLEN *is professor of urban planning and public policy at New York University's Wagner Graduate School of Public Service and co-director of the Furman Center for Real Estate and Urban Policy. She joined the Wagner faculty in the fall of 1997 and presently teaches courses in microeconomics, urban economics, and housing and urban policy. Professor Ellen's research interests center on urban social and economic policy. She is author of* Sharing America's Neighborhoods: The Prospects for Stable Racial Integration *(Harvard University Press, 2000) and has written numerous journal articles and book chapters related to housing policy, neighborhood change, urban growth, and*

8 Jens Ludwig et al., "Neighborhoods, Obesity and Diabetes: A Randomized Social Experiment," New England Journal of Medicine 365 (16) (2011): 1509–1519.

school and neighborhood segregation. Before coming to NYU, Professor Ellen held visiting positions at the Urban Institute and the Brookings Institution. She attended Harvard University, where she received a bachelor's degree in applied mathematics, an MPP, and a PhD in public policy.

EARLY CHILDHOOD DEVELOPMENT:
Creating Healthy Communities with Greater Efficiency and Effectiveness

Gabriella Conti and James J. Heckman[1]
University of Chicago

Healthy communities are catalysts for personal health and economic success. Creating healthy communities by transforming disadvantaged ones, is an enormous challenge. Possible solutions are myriad. Or so it seems. Thanks to developmental, social, and economic science, we know more than many think about how to effect change. We can apply what we know for the public good. The most effective strategies for building healthy communities are based on a causal framework that shows how family, community and institutions matter, how they create health, and where and

1   We gratefully acknowledge support from NIH R01-HD054702 and R37-HD065072; the JB and MK Pritzker Family Foundation; the Institute for New Economic Thinking (INET); a European Research Council grant DEVHEALTH-269874; the Smith Richardson Foundation; the Buffett Early Childhood Fund; the California Endowment; the Commonwealth Foundation; the Nemours Foundation; and an anonymous funder. The views expressed in this paper are those of the authors and not necessarily those of the funders.

when interventions in the life cycle of human development are most effective.

The most important step in developing sound policies and practices is to move past correlations to understand causal mechanisms. For example, it is often noted that more education leads to better health. Taken at face value, that looks to be the case. Yet, do we really know if education alone is the catalyst for better health, or might there be other, earlier factors, in the developmental lifecycle—for example, prenatal health, family environments, or early childhood development that promotes the education that is positively associated with health outcomes and that also have independent effects on health.

Determining causal mechanisms is important because relying on correlations often leads to poor decisions. One famous example is taken from the Russian peasants in the 19th century. Some peasants noticed that a lot of doctors were present when epidemics spread through the community. They concluded that their health depended on rising up and killing the doctors.[2] We laugh at this type of causal reasoning today, but we are something like Russian peasants in addressing our own vexing problems. Consider our current debate over the causes of obesity. Some blame corn syrup, others carbohydrates, others fat, others processed food, others food deserts, and still others total caloric intake. Some of this analysis is scientific, but most is guilt by association. As a result, food is rapidly becoming part of a culture war. Without hard causal analyses grounded in data, we are at the whim of speculation in making policy.

In addition to determining causality, it is critical to assess optimal timing. Where in the lifecycle of individuals is an intervention most effective? Budgets are tight and resources are scarce. To do the most with our money, we need to know what is best to do and when to do it. We need to be courageous enough to let solid causal evidence drive public and private investments in human capital.

---

2   See F. Fisher, The Identification Problem in Econometrics (New York: McGraw-Hill, 1966).

A case in point is research conducted by the Robert Wood Johnson Foundation over a decade ago into the causes of early deaths. They estimated that the behavior of individuals and the lack of self-care accounted for 40 percent of early deaths. Thirty percent were due to genetic predispositions, 15 percent were due to social circumstances and 5 percent to environmental exposures. Only 10 percent of early deaths stemmed from shortfalls in medical care. In light of this, it makes little sense that, prior to recent health care reforms, 95 percent of the health budget was spent on treatment, and not prevention in all of its forms.[3] Now, more than a decade later, we focus more resources on prevention, yet we are still not looking analytically at timing. If 40 percent of early deaths are caused by behavioral patterns, when is an investment in prevention most efficient and productive? When can positive behaviors be formed, or when do negative behavior patterns become evident? The answer to these questions can make or break budgets.

Fortunately, empirical analysis provides clear answers when it comes to effective strategies for developing healthy communities. The contributing factors are the things that make for a productive person—strong families, effective early childhood development that includes health and developmentally appropriate education, quality schools, and access to preventive health care. If one were to prioritize resources, evidence suggests we should place greater emphasis on strengthening early childhood development, with families and early health playing essential roles. K-12 education is important, and it is imperative that we fix what is currently wrong. However, waiting until age 5 when children enter formal schooling to influence the cognitive and character skills necessary for a healthy and productive life—and, by extension, a healthy and productive community—is far too late. The evidence is quite clear: Early health and early childhood development from birth to age 5 is a form of preventive health *and* economic investment that drives achievement and economic returns.

---

3 See J. McGinnis, P. Williams-Russo, and J. Knickman, "The Case for More Active Policy Attention to Health Promotion," Health Affairs 21(2) (2002): 78-93.

This finding cuts across the grain of the widely held belief that more education produces better health. To a certain extent, that is true. More highly educated people tend to select higher-paying jobs that come with greater health, social, and economic benefits. They also tend to be more careful about their health. As a result of this belief, many of our current policies to advance healthier individuals and communities promote more education. It is a good strategy, but by itself it is not the most effective strategy.

Careful studies establish that education is a causal factor producing better health. But the traits shaped before children enter school produce success in school and have independent effects of their own. Important early traits include health and socioemotional or character development that enhances cognitive development and generates achievement in school, career, community, and life. These findings suggest that those looking to build healthier communities should incorporate early interventions as an important part of the strategy to catalyze greater returns.

A key piece of evidence for this is our research based on the British Cohort Study (BCS).[4] We use it to examine the causal effect of education on healthy behaviors and on labor market outcomes.

The British Cohort Study is a survey of all babies born after the 24th week of gestation from Sunday, April 5 to Saturday, April 11, 1970 in Great Britain. There have been seven follow-ups to trace all members of this birth cohort: 1975, 1980, 1986, 1996, 2000, 2004, and 2008. We looked at information from the birth survey in 1970, measurements from the second sweep in 1980 and outcomes from the fifth follow-up sweep in 2000.

---

4 See G. Conti and J. Heckman, "Understanding the Early Origins of the Education-Health Gradient: A Framework That Can Also Be Applied to Analyze Gene-Environment Interactions," Perspectives on Psychological Science, 5(5) (2010): 585–605; and G. Conti, J. Heckman, and S. Urzua, "The Education-Health Gradient," American Economic Review: Papers & Proceedings, 100(2) (2010): 234–238.

Birth information took "family endowments"—parental resources that formed the foundation for early learning experiences—into account. These included the mother's age, education, father's social class, and parity at birth. This was supplemented with family information at age 10 (the second follow-up sweep in 1980) that included the gross family income, whether the child had lived with both parents since birth, and the number of children in the family at age 10.

Measurements in the second follow-up sweep included scores on standard cognitive tests such as math, English, language comprehension and word definition. Also included were measurements of social and personality—character—skills from tests on control, perseverance, cooperativeness, attentiveness, and persistence. These were supplemented by basic physical measurements in height, weight, head circumference, and the height of the child's parents. The fifth follow-up sweep in 2000 surveyed the adult outcomes of the child, taking into account the length of schooling, labor market outcomes in employment and wages, healthy behaviors, and health status.

We study the measured effect of education on employment and key indicators of health, such as smoking, depression, and obesity. We control for the selective factors that cause some to go to school and others not to—early life experiences (parental endowments, early health, early childhood development, and effective character skills). We find that skills acquired early in life—particularly the early development of the character skills of impulse control, persistence, and sociability—greatly contribute to persistence in education, career attainment, and health. While schooling has a substantial impact on health outcomes, the causal factor and weight of its impact varies by issue and gender. In some cases, schooling plays a greater role; in others, skills acquired early on have more impact. In the majority of cases, the skills acquired early in life explain a greater proportion of the measured effect of education than does the true causal effect of education—the effect of education on outcomes controlling for the influence of early life factors on the studied outcomes.

The chart below shows a clear relationship between education and health. The height of the bars including the light and dark portions displays mean differences in a variety of outcomes between those who stop their education at the compulsory level and those who go on to attain a higher level of education. More educated individuals are more likely to work full-time, earn higher wages, and exercise regularly. In addition they are less likely to be obese, smoke daily, be in poor health and suffer from depression. But how much of the difference between highly and less-educated individuals is caused by education, and how much reflects early life factors (cognitive ability, social skills and early health) and family background characteristics? If education has a causal effect, then increasing the educational level of the population would be an effective health policy. If, instead, more educated individuals are healthier because they have better skills developed as children, then early intervention is a more effective strategy for reducing health disparities in adulthood.

Figure 1 decomposes the drivers of a variety of outcomes by gender. The dark portion of each bar in the graph is the causal contribution of education, and the light portion quantifies the contribution of cognitive and noncognitive skills, early health, and family endowments shaped by early environments. For example, early life factors (cognitive and social skills as well as family endowments) account for at least half of the adult dispari- ties in poor health, depression, obesity, and wages. In addition, the early life factors promote education which has independent effects on outcomes.

Studying the contributions of early life factors and the causal effect of education leads to a solid conclusion: Quality early childhood development can close the income gap, reduce health disparities, and save taxpayers a bundle in lower health and social costs. It saves lives, and it saves money. Early childhood development has substantial health and economic payoffs.

Three important lessons emerge from recent research that should shape future policies to improve the health of individuals, communities, and the American economy.

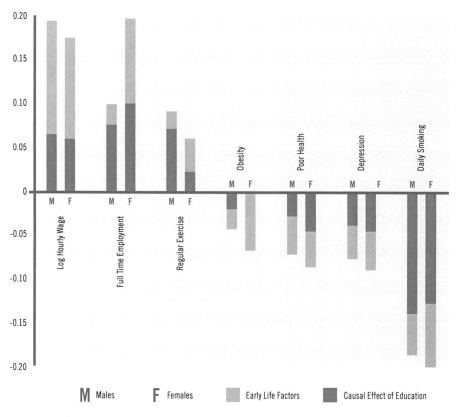

Figure 1: Mean Differences in Outcomes Due to Early Life Factors versus the Causal Effect of Education

Source: Conti and Heckman (2010)

NOTE: The figure displays mean differences by gender in health, health behaviors and labor market outcomes due to early life factors and due to the causal effect of education (post-compulsory schooling level vs. compulsory schooling).

LESSON 1: DEVELOP THE WHOLE CHILD

Many major economic and social problems such as crime, teenage pregnancy, dropping out of school, and adverse health are linked to low levels of skill and ability. Those with high levels of skill and ability more often succeed in life.

To promote successful lives and healthy communities, policy-makers should recognize the multiplicity of human abilities.

Currently, public policy in the United States focuses primarily on promoting and measuring cognitive ability (typically captured by achievement tests). That emphasis is wrong. We must also promote and assess cognitive, character, and health skills necessary to be a highly adaptive, productive, and valuable adult.

In many ways, we are failing the economic test of our times because our tests are failing us. There is no question that cognitive abilities are important determinants of socioeconomic success. But we must also heed the decisive evidence that skills other than cognition—physical and mental health, perseverance, attention, motivation and self-confidence—are as important in predicting success in life. In many tasks in life, they are more important. They contribute greatly to performance in society at large, to workforce productivity and to stronger, more prosperous communities.[5]

In their quest for accountability in public investments, policymakers must hold themselves accountable for developing the whole child and evaluating progress based on measurements that reflect the full range of skills and abilities that are essential for success in life and that are highly valued in the labor market.

LESSON 2: INEQUALITIES OPEN UP EARLY IN LIFE

We live in an era of substantial and growing social and economic inequality. Research in economics, psychology, neuroscience and genetics examines the origins of inequality and analyzes policies to alleviate it. A large body of research confirms that the accident of birth is a primary source of inequality. Families play a powerful role in creating adult outcomes. Parental resources, skills and abilities matter greatly in shaping the skills of children.

It is widely documented that American mobility across generations is lower than in most European countries. Horatio Alger's "rags to riches" story is not true in contemporary American society. A father's long-run income and social position

---

5   Mathilde Almlund, Angela Duckworth, James J., Heckman, and Tim Kautz, "Personality Psychology and Economics." In Handbook of the Economics of Education, edited by in E. Hanushek, S. Machin, and L. Woessman (Amsterdam: Elsevier, 2011).

is a powerful determinant of the income and social position of the son.

Gaps in cognitive, character, and health skills between the advantaged and the disadvantaged open up early in the lives of children, well before they enter school. Parenting and family environments of young children are major causal factors.

Family environments in the United States have deteriorated over the past 40 years. A greater fraction of children is being born into disadvantaged families with fewer parenting resources. At the same time, parents in the top-earning families invest far more in parenting and schooling for their children than ever before. Due to growing inequality in parental resources and child-rearing environments, the disparity of resources between the haves and the have-nots has increased substantially.

As a group, children from families at the top of the income distribution receive far more investment in parenting and schooling than ever before, and the disparity between the haves and the have-nots is widening.

This trend shows no sign of abating. In fact, the current economic downturn has accelerated it. Unchecked, it will further reduce social mobility and create greater economic and social polarization in the next generation. It will also increase the burdens of ill health, crime, and educational and skill deficits for future generations of Americans. Supplementing at-risk families with quality early childhood development resources can help stem this inequality and promote social mobility. Failure to address this problem will result in greater economic deficits with fewer chances to generate revenue through a more productive workforce.

LESSON 3: EARLY INTERVENTION IS FAR MORE EFFECTIVE THAN LATER REMEDIATION

The skills that matter can be created. That is the solid promise for alleviating poverty, promoting health, and creating upward mobility through opportunity and talent. Child poverty is not solely determined by family income. It is most accurately measured by the parenting resources—the attachment, the guidance and the supervision accorded to children, as well as the quality of the schools and the neighborhoods that parents can draw on.

Investments in early childhood development, from birth to age 5, can improve cognitive and character skills and the health of disadvantaged children. Such early efforts promote schooling, reduce crime, foster workforce productivity, reduce teenage pregnancy, and foster healthy behaviors. The rates of return on these investments are higher than stock market returns, even in normal times.

The substantial benefit from early investments arises because life cycle skill formation is dynamic in nature. Skill begets skill; motivation begets motivation. Motivation cross-fosters skill and skill cross-fosters motivation. Early health is critical to this development process. A healthy child free of asthma and lead poisoning is a child who is ready to engage, who will learn more, and who is more likely to be a productive adult. The longer society waits to intervene in the life of a disadvantaged child, the more costly it is to remediate disadvantage in the form of public job training, convict rehabilitation programs, adult literacy programs, treatment for chronic health conditions or tuition subsidies.

In conclusion, if we truly seek to build healthier communities, we must significantly refocus public policy to capitalize on the importance of the early years in creating opportunity, building capabilities and producing skills that create healthier people, a highly productive workforce, and an economically competitive nation.[6] The path forward is clear: Governments, the community development industry, foundations, and other private organizations should work together to invest in early childhood

---

6 For further evidence, see James J. Heckman, "Schools, Skills, and Synapses," Economic Inquiry, 46 (2008): 289–324. This paper is also available as a discussion paper through IZA available at http://ftp.iza.org/dp3515.pdf.

development that will promote better education, health, social and economic outcomes for all—and for many years to come.

GABRIELLA CONTI *is an assistant professor at the Irving B. Harris School of Public Policy, University of Chicago. She is a cofounder of the Health Inequality Network. Among other research she also works with health effects of early life adversity in rhesus monkeys.*

JAMES J. HECKMAN *is the Henry Schultz Distinguished Professor of Economics at the University of Chicago. In 2000, he shared the Sveriges Riksbank Prize in Economic Sciences in Memory of Alfred Nobel with Daniel McFadden. Heckman directs the Economics Research Center and the Center for Social Program Evaluation at the Harris School for Public Policy, and is professor of law at the University of Chicago School of Law.*

MOBILIZING SCIENCE TO REDUCE INTERGENERATIONAL POVERTY

James M. Radner
University of Toronto

Jack P. Shonkoff
Harvard University

T he proposition that local communities can generate innovative strategies to rise out of poverty has a long pedigree. Its roots are embedded in a rich combination of scholarly thought and popular conviction. Its growth is marked by parallel processes of rigorous evaluation and partisan advocacy. A wide variety of place-based initiatives have been inspired by organizing concepts such as collective efficacy and social empowerment and by deep commitments to eliminating structural inequities, combating institutionalized discrimination, building social capital, and advancing social justice. In this context, generations of efforts that began during the War on Poverty of the 1960s and continue to the present day have underscored both the promise and the challenges of community-based efforts to combat entrenched poverty.

As we ponder the future of place-based approaches to social change, four themes provide a promising framework for fresh thinking about the challenges. The first is the *complexity* of neighborhood poverty, whose diffuse burdens (such as jobs short-ages, social and racial exclusion, transportation gaps, violent crime, poor public health, and deficient educational opportunities) all affect each other and demand simultaneous attention.[1] The second theme is *conflict*, which is fueled by disagreements among key stakeholders about objectives, resources, time horizons, and messaging (among others) that can result in deeply entrenched positions that block innovation.[2] For example, the War on Poverty's community action program quickly encountered tensions among public officials and neighborhood leaders over the extent to which the purpose was policy change or program implementation.

The third theme is *context*, which refers to the challenge of widely applying innovations developed in a particular community that depend on its unique aspects and are therefore difficult to incorporate into sustainable, large-scale policies.[3] The fourth and final theme is *time*, which is reflected in the simple reality that effective community development requires patience for listening and relationship building, while it faces intense pressure for rapid results.[4]

The aim of this essay is to describe a new approach to reducing intergenerational poverty by mobilizing science to stimulate community-driven innovation. This approach is premised on effective collaboration among scientists, community leaders, and

---

1 This challenge was recognized in the 1960s as policymakers worked to improve on early War on Poverty results; Robert Kennedy famously called it the need to "grasp the web whole."

2 For a recent account of pitfalls and strategies in this arena, see Xavier de Souza Briggs, Networks, Power, and a Dual Agenda: New Lessons and Strategies for Old Community Building Dilemmas (Boston: MIT, 2007). Available at http://web.mit.edu/workingsmarter/media/pdf-ws-kia-brief-0703.pdf (retrieved March 2012).

3 For an insightful review of this challenge, see Lisbeth B. Schorr, Common Purpose (New York: Anchor Doubleday, 1997).

4 This challenge, too, was encountered by community efforts in the 1960s, as Schorr (ibid., p. 311) notes.

other stakeholders, starting with agreement on ambitious goals and hypotheses about how they can be met. Connected in this shared purpose, communities and their partners can then begin to move along a pathway of practical action and continuous learning toward the co-discovery of effective strategies. This essay elaborates on the four themes outlined above and draws on recent experiences in diverse settings where people are applying this approach to enhance the healthy development of young children.

TAMING COMPLEXITY

Advances in the science of early childhood development, including its underlying neurobiology, offer an unprecedented opportunity for communities, families, and their partners to bring sharper focus to their efforts on behalf of vulnerable young children. Although it may appear that introducing new frameworks into an already complex set of dynamics can only complicate the challenges we described above, multiple stakeholders can capitalize on advances in science if they focus on a shared commitment to an explicit set of "stretch outcomes" and then work jointly on developing and testing a "causal theory of change" that links specific actions to those outcomes.

Stretch outcomes are results that represent high but potentially achievable aspirations for the well-being of a defined population.[5] Setting stretch outcomes entails agreeing on measurable goals along dimensions that matter to the community and specifying achievement targets (for example, in terms of population percentages) that represent substantial gains over what current practice yields. This is a distinctly different philosophy from the approach adopted by most poverty reduction efforts, which center on the effectiveness of an individual *program*, assessed by a combination of programmatic outputs, anecdotal examples, and the discovery of measured impacts that are statistically significant yet typically modest in magnitude. In contrast, a stretch outcomes approach

---

5   "Population" in this essay refers to a definable group of vulnerable children or families in a geographic area.

focuses on the *well-being of a population*, as defined by community-specified objectives, which serve as the central criteria for success and drive constant experimentation with combinations of program inputs. Stretch outcomes for a city might include, for example, cutting infant mortality in half over three years, and halving it again over the next three.

The concept of a *causal theory of change* refers to a testable notion of how a set of new or modified policies and programs can produce specifically targeted stretch outcomes. It begins by identifying assumptions and hypothesized pathways, drawn from a combination of scientific research and community experience, about how to reach important goals, beyond incremental improvement over the status quo. At its best, a productive theory of change serves as a continuously evolving tool for playing with new ideas and promoting collaborative discovery. While relentlessly focusing on stretch outcomes, good theories of change for reducing poverty reflect the complex interactions and reciprocal feedback loops that characterize human development.

When we began collaborating to catalyze innovation in the early childhood arena, we started with extensive interviews of leading researchers, practitioners, and policymakers. These conversations generated a range of potential stretch outcomes, from maternal mental health to family economic stability, but most pointed toward the importance of assuring that every child in each participating community arrives in kindergarten sufficiently prepared to succeed in school. Our plan was to begin with this concept in a variety of settings and encourage each community to develop its own consensus on what specific stretch outcomes it would pursue toward that goal. With that focus in hand, we proceeded to search for barriers to kindergarten readiness in vulnerable children, including variable availability of early learning services. This led to the hypothesis that the problem is not simply access to programs but that the effectiveness of existing services is constrained by the biological consequences of *toxic stress*—frequent, prolonged activation of the body's stress response systems—that children experience when their families are facing significant economic hardship.[6]

Our initial theory of change therefore hypothesized that better outcomes would emerge if the current policy emphasis on enriched learning environments for children and parenting education for mothers were augmented by the complementary implementation of specific strategies designed to protect the developing brains of vulnerable young children from the disruptive effects of toxic stress. The knowledge base driving this approach was derived from advances in neuroscience, molecular biology, and epigenetics (the study of biological mechanisms through which environmental influences affect the activation or suppression of gene expression), combined with the cumulative wisdom of decades of practical experience and evaluation data from the field, which highlighted the extent to which significant adversity disrupts brain circuitry and precipitates cognitive, emotional, and behavioral difficulties that interfere with learning.[7] As we introduced this theory of change to diverse stakeholders, we found substantial resonance, but also some resistance, as we describe below.

LEVERAGING CONFLICT

Coalescing around stretch outcomes and a causal theory of change is a community development task that ought to benefit from decades of practical experience and systematic research. In this spirit, the determination of appropriate outcomes requires

---

6 Environmental sources of toxic stress include deep poverty, child maltreatment, social exclusion, chronic exposure to violence, and parental substance abuse. See the recent American Academy of Pediatrics (AAP) technical report: J.P. Shonkoff, A.S. Garner, the Committee on Psychosocial Aspects of Child and Family Health, Committee on Early Childhood, Adoption, and Dependent Care, Section on Developmental and Behavioral Pediatrics, "The Lifelong Effects of Early Childhood Adversity and Toxic Stress," Pediatrics 129 (1) (January 2012): e232–246, and the AAP policy statement: Committee on Psychosocial Aspects of Child and Family Health, Committee on Early Childhood, Adoption, and Dependent Care, Section on Developmental and Behavioral Pediatrics, "Early Childhood Adversity, Toxic Stress, and the Role of the Pediatrician: Translating Developmental Science into Lifelong Health," Pediatrics 129 (1) (January 2012): e224–231.

7 See National Scientific Council on the Developing Child, Excessive Stress Disrupts the Architecture of the Developing Brain: Working Paper No. 3 (updated 2009). Available at http://developingchild.harvard.edu.

a consensus definition supported by families, civic leaders, and community-based service providers, as well as policymakers at multiple levels and academic researchers in an array of relevant disciplines. Indeed, the opportunity to define multiple pathways for different subpopulations and outcomes invites inclusion and becomes a way to build shared purpose.

The complexity of this process means that everything could and should be on the table at the outset. Heterogeneous groups can navigate inevitable sources of conflict and work toward consensus if the task is defined from the start as joint discovery, rather than power brokering or winner-take-all decision-making. For example, when a group of initially skeptical community leaders and other stakeholders discussed kindergarten readiness outcomes, they quickly agreed that classroom chaos is an important barrier. This provided an entry point for exploring the role of executive function[8] and self-regulation skills, which resonated with practitioners' observations[9] that they are dealing with disrupted development that needs expert management, not "bad" children who should be medicated or expelled from programs.

A broadly embraced theory of change must be co-created, beginning with high aspirations, population-based outcomes, and revisable causal hypotheses. The aim is not to decide whether the community accepts or rejects a predefined program imposed from the outside, but rather to create a welcoming environment that supports the joint development of evolving strategies. One of us recently observed such a process in a neighborhood facing poor health outcomes among immigrants, where health care providers and community residents were able to bridge their

---

8 Examples of executive functioning skills include working memory (such as ability to hold in mind and follow a sequence of instructions), inhibitory control (such as ability to delay gratification), and cognitive flexibility (such as ability to adapt to changes in rules). See Center on the Developing Child at Harvard University, "Building the Brain's 'Air Traffic Control' System: How Early Experiences Shape the Development of Executive Function." Working Paper No. 11 (2011). Available at http://developingchild.harvard.edu.

9 Such practitioner observations, which we heard frequently, are in turn well supported by relevant research. See, e.g., Linda S. Pagani et al., "Relating Kindergarten Attention to Subsequent Developmental Pathways of Classroom Engagement in Elementary School," Journal of Abnormal Child Psychology 40(5) (2012): 715-725.

differing perspectives by identifying gaps in access to services and then working jointly to develop practitioner checklists and multilingual, immigrant-oriented reference sheets to close those gaps from both ends.

In short, conflict challenges can be transformed into assets by devoting substantial collective effort up front to the invigorating task of defining a set of jointly owned stretch outcomes and a shared theory of change. When these are both in place, the work can shift to collaborative discovery, where heterogeneity is an advantage, as each participant makes distinctive contributions to the learning process. In this context, the community itself plays a vital, ongoing role, not only in co-creating innovative interventions but also in monitoring progress toward stretch outcomes and in stimulating revisions to the theory of change until results match aspirations for all families.[10]

After consultations among early childhood stakeholders as we described above, we shared the preliminary goal (i.e., assuring school readiness) and theory of change (complementing enrichment with protection) at a workshop including researchers, practitioners, policymakers, and philanthropists. Although the participants were largely from the field of early learning, a strong reaction emerged that stretching on the learning dimension only—even merely as an initial step—was not sufficient, given the way early experiences also affect physical and mental health. Consequently, the group's overall goal now includes *both* building readiness for school success *and* strengthening foundations for lifelong health, and community partners are currently defining stretch outcomes on both dimensions.

In a parallel fashion, in order to narrow the focus for designing pilots, the workshop identified causal pathways that would serve both learning and health objectives simultaneously. The theory of change thus progressed from a general emphasis on the need

---

10 We have seen this approach work in complex settings, such as when a community bridged racial and ethnic differences by following this sequence both in plenary sessions and in small working groups that reflected the diversity of the whole. However, it is far too early to report results against stretch outcomes.

to balance developmental enrichment with protection against the burdens of severe adversity to a more nuanced strategy designed to build the capacities of caregivers to buffer stress. Two sources of such capacity then stood out: (1) children's and adults' executive functioning and self-regulatory skills, and (2) family economic stability. Because adult executive functioning and related skills are important to both parenting and employability (hence economic stability), participants saw exciting leverage[11] in targeting such skills.[12]

EMBRACING CONTEXT

If an innovation strategy is aligned around the needs of a specific population or subgroup in a single community, the task of producing comparable results in other places can be formidable. That said, successful mastery of this challenge begins with embracing it. Private sector experience suggests that innovation most often emerges from problem solving in a specific context. A good place to start in the social sphere is to formulate stretch outcomes in a single community that is open to new ideas and to take the distinctive constraints and opportunities within that setting as the basis for collaborative problem solving aimed at those outcomes.[13]

Paradoxically, the very approach that engages problem solvers in a unique local environment can also position them to achieve broader impact. If the stakeholder model includes clusters of communities working with external stakeholders (such as policymakers, researchers, or social entrepreneurs), then goals can be defined for multiple subpopulations through an inclusive

---

11 For example, a community-based team, including agency and civic leaders, single-parent mothers, public officials, and researchers is currently considering an intervention strategy that aims to build such skills through a combination of parent (and parent-child) mental health services with employment and life coaching.

12 See E. J. Costello et al., "Relationships between Poverty and Psychopathology: A Natural Experiment," Journal of the American Medical Association 290 (15) (2003): 2023–2029.

13 It is thus helpful to begin in settings where effective community work has already created a functioning planning forum, including a full range of stakeholders from families to public officials. A good example is the New Haven, CT, MOMS Partnership, http://researchforher.com/current-studies/moms-project.

theory of change. Within this framework, each community can set its own stretch outcomes, and multiple communities can share hypotheses, strategies, and results. Researchers and other external stakeholders are then positioned to broadly apply discoveries from their participation in specific community settings.

When we met with a community agency providing child care for vulnerable children and jointly reviewed their outcomes— applying formal data and staff experience—we found that one inhibitor of success was the tendency to lose ground after program exit. Working with researchers to apply the broader theory of change described above, the agency is now designing tailored interventions to support families as their children transition to kindergarten or Head Start. This can involve the application of insights[14] and tools developed by researchers in other contexts (for example, an experimental set of manual or electronic games that parents and children can play together to build cognitive and executive functioning skills)[15] as well as adaptations to the specific "transition" problem (such as through specially supported family game nights for alumni).[16] Concurrently, researchers can draw lessons from experiences in this particular context as they design broadly applicable learning tools for other purposes. Finally, with state policymakers at the table, further discussions could focus on how these intervention

---

14 For example, based on laboratory results reported in Allyson P. Mackey et al., "Differential Effects of Reasoning and Speed Training in Children," Developmental Science 14 (3) (2011): 582–590. See also S. B. Nutley et al., "Gains in Fluid Intelligence after Training Non-Verbal Reasoning in 4-Year-Old Children: A Controlled, Randomized Study," Developmental Science 14 (3) (2011): 591–601.

15 Relevant background includes research on computer tools to train and measure executive functioning, and on the role of parent-child interaction, including play, in cognitive development. In addition to the two Developmental Science studies cited above, see, for example, G. B. Ramani and R. S. Siegler, "Promoting Broad and Stable Improvements in Low-Income Children's Numerical Knowledge through Playing Number Board Games," Child Development 79 (2) (2008): 375–394; and A. Bernier et al., "Social Factors in the Development of Early Executive Functioning: A Closer Look at the Caregiving Environment," Developmental Science 15 (1) (2012): 12–24.

16 As the agencies recognize, families will need logistical support to make it to game nights, and these evening programs themselves need thoughtful structure to engage parents, teachers, and children. Some families will need significant therapeutic support before regular participation in events like this would be feasible for them.

strategies could benefit from policy reforms (such as in transition regulations governing the child welfare system).

RESPECTING TIME

Effective connections rarely happen spontaneously. They require active support that can be generated through face-to-face meetings, web linkages, and collaborative problem solving. Most important, however, productive connection takes time.

Constructive dissatisfaction with the status quo serves as an engine for innovation. Impatience for impact at scale for multiple populations simultaneously, however, nearly guarantees frustration. Fast, large-scale program gains depend on the rare phenomenon of already existing transformative ideas that are immediately acceptable to key (and typically entrenched) actors. Consequently, innovators need time. However, they must also work fast, not only because of stakeholder pressures but also because success requires trying many new things, learning from both progress and setbacks, and testing modified interventions repeatedly in quick cycles.

Stated simply, effective stakeholders must strike a balance between the patience required for large-scale change and the impatience that drives discovery, especially when it is guided by visionary stretch outcomes and measured against testable theories of change. In this spirit, current efforts to promote innovation in early childhood policy and practice are being designed to include both a *connection* function (to leverage conflict and embrace context) and an *acceleration* function (to both respect and push the dimension of time).

Washington State, for example, has developed connection through a cross-agency working group of policy leaders who are collaborating with 11 community sites across the state and a team of participating scientists. An early product of this collaboration, now heading for field testing, is a new curriculum on executive functioning with a video tool designed for state program leaders, community-service providers, and caregivers.

This will enable programs across the state to begin acting on the theory of change we described above, so shared knowledge can accumulate without each intervention having to wait for results from another.

Meanwhile, on the acceleration front, two of those 11 community agencies are now working more closely with scientists and policymakers to design pilot interventions geared to stretch outcomes for the most vulnerable populations they serve (such as families needing transition support, as we described above). Seeking the investment of local philanthropists, each team is developing a funding strategy that can, with full accountability, catalyze a quick launch and ongoing empirical revision of program designs. In short, the aim is to accommodate and even nurture impatience for discovery.

Impatience for discovery of pathways to stretch outcomes is well served by close attention to early feedback at the community level. That feedback gains power from an innovation design that works backward from stretch outcomes through the formulation of a provisional theory of change to hypotheses about what must be true about a specific intervention to actually achieve those goals. These are the assumptions that need quick testing. As Scott Anthony observed about business innovation, "No matter how smart you are, your first plan is sure to be wrong—test and learn to figure out *how*."[17] From university laboratories to community antipoverty coalitions, early learning about what's wrong is a critical challenge that all successful innovators must master.

CONCLUDING THOUGHTS

Community-based strategies occupy an important niche in the effort to combat intergenerational poverty. Although the rationale for such strategies remains strong, the complexity of the challenges and the diversity of the interventions that have been tried (with variable success) have made it difficult to build cumulative impact. Advances in the biology of adversity, linked

---

17 Scott D. Anthony, The Little Black Book of Innovation (Cambridge, MA: Harvard Business Review Press, 2012), p. 206.

to practical experience, offer an opportunity to develop new community-based strategies that could catalyze greater impact and sustained progress.

To capitalize on this opportunity, many communities would benefit from a focused approach to innovation that enables direct engagement with researchers and other stakeholders. This could begin productively with a commitment to ambitious outcomes for defined subpopulations and collaborative development of a theory of change that is sufficiently inclusive to overcome stakeholder conflict and geographic separation. When resources are provided by investors who understand the need for "intellectual venture capital," innovative thinkers and doers could then design pilot interventions geared to those outcomes and subpopulations, and ignite fast-cycle action learning to deliver local results while testing and enhancing the broader theory of change. A compelling new framework for such collaborative action beckons. Through focused reduction of neighborhood sources of toxic stress, communities can apply converging biological and experiential knowledge to dramatically curtail the cycle of intergenerational poverty that still threatens the learning, health, and life prospects of millions of young children.

JAMES M. RADNER *is assistant professor at the School of Public Policy and Governance, University of Toronto; senior fellow at the Center on the Developing Child at Harvard University; executive director and co-founder of The Boreal Institute for Civil Society; and senior fellow at the Munk School of Global Affairs. His teaching and action research engage with challenges in domestic and international social and economic development, and applications of quantitative and qualitative tools to improve the effectiveness of social initiatives at local, national and international levels. He works extensively with programs focused on children and youth and is partnering with the TruePoint Center for Higher Ambition Leadership and the Center on the Developing Child at Harvard University in the design and development of the "Frontiers of Innovation" initiative, from which many of the examples in this essay are drawn.*

JACK P. SHONKOFF, MD, is the Julius B. Richmond FAMRI Professor of Child Health and Development at the Harvard School of Public Health and Harvard Graduate School of Education; professor of pediatrics at Harvard Medical School and Boston Children's Hospital; and director of the Center on the Developing Child at Harvard University. He currently chairs the National Scientific Council on the Developing Child and the National Forum on Early Childhood Policy and Programs. He has served as chair of the Board on Children, Youth, and Families at the National Academy of Sciences and headed an Academy blue-ribbon committee that produced the landmark report From Neurons to Neighborhoods: The Science of Early Childhood Development. *He has received elected membership to the Institute of Medicine of the National Academy of Sciences, the C. Anderson Aldrich Award in Child Development from the American Academy of Pediatrics, and the Distinguished Contributions to Social Policy Award from the Society for Research in Child Development.*

III

MAPPING THE FUTURE

Synthesizing Themes and Ideas for Next Steps

INTEGRATION AND INNOVATION IN A TIME OF STRESS:
Doing the Best for People and Place

Ellen Seidman
Visiting Scholar at the Federal Reserve Bank of San Francisco

O ver the past decade, amid bubble and bust, community development has undergone a subtle but important transformation, broadening its outlook from a primary focus on investment in real estate, especially affordable housing, to include other types of real estate, such as charter schools and health clinics. But perhaps more importantly, it has broadened its outlook to encompass what goes on in those places (the quality of services); the total physical and social structure of the community (including issues such as transportation and public safety); and the physical, financial, and mental health of the people who live in those communities. As Alex von Hoffman demonstrates in his history of community development, the field has long pulsed between tighter focus, whether by geography or sector, and the search for comprehensive solutions. What may distinguish the current transformation, in which two leading organizing principles are "integration" (focused on process) and "healthy communities" (focused on results), is the coming together of so many fields in so many places, at a time when financial strain and advances in technology encourage true innovation in solving ever-more-difficult problems.

The essays in this book look at community development from many perspectives, but several themes emerge with some regularity. Perhaps the most profound is the recognition that community development is about the entire life of the community. That recognition generates a series of important corollaries: (1) a focus on the health and well-being of individuals and families, especially children, as well as of the places in which they live; (2) the need to bring many disciplines to the table and "bust silos," including in particular the silos of government programs; and (3) the essential role of effective participation of residents in developing and implementing the strategies that will help their communities prosper. Several of the essays explore the role of the community beyond participation in decision-making to include community ownership and control of assets.

A second theme is that community development, although still largely focused in neighborhoods, must connect those neighborhoods with the broader economy to be effective. Families can neither live well in the present nor focus on the future without a stable household income. And because the jobs that can generate a stable income are often unavailable in sufficient quantity in a particular neighborhood, that neighborhood must be effectively connected to the broader regional economy, both physically (such as through transit) and organizationally (by having a true voice in the decisions that are implemented outside the neighborhood but affect it profoundly). Connection beyond the neighborhood can also help provide access to the education needed to obtain jobs that provide a steady income, as well as to other goods, services, and amenities not available in every neighborhood. Connection is also vital if people are going to have real choice in where they want to live.

A third theme is that because funding is severely constrained, the field must find new sources of financing and put what has been available to better use, both by focusing on what works and by establishing and using new financing systems and structures. Impact investors, who are interested in values beyond simple financial return—including foundation endowments, corporations and other institutions, and individuals—may be new sources of investment, but their demands for efficient investment vehicles combined with measurable financial and social returns raise serious challenges for an industry used to relying for subsidy sources on a combination of government programs, regulation-driven bank investment, and philanthropy.

Other potential new sources of funds arise from the recognition of the broader scope of community development: the fields of health care, transportation, and energy efficiency may have new funds available for well-integrated investments that meet multiple goals. Moreover, the sector is itself a job creator, in construction and the activities (such as education, health care, and supportive housing services) that are enabled by that construction, and in its support for business development in underserved communities, and thus should be able to benefit from funding for job creation. Both impact investors and new funding sources will require innovation in capital management, to reduce both the amount of funds needed and the risk of investment. In addition, the field will need to better leverage impact investments by making the most efficient use of subsidy sources and by accessing broader markets, including the capital markets, for nonsubsidy dollars. Over the past 10 years, and through the Great Recession, community development financial institutions (CDFIs) have proven their prowess in this area, but the future will challenge them, and others, to use capital more efficiently, think more broadly, and tap new resources in order to operate at the larger scale that will be necessary.

But more money cannot be the entire answer, partly because in a time of fiscal stress and greater need coming out of the Great Recession, it is unlikely to be available, at least to the extent needed. The field must also get better at directing money where it will be most effective. This requires collection, aggregation, and analysis of data at many levels—project and program; neighborhood, city, and region; national and international. Modern technology, including social networking, can facilitate this, especially through use of government data and open sources of private data. Several essays raise the exciting prospect that the methodologies of public health and the use of biomarkers can give us quicker and more accurate insights into the effectiveness of strategies than previously possible. But analysis is not enough. It will be essential to use the data and analysis to make difficult choices, including discontinuing programs that fail to produce results. A number of essays focus on establishing decision-making structures that improve our ability to make those choices, including the greater use of pay-for-performance funding.

A final theme is community development's need to regain the entrepreneurial spirit that characterized its early years, which it lost for a host of reasons including funder risk aversion and excessive regulation. As Federal Reserve Governor Elizabeth Duke points out in the foreword to this book, the skills of entre-preneurship—spotting opportunities, managing complexity, rapid prototyping and revision, willingness to experiment and fail, and networking—are also the skills of effective community develop-ment. This is especially critical given the variation in circum-stances and challenges of lower-income communities around the country. Many of the essays build on the entrepreneurship theme.

The remainder of this chapter explores the problems that community development is attempting to solve and the challenges and opportunities that face the field, using the themes the authors raise to suggest future directions for the field.

WHAT PROBLEM IS COMMUNITY DEVELOPMENT TRYING TO SOLVE?

The term "community development," as this book demonstrates, means many things to its practitioners. However, it appears that the field is attempting to solve three main problems. First—and as von Hoffman points out, first in time as well—is the goal of lifting individuals and families out of poverty. Alan Berube demonstrates that although the nature of poverty is changing, especially with respect to age, ethnicity, location, and participation in the workforce, the amount of poverty in the United States is increasing in absolute terms and in terms of the percentage of the population who live in poverty. Moreover, although poverty did decline during the economic growth of the late 1990s, it increased in the first decade of the twenty-first century during both recessions and recoveries.[1]

The authors highlight different aspects of this persistent poverty: Clara Miller, Ben Hecht, and Angela Glover Blackwell point to the systemic nature of poverty in the United States—poverty is no longer a matter of the poor being at the edge of a prosperous society; Peter Edelman, Shirley Franklin and David Edwards, and Blackwell focus on the particular problems of concentrated urban poverty, especially among African Americans; Secretaries Shaun Donovan, Arne Duncan, and Kathleen Sebelius (together "the Secretaries") highlight both concentrated poverty and homelessness; Gabriella Conti and James Heckman and Ted Howard pay special attention to growing inequality; and Cynthia Mildred Duncan cites the persistent poverty of the Mississippi Delta, Appalachia, and Native American reservations and the newer poverty of the depopulating areas of the Midwest and Great Plains. Community development is in part about overcoming persistent poverty and providing individuals and families with, among other things, long-term financial stability, reduced stress, and opportunities for both forward-thinking[2] and intergenerational wealth transfer.

A second problem community development is attempting to solve is the creation of communities that work. The work of Purpose Built in Atlanta, the Neighborhood Centers in Houston, and the Cleveland Initiative (described in Part 2), as well as most of the

---

1 For more information see http://census.gov/hhes/www/poverty/data/historical/families.html.

2 See Abhijit V. Banerjee and Esther Duflo, Poor Economics: A Radical Rethinking of the Way to Fight Global Poverty (New York: Public Affairs, 2011), p. 233.

other integrated activities that Eric Belsky and Jennifer Fauth describe in Part 1, is focused on turning individual communities into places where people, especially those of limited economic means, can live in safety and dignity and with access to economic opportunity and quality services.[3] Edelman, tracing the history of community development from the early 1960s, emphasizes the importance of choice, in the sense both of people being able to freely choose where to live (which discrimination and related issues continue to make challenging) and of the neighborhoods in which many lower-income people live having qualities that would make them neighborhoods of choice. Edelman, John Robert Smith and Allison Brooks, Hecht, and Blackwell point out, however, that neighborhoods exist within the context of their cities and regions, particularly when it comes to jobs, and that a healthy neighborhood is a connected neighborhood. Duncan emphasizes that for rural America, connection to urban areas and the greater region is essential to community vitality.

Miller and Hecht, as well as the Secretaries, take community development one step further, tying the field to the bigger issues of establishing a base for a far more vibrant and inclusive economy over the long term. As Miller says, those working in community development must acknowledge "the need to rebalance the economy itself so it can fulfill the traditional American promise: full livelihood, democracy, and opportunity for all." And Blackwell, citing both disproportionate and growing poverty among African Americans and Latinos and their increasing proportion of the population, makes the case that "equity . . . has become more than a moral issue. It is now an economic imperative."

WHAT ISSUES ARE PARTICULARLY CONFOUNDING FOR COMMUNITY DEVELOPMENT TODAY?

Community development has always been about poverty, frequently concentrated urban poverty. But as Berube points out, the nature of poverty is changing. Concentrated urban poverty,

---

3 See also Robert J. Sampson, *Great American City: Chicago and the Enduring Neighborhood Effect* (Chicago: University of Chicago Press, 2012), p. 421.

in particular among African Americans, remains a serious problem (as Edelman, Franklin and Edwards, Blackwell, and others discuss), and in recent decades it has been compounded by increasing and persistent income inequality and an increase in severe poverty and intergenerational poverty. But Berube suggests that other dynamics are also at work: those in poverty are more heavily Latino, more suburban, more concentrated in the South and West, younger, and less connected to the workforce (and in particular to a steady job).

Duncan adds that although some rural poverty has been persistent, other rural areas have fallen into poverty as changes in agricultural and natural resources technology have combined with the lack of employment opportunities to depopulate whole regions. Each of these changes challenges some of the existing responses to poverty alleviation. In particular, the increasing number of poor people in suburbs, especially those beyond transit systems, makes service delivery more difficult and reduces the effectiveness of some of the old and new tools of community development, such as concentrated redevelopment of a single neighborhood.[4] There may be opportunities to learn from rural America, where, as Duncan points out, poverty has always been exacerbated by distance and lack of concentrated resources.

Moreover, the Great Recession has amplified the challenges of poverty. Not only have individuals been affected by lost income from unemployment but, as Jennifer Tescher writes, the recession has resulted in depleted balance sheets (in particular, the loss of home equity and savings) and a reduced ability to access financial services in general, including credit. These problems have been especially acute in the African American and Latino communities.[5] Berube and Miller discuss additional impacts on individuals

---

4 See also Matthew Soursourian, "Suburbanization of Poverty in the Bay Area" (San Francisco: Federal Reserve Bank of San Francisco, January 2012).

5 See Pew Research Center, "Wealth Gaps Rise to Record Highs Between Whites, Blacks and Hispanics" (Washington, DC: Author, July 2011); Debbie Bocian et al., "Lost Ground, 2011: Disparities in Mortgage Lending and Foreclosures" (Durham, NC: Center for Responsible Lending, November 2011); and Ray Boshara, Testimony to the United States Senate, Federal Reserve Bank of St. Louis, October 2011, available at http://stlouisfed.org/publications/br/articles/?id=2208.

of long-term unemployment, including its psychological impact and the increasing mismatch between an unemployed worker's skills and the needs of potential new employers.

The Great Recession has also greatly harmed lower-income communities, including some that had made significant progress during the previous 30 years. House prices have collapsed and are showing no sign of recovery in many lower-income communities, record levels of vacant and foreclosed homes have attracted speculative buyers with little interest in the continued health of the community, and rental vacancies (especially for lower rent and larger apartments) are down while demand is up. As former Assistant Secretary for Policy Development and Research at the Department of Housing and Urban Development Raphael Bostic put it, in many places "there is no functioning real estate market."[6] This situation has in turn ignited a debate about one of the major tenets of community development: the value of homeownership. Whereas some have questioned whether both the country and the field have put excessive emphasis on home-ownership as the key to "the American Dream," others have pointed out that lower-income homeowners with well-designed loans, in particular long-term fixed-rate mortgages, were generally able to weather the recession successfully and to provide important stability to their communities.[7]

A related challenge is the uncertain state of the housing finance system. With Fannie Mae and Freddie Mac in conservatorship, more than 90 percent of home mortgage loans backed in some

---

6 Raphael Bostic, "The Future of Affordable Housing" (panel presentation at the National Interagency Community Reinvestment Conference in Seattle, WA, March 25–28, 2012) and slides presented at that panel, available at http://frbsf.org/community/seattle2012/presentations/CommunityDevelopment_Track/FutureofAffordableHousing.cfm. See also US Census Bureau, "Residential Vacancies and Homeownership in the First Quarter 2012," April 30, 2012.

7 See Lei Ding et al., "Risky Borrowers or Risky Mortgages: Disaggregating Effects Using Propensity Score Models" (Durham: Center for Community Capital, University of North Carolina, May 2010); Mark R. Lindblad, Kim Manturuk, and Roberto Quercia, "Sense of Community and Informal Social Control Among Lower-Income Households: The Role of Homeownership and Collective Efficacy in Reducing Subjective Neighborhood Crime and Disorder" (Durham Center for Community Capital, University of North Carolina, March 2012).

way by the government, a moribund market for private securities backed by mortgages, regulatory uncertainty, and mortgage originations drastically down both in general and among lower-income borrowers,[8] the future of housing finance—especially for affordable housing, whether ownership or rental—is less clear than at any time since the 1930s. Although one of the major breakthroughs in community development over the past 10 years has been to consistently broaden the field's interest beyond housing, as Sister Lillian Murphy and Janet Falk point out in their essay, "the need for quality, affordable housing is still a crucial part of the equation." Unless and until the housing finance issue is settled in a way that continues to support affordability, real progress in rebuilding stable mixed-income communities, especially in the communities hard hit by the recession and in newly-attractive city centers where rebuilding can lead to the displacement of long-time residents, will be especially difficult.

Community development also faces significant fiscal challenges. At the federal level, the twin challenges of a growing deficit and political gridlock threaten four critical sources of support for community development—funds to support construction of, for example, affordable rental housing; operating subsidies; tax credit programs for low-income housing and for facilities and commercial development in low-income communities; and support for innovation. Although there may be new sources of federal funding (such as from the Affordable Care Act), and the Obama administration has tried to protect community development programs and make them more efficient through such integrative efforts as Choice Neighborhoods and Promise Neighborhoods, there is little doubt they are under threat. The threat is both direct, through a reduction in appropriations, and indirect, such as through tax reform that might lower the tax rate or do away with the Low Income Housing Tax Credit and New Markets Tax Credit, both of which are important to community development finance. The challenges at the federal level are replicated and amplified at the state and local levels, where both

---

8   For more information see http://federalreserve.gov/pubs/bulletin/2011/pdf/2010_
HMDA_final.pdf.

funds specifically targeted to lower-income communities and monies to support broader infrastructure development, upkeep, and basic services (such as police, fire, and schools) have been hard hit by a stagnant economy, reduced property values and property tax revenues, and reduced transfers from the federal and state government, at a time when the demand for services is increasing.[9]

Although government and philanthropic support has always been critical to community development—especially to provide scarce equity, credit enhancement, and operating support—most of the money that flows into community development real estate projects comes from banks subject to the Community Reinvestment Act (CRA), which is also under severe pressure. The number of banks in the United States has declined by 40 percent since 1995, when the regulations governing the CRA were last seriously revised. Moreover, the 10 largest banks now hold 43 percent of system assets and the 100 largest hold 79 percent.[10] This means that not only are there fewer institutions subject to the CRA, but those that remain have less local knowledge and decision-making is further removed from communities. These changes have been exacerbated by increased capital and regulatory demands on the remaining banks, often resulting in diminished funds for community development.

Finally, banks are finding it more difficult to get CRA credit for targeting funds to the communities and investments most in need because the CRA regulations, adopted before the wave of coast-to-coast mergers and acquisitions that have transformed the banking system, are outdated for today's needs. And, as Antony Bugg-Levine points out, the CRA is less important to bank senior management in a world in which regulators are more focused on safety and soundness. The financial stresses on banks aren't over, especially for smaller institutions that serve lower-income and

---

9 See Conner Dougherty, "States' Tax Collections Inch Upward," Wall Street Journal, April 19, 2012. Available at http://online.wsj.com/article/SB10001424052702303513404577354161334500688.html?mod=WSJ_economy_LeftTopHighlights.

10 Details available at FDIC.gov.

minority communities. There were more than 400 bank failures from 2008 through 2011, and as of the end of March 2012, there were still 772 banks on the "problem institutions" list.[11]

WHAT TOOLS DOES COMMUNITY DEVELOPMENT HAVE TO RESPOND TO THESE CHALLENGES?

The essential building blocks of community development are physical, human, and financial capital. Each is changing in ways that will continue to evolve over the next several decades. With respect to physical capital—in many ways what community development has been focused on for much of the past 30 years—affordable housing continues to be critical. With the housing and housing finance markets in continuing disarray, the Low Income Housing Tax Credit threatened, and (as Murphy and Falk point out) the business model of most nonprofit affordable housing developers unsustainable, this will be more of a challenge than it would have appeared eight to 10 years ago.

What's more, as the essays in this book make clear, healthy communities demand more than housing. Franklin and Edwards' description of Purpose Built's work in Atlanta emphasizes the need to integrate mixed-income housing with high-quality cradle-to-career education and supportive public services. The work of Neighborhood Centers, Inc. in Houston, which Blanchard describes, focuses largely on empowering a community to work together to discern and accomplish its goals, but the physical structure that holds it all together in the end is a "bricks and mortar" multipurpose community center. Others emphasize the broader nature of the built environment, including the structure of the community to encourage a healthy lifestyle (Risa Lavizzo-Mourey, Nancy Adler), the connection of the community to transit and to anchor institutions (Smith and Brooks, Howard), and the integration of the community into the broader regional economy (Edelman, Hecht, Smith and Brooks, Duncan, Blackwell).

---

11 FDIC Quarterly Banking Profile, first quarter 2012, p. 4 available at http://www2.fdic.gov/qbp/2012mar/qbp.pdf.

Beyond physical capital, healthy communities focus on human capital—improving the quality of life for lower-income people, whether focused specifically on a place or not. As Federal Reserve Governor Elizabeth Duke writes in her foreword, "At one time, policy discussions revolved around whether community development was about people or places. I would argue that the debate is over and both sides won." Thus, as both Conti and Heckman and Jack Shonkoff and James Radner state in their essays, interventions to ensure early childhood health and the development of social and character skills are critically effective in improving outcomes for children, families, and communities. Ingrid Gould Ellen focuses on the importance of public safety in part simply because people care about it, but also because crime destroys the fabric of the neighborhood and increases individual and family stress. Tescher points out that quality financial services are key to moving families beyond a cash economy and enabling them to build both a financial cushion and a strong credit history. And several authors, including Miller, Howard, Edelman, Hecht, the Secretaries and Blackwell, focus on the importance of jobs that provide a stable income and security.

Finally, healthy communities need financial capital. For individuals, as Tescher states, this means having financial services—including transactions, savings, investing, and borrowing—that are well-priced, well-designed, well-marketed, and accessible. Technology such as smartphones and unconventional distribution channels such as nonprofit organizations like the AARP and retailers like Wal-Mart may complement (and in some cases supersede) traditional banks and credit unions.

Healthy communities also need access to new forms of capital and to make better use of what is available. During the past 50 years, several thousand community development corporations (CDCs) have developed, acquired, and managed more than a million units of affordable housing. Murphy and Falk find that in an era of reduced federal funds, the CDC business model is outdated and unsustainable. They call for a new model that allows for innovation, collaboration, and diversification and that is sustained to a far greater extent by low-cost enterprise funding instead of the project-based funding on which the current model is based.

At the same time, CDFIs, including nonprofit loan funds and credit unions and for-profit banks dedicated to working in lower-income neighborhoods, have grown increasingly sophisticated at accessing and using public and philanthropic funds to leverage private money, largely from banks, to support housing, facilities, and economic development. CDFIs largely came through the recession in relatively strong financial condition. But as Bugg-Levine and others point out, their ability to access the larger pools of capital necessary to bring greater scale to their activities—including social impact investors and new sources of public funds—will depend on enhancing their efficiency, transparency,[12] and ability to demonstrate impact. This will likely require industry consolidation, or at least far more robust networks of shared services, and, according to Mark Pinsky, focus on a brand that emphasizes strength, effectiveness, and "solution," rather than "community development."

Technology can also help increase access to capital. Before 2008, community development was beginning to find ways to tap the broader capital markets through securitization; as Hecht suggests, this may once again become possible. But beyond that, social networks enabled by technology may provide access to capital for community development through techniques ranging from person-to-person lending to the type of equity fundraising authorized by the recently enacted Jumpstart Our Business Startups (JOBS) Act. Focusing on foundations, both Miller and Lavizzo-Mourey assert that to be effective, foundations supporting community development will need to use more—perhaps all—of

---

12 See Michael Swack, Jack Northrup, and Eric Hangen, "CDFI Industry Analysis Summary Report" (Durham, NH: Carsey Institute, Spring 2012). Available at http://cdfifund.gov/docs/CBI/2012/Carsey%20Report%20PR%20042512.pdf. This report, which studied 282 CDFI loan funds as well as CDFI credit unions and banks, concludes that CDFI loan funds are not most efficiently leveraging their capital and that "inadequate data and non-standardized auditing practices may present a barrier to CDFI capitalization."

their financial and human assets and intellectual capital to support their mission, in better collaboration with others.

Although only Paul Grogan and Blackwell take on the issue of policy advocacy directly, it will be impossible for community development to retain and gain increased access to the public monies and systems (such as the CRA) on which it has relied unless those involved in the field, including those in communities, make their needs known and voices heard. This encompasses advocacy to ensure that the outcomes of deficit reduction and tax reform, banking regulation and land use planning, health care reform and energy efficiency, enhance the country's ability to serve its entire population. While many authors assert the need for increased direct funding for community development, Mark Calabria argues that programmatic funding for community development may in fact be holding communities back from choosing to do what is in their own best interests, and that a more market-based solution is needed.

WHAT STRATEGIES CAN COMMUNITY DEVELOPMENT USE?

The essays in this book suggest a series of strategies that will be essential if the field is to accomplish its goals relating to poverty, community, and the broader economy. Key concepts are that solutions must be integrated, broadly collaborative, data-driven and focused on what works, and entrepreneurial.

In Part 1, Belsky and Fauth discuss the increasing focus on integrated community development, ranging from the highly directive strategies of Purpose Built and the Harlem Children's Zone to the more resident-driven Neighborhood Centers and LISC's Better Communities Initiative. As von Hoffman makes clear, "comprehensive" community development strategies have a long history. What distinguishes the newer strategies is a conscious effort to understand the linkages among, for example, housing, health, education, public safety, and economic development, and to tackle them in a manner that strengthens them in concert. As the Secretaries put it, "As community developers have long recognized, the problems that contribute to poverty are very much interconnected. While poverty cannot be explained as merely a consequence of housing, education and health, each poses unique challenges to low-income families at the community level and none can be understood independently of one another." Blanchard says "real transformation comes from an integrated, focused approach to neighborhood transformation, not from an 'either/or' set of choices like housing or school, health or finan- cial, infrastructure or immigration," whereas Lavizzo-Mourey states that "what we've learned is that factors that are integral to poverty—such as insufficient education, inadequate housing, racism, and food insecurity—are also indicators of poor health." Edelman, Franklin and Edwards, and others also stress the need for integrated solutions. Similarly, Bugg-Levine emphasizes the need to integrate financing strategies, involving both human and financial capital and focused on solving problems, with invest- ment as one tool rather than the focus of action.

Integration of necessity requires collaboration across many disciplines, types of programs, and funding sources, and among a wide range of stakeholders, from residents to the most powerful actors in a community or region. Xavier Briggs and Phillip Thompson call for "deep democracy" or "empowerment 2.0," collective problem-solving that "hinges on developing and using 'civic capacity' with and beyond the government" to ensure sustained effort, trust, and "the creative exchange of ideas." Radner and Shonkoff emphasize the need for broad-based collaboration, including in particular for community involve- ment in both goal setting and strategy development. Blanchard summarizes this line of thought: "The people are the asset. . . . Community development is about unlocking that asset, releasing the potential of people to move forward together." Briggs and Thompson and Howard extend this concept to community control over capital through, for example, worker-owned busi- nesses and greater accountability for owners, managers, and users of capital, a concept also present in Blackwell's focus on equity.

"One table" collaboration requires facing issues such as determining who is at the table, finding local leadership and keeping it relevant, the impact of race and poverty on effective participation, and the extent to which organizations or individuals will be at the table. Calabria raises the question whether it is possible to accomplish this in a manner that is not captured by elites who act in their own interest even when they think they are acting in the community interest. Calabria suggests that neighborhoods might in fact be better off with fewer participation requirements, but also less discretion on the part of officials and more reliance on rules and the market to make investment decisions.

However residents make their views known, integration requires new relationships among more institutional players.[13] The Secretaries point to integration initiatives across the country, under the umbrellas of the Neighborhood Revitalization Initiative and Strong Cities, Strong Communities. Hecht, citing Living Cities' Integration Initiative, stresses the need for a systematic change in approach, rebuilding the civic infrastructure, systems innovation, engaging the private market by focusing on shared value, and using "big data," social media, and distributed leadership to make it all happen. Smith and Brooks, focusing on transportation systems, which are typically large in geography, cost, and time, state that collaboration and integration across disciplines and timelines is essential, especially to influence both transportation infrastructure and the location decisions of major employers. Howard looks at the same issue from a slightly different perspective, discussing how "anchor institutions" in a community, such as universities and hospitals, can become drivers of major change in collaboration with both the community and civic and philanthropic leadership.

Several of the essays note that notwithstanding the expenditure of trillions of dollars to help low-income communities, poverty has not declined in either rate or numbers. As Edelman and others point out, much has indeed been accomplished. But our ability to

---

13 See also John Kania and Mark Kramer, "Collective Impact." Stanford Social Innovation Review (Winter 2011).

fully understand the impact of the accomplishments of community development—affordable housing units, charter school seats, health clinic spaces, square feet of commercial space, and similar metrics—on the lives of those living in the communities has been limited. One of the major goals of the new community development efforts, aided by significant advances in information technology, life sciences, and other fields, has been to collect, analyze, and use data to drive investment to activities with the greatest impact, a point emphasized by Conti and Heckman, Lavizzo-Mourey, Smith and Brooks, and Murphy and Falk. Although there are concerns, some of which Belsky and Fauth raise, that too great a focus on metrics can disadvantage the small (including the rural), the new and difficult to achieve, and things that take a long time to accomplish, the pressure to demonstrate impact suggests the value of developing strategies to overcome these concerns.

Adler's essay makes some useful suggestions. Saying that it is time to test the link between community development and health outcomes, Adler focuses on the need to agree on data measures and research protocols and to establish databases that are of wide use. Adler recognizes the challenges this presents but points out that existing data sets and focusing on biomarkers and risk factors can reduce cost and overcome the problem that the impacts of community development activities may be slow to manifest themselves other than through health indicators, a point that Radner and Shonkoff also make. For example, Adler states that one widely asked survey question—"How would you rate your health relative to others your age?"—is extremely good at predicting actual health outcomes, and may be a key to measuring at least a portion of the impact of community development activities.

Pulling these strategies together successfully requires competencies beyond the professionalism, especially concerning investment, that has been the hallmark of successful community development for the past 30 years. Sister Lillian Murphy of Mercy Housing, one of the field's most effective and successful practitioners, flatly asserts that the current business model, at least for producers and managers of affordable housing, "is not sustainable" and that a paradigm shift is needed "to develop a system that allows housing developers—those with a holistic, community approach to housing, including the commitment to long-term ownership—to get to scale." She says the new model should allow for flexibility and diversification, encourage innovation, be funded at the enterprise level, encourage collaborations across sectors, promote public/private/nonprofit partnerships, and develop comprehensive impact measurement. Blanchard, Belsky and Fauth, Grogan, Pinsky and others echo this need for financially strong, highly competent institutions that can do the work of community development.

Other authors join in the call for elements of entrepreneurship—experimentation; rapid prototyping (including testing and modifying interventions in short cycles); networking and knowledge sharing; and dealing effectively with complexity, conflict, and the difficulty of replication. Whether, to what extent, and how entrepreneurship and enhanced institutional scale can emerge simultaneously in the field are major questions for the future.

Scale is made even harder by a theme that runs just under the surface of much of this book: there is immense variability among communities, reflecting different needs, different resources and opportunities, and different strategies that will likely be successful. The most extreme differences may be between the community development needs of rural areas that Duncan discusses and those of the urban neighborhoods that most of the other authors examine. But the differences don't end there. As Howard and Berube suggest, major central cities, even those hardest hit by the Great Recession, have resources that are lacking in smaller cities and suburbs. Areas that came through the recession relatively unscathed have the opportunity to focus beyond rebuilding communities devastated by foreclosures and vacancies. But even within a city or metropolitan area, individual neighborhoods are subject to immense variability.[14]

---

14 Sampson, Great American City.

These differences must necessarily lead to different strategies for community development, even within the common themes of integration and collaboration, connection, focus on what works, and entrepreneurship. For example, Franklin and Edwards are careful to point out that although Purpose Built's highly successful intervention at East Lake in Atlanta is replicable, successful replication is most likely in a community that has some of East Lake's characteristics, particularly the opportunity to completely rebuild a significant amount of mixed-income housing and to establish a neighborhood-targeted high-quality educational system. The Parkside-Kenilworth Promise Neighborhood in Washington, DC, for example, has had difficulty replicating Purpose Built's success in part because open enrollment in the District of Columbia's schools means that half the neighborhood children attend school elsewhere and half the children in local schools are from out of the neighborhood.[15] As Hecht points out, the "one table" collaborations that Living Cities has undertaken have focused on different needs in different places, such as equitable transit-oriented development in the Twin Cities and the Bay Area, education in Cincinnati, and energy efficiency in Portland, OR. Living Cities has also discovered that each area has a different "capital absorption capacity," which they define as "the ability of communities to make effective use of different forms of capital to provide needed goods and services to underserved communities."[16]

SOURCES OF OPPORTUNITY

Although the challenges for community development are daunting, new opportunities will come from greater awareness of the issues community development tackles, new forms and sources of capital, and the focus on energy efficiency and environmental sustainability. Not long ago, there was little discussion of income inequality and less understanding of the

---

15 Jennifer Comey et al., "Bringing Promise to Washington, DC, The DC Promise Neighborhood Initiative" (Washington, DC: Urban Institute, January 2012).

16 "The Capital Absorption Capacity of Places, A Research Agenda and Framework," Living Cities and Initiative for Responsible Investment, 2012. Available at http://livingcities.org/knowledge/media/?id=74.

wide and widening gap between rich and poor and the long-term income stagnation and more recent loss of wealth that has exacerbated the condition of those in the bottom half of the income distribution. The Occupy movement has been instrumental in changing that and in substantially raising awareness of both poverty and inequality. At the same time, the work of the Robert Wood Johnson Foundation on healthy communities and the Harlem Children's Zone, James Heckman, and others on early childhood development has put the community—both social and physical—into the ongoing discussions in those fields. Integrated strategies at the federal, regional, and local levels, such as Choice Neighborhoods, Living Cities' Integration Initiative, and Cleveland's Greater University Circle Initiative, have significantly broadened awareness of the usefulness of community development to a broad array of programs and goals that benefit lower-income populations within the context of benefitting the broader community. The field's greater interest in measuring impact and telling its story is likely to result in greater awareness and greater understanding of what community development can and cannot accomplish.

Although the field is under significant financial pressure from traditional sources, there are also opportunities in potential new sources of capital. As discussed above, CDFIs came through the recession in relatively strong condition, and several statutory changes, most notably those in the Small Business Jobs Act of 2010, including the CDFI bond guarantee program,[17] create an opportunity for significantly more well-priced capital to flow into CDFIs. In addition, and most visibly in the Starbucks Create Jobs for USA initiative,[18] corporations other than banks and local anchor institutions have begun to take an interest in helping to finance, as Pinsky puts it, disciplined and effective solutions to community problems. Whereas some impact investors, such as the F. B. Heron Foundation, with its focus on equity investment

---

17 See Pub. L. 111-240 (September 27, 2010); see especially section 1134.

18 For more information see http://starbucks.com/responsibility/community/create-jobs-for-usa-program.

and its breakthrough strategy of using all its financial resources for mission accomplishment, as described by Miller, will be interested in enterprise-based equity investment, others will focus their attention on specific projects. Structures such as performance bonds may be useful to ensure that the projects "work," but these structures are still in the exploratory stage and will not necessarily focus funds on areas most in need, especially when those needs are less susceptible to impact measurement within a reasonable time.[19]

Finally, as Howard and Duncan point out, the interest in energy efficiency and environmental sustainability opens some new opportunities for community development in both urban and rural America. To start, both strategies have the possibility to significantly reduce both capital and operating costs and improve quality of life in low-income communities, as the work of the Enterprise Green Communities and others have demonstrated.[20] And Duncan cites opportunities in energy, "ecosystem services," and local food production as three potential rural development strategies. A critically important role for community development as this opportunity develops will be to ensure that the costs and benefits are shared equitably; if improvements in technology or transportation merely serve to displace lower-income residents or communities or to increase their cost of living, the field will have not only squandered an opportunity but failed those who depend on it.

EMERGING MODELS

How does all of this fit together? That is the topic of the next chapter, but the essays in this book describe a number of strategies that fit the emerging themes in community development.

---

19 See Jeffrey B. Liebman, "Social Impact Bonds: A Promising New Financing Model to Accelerate Social Innovation and Improve Government Performance" (Washington, DC: Center for American Progress, February 2011). Available at http://payforsuccess.org/sites/default/files/social_impact_bonds_-_a_promising_new_financing_model.pdf; see also Nonprofit Finance Fund, Pay for Success Initiative, available at http://nonprofitfinancefund.org/pay-for-success.

20 For more information see http://enterprisecommunity.com/solutions-and-innovation/enterprise-green-communities.

First, there are the intensely community-oriented programs, with an integrated focus. These include Purpose Built, Neighborhood Centers, the Harlem Children's Zone, Promise Neighborhoods, Choice Neighborhoods, and LISC's Better Communities Initiative. In each case, the focus is on a specific neighborhood of relatively small size. But in each case, the program is designed to respond in an integrated fashion to a broad range of community needs and opportunities. The anchor institution based strategies that Howard describes also fit into this group, with the additional focus of community ownership of the community's capital, including through cooperatives.

A second group of strategies involves cross-agency coordination and "one table" to break through silos of both substance and strategy. Although Strive is focused solely on education, it is a broad initiative involving a large geography; public, private, and philanthropic entities; and those engaged in education of every type and at all levels. Some of the tables set by Living Cities' Integration Initiative are similar, such as the transportation-oriented work in the Twin Cities, but others, as in Detroit, are broader. The federal programs encouraging this trend, such as the Neighborhood Revitalization Initiative and Strong Cities, Strong Communities (both described by the Secretaries), focus on bringing together federal, regional, and local officials with a wide range of responsibilities to break barriers to effectively meeting community needs and sparking economic development.

Finally, we cannot forget that one reason the community development field has accomplished so much over the past 30 years is because of the presence of institutions—both direct providers and intermediaries—with strong finances and highly competent and innovative staff. As Murphy and Falk (with respect to CDCs), Grogan (with respect to national intermediaries), and Bugg-Levine and Pinsky (with respect to CDFIs) point out, these institutions will continue to be critical to the field. Ensuring they have a business model that is consistent with new challenges and new opportunities is key.

ELLEN SEIDMAN *was a visiting scholar with the Community Development Department of the Federal Reserve Bank of San Francisco in 2012. From 1997 to 2001, Seidman served as the director of the Office of Thrift Supervision. She has also held senior positions at the US Departments of Treasury and Transportation, the National Economic Council, Fannie Mae and ShoreBank Corporation. She currently serves on the boards of three community development financial institutions and the CDFI Assessment and Ratings System (CARS), and chairs the board of the Center for Financial Services Innovation.*

ROUTINIZING THE EXTRAORDINARY[1]

David Erickson, Ian Galloway, and Naomi Cytron
Federal Reserve Bank of San Francisco

I t is hard not to be inspired by the community-revitalizing work highlighted in this book. Geoffrey Canada, Angela Blanchard, Tom Cousins, and many others are lifted up as extraordinary leaders who are making their communities thrive despite difficult circumstances. But we cannot rely on saints to achieve systemic change in the thousands of low-income communities in America that need help; we need new policies, practices, and products to create a next-generation system that empowers everyday people to achieve extraordinary results.

The views expressed in this chapter belong to the authors and do not necessarily represent the views of the Federal Reserve Bank of San Francisco or the Federal Reserve System. We would like to thank the following people who gave such good advice on how to improve this chapter: Nancy O. Andrews, Ellen Seidman, and Scott Turner.

1 We are borrowing this title from a subtitle in Langley Keyes' book, Strategies and Saints: Fighting Drugs in Subsidized Housing (Washington, DC: Urban Institute Press, 1992), 226.

How do we create a system like this? What is necessary to build on the examples of strong leaders and to create intervention strategies using the best ideas possible? In this chapter we try to reverse-engineer some of the leadership examples highlighted in this book and draw on lessons from community development's achievements to outline a new approach to community development. It will play out differently in different communities, but at its core, this new approach must be:

1 entrepreneurial in nature and fundamentally cross-sectoral, engaging more partners than are currently involved in community development;

2 data-driven and capable of sense-and-respond adjustments; and

3 composed of both people- and place-based interventions.

At root, this approach to community development is focused on leadership that is able to promote a compelling vision of success for an entire community, marshal the necessary resources, and lead people in an integrated way. It must be accountable for outcomes, not just specific outputs (such as the number of apartments built). The outcome goals for the entire community should be bold: doubling the high school graduation rate, halving the number of people living below the poverty line, cutting emergency room visits by 75 percent, or making sure 100 percent of kindergarteners arrive at school ready to learn.

The type of coordination required to change a whole neighborhood—as we have seen in the examples in Harlem, or Atlanta, or Houston in this book—requires bringing together dozens of institutions and thousands of people inside and outside a community. Angela Blanchard once said that her organization, Neighborhood Centers, Inc. (which started as a Settlement House), relies on many pillars of support to be effective. The pillars are multiple; it's not just a three-legged stool or a four-legged table, she explained. It is a millipede with hundreds of legs.

It may seem impossible to take Angela Blanchard's spirit and leadership and inject it into an institution or a system, but that is exactly what community development was able to do in the 1980s. Alex von Hoffman's chapter in this book shows how community revitalization work in that era was driven by charismatic leaders with few resources. People like Don Terner, Dorothy Mae Richardson, Paul Grogan, and Sister Lillian Murphy dove into their work and others followed. Perhaps even more remarkable than any one of their stories, however, was that they contributed to building a network of actors that grew in professionalism and capacity over time. These entrepreneurs built institutions that began to link up in new ways with new partners in government and the private sector. This network had the vision and provided leadership that was modeled on the individuals who were its pioneers. Those pioneers started a "movement" and transformed it into an "industry."

THE HISTORIC ROLE OF THE COMMUNITY DEVELOPMENT INDUSTRY

The backbone of and the community development industry for the past 25 years has been affordable housing development. Affordable housing serves as more than just shelter. These projects are often anchors in their communities; they physically revitalize the neighborhood around them. Often a new apartment building will serve a target population that has special needs, such as tenants who were formerly homeless. Or the housing might be built in an ethnic enclave and have culturally sensitive services and language instruction. In these and many other examples, affordable housing becomes a platform for delivering other social services and promoting community in ways that go far beyond simply providing a roof over one's head.

The community-tailored approach to affordable housing production emerged in response to previous policy regimes in which much of urban renewal was orchestrated by large bureaucracies like the U.S. Department of Housing and Urban Development (HUD). These top-down regimes gave way to a more decentralized approach that used local groups—often nonprofit community development corporations (CDCs)—to identify local housing needs and then plug into larger systems of support. Those larger systems might include subsidy programs through the tax code (i.e., the Low Income Housing Tax Credit [LIHTC]) or other government subsidy programs, or they might include loans and investments from banks motivated by the Community Reinvestment Act (CRA). Foundations also played an important role in funding this new network of affordable housing developers.[2] This new funding approach made it common for an apartment building to have six (or more) different public and private funders.

The housing that has been built under this approach is high quality and often beautiful. And even though the buildings are tailored to the needs of a specific neighborhood, this is not a boutique activity. The community development industry has used the LIHTC program to build more than 2.5 million apartments.[3] That number is nearly as many apartments still standing today from all prior public housing and other government-subsidized building programs combined, dating back to 1937.[4]

As successful as this industry has been, it must evolve if it is to continue to make progress toward its ultimate goal of improving the life chances of low-income people. One important change that we will address in this chapter is a topic that Paul Grogan, president of the Boston Foundation, considers in this book. In looking to the future of community development, he writes:

> *What then is the future of community development? It lies in turning the architecture of community development to meet urgent challenges of human development. How to turn a*

2 For a more detailed discussion of this history, see David J. Erickson, Housing Policy Revolution: Networks and Neighborhoods (Washington, DC: Urban Institute Press, 2009).

3 National Council of State Housing Finance Agencies, HFA Factbook: 2010 Annual Survey Results (Washington, DC: The National Council of State Housing Finance Agencies, 2012), p 92 and 100. We recognize that these apartments were built by both nonprofit and for-profit developers. All the units, however, serve low-income tenants and their families.

4 Erickson, Housing Policy Revolution, p. 163.

successful community organizing and real estate development system toward the goal of increasing educational outcomes, employment success, family asset building, individual and community resilience to weather setbacks? As an industry, we need new strategies to face these challenges.

The following is one attempt to grapple with these questions and to suggest new strategies. We believe it is possible to use key elements of the current community development industry to both build out an expanded approach to revitalizing low-income communities and integrate people- and place-based strategies. This new approach needs a lead organization at the local level—a millipede, or a quarterback—and the following is an exploration of how that entity might work.

THE NEED FOR A NEW APPROACH

It may seem obvious, but the most important reason why community development needs to evolve is that it is not solving the problem it was set up to fix-namely, reducing the number of people living in poverty. The percentage of Americans living in poverty when the War on Poverty was underway was about 15 percent, and it is about 15 percent today.[5] That is not entirely the fault of community development, as Peter Edelman explains in his essay in this book. Changes in the economy—in terms of technology and globalization—in addition to swings in political support for antipoverty programs and a significant influx of very low-income immigrants, has made fighting poverty an uphill battle.

Moreover, poverty itself has changed dramatically in the last 40 years, and as Alan Berube explains in his chapter, the needs of low-income communities—and where those communities are located—are very different now than they were when our current antipoverty and community development programs were put into place.

---

5 Carmen DeNavas et al., "Income, Poverty, and Health Insurance Coverage in the United States: 2010" (Washington, DC: U.S. Department of Commerce, 2011), 15. Available at: www.census.gov/prod/2011pubs/p60-239.pdf.

The suburbanization of poverty, for instance, compels us to rethink the work of community development. The older community development approach that focused on project-by-project interventions worked well when the goal was to revitalize a relatively small inner-city geography that had experienced an exodus of middle-class residents and capital. But it is now out of step with the new reality of where poor people live and the choices they have there.

All of this suggests that there may be better ways to organize our efforts in alignment with our understanding that poverty today is a complex system. It is the result of many interlocking and reinforcing negative inputs. The current practice of making a few interventions—in food security, affordable housing, or some income supplement—in a piecemeal way will not resolve the problem.

A POSSIBLE NEW PLAYER FOR COMMUNITY DEVELOPMENT: THE QUARTERBACK

We are proposing a new local entity to coordinate local interventions in low-income communities. For the sake of argument, we are calling this entity the quarterback, although we recognize this metaphor has limitations. The quarterback's role is similar in important ways to how a CDC operates at the level of developing an affordable housing project. Like the CDC, the quarterback must articulate the vision it is managing to (the outcome of reduced poverty, for example) and then marshal the funding sources and manage multiple partners to execute on that vision. The difference, of course, is that instead of managing banks, architects, and contractors, as a CDC might to construct a building, the quarterback is trying to enhance life chances for neighborhood residents by orchestrating the development and deployment of an array of high-quality human and physical capital interventions. The scope of work includes not only traditional community development activities, such as affordable housing and small business financing, but also educational improvements, workforce development, and health care, among

Figure 1. The Quarterback as Integrator[6]

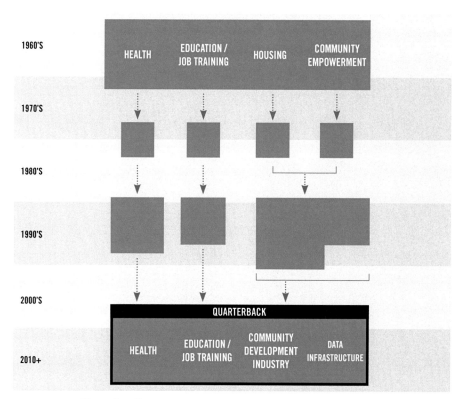

The earlier efforts at comprehensive community revitalization during the War on Poverty in the 1960s splintered off into separate policy areas that lacked coordination. Over time, those siloed policy domains grew in capacity and capability; some merged. The promise of the quarterback is to knit the better-equipped separate silos back together into a more effective and integrated effort.

others. The quarterback will thus primarily serve in a coordinating role, managing a diverse coalition of players in order to achieve community betterment.

The quarterback can take many forms depending on the needs or the circumstances of the community. In some communities, there

---

6 David Erickson first presented this graphic and the idea of a quarterback organization at the "Exploring New Models for Affordable Housing" conference, Federal Reserve Bank of San Francisco, September 12, 2011. Available at: www.frbsf.org/cdinvestments/conferences/affordable-housing/.

may be a rich variety of strong institutions in the government, nonprofit, and for-profit sectors. In this case, what might be needed is to bring all those groups together in common cause. A fitting example of this type of coordination is Living Cities' Integration Initiative in Minnesota. There, the Twin Cities of Minneapolis and St. Paul have very strong institutions, but they need better coordination if they are to achieve the community-wide benefits they desire. In this case, Living Cities employs what they call "one table" to bring together all the parties to work together. They are able to facilitate this process by providing resources to organize the table's work—administrative support as well as grants and below-market-rate capital that are made available to the participants to create incentives to cooperate. In this case, the quarterback is a bridge builder and coordinator who uses a light touch.

On the other end of the spectrum are communities that lack high-functioning institutional partners. For these places, a quarterback may need to be far more aggressive in organizing what resources are present in addition to building up new capacity in places where it did not exist before. Here you might think about Harlem Children's Zone, an organization that created many of the institutions that ultimately were essential to its success.

Clearly there are communities in between the high and low ends of the community viability spectrum, and they will require unique combinations of integration and institution-building. There are many examples of quarterback-like entities across the country that fall along that spectrum, including: Strive Partnership in the Greater Cincinnati area;[7] Magnolia Place Community Initiative in South Central Los Angeles;[8] LISC's Building Sustainable Communities Initiative, which sponsored quarterback-like entities

---

7   Jeff Edmondson and Nancy L. Zimpher, "The New Civic Infrastructure: The 'How To' of Collective Impact and Getting a Better Return on Investment," Community Investments, 24 (1) (Spring 2012): 10-13.

8   More information available at: www.magnoliaplacela.org.

such as the Quad Communities Development Corporation in Chicago;[9] and Codman Square Health Center in Boston.[10]

Any Community Can Produce a Quarterback

For those communities that fall on the low-capacity end of the spectrum, the quarterback concept holds particular promise. Consider, for example, findings from the Federal Reserve's Community Affairs Offices and the Brookings Institution's Metropolitan Policy Program, which profiled 16 high-poverty communities in a study on concentrated poverty in 2008. The results showed that only a few of those communities had even minimal community development capability in the form of CDCs, community development financial institutions (CDFIs), strong local banks, or effective local government.[11] In most of the communities, however, there was leadership in unlikely places: schools, churches, charities, clinics, and elsewhere. It would be the job of the quarterback to identify and build on those areas of leadership and strength, as well as to build capacity in the gaps. In that sense, the quarterback is really a facilitator who brings out the strengths of service providers and leaders in the community. This is a delicate balance, of course. The quarterback must respond to, and have support from, the community to succeed. At the same time, it must also lead and provide vision and a structure for moving forward.

Another instructive example is the recent effort to better coordinate antipoverty work in Las Vegas. Stakeholders there hosted a Healthy Communities conference as part of the social determinants of health and community development series (a partnership of the Federal Reserve and the Robert Wood Johnson

---

9 LISC, "Building Sustainable Communities: A Progress Report on Meeting LISC's Next Generation of Challenges and Fulfilling the Promise of Community Development" (New York: LISC, 2009). Available at: www.lisc.org/files/17689_file_sep_bsc_prog-ress_report.pdf.

10 More information available at: www.codman.org/.

11 Community Affairs Offices of the Federal Reserve System and Brookings Metropolitan Policy Program, "The Enduring Challenge of Concentrated Poverty in America" (Richmond, VA: Federal Reserve System, 2008). The full report is available at: www.frbsf.org/cpre-port/index.html.

Foundation).[12] Local leaders came forward from HUD's regional office, local government, the Nevada Bankers' Collaborative, the United Way, the University of Nevada, and other nonprofits.[13] They identified collaboration and integration as fundamental to developing an initiative to address the needs of struggling Las Vegas communities. Subsequent to the meeting, these local leaders hired the Strive Network to help organize cross-sector antipoverty and community revitalization efforts. In essence, they hired their own quarterback.

THE QUARTERBACK EMPLOYS BOTH PEOPLE- AND PLACE-BASED STRATEGIES

The quarterback responds to community input and community need by choosing from an array of service providers. Although the choices can be overwhelming, they are also liberating. The quarterback is not wedded to any one approach, but instead is agnostic about which strategies to employ to get the best outcome. That feature makes the quarterback the ultimate silo-busting institution and one that is perfectly poised to solve the age-old question of whether we should focus on people or places in helping low-income communities. As Federal Reserve Governor Elizabeth Duke says in the foreword to this book, that debate is over and both sides won. The quarterback must choose strategies from both sides, including:

- human capital/people: early childhood interventions, schools, health, recreation, workforce development (including connecting people to good quality jobs); and

- physical capital/place: affordable housing improvements, community facilities, well-lit and safe community spaces, transportation, health clinics, parks, grocery stores and other essential businesses, and anchor institutions (e.g., hospitals,

---

12 More information on this initiative can be found at: http://www.frbsf.org/cdinvestments/conferences/healthy-communities/.

13 Culinary Training Academy, "Healthy Communities: Las Vegas,"(North Las Vegas, Culinary Training Academy, January 19, 2012). Available at: www.frbsf.org/cdinvestments/conferences/healthy-communities/2012-las-vegas-nv/.

universities) that may play a special role in creating good-paying local jobs.

Human Capital

Two recent developments underscore the promise of having community development quarterbacks address the people side of the equation. The first centers on a growing body of research on the importance of early childhood interventions, as outlined by Gabriella Conti, James Heckman, James Radner, Jack Shonkoff, and others in this volume. It is increasingly clear from this research that children who are exposed to the corrosive effects of poverty early in life begin to develop a thick shell that makes it very hard to influence them in later life. Therefore, any community intervention must start with a special focus on keeping children motivated and inspired to learn and helping them grow in the healthiest way possible.

Second is the increasing recognition of the intersection between concerns over the economic, political, and social conditions that influence individual and population health (the "social determinants of health") and the goals of community development. As Risa Lavizzo-Mourey, president of the Robert Wood Johnson Foundation, writes in her essay in this volume, "we are likely to look back at this time and wonder why community development and health were ever separate industries." Abundant research shows that people who feel a sense of community, who live in safe and vibrant neighborhoods, and who have some sense of control over their lives live longer and healthier.[14] From this perspective, community development plays an important role in improving health for low-income people.

The partnership between health and community development could be the single most important recent development for community revitalization. It brings new partners, new resources, and especially, new ideas. For example, the Robert Wood

---

14 For a good overview of these studies, see Robert Wood Johnson Foundation, "Beyond Health Care: New Directions to a Healthier America" (Princeton, NJ: Robert Wood Johnson Foundation Commission to Build a Healthier America, 2009). Available at: www.commissiononhealth.org/Report.aspx?Publication=64498.

Johnson Foundation's Commission to Build a Healthier America characterizes the social and environmental circumstances that influence health as follows:

> Where we live, work, learn and play dramatically affects the health of all Americans for better or for worse. The sometimes toxic relationship between how we live our lives and the economic, social and physical environments that surround us has resulted in some of America's most persistent health problems. At the same time, improving conditions in our homes, schools, workplaces and communities can help create greater opportunities for healthy lives.[15]

Improving peoples' lives as a way to improve their health is a powerful concept, which points to a clear role for community development as the action arm for the analysis and research from those who study population health.[16] Working hand in glove, these two fields can be far more successful in their mutual goal of reducing the negative effects of poverty.

There are other ideas and developments around human capital strategies that are pushing in the direction of the quarterback concept. The community schools movement, for example, is an approach that positions a school as a neighborhood hub, where partnerships between the school and other community resources allow for much needed alignment across academics, health, and social services, youth and community development, and community engagement.[17] As a neighborhood hub, the community school can play the role of quarterback by strategically aligning a variety of services in a location that is familiar and convenient for community members. For example, throughout Multnomah County, Oregon, a network of SUN (Schools Uniting Neighborhoods) community schools provides educational,

---

15 Robert Wood Johnson Foundation, "What Drives Health" (RWJ web page). Available at: www.commissiononhealth.org/WhatDrivesHealth.aspx.

16 This characterization comes from Dr. Douglas Jutte, director of the Center for Community Development and Health.

17 Coalition for Community Schools. "What is a Community School?" (web page). Available at www.communityschools.org/aboutschools/what_is_a_community_school.aspx.

recreational, social, and health services across six school districts, representing a collaboration of County Department of Human Services, the City of Portland Parks and Recreation, nonprofits, and local school districts. The schools offer extended-day academic and enrichment programs, as well as direct services supported by partnerships with other community institutions, such as libraries, parks, and community centers, neighborhood health clinics, and area churches and businesses.[18] In essence, the community school acts as a quarterback in aligning these entities for community advancement.

Physical Capital

The roots of community development are still firmly in real estate—developing affordable housing, charter schools, community clinics, and more—that improves the places where low-income people live. This should remain an important focus of the quarterback, but we must be honest about when to make tradeoffs if other investments—such as people-based strategies—have a greater likelihood of increasing the life chances of community residents.

It is also true that community development needs to use the skills and professionalism it developed in building affordable housing to finance a much broader array of physical investments. Of course, there has been some progress in this area with more CDFI financing for charter schools and for grocery stores located in food deserts, for example, but the need for community development to finance more and different types of facilities is pressing. Health clinics are a prime example. The Affordable Care Act will necessitate building thousands of new Federally Qualified Health Centers in low-income communities, and the Act provides $11 billion in additional funding for this work (although it will not be enough for all the building that is needed).[19] This building

---

18 Coalition for Community Schools, "Community Schools Across the Nation: A Sampling of Local Initiatives and National Models" (Washington, DC: Coalition for Community Schools, n.d.).

19 Ronda Kotelchuck, Daniel Lowenstein, and Jonathan N. Tobin, "Community Health Centers and Community Development Financial Institutions: Joining Forces to Address Determinants of Health," Health Affairs 30 (2011): 2090-2093.

boom of clinics is a significant opportunity for community revitalization.

These next-generation health clinics are additionally compelling in light of their ability to play a quarterback role. Consider the inspiring example of Codman Square Health Center in Boston, a community clinic that serves the city's poorest and most vulnerable populations. It is driven by a recognition that individual physical and mental health is dependent on the social well-being of the entire community, and accordingly offers an array of community services including adult education, financial counseling, and youth programs either in-house, or through partners. In mirroring this approach, the next-generation community clinics would hew more closely to the War on Poverty vision of "community-oriented primary care" that stipulates that the whole neighborhood is the clinic's patient. This approach, promoted by public health leaders such as John Cassel, tries to reduce the negative effects of poverty-induced stress by building up community ties and overall resilience.[20] Attacking the "upstream" sources of poor health is essential to improving the health of low-income communities, as both Risa Lavizzo-Mourey and Nancy Adler argue in this book.

The community development finance industry will need to learn to fund many other additional community enhancements in addition to clinics, including parks, community centers, and better connections to transit. The Bay Area Transit-Oriented Affordable Housing Fund, which provides flexible capital to develop affordable housing and vital services near transit lines, offers a prime example of blending many different sources of capital from foundations, banks motivated by the CRA, CDFIs, and perhaps most surprisingly, a regional transportation agency.[21] This fund allows the transportation sector to join with the community

20 For an overview of Cassel's groundbreaking work, see his lecture on the subject at: J.C. Cassel, "The contribution of the social environment to host resistance: The Fourth Wade Hampton Frost Lecture." American Journal of Epidemiology 104 (1976): 107-123.

21 Center for Transit-Oriented Development, "CDFIs and Transit Oriented Development" (San Francisco: Federal Reserve Bank of San Francisco, 2009), Appendix B. Available at: www. frbsf.org/publications/community/wpapers/2010/cdfi_transit_oriented_design.pdf.

development industry and philanthropic organizations to work together for a mutual goal: more vibrant and connected low-income communities.

Core Set of Interventions Needed in Every Community

As wide-ranging as the above people- and place-based strategies are, the quarterback must focus on a set of core needs that are a high priority in every community. These include: (1) safety and security in the home, (2) highly engaging early learning for children, (3) continuing access to high-quality education, (4) at least one living wage job in every household, and (5) community design and services that allow residents to make healthier choices in their daily lives.[22] These core principles allow for the home to be a base for an experience-rich and stable environment for children. This base better ensures that children arrive ready to learn at school. As the landmark early education studies that Gabriella Conti and James Heckman discuss in their chapter demonstrate, investments like those in the Perry Preschool and the Abecedarian projects have enormous payoffs in the long run in terms of more capable workers and better prepared parents and community leaders. Furthermore, ensuring that every household is connected to the labor market is a source of stability and pride, which is also critical, as Clara Miller describes in her essay in this book. Finally, building communities and providing services in such a way that make the healthy choice the easy choice is essential to overcoming crippling health disparities. The quarterback will need to focus on these core strategies and build out other interventions tailored to local needs, but in concentric circles beyond the core described above.

THE QUARTERBACK NEEDS ACTIONABLE DATA

Assembling a set of interventions that is sharply tailored to local needs is no easy task. Akin to Tolstoy's assertion that happy families are all alike, but every unhappy family is unhappy in its own

---

22 Although a job is key to the viability of an individual or family, there are limited ways in which community development can create them. To a large degree, job creation has more to do with the macro economy. Although community development can play a significant role in overcoming a skills mismatch between what jobs are available and the skills of potential workers.

way, functional neighborhoods share common characteristics, but each struggling neighborhood has its own particular constellation of challenges and assets. The multi-dimensional nature of neighborhood distress, taken together with the variability in assets that influence the prospects for neighborhood recovery, means that a "best practice" for one neighborhood is not necessarily the best practice for another. This is a particular challenge for the quarterback. To be effective, the quarterback must identify and respond to the conditions, context, and changes over time in each of the areas in which it works.

In essence, the quarterback needs a sense-and-respond system that has at its core reliable, frequently updated data that are consistently assembled and aligned from myriad sources. Ideally, these data could be flexibly organized into a number of analytical frameworks, each useful for different reasons. Using the data in a neighborhood indicators framework, for instance, would allow the quarterback to "diagnose" community conditions and monitor multiple dimensions of change over time. Further assembling these data into a community dashboard would allow the quarterback to evaluate a community at a specific moment in time to determine its standing along a specific dimension of change, and to compare progress across similarly situated communities and build community support for change.[23] These data could also be employed by academic researchers investigating the still-vexing questions of which community development interventions work best and why.

Several tools and approaches that fit within each of these frameworks have emerged in recent years to help gauge both the "investment environment" and the results of particular

---

23 There are many interesting examples of community dashboards, including the work of Neal Halfon from the UCLA Center for Healthier Children using a dashboard of key data to monitor the progress of wellbeing in children in the Magnolia Place Community Initiative. More details are available in the report "Getting to Scale: The Elusive Goal," Annie E. Casey Foundation, Family Programs, available at http://www.casey.org/Resources/Publications/magnoliaplace.htm.

community development interventions.[24] However, what we still lack is a mechanism that is capable of more systematically aligning these tools to help us understand community conditions and context, and to assess the changes that flow from our work. This kind of mechanism could help a quarterback make better decisions about the type and scale of investment needed in a given place.

Linking Data Across Silos

The foundation of such a mechanism would be a sophisticated data infrastructure that enables input and output of varying types of small area data. We can look to the National Neighborhood Indicators Partnership (NNIP) for guidance on developing this data infrastructure. For more than 15 years, NNIP has helped develop data systems with 36 partner organizations in cities around the nation, each of which collects local area data and facilitates their direct use by local entities. If adapted to capture both qualitative and financial data, these platforms could help monitor conditions that have been historically difficult to capture, such as community capacity as well as costs and savings across sectors. If built out in more places, they could serve as the local data infrastructure needed to help gain clarity about baseline conditions in an area and changes over time, and to ultimately help identify not only effective strategies, but cost-efficient ones as well.[25]

These data could be augmented by the information gathered via platforms and systems already in use by nonprofits and foundations across the nation for gauging the reach and effectiveness

---

24 Some examples: The Reinvestment Fund's Market Value Analysis and PolicyMap tool, RW Ventures' Dynamic Neighborhood Taxonomy, Social Compact's DrillDown profiles, NeighborWorks' Success Measures Data System, and Social Solutions' Efforts to Outcomes software, as well as various neighborhood indicator projects supported by the National Neighborhood Indicators Partnership.

25 Ideas from the public health research field to link administrative data records at an individual level could also be of use here. For more information, see Douglas Jutte et al. "Administrative Record Linkage as a Tool for Public Health Research," Annual Review of Public Health 32 (2011): 91-108.

of their programs and service delivery.[26] If the proprietary data collected through these systems were shared in some format and integrated with baseline data available through local data intermediaries, the network of organizations that serve a given neighborhood could use this information to better assess their capacity and activities.

Although local area data is a core requirement for a sense-and-respond system, forces outside a neighborhood, such as housing market dynamics, regional economic trends, and the spatial allocation of public and private resources, play a significant role in shaping results of local interventions. Small area data do not provide enough information to fully understand these conditions, but increasingly, relevant administrative data on both regional and national scales are becoming accessible through online tools such as PolicyMap, a subscription-based mapping application from The Reinvestment Fund, or HUD's Consolidated Planning mapping tool. Each of these platforms assembles longitudinal data from diverse sources, including HUD, the IRS, Home Mortgage Disclosure Act (HMDA), and the U.S. Census. Systematically integrating small area data with these regional and national data would represent a big step forward in enabling community developers to gauge the context of their investments and make adjustments for what is working and what is not.

Turning Data Into Usable Information

Already though, we are talking about a considerable quantity of information, unwieldy at best and crushing at worst. And a quarterback's job of managing to a specific outcome would be enormously complicated if there were hundreds of data points to consider in making any given decision. One way to make sense of the plethora of data available would be to organize them

---

26 Increasingly, nonprofits and foundations are maintaining private data collection and analysis systems to track their programs and investments, or use Success Measures or Efforts to Outcomes tools. The exclusive nature of these efforts minimizes their potential to broadly inform community-wide revitalization strategies.

into a set of indices and dashboards.[27] Here we can look to the Fair Housing and Equity Analysis (FHEA) tools issued recently by HUD for guidance. The FHEA assembles carefully selected indicators on related topic areas into a number of indices on various dimensions of community stability, including poverty, health, housing conditions, job access, employment, and education. The "scores" help quantify and standardize the social and economic conditions in a given neighborhood relative to those in other areas.[28]

This basic structure could be adapted to develop indices of a broader range of neighborhood factors that we know influence social and economic outcomes, and they could include both quantitative and qualitative data collected through our integrated data systems. For example, indices of educational opportunity and job access could be constructed as follows:

EDUCATIONAL OPPORTUNITY INDEX

- Reading proficiency
- Math proficiency
- Percentage of students on Free and Reduced Price Meals
- Survey data on enrichment services/resources, etc.

JOB ACCESS INDEX

- Ratio of jobs counts to worker counts
- Car ownership rates and/or level and frequency of transit access
- Commute time
- Survey data on child-care availability during workshifts, etc.

---

27 Indices and dashboards are increasingly being used to gauge social, economic, and/or health conditions at varying geographic scales. Some examples: The Social Science Research Council's Measure of America maps and tools, as well as local projects like Austin's Community Action Network Community Dashboard, San Francisco's Healthy Development Measurement Tool, and the Community Dashboard established by the Magnolia Place Community Initiative in Los Angeles.

28 Another good example here is the County Health Rankings, available at: www.county-healthrankings.org/.

A dashboard of scores along each dimension for both a neighborhood in question and its surrounding areas offers a quick means to grasp a community's main concerns, needs, and opportunities. A hypothetical example is provided in the sample below. The scores indicate that the neighborhood is considerably behind the surrounding city in terms of educational opportunity, economic integration, and organizational capacity. This kind of scoring can be powerful in helping a quarterback identify priorities and target community development interventions to specific communities and populations in need. If scores are tallied over time, such a system can also help monitor progress, or lack thereof, along each dimension.

	Any City, USA	Low-Income Neighborhood	Black-White Disparity	Hispanic-White Disparity	Asian-White Disparity
Educational Opportunity Index	5.3	2.6	1.4	1.1	0.5
Integration Index	4.9	2.7	1.8	1.2	0.4
Job Access Index	6.2	4.4	2.1	1.3	1.1
Housing Stability Index	5.4	3.6	1.1	1.4	0.7
Health Index	5.5	4.5	1.6	1.3	0.8
Organizational Capacity Index	5.8	2.2			

To be sure, though, the task of identifying the most appropriate interventions for a given place cannot be reduced to a simple math problem.[29] More sophisticated analysis is needed if we are

---

29 For a more detailed discussion of the various challenges of employing data to understand social and community change, see Naomi Cytron, "Doing the Math: The Challenges and Opportunities of Measuring Results in Community Development," Community Investments 24 (1) (Federal Reserve Bank of San Francisco: 2012).

to identify the highest and best uses of community development resources. This points to an additional benefit of integrated data made available through improved data infrastructure. Enhanced qualitative and quantitative data would be of significant use to researchers studying the process, reach, outcomes, and impact of complex community development interventions. This research would help build the industry's knowledge base and guide resources toward what works.

BUILDING AN ENABLING ECOSYSTEM TO PRODUCE MORE QUARTERBACKS

How do we create an environment that makes it easier to develop many more quarterbacks? To do this, we must think seriously both about incentives and ways to pay for the quarterback's interventions.

Getting The Incentives Right

The quarterback will be held responsible for improving the life chances of an entire community. To do that, the quarterback needs to traverse the sinews of the community development network. The quarterback must operate *in between* silos. This is easier said than done. We know, for example, that stable housing improves educational achievement. And yet housing developers rarely interact with educators. Likewise, we know that violence stunts early brain development. Yet pediatricians rarely consult public safety officials. The quarterback can alter this dynamic with the proper incentive structure. The structure may not be a market per se, but market-like forces, similar to the ones that guide community development's project-by-project work (e.g., affordable housing), should reward community-transforming quarterbacks over less successful ones. The quarterback should also have the resources to either build its own capability to deliver a certain service or product (start a charter school, for example) or contract out for that work (hire the Knowledge is Power Program, for example, to do it). This is the business world's classic "make or buy" decision.

Successful quarterbacks will also need to facilitate cross-sector partnerships. If the quarterback is tasked with improving fifth grade reading scores, for example, it may look to educators, doctors, and affordable housing organizations for support. Absent an incentive, however, it is unlikely these partners will fully engage. Alternatively, if the quarterback could reward them for collaborating, more housing projects may have libraries and more schools may have health clinics. By creating a reward structure to pay for broad outcomes, collaboration becomes more natural.

Consider, for example, how the LIHTC rewards collaboration. The LIHTC is the primary federal financing vehicle used to build and rehabilitate multifamily affordable rental housing. The federal government allocates LIHTCs to affordable housing developers, who sell them to investors, usually at a discount.[30] This discount reflects various risks. Will the project be completed on time? Will the financing be adequate? Most important, will the project serve low-income people (the major aspect of program compliance)? These risks have material consequences. If the project lags, the developer can be replaced. If the financing is inadequate, the project can be scrapped. And if the rents are too high, or the project does not serve low-income people, the credits can be recaptured by the IRS. This aligns the incentives of the project participants. In a LIHTC transaction, the developer, investor, and government all share the same goal: financially viable, high-quality housing that serves low-income people.

A similar structure could be used to align the quarterback with its community partners—a "Neighborhood Improvement Tax Credit," perhaps.[31] Or, if not a tax credit, another outcome-based financing structure such as the Social Impact Bond, Minnesota Human Capital Performance Bond, or the newly created Robin

---

30 Michael D. Eriksen, "The Market Price of Low-Income Housing Tax Credits," Journal of Urban Economics, 66:2 (2009), p. 141-149.

31 A school-based variation of this idea is explored by Ian Galloway in "Charter School Tax Credit: Investing in Human Capital," Working Paper Series (Federal Reserve Bank of San Francisco: December, 2011) available at http://www.frbsf.org/publications/community/wpapers/2010/working_paper_2010_08_galloway.html.

Hood X Prize.[32] More important than the financial tool, though, is the mechanism: it must reward outcomes over outputs. Only outcomes-based funding will afford the quarterback the financial flexibility to align the incentives of a broad range of community collaborators.

HOW TO PAY FOR THE QUARTERBACK

There is a strong rationale for using community development funds to support a quarterback. A quarterback can blend existing sources of subsidy and market-rate capital similarly to how a CDFI or CDC might build an affordable housing project. Perhaps even more important in the long run, using a quarterback provides a stable and trusted partner that reduces the risk for new sources of capital participating in a community-improving effort, which may be a key in attracting socially motivated or impact investors, along with other nontraditional community development investors.

Existing Funding Sources

Although government funding at all levels—federal, state, and local—has declined and may continue to fall, community development finance still has significant resources at its disposal. The exact numbers are hard to establish, but our estimate of the core funding programs (block grants and investment tax credits) in 2006 put the number at $11 billion for affordable housing and another $4.1 billion for small business and real estate development through the New Markets Tax Credit.[33] These subsidies are almost always combined with capital from other sources. Most notable is the money that banks loan and invest in community development projects as part of their obligation under the Community Reinvestment Act of 1977. Community development

---

32 For a more in-depth discussion of pay-for-success financing see Volume 8, Issue 1 of the Community Development Investment Review (forthcoming) published by the Center for Community Development Investments at the Federal Reserve Bank of San Francisco.

33 Erickson, "Housing Policy Revolution," p. xvi; and Department of the Treasury, "NMTC Qualified Equity Investment Report." (Washington, DC: DOT, Community Development Financial Institutions Fund: New Markets Tax Credits Program, October 4, 2010). Available at: www.cdfifund.gov/docs/nmtc/2010/NMTCQEIReport-October-2010.pdf. The New Markets Tax Credit figure is what was allocated in that year.

lending activity since 1996, reported as required by the CRA, is about $516 billion, or about $37 billion per year on average.[34] Larger banks are also required to make investments into low-income communities, so the yearly average is certainly higher than this number would suggest. On top of those annual numbers are other sources that amount to billions of dollars a year from foundations, state and local government, and other institutional investors such as pension funds and insurance companies. These resources are considerable, but not sufficient to fund the needs of all struggling low-income communities.

The community development finance system could be the foundation, though, for a larger and more complex web of other funding sources and income streams, which would make the community-wide improvement activities possible. In this larger structure, one might imagine combining funding streams for schools, health promotion programs, community policing programs, transit, and others that are currently not yet coordinated for an individual, group, or neighborhood.[35] It will be a central challenge for the quarterback to weave these different funding streams together for the maximum impact.

Additional Funding Sources

Funding this new system cannot simply come from existing sources of capital, even if they were all spent in the best way possible. A comprehensive, place-based, multisector intervention is expensive, but it is also a good long-term investment to reduce the negative social costs of poverty. By incorporating a broader and more comprehensive framework for community interventions, it opens the possibility that funding streams that were previously not seen as relevant now might not only fit, but be made more effective as they are blended for stronger outcomes.

---

34 This estimate is from Phil Daher, manager, Information Management, Division of Consumer and Community Affairs, Federal Reserve Board of Governors. Email exchange Sept. 16, 2011.

35 There are some promising examples of this type of coordination, such as the United Way Bay Area SparkPoint centers that bring together, credit and money management services, income tax help, and help enrolling in social services along with getting housing and medical assistance. They also provide violence prevention services and counseling and job training and placement. The innovation here is focusing on the individual.

Aligning funding streams may fix the pervasive "wrong pocket problem," where investments from one part of the government are not reimbursed by the benefits that accrue to another part of government, discouraging cross-agency investment. Consider, for example, an investment by HUD or the Department of Transportation that ultimately keeps a community healthier in the long run. These investments create savings for the Medicaid and Medicare programs, but the Department of Health and Human Services is not able to take that savings and redirect it back to the agencies that made the cost-saving investment in the first place. We need new mechanisms to allow for smarter investing of public resources that get away from siloed budgets. As Xavier de Sousa Briggs said at a Federal Reserve community development conference, we need to "change the DNA of government" so funds flow to experiments and then get redirected to successes.[36]

Socially motivated investors are also a promising new source of capital; they are interested in making a financial return on their money, but are also interested in promoting a social goal. It is hard to estimate the market for this source of capital, which is often targeted to overseas investments in poor countries, but one study by J.P. Morgan puts the potential investment amount at $400 billion to $1 trillion.[37] Another study by Hope Consulting that focuses on individual retail investors gauges a demand of about $120 billion.[38] As Antony Bugg-Levine explains in his essay in this volume, these investors might be attracted to community development, particularly if it were able to explain its value and

---

36 Federal Reserve Board of Governors, "Healthy Communities Conference," (Washington, DC: Federal Reserve Board of Governors, July 10, 2010). Transcripts available at: www.frbsf.org/cdinvestments/conferences/healthy-communities/2010-washington-dc/nextsteps.html.

37 Estimate is over ten years. J.P. Morgan, "Impact Investments: An Emerging Asset Class," Global Research Report (New York: J.P. Morgan, November 29, 2012), p. 6, available at https://www.jpmorgan.com/cm/BlobServer/impact_investments_nov2010.pdf?blobkey=id &blobwhere=1158611333228&blobheader=application%2Fpdf&blobcol=urldata&blob table=MungoBlobs.

38 Not an annual number. Hope Consulting, "Money for Good," (San Francisco, CA: Hope Consulting, May 2010), p. 62. Available at http://www.hopeconsulting.us/pdf/Money%20 for%20Good_Final.pdf.

impact—in terms of better health, education, and life-chances for low-income people—in more compelling ways by developing new approaches to data and measurement along with more effective communication strategies. "Telling the story" effectively to would-be investors is crucial.

The health care world also has two exciting new sources of capital, in addition to funding for clinics, that could be blended with community development resources to promote the mutually reinforcing goals of improving low-income communities and improving health outcomes for high-need populations. They are: (1) community benefit dollars from nonprofit hospitals, and (2) the money for health promotion from sources such as Accountable Care Organizations (ACOs).

Currently, nonprofit hospitals are required to spend a certain amount of their revenue on the community to maintain their nonprofit status. The dollar figure for total investments nation-wide varies, but most estimates put this community benefit at more than $12 billion annually.[39] Today, most is spent on covering the medical care costs of people who are uninsured. In the future, if most people have health insurance, the hospitals will need to find new investments that promote health in their communities. Increasingly, hospitals are looking to invest in improving the social determinants of health, which naturally leads them to the universe of community development invest-ments. This could be a significant new source of funding for the quarterback, particularly if the data infrastructure were in place to show that improving housing, schools, and access to jobs yielded the expected health improvements within a certain targeted community.

ACOs were created as part of the Affordable Care Act and work like a health maintenance organization (HMO), with the similar

---

39 This figure is somewhat dated as it was calculated by the Congressional Budget Office for 2002. U.S. Congressional Budget Office, "Non-profit Hospitals and the Provision of Community Benefits" (Washington, DC: CBO, December 2006). Available at www.cbo.gov/ sites/default/files/cbofiles/ftpdocs/76xx/doc7695/12-06-nonprofit.pdf. For a more up-to-date and nuanced analysis of this issue, see Erik Bakken and David Kindig, "Is Hospital Community Benefit Charity Care?" Wisconsin Medical Journal (forthcoming).

incentives of keeping their fee-paying members healthy. "ACOs are groups of doctors, hospitals, and other health care providers, who come together voluntarily to give coordinated high quality care to the Medicare patients they serve," according to the Center for Medicare and Medicaid Innovation. "When an ACO succeeds in both delivering high-quality care and spending health care dollars more wisely, it will share in the savings it achieves for the Medicare program."[40] Some forward-thinking ACOs are now considering how they can make investments to improve their patients' communities as a strategy to save medical care costs in the long term.[41]

In addition, there are many other emerging financial tools and vehicles, like the Social Impact Bond mentioned earlier, that can be used to support community improvement. Foundations, for example, are increasingly using the corpus of their endowments to make investments that promote the goals of community development. These "mission-related investments," or MRIs, are designed to deliver a financial return and achieve a social return at the same time. Clara Miller, president of the F.B. Heron Foundation, in her essay in this book, offers a clarion call to all her sister foundations to tap this $590 billion source of capital to finance antipoverty work.[42]

Finally, there are some potential and in-the-works changes to the rules for bank and other institutional investors that could unlock additional capital for community development. Changes to the CRA that make it easier to invest in community-wide outcomes would be a significant step in the right direction. Additionally,

---

40 Center for Medicare and Medicaid Innovation, "Accountable Care Organizations" (website). Available at: http://innovations.cms.gov/initiatives/ACO/index.html.

41 This idea was explained by Jim Hester, acting director, Population Health Models Group, Center for Medicare and Medicaid Innovation. Congress created the Innovation Center under the Affordable Care Act, giving the center the authority and direction to "test innovative payment and service delivery models to reduce program expenditures, while preserving or enhancing the quality of care" for those who receive Medicare, Medicaid, or Children's Health Insurance Program (CHIP) benefits. More information is available at: www.innovations.cms.gov/About/index.html.

42 Foundation Center. "Aggregate Fiscal Data by Foundation Type, 2009." (San Francisco, CA: Foundation Center, 2011). Available at: http://foundationcenter.org/findfunders/statistics/pdf/01_found_fin_data/2009/02_09.pdf.

some changes already reflected in the JOBS Act of 2012 allow for smaller investors to participate in crowdfunding efforts, which could be an important new source for community development finance as well.[43]

CONCLUSION

In many ways, it was the 1960s War on Poverty, which Alex von Hoffman describes in his chapter, which created the vision of a coordinated approach to revitalize struggling communities. On the ground, however, efforts did not yield the desired results in part because the institutions that were created to execute the programs were underfunded and underdeveloped, and they struggled to meet the ambitious goals of programs such as Model Cities. In the years following those experiments, the War on Poverty's "war chest" splintered into multiple silos (see Figure 1). Over time, however, those siloed entities, through trial and error, emerged as stronger institutions that are capable of remarkable feats of organizational and financial complexity. Community development finance, for example, is much more capable and adept at blending all types of public and private capital sources to serve certain needs of low-income communities. There have been similar advances in capability in other important industries and sectors, including health, education, public safety, and others. The time has come to bring all those fields back into better integration and not simply half-hearted cooperation.

One theme this book hopes to drive home is that there are no silver bullets, as Ben Hecht writes in his essay. In addition to the core set of interventions (many of which are focused on children) outlined above, there will be unique solutions for each low-income neighborhood. And the initial intervention will create new realities within a community that will require the quarterback to adapt. The interventions will need to be changing constantly to be relevant to the changing nature of the problem. In other words, neighborhoods are complex adaptive systems,

---

43 For a discussion about how crowdfunding could support community building, see Ian Galloway, "Peer-to-Peer Lending and Community Development Finance." Working Paper 2009 - 06 (San Francisco: Federal Reserve Bank of San Francisco, August 2009).

and the interventions in one area will cause changes and adjustments throughout the web of connections (of opportunities and challenges) in the neighborhood and in the connections that neighborhood has to the region and other linked systems. In this aspect, community development could look to and learn from the emerging field of complexity science, which examines how relationships between parts of a system produce aggregate outcomes. It is past time that we recognize that poverty is a complex and emergent system that requires a dynamic and adaptive response.[44]

The work of the quarterback is a process and not a single idea or program. It is based on the latticework that the community development industry developed during the past 40 years, but it expands the scope dramatically to bring in new players, new sources of capital, and new ideas. The greatest challenge will be integration, which is why we have placed such a premium on the role of the quarterback in this chapter. A flexible and dynamic quarterback with sufficient resources, backed with data and the ability to constantly refine strategy, would be a significant benefit for low-income communities. It would, in short, be an institutional and policy breakthrough that would empower thousands of communities across the country to do what a few saints have accomplished: routinize the extraordinary.

DAVID ERICKSON *is director of the Center for Community Development Investments at the Federal Reserve Bank of San Francisco. He has a PhD in history from the University of California, Berkeley and his book on the history of community development,* The Housing Policy Revolution: Networks and Neighborhoods, *was published by the Urban Institute Press in 2009.*

IAN GALLOWAY *is a senior research associate at the Federal Reserve Bank of San Francisco. He is the author of "Peer-to-Peer Lending and Community Development Finance" and "Charter School Tax Credit: Investing in Human*

44 For more information on complex systems, particularly how some of the theories in science have been applied to human issues, see Geoffrey West, "The Hidden Laws That Pervade Complex Biological and Social Phenomena" (Santa Fe, NM: Santa Fe Institute, 2012). Available at http://www.santafe.edu/templeton/hidden-laws/detail/. An interesting treatment of complexity theory applied to public administration is Jocelyne Bourgon, A New Synthesis of Public Administration: Serving in the 21st Century (Montreal: McGill-Queen's University Press, 2011).

Capital" and was recognized as a "future industry leader" by the Opportunity Finance Network in 2010. Ian holds a master's degree in public policy from the University of Chicago and a bachelor's degree in political science and philosophy from Colgate University.

NAOMI CYTRON *is a senior research associate at the Federal Reserve Bank of San Francisco. Her primary research interests are neighborhood revitalization and regional equity, and she has authored numerous articles and reports on topics ranging from concentrated poverty to transit-oriented development. She has a master's degree in city and regional planning from the University of North Carolina at Chapel Hill, and a bachelor's degree in biology from Macalester College.*

INFLECTION POINT:
New Vision, New Strategy, New Organization

Nancy O. Andrews
Low Income Investment Fund

Nicolas P. Retsinas
Harvard Business School

W hat does it cost to build a great society? More pointedly, what does it cost to lose a great society? Since the War on Poverty began almost 50 years ago, investments in America's communities have spurred those questions. Today, we face a society more unequal than at any time since the Great Depression: almost every person knows at least one family member, neighbor, or friend in danger of losing a home, and the number of people living in poverty has grown by half in a decade. Today, a child's ZIP code is one of the most powerful predictors of her future life—health, education, longevity. As Federal Reserve Chairman Ben Bernanke has warned, "income inequality is a very bad development. It's creating two societies....It leads to...a society that doesn't have the cohesion we'd like to see."[1]

So these questions rise to a new urgency.

Civil, social, and political justice is entwined in the persistence of poverty. We cannot speak of a just society when an individual's birthplace determines whether he or she will thrive. If the United States intends to remain the most prosperous economy in the world, we can no longer afford to see 20 percent of our children ill-housed and poorly educated. We can no longer afford an achievement gap estimated at $1–2 trillion annually and between 9 percent and 13 percent of lost gross domestic product, or what McKinsey & Company has called the "equivalent of a permanent national recession."[2]

This book is a call to action. Our work in America's communities is at an inflection point, propelled by the magnitude of change in the world around us and the hard-won knowledge of the past five decades. This new knowledge on what works best for people and places is at the center of our work. This book also calls for a way forward, built on a vision that integrates people and place and that champions collaborative networks of organizations with diverse expertise and ways of working that reward success.

Each chapter in this book is intended to inspire thought. We created an open forum for practitioners, policymakers, and thinkers to re-imagine community development, without constraint. Our contributors represent diverse philosophies, practice, and regions. Our goal is to create new insights about what the future should be. Above all, this book urges you, our readers, to re-imagine your work and to embrace a vision that

---

1 Federal Reserve Chairman Ben Bernanke in a December 10, 2010 interview on 60 Minutes, available at www.cbsnews.com/stories/2010/12/03/60minutes/main7114229_page4.shtml?tag=contentMain;contentBody.

2 "The Economic Impact of the Achievement Gap in America's Schools," McKinsey & Company, April 2009. Achievement gap is defined as educational achievement levels between the U.S. and other top-performing industrialized countries. The gap for black, Latino, and low-income children is estimated to be approximately $700 billion to $1.3 trillion annually, or 5–9 percent of GDP. Available at http://mckinseyonsociety.com/downloads/reports/Education/achievement_gap_report.pdf.

uses and harmonizes contributions from diverse sectors across the spectrum of people and place.

STANDING ON THE SHOULDERS OF GIANTS

The American belief in community as the center of social action is special, perhaps unique in the world for its scale and scope. During the past 50 years, community developers have organized, invested, built, and nurtured renewal in the places that fell to the sidelines of our national prosperity. In the 1960s, we created an inflection point in American social policy when we asserted that neighborhoods and communities are an appropriate focal point for national policy. More than any other country, the United States has created a national delivery system of entrepreneurial local organizations, working in every state, major city, and rural area. This infrastructure is now woven into the fabric of our social response. We are a partner to the private sector, to private capital markets, and to federal, state, and local governments. Every year, this remarkable American experiment with community development delivers billions of dollars in private and public capital investments to poor neighborhoods, creating thousands of jobs, homes, schools, early learning centers, and health and recreational facilities.

In the early days of the community development movement, we knew little about what worked or what was possible. We experimented boldly. The first decade of this movement was dedicated to people power: creating energy within communities to *demand* fairness and opportunity. The next three decades were spent building the institutions, the partnerships, and the practices to *create* fairness and opportunity through an emerging network of community-based organizations, community development corporations, and the community capital movement that serves them. In this past decade, the field has achieved scale and professionalism, becoming a bona fide pillar within the American social delivery system. Our work changed many lives for the better, but more important, it generated a body of knowledge that helps us understand what works. With 50 years behind us, we now ask:

- What did we get right?

- What did we get wrong?

- How shall we remake ourselves?

What we have learned over the past five decades calls us toward reflection. In Abraham Lincoln's words, "As our case is new, we must think anew."[3] Where once we believed that economic advances within the four corners of the most distressed neighborhoods would reverse poverty, we now understand the importance of connecting communities and their residents to broader opportunities in regional economies. Where once we believed that a few powerful drivers—housing, physical, and economic revitalization—could change the life chances of the poorest Americans, we now understand that poverty is a complex swirl of forces, bathing people and places in a corrosive influence 24 hours a day, seven days a week. Single solutions by themselves will not work. Silver bullets have gone the way of the six-shooter, even though the legacy of that perspective remains in the segregated array of federal and local programs that were created to help low-income communities.

For the past decade, knowledge has emerged that shines a bright light on the people side of the equation. We have learned that often the "soft stuff" makes the biggest difference. Yet, the practice and mindset of community development remains rooted in the place-based tradition of physical and economic revitalization. The people-based side of the equation has often been accorded second-class status. We have been so drawn to the tangible, to the built environment, that we sometimes forget why we do this work. We have invested so much in the buildings within a place that we have not always remembered to invest in the people who live in them.

Now is the time for change. The knowledge revolution of the past decade teaches us that we cannot separate community-building

---

3 "Annual Message to Congress: Concluding Remarks, Washington, D.C., December 1, 1862," Collected Works of Abraham Lincoln, edited by Roy P. Basler.

strategies from human capital strategies. As Federal Reserve Governor Elizabeth Duke wrote in the foreword of this book, the age-old people versus place debate is over: both sides have won.

ESCAPE VELOCITY: TWENTY-FIRST CENTURY COMMUNITY DEVELOPMENT

The places where we live, learn, work, and play transform us; our communities seed our futures, and we seed the future of our communities. People and place exist within a continuum of influences, changing one another over time. There is little debate that the twenty-first century is bringing change with amplitudes not seen in many decades. Economic shifts are tectonic in scale and the resulting challenges to social policy will persist for many years. We are at another inflection point in our evolution.

Forces within community development today create a push-pull dynamic that has been building for some time. We are pushed by sharp economic challenges that will limit future resources, and we are pulled by an emerging knowledge revolution, where all evidence drives to the integration of people- and place-based investments. Because community development is uniquely positioned at the nexus of people and place, we can be at the center of these currents. But to remain at the center requires a renewal of our vision of social progress within America's communities, one built on models of success and accountability, on collaboration, and on networks of organizations working beneath an umbrella vision of integration, learning, sharing, and working together. Above all, the future will require that we do more with less. We will face fiscal constraints that will increase the pressure to invest in the projects with the biggest bang for the buck.

The world will be more competitive than in the past. With only 300 million people to compete within a world of more than 7 billion people, the future prosperity of the United States rests on the skill and capability of all our people. Every person, every mind must give at his or her highest level.

The question of impact—what measurable difference did a given social investment make—looms large. Expressing our social value in terms of "return on taxpayer (or social) investment" will be vital to ensure continued public investment in community development. Answering convincingly the questions of outcomes, impact, and return on public investment will be the key to continued success. Where we traditionally described our value to society in outputs— dollars invested, homes built, jobs created— we will now be asked what these inputs add up to. What do they deliver to society at large? What is the case for ongoing investment in community development? How do we prove to the American taxpayer or the social investor that community investment delivers value for their money?

Answering these questions requires a twenty-first century model of community development, one that stands on the shoulders of the past, that learns from past accomplishments and one that is organized beneath the umbrella of an *integrative, collaborative vision for impact.*

While the idea of a comprehensive vision for community development has been around for several decades, what is new today is the knowledge revolution that sheds greater light on what works and why. The growth in scale, professionalism, and excellence among community development practitioners is also new. And finally, promising new models based on accountability, like pay for success innovations and Human Capital Performance Bonds, are emerging and create a win-win for our investors, from the taxpayer to private capital. Accordingly, we believe that a renewed vision for our future investments in America's communities will rest on three pillars of practice:

- Invest in what works – evidence matters

- Networks of learning, flexible, adaptive organizations among sectors of practice

- Scale with impact – getting the job done

We take each of these points in turn.

Integrative, collaborative vision for impact. The evidence leaves little doubt that a more holistic vision and practice is necessary to lift people and places to their potential. But, the needs of people and their communities do not fall neatly within the jurisdictional lines of Congressional committees or government funding streams. We need to cross traditional boundaries, recognizing that people and their communities require holistic solutions. This may require us to accept inconvenient truths about what works best and what doesn't work. It will require understanding the role of the regional economy and connecting to it as a source of strength for future opportunity. It will require "cross border" thinking that relies on networks of expertise and skills, striving toward a synthesized vision. And we believe that the future must be animated by a commitment to impact, to getting the job done in lifting people and places out of poverty.

Imagine the skills and expertise needed to build the space shuttle. No single discipline, no single company, and no single leader could succeed in such a complex undertaking. Astronautic experts were required to work with human behavior experts; health and medical professionals were required to work with thermodynamics engineers; pilots teamed up with cosmologists. This diverse array of teammates could have produced a cacophony, rather than a functioning, magnificent machine that broke barriers and opened new chapters in space exploration. Importantly, the teams that created the space shuttle were united by a master plan that was created to realize a common vision. The vision was clear, tangible; the outcomes were clearly specified and evidence was used to measure success. How to achieve the mission was not known with certainty in the beginning. When the planners began, there was no assurance of success. In fact, the goal of creating a space shuttle was so complex that it was described as a mission not a product or a project, but a mission.

A Mission to Integrate: Already, several community development efforts in the United States are working with integrative development models. Indeed, a number of the authors in this book represent this trend, in particular, Purpose Built Communities (Shirley Franklin and David Edwards) and Neighborhood Centers, Inc. (Angela Blanchard). These organizations coordinate a consortium of disciplines across the spectrum of human and community development, with a master vision for a community and its residents.

Purpose Built Communities in Atlanta has created a holistic program that combines mixed-income housing, early learning programs, high-performing charter schools, and supportive programs for community residents. The effort is guided by an oversight body that is accountable to the community and sees its responsibility as getting the job done in improving life chances and the quality of the neighborhood. In Purpose Built's pilot site—the East Lake neighborhood in Atlanta—this cross-sectoral coordination led to a 95 percent reduction in violent crime, an almost five-fold increase in employment, and extraordinary improvement in school achievement. In 2011, 98 percent of East Lake's charter school students performed at or above grade level, compared with 30 percent in 2001.

Neighborhood Centers, Inc. (NCI) in Houston is achieving similar outcomes, also with a holistic integrated cluster of programs that range from schools to early learning to health services and has recently begun to tackle the problem of physical blight.

The Integration Initiative, Strive, Building Sustainable Communities, Choice Neighborhoods, and Promise Neighborhoods are other examples. These are relatively new approaches and a great deal remains to be learned about how to create success. Success may ultimately vary from one place or time to another; such is the nature of trying new approaches and learning from trial and error. One point is clear, however: the siloed, mono-line approaches of the past will not work. We need a more complete, integrated vision and ways of working that support such a vision. We also need ongoing learning and adaptation to emerging knowledge.

PILLARS OF A NEW VISION FOR COMMUNITY DEVELOPMENT

Pillar I. Invest in What Works-Evidence Matters

In the past, we believed that access to opportunity and services was enough to improve lives. With access as our primary mental model, it made sense to focus on outputs. Simply providing the outputs would cause the desired change, we believed. Of course, this idea was rooted in an earlier understanding of how poverty emerged. After 50 years of trial and error, we know much more about what works and what does not. Focusing on outcomes, rather than just outputs, requires a system of learning and self-reflection, with a commitment to accountability. We must be willing to test, to err, to adjust course. To learn, there must be clear benchmarks and data linked to the desired outcome. Focusing on outcomes and impact will be a paradigm shift not only for community development, but for much of American social policy.

Accountability is the elixir of success. In our view, the ultimate evidence of success is moving the dial on poverty, and the most powerful predictor of this is closing the achievement gap between poor and affluent children. But there are other measures along the way, including health improvements; improvements in child development, particularly by age 5, so that children enter school ready to learn; a greater sense of personal safety; reduced violent crimes; and social efficacy.

There are also exciting new examples of social models with built-in accountability. For example, pay-for-success approaches, now emerging in several fields, are a good step in this direction. Experiments with Social Impact Bonds in the United Kingdom, pay-for-success programs in New York City and Boston, and Human Capital Performance Bonds in Minnesota are all early-stage trials of a new way of working. By investing in what works, we hold our feet to the fire, we ensure that evidence is the basis for decision making, and we create an atmosphere that rewards learning. These approaches will pave a path for sustained social investments in the future. They are the beginnings of an outcomes-based vision. Outcomes, social metrics, and measurement are part and parcel of learning, adaptive practice. Pay-for-success and evidence-based models will amplify our success by many fold.

Solving the problem of poverty and inequality is not a simple task, but today we understand a great deal about how to get the job done. At this stage, community development can and should be accountable to this standard, as a matter of integrity to our mission and as a means of creating buy-in for our work. The access-based models of the past will be overtaken by ways of working that reward success and are validated by evidence.

Pillar II. Networks of Organizations across Sectors

Recently, after listening patiently to the case for integrative models, Mary Kaiser, CEO of the California Community Reinvestment Corporation and a seasoned community development practitioner, penned an essay humorously entitled "Siloes of the World, Unite!" It is hard enough to learn how to do one thing well, she argued. Entire careers have been devoted to mastering the skills needed for success in a single sector—building or financing affordable housing, for example. We have spent decades creating excellence in our practice. Isn't an integrative approach that expects community developers to perform too many roles a recipe for mediocrity?

The answer is likely yes. Poverty may be a complex integrated problem, but the solution cannot be layering myriad expectations onto a single organization, or even on a single strategy. This is where networks or teams of organizations come in. Community development's goal can be holistic, but its execution strategy requires a network of expert and professionalized organizations working toward a common purpose and vision. One of the critical questions we face is who creates and who is accountable for the master vision?

In answer to that, we imagine a symphony of players, working from a common score, guided by a conductor who holds the vision for the whole and harmonizes the unique qualities of individual instruments. In the Purpose Built example, a governing board of civic leaders plays this role. The board monitors the quality of the physical development, the schools, the early learning centers, and holds the authority to remove poor-performing operators. In other examples, such as NCI or the Harlem Children's Zone, a nonprofit organization plays this role. In all cases, some entity must take ownership and be the advocate for the community and its residents, with responsibility and authority for outcomes.

Pillar III. Scale with Impact

Community development has created a national platform that is networked, local in its roots, yet scaled and professional. We are a national asset in the country's response to social need. Over the past few decades, we have leveraged hundreds of billions of dollars in capital into low-income communities. We are poised to reach a far greater scale and to play a much broader role in changing the lives of the poor. We have become outstanding practitioners, with success in building affordable housing, creating strong and vibrant communities, running high-performing schools that see their graduates into and through college. We have created innovative capital tools, such as the Low Income Housing Tax Credit and the New Markets Tax Credit, and annually deliver goods and services to millions of Americans. We are now creating partnerships with new sectors within the economy, such as the health care industry, insurance companies, and social venture capital. For the past several decades, we have built organizations that possess the know-how and the assets to be first responders in hard times for low-income communities and individuals.

Many community development organizations have billions of dollars in delivery track records, with decades of successful operations. We possess sizable balance sheets and are well respected by private investors. We have the skills, the knowledge, and the capital to make a difference. We are ready to be a partner to the private and the public sectors at a far larger scale. We are ready to embrace models that reward success for impact as well as quality outputs. We are entrepreneurial and confident enough to learn from trial and error. We are ready to deliver scale *with* impact.

CONCLUSION

By all measures, the community development field has reached scale and is poised at an inflection point. We see a future where we will channel hundreds of billions of dollars annually into mission-related work, where we will help millions of people with a firm hand up, and where we are a steady partner to private capital markets. Banks, insurance companies, Accountable Care Organizations, and others will turn to us as a reliable platform to deliver social improvements in addition to financial return. As we develop an integrated vision of what works, and hold that ideal accountable to data and measurement, community development should become the "go to" partner for improving the life chances of individuals and fostering healthier communities. We will deliver scale with clear and measurable impact, with evidence of "return on taxpayers' and social investment."

The future will champion a vision of social progress based on integration and collaboration across sectors, on accountability to evidence-based outcomes, and on models that reward success. Community development is poised to be at the center of this, offering scale and quality. We are entrepreneurial, willing to innovate, to test, to learn by trial and error, and to be account-able to results. We are ready, willing, and able to be a partner to the private sector, to private capital markets, and to the public sector. We have the know-how, the scale, and the skills to invest hundreds of billions of dollars toward an agenda of progress in America's communities. We are ready to build a twenty-first century platform for investment in what works in America's communities, a platform that allows all Americans to achieve at their highest potential and to give their very best to our nation's future prosperity.

NANCY O. ANDREWS *is the president and CEO of the Low Income Investment Fund (LIIF), which is a community capital organization dedicated to poverty alleviation* *in the United States. LIIF recently celebrated investing $1 billion in low-income communities and serving one million people.*

NICOLAS P. RETSINAS *is a senior lecturer in real estate at the Harvard Business School, the director emeritus of the Joint Center for Housing Studies of Harvard University, and the former Assistant Secretary for Housing and Federal Housing Commissioner at the United States Department of Housing and Urban Development. He also served as director of the Office of Thrift Supervision.*